Software Engineering: Contemporary Approach

Edited by Jeff Smith

www.statesacademicpress.com

States Academic Press,
109 South 5th Street,
Brooklyn, NY 11249, USA

Visit us on the World Wide Web at:
www.statesacademicpress.com

ISBN: 978-1-63989-693-6

Cataloging-in-publication Data

Software engineering : contemporary approach / edited by Jeff Smith.
p. cm.
Includes bibliographical references and index.
ISBN 978-1-63989-693-6
1. Software engineering. 2. Computer programming. 3. Computer networks. 4. Computer science.
5. Information science. 6. Automatic programming (Computer science). I. Smith, Jeff.
QA76.758 .S64 2023
005.1--dc23

Contents

Preface

A program is a type of executable code that performs some computational function. Software is defined as a group of executable programming code, along with related documentation and libraries. Software engineering is a discipline of engineering concerned with the creation of software products based on scientific procedures, principles and methods. It produces an effective and dependable software product. The requirement for software engineering rises as a result of the increased rate of change in user needs and the environment in which the software operates. Some of the major functions of software engineering are software testing, software architecture and software analysis. This book traces the progress of software engineering and highlights some of its key concepts and applications. There has been rapid progress in this field and its applications are finding their way across multiple industries. The book will provide comprehensive knowledge to the readers.

Various studies have approached the subject by analyzing it with a single perspective, but the present book provides diverse methodologies and techniques to address this field. This book contains theories and applications needed for understanding the subject from different perspectives. The aim is to keep the readers informed about the progresses in the field; therefore, the contributions were carefully examined to compile novel researches by specialists from across the globe.

Indeed, the job of the editor is the most crucial and challenging in compiling all chapters into a single book. In the end, I would extend my sincere thanks to the chapter authors for their profound work. I am also thankful for the support provided by my family and colleagues during the compilation of this book.

Editor

SMT-Based Bounded Schedulability Analysis of the Clock Constraint Specification Language

Min Zhang[1], Fu Song[2(✉)], Frédéric Mallet[3], and Xiaohong Chen[1]

[1] Shanghai Key Laboratory of Trustworthy Computing, ECNU, Shanghai, China
[2] ShanghaiTech University, Shanghai, China
songfu@shanghaitech.edu.cn
[3] Université Cote d'Azur, CNRS, Inria, I3S, Nice, France

Abstract. The Clock Constraint Specification Language (CCSL) is a formalism for specifying logical-time constraints on events for the design of real-time embedded systems. A central verification problem of CCSL is to check whether events are schedulable under logical constraints. Although many efforts have been made addressing this problem, the problem is still open. In this paper, we show that the bounded scheduling problem is **NP**-complete and then propose an efficient SMT-based decision procedure which is sound and complete. Based on this decision procedure, we present a sound algorithm for the general scheduling problem. We implement our algorithm in a prototype tool and illustrate its utility in schedulability analysis in designing real-world systems and automatic proving of algebraic properties of CCSL constraints. Experimental results demonstrate its effectiveness and efficiency.

Keywords: SMT · CCSL · Schedulability · Logical time · Real-time system

1 Introduction

Model-based design has been widely used, particularly in the design of safety-critical real-time embedded systems. It has achieved industrial successes through languages such as SCADE [12], AADL [15] and UML MARTE [26]. For example, UML MARTE provides syntactic annotations to implement, when the context allows, classical real-time scheduling algorithms such as EDF (Earliest Deadline First). It also provides a domain-specific language–Clock Constraint Specification Language (CCSL) [3], to express the real-time behaviors of a system under development as logical constraints on system events, but independently of any physical time and classical real-time scheduling algorithms. CCSL has been used on several industrial scenarios such as vehicle systems [16] and cyber-physical systems [10, 22].

Model-based design usually starts with coarse-grained logical models that are progressively refined into more concrete ones until the final code deployment. It is well-known that the earlier one can detect and fix bugs in the refinement process, the better [7]. Therefore, it is critical to provide efficient methods and tools to check safety, liveness and schedulability on the logical models and not only on the definite deployed system. This has motivated a large body of works on verifying whether events are schedulable under a set of constraints expressed in CCSL [11, 21, 28, 33, 35, 36, 38], though its decidability is still open. These works first transform CCSL constraints into other formal representations such as transition systems [21], Promela [35], Büchi automata [36], timed automata [33], rewriting logics [38], instant relations [28], or timed-interval logics [11], and then apply existing tools. However, their approaches usually suffer from the state explosion problem. Moreover, most of these works only deal with the so-called safe subset of CCSL and the other ones only provide semi-algorithms. In our earlier work [39], we proposed an SMT-based verification approach to CCSL and demonstrated several applications of the approach to finding schedules, verifying temporal properties, proving constraint entailment, and analyzing the validity of system traces. Based on the approach, we implemented an efficient tool for verifying LTL properties of CCSL [40].

In this work we are focused on the scheduling problem of CCSL, a fundamental problem to which the aforementioned verification problems of CCSL can be reduced. We first prove that the *bounded* scheduling problem of CCSL with fixed bounds is **NP**-complete. To our knowledge, this is the first result regarding the complexity of the scheduling problem with CCSL. Then, we propose a decision procedure for the bounded scheduling problem with a given bound. The decision procedure is based on the transformation of CCSL into SMT formulas [39]. Our decision procedure is sound, complete, and efficient in practice. Based on this decision procedure, we turn to the general (i.e. unbounded) scheduling problem and present a binary-search based algorithm. Our algorithm is sound, i.e., if it proves either schedulable or unschedulable, then the result is conclusive. We implemented our algorithms in a prototype tool. The tool was used to analyze a real-world interlocking system in a rail transit system. Using the proposed approach, we also prove some algebraic properties of CCSL. The experimental results demonstrate the effectiveness and efficiency of the SMT-based approach.

The rest of this paper is organised as follows: Section 2 introduces CCSL. Section 3 defines the (bounded) scheduling problem of CCSL and shows that the bounded case is **NP**-complete. Section 4 presents an SMT-based decision procedure for the bounded scheduling problem and a sound algorithm for the general scheduling problem. Section 5 shows a case study and experimental results. Section 6 discusses related work, and Section 7 concludes the paper.

2   The Clock Constraint Specification Language

2.1   Logical Clock, History and Schedule

In CCSL, clocks are used to model occurrences of events, where a clock ticks when the corresponding event occurs. For instance, a clock may represent an event that is dispatch of a task, communications between tasks or acquisition of a shared resource by a task. Constraints over clocks are used to specify causal and temporal relations between system events. No global physical time is presumed for the clocks and their constraints. This feature allows CCSL to define a polychronous specification of a system at a logical level.

Definition 1 (Logical clock). *A (logical) clock c is an infinite sequence of ticks $(c^i)_{i \in \mathbb{N}^+}$ with each c^i being* tick *or* idle, *where $\mathbb{N}^+$ denotes the set of all the non-zero natural numbers.*

The value of c^i denotes whether an event associated with c occurs or not at step i. If c^i is *tick*, then the event occurs, otherwise not. In particular, we denote by **1** a global reference logical clock that always ticks at each step.

Definition 2 (Schedule). *Given a set C of clocks, a* schedule *of C is a total function $\delta : \mathbb{N}^+ \to 2^C$ such that $\forall i \in \mathbb{N}^+$, $\delta(i) = \{c \in C \mid c^i = tick\}$ and $\delta(i) \neq \emptyset$.*

Intuitively, a schedule δ defines a partial order between the ticks of the clocks. $\delta(i)$ is a subset of C such that $c \in \delta(i)$ iff c ticks at step i. The condition $\delta(i) \neq \emptyset$ expresses that step i cannot be empty. This forbids stuttering steps in schedules. As one can add or remove finite number of empty steps without effect on schedulability, we exclude them from schedules for succinctness.

A clock can memorize the number of ticks that it has made. We use *history* to represent the memorization.

Definition 3 (History). *Given a schedule δ for a set C of clocks, a* history *of δ is a function $\chi_\delta : C \times \mathbb{N}^+ \to \mathbb{N}$ such that for each $c \in C$ and $i \in \mathbb{N}^+$:*

$$\chi_\delta(c, i) = \begin{cases} 0, & \text{if } i = 1; \\ \chi_\delta(c, i-1), & \text{if } i > 1 \land c \notin \delta(i-1); \\ \chi_\delta(c, i-1) + 1, & \text{if } i > 1 \land c \in \delta(i-1). \end{cases}$$

$\chi_\delta(c, i)$ represents the number of the ticks that the clock c has made immediately before step i. (Note that the tick of c at step i is excluded in $\chi_\delta(c, i)$.) For simplicity, we may write χ for χ_δ if it is clear from the context.

2.2 Syntax and Semantics of CCSL

CCSL consists of 11 kinds of constraints, 4 of them are binary relations for specifying the *precedence*, *causality*, *subclocking*, and *exclusion* relations between clocks, and the others are used to define clocks from existing ones. Clocks defined by constraints may correspond to system events or are just introduced as auxiliary clocks without corresponding to any events.

Table 1. Semantics of CCSL with respect to schedules

	ϕ	$\delta \models \phi$
Precedence	$c_1 \, [b] \prec c_2$	$\forall n \in \mathbb{N}^+ . \chi(c_2, n) - \chi(c_1, n) = b \Rightarrow c_2 \notin \delta(n)$
Causality	$c_1 \preccurlyeq c_2$	$\forall n \in \mathbb{N}^+ . \chi(c_1, n) \geq \chi(c_2, n)$
Subclock	$c_1 \subseteq c_2$	$\forall n \in \mathbb{N}^+ . c_1 \in \delta(n) \Rightarrow c_2 \in \delta(n)$
Exclusion	$c_1 \, \# \, c_2$	$\forall n \in \mathbb{N}^+ . c_1 \notin \delta(n) \vee c_2 \notin \delta(n)$
Union	$c_1 \triangleq c_2 + c_3$	$\forall n \in \mathbb{N}^+ . c_1 \in \delta(n) \Leftrightarrow c_2 \in \delta(n) \vee c_3 \in \delta(n)$
Intersection	$c_1 \triangleq c_2 * c_3$	$\forall n \in \mathbb{N}^+ . c_1 \in \delta(n) \Leftrightarrow c_2 \in \delta(n) \wedge c_3 \in \delta(n)$
Infimum	$c_1 \triangleq c_2 \wedge c_3$	$\forall n \in \mathbb{N}^+ . \chi(c_1, n) = \max(\chi(c_2, n), \chi(c_3, n))$
Supremum	$c_1 \triangleq c_2 \vee c_3$	$\forall n \in \mathbb{N}^+ . \chi(c_1, n) = \min(\chi(c_2, n), \chi(c_3, n))$
Periodicity	$c_1 \triangleq c_2 \propto p$	$\forall n \in \mathbb{N}^+ . c_1 \in \delta(n) \Leftrightarrow (c_2 \in \delta(n) \wedge \exists m \in \mathbb{N}^+ . \chi(c_2, n) = m \times p - 1)$
Filtering	$c_1 \triangleq c_2 \blacktriangledown w$	$\forall n \in \mathbb{N}^+ . c_1 \in \delta(n) \Leftrightarrow (c_2 \in \delta(n) \wedge w[n])$
DelayFor	$c_1 \triangleq c_2 \, \$ \, d \, on \, c_3$	$\forall n \in \mathbb{N}^+ . c_1 \in \delta(n) \Leftrightarrow (c_3 \in \delta(n) \wedge \exists m \in \mathbb{N}^+ . (c_2 \in \delta(m) \wedge \chi(c_3, n) - \chi(c_3, m) = d))$

Definition 4 (Syntax). *A* CCSL *constraint* ϕ *is defined by the following form:*

Precedence: $c_1 \, [b] \prec c_2$ | *Causality:* $c_1 \preccurlyeq c_2$
Subclock: $c_1 \subseteq c_2$ | *Exclusion:* $c_1 \, \# \, c_2$
Union: $c_1 \triangleq c_2 + c_3$ | *Intersection:* $c_1 \triangleq c_2 * c_3$
Infimum: $c_1 \triangleq c_2 \wedge c_3$ | *Supremum:* $c_1 \triangleq c_2 \vee c_3$
Periodicity: $c_1 \triangleq c_2 \propto p$ | *Filtering:* $c_1 \triangleq c_2 \blacktriangledown w$
DelayFor: $c_1 \triangleq c_2 \, \$ \, d \, on \, c_3$

where $b \geq 0$, $d \geq 0$ *and* $p > 0$ *are natural numbers,* c_1, c_2, c_3 *are logical clocks and* w *is a (possibly infinite) word over* $\{0, 1\}$ *expressed as a (ω-)regular expression.*

For simplifying presentation, we denote by $c_1 \prec c_2$ the constraint $c_1 \, [0] \prec c_2$, and $c_1 \triangleq c_2 \, \$ \, d$ the constraint $c_1 \triangleq c_2 \, \$ \, d \, on \, c_3$ such that $c_2 = c_3$.

The semantics of CCSL constraints is defined over schedules. Given a CCSL constraint ϕ and a schedule δ, the satisfiability relation $\delta \models \phi$ (i.e., δ satisfies constraint ϕ) is defined in Table 1.

The precedence constraint $c_1 \prec c_2$ (i.e., $c_1 \, [0] \prec c_2$) expresses that the clock c_1 precedes the clock c_2. Suppose there is an unbounded buffer with two operations *fetch* and *store*, which respectively fetch data from and store data into the buffer. Fetch is only allowed when the buffer is nonempty. If the buffer is initially empty, store operation must strictly precede fetch operation. This behavior can be expressed by the constraint: *store* $\prec$ *fetch*. Likewise, the precedence constraint can be used to represent reentrant tasks by replacing *store* with *start* and *fetch* with *finish*.

The general precedence constraint $c_1 \, [b] \prec c_2$ that can specify the differences b between the number of occurrences of two clocks before the precedence takes effect. Hence, it is able to express more complicated relations. For instance, if the buffer initially is nonempty, fetch operations can be performed prior to any store operation. Figure 1 shows such a scenario where 4 elements are initially presented in the buffer. This behavior can be represented as: $store\ [4] \prec fetch$.

The causality, subclock and exclusion constraints are straightforward. The causality constraint $c_1 \preccurlyeq c_2$ specifies that the occurrence of c_2 must be caused by the occurrence of c_1, namely at any moment c_1 must have ticked at least as many times as

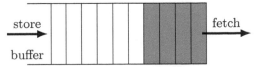

Fig. 1. Example for $store\ [4] \prec fetch$

c_2 has. The subclock constraint $c_1 \subseteq c_2$ expresses that c_1 occurs at some step only if c_2 occur at this step as well. The exclusion constraint $c_1 \# c_2$ specifies that two clocks c_1 and c_2 are exclusive, i.e., they cannot occur simultaneously at the same step.

The union and intersection constraints are used to define clocks. $c_1 \triangleq c_2 + c_3$ defines a clock c_1 such that c_1 ticks iff c_2 or c_3 ticks. Similarly, $c_1 \triangleq c_2 * c_3$ defines a clock c_1 such that c_1 ticks iff both c_2 and c_3 tick. The infimum (resp. supremum) constraint $c_1 \triangleq c_2 \wedge c_3$ (resp. $c_1 \triangleq c_2 \vee c_3$) is used to define a clock c_1 that is the slowest (resp. fastest) clock that is faster (resp. slower) than both c_2 and c_3. These two constraints are useful for expressing delay requirements between two events. Remark that clocks c_1 defined by constraints may correspond to system events, otherwise are auxiliary clocks. In the former case, these constraints can be seen as constraints specifying relations between clocks c_1, c_2 and c_3.

The periodicity constraint $c_1 \triangleq c_2 \propto p$ defines a clock c_1 such that c_1 has to be performed once every p occurrences of clock c_2. It is worth mentioning that the periodicity constraint defined in such a way is relative because of the logical nature of CCSL clocks. That is, clock c_1 is relatively periodic with respect to clock c_2. CCSL does not assume the existence of a global reference clock, most relations are defined relative to other clocks. These notions extend the equivalent behaviors which are usually defined relative to physical time. If c_2 represents a sensor that measures physical time, then c_1 becomes physically periodic.

The filtering constraint $c_1 \triangleq c_2 \blacktriangledown w$ is used to define a clock c_1 which can be seen as snapshots of the clock c_2 at some steps according to the (ω-)regular expression w. For instance, $c_1 \triangleq c_2 \blacktriangledown (01)^\omega$ expresses that c_1 simulates c_2 at every even step. It defines a logically periodic behavior of c_1 with respect to c_2.

The delayFor constraint $c_1 \triangleq c_2 \$ d$ (i.e., $c_1 \triangleq c_2 \$ d\ on\ c_2$) defines a new clock c_1 that is delayed by the clock c_2 with d steps. The general form $c_1 \triangleq c_2 \$ d\ on\ c_3$ defines a new clock c_1 that is delayed by c_2 with d times of the ticks of c_3. c_1 can be seen as a *sampled* clock of c_2 on the basis of c_3. For instance, $c_1 \triangleq c_2 \$ 1\ on\ c_3$, denotes that whenever c_2 ticks at least once between two successive ticks of c_3 at steps m and n, c_1 must tick at step n.

3 Scheduling Problem of CCSL

3.1 Schedulability

Given a set Φ of CCSL constraints, a schedule δ satisfies Φ, denoted by $\delta \models \Phi$, iff $\delta \models \phi$ for all constraints $\phi \in \Phi$.

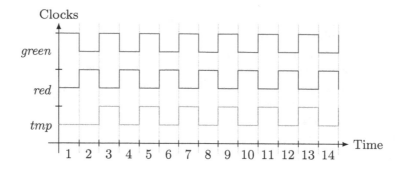

Fig. 2. The unique schedule that satisfies the three constraints in the example

Definition 5 (Logical time scheduling problem). *Given a set Φ of* CCSL *constraints, the (logical time) scheduling problem of* CCSL *is to determine whether there exists a schedule δ such that $\delta \models \Phi$.*

We illustrate the scheduling problem by a simple example. Consider alternative flickering between the green and red light using CCSL. We assume that green light starts first. The timing requirements can be formalized by the following three constraints:

$$green \prec red, \qquad tmp \triangleq green \, \$ \, 1, \qquad red \prec tmp,$$

where *green* and *red* are clocks respectively representing whether the green (resp. red) light is turned on, the clock *tmp* is an auxiliary clock used to help specify the constraints on clocks.

There exists exactly one schedule satisfying the three constraints, as shown in Fig. 2. In this schedule, the clock *tmp* has the same behavior as *green* from step 2, while the clock *red* has the opposite behavior to *green*. Namely, *red* and *green* operates in an alternative manner. For simplicity, we also write *green $\sim$ red* to denote the *alternation* relation of the two clocks.

Although one may be able to find one or more schedules for some simple constraints, to our knowledge, there is no generally applicable decision procedure solving the scheduling problem of full CCSL. There are two main challenges. First, schedules are essentially *infinite*, i.e., defined on all the natural numbers. Second, the *precedence* is *stateful*, i.e., it depends on the history, and there is no upper bound on how far in the history one must go back. It may then require an infinite memory to store the history. As a first step to tackle this challenging problem, in this work, we first consider the *bounded* scheduling problem.

3.2 Bounded Scheduling Problem

Given a bound $k \in \mathbb{N}^+$, let $\sigma : \mathbb{N}^+_{\leq k} \to 2^C$ be a function. σ is an k-bounded schedule of a set Φ of CCSL constraints, denoted by $\sigma \models_k \Phi$, iff there exists a schedule δ such that $\delta(i) = \sigma(i)$ for every $i \in \mathbb{N}^+_{\leq k}$ and $\delta \models \Phi$ from step 1 up to k, where $\mathbb{N}^+_{\leq k} := \{1, \cdots, k\}$.

Definition 6 (Bounded scheduling problem). *The* bounded scheduling problem *is to determine, for a given set Φ of CCSL constraints and a bound k, whether there is an k-bounded schedule σ for Φ, i.e., $\sigma \models_k \Phi$.*

Theorem 1 (Sufficient condition of unschedulability). *If a set Φ of constraints has no k-bounded schedule for some $k \in \mathbb{N}^+$, then Φ is unschedulable.*

The proof is straightforward by contradiction.

It is easy to see that the bounded scheduling problem is decidable, as there are finitely many potential k-bounded schedules, i.e., $(2^{|C|} - 1)^k$, where $|C|$ denotes the number of clocks. Furthermore, the satisfiability problem of Boolean formulas can be reduced to the bounded scheduling problem in polynomial time.

Theorem 2. *The k-bounded scheduling problem of CCSL is NP-complete, even if $k = 1$.*

Proof. The NP upper bound can be proved easily based on the facts that the number of possible k-bounded schedules is finite and the universal quantification $\forall n \in \mathbb{N}^+_{\leq k}$ can be eliminated by enumerating all the possible values in $\mathbb{N}^+_{\leq k}$.

We prove the NP-hardness by a reduction from the satisfiability problem of Boolean formulas which is known NP-complete. Consider the Boolean formula $\phi = \bigwedge_{i=1}^m (l_i^1 \vee l_i^2 \vee l_i^3)$, where $m \in \mathbb{N}^+$ and l_i^j for $j \in \{1, 2, 3\}$ is either a Boolean variable x or its negation $\neg x$. Let $\mathsf{Var}(\phi)$ denote the set of Boolean variables appearing in ϕ. We construct a set of CCSL constraints Φ as follows.

For each $x \in \mathsf{Var}(\phi)$, we have two clocks x^+ and x^-. Let $\mathsf{enc}(x) = x^+$ and $\mathsf{enc}(\neg x) = x^-$. Each clause $l_i^1 \vee l_i^2 \vee l_i^3$ in ϕ is encoded as the CCSL constraint $c_i \triangleq \mathsf{enc}(l_i^1) + \mathsf{enc}(l_i^2) + \mathsf{enc}(l_i^3)$, denoted by ψ_i. Note that $c_i \triangleq \mathsf{enc}(l_i^1) + \mathsf{enc}(l_i^2) + \mathsf{enc}(l_i^3)$ can be transformed into CCSL constraints by introducing one auxiliary clock c, i.e., $\{c_i \triangleq \mathsf{enc}(l_i^1) + \mathsf{enc}(l_i^2) + \mathsf{enc}(l_i^3)\} \equiv \{c_i \triangleq \mathsf{enc}(l_i^1) + c, c \triangleq \mathsf{enc}(l_i^2) + \mathsf{enc}(l_i^3)\}$.

Let $\mathsf{enc}(\phi)$ denote the following set of CCSL constraints

$$\{\mathbf{1} \triangleq *_{i=1}^m c_i, \psi_1, ..., \psi_m, x^+ \# x^-, \mathbf{1} \triangleq x^+ + x^- \mid x \in \mathsf{Var}(\phi)\}$$

where $x^+ \# x^-$ and $\mathbf{1} \triangleq x^+ + x^-$ enforce that either x^+ or x^- ticks at each step, but not both. This encodes that either x is true or $\neg x$ is true. Note that $\tau \triangleq *_{i=1}^m c_i$ is a shorthand of $\tau \triangleq c_1 * \cdots * c_m$, and can also be expressed in CCSL constraints by introducing polynomial number of auxiliary clocks. For instance, $\{c \triangleq c_1 * c_2 * c_3\} \equiv \{c \triangleq c_1 * c', c' \triangleq c_2 * c_3\}$. We can show that ϕ is satisfiable iff $\mathsf{enc}(\phi)$ is 1-bounded schedulable. The satisfiability problem of Boolean formulas is NP-complete, we get that the 1-bounded scheduling problem of CCSL is NP-hard. The k-bounded scheduling problem for $k > 1$ immediately follows by repeating the ticks of clocks at the first step. $\square$

Theorem 2 indicates the time complexity of the bounded scheduling problem. Thus, we need to find practical solutions that are algorithmically efficient for it. In the next section, we propose an SMT-based decision procedure for the bounded scheduling problem and a sound algorithm for the scheduling problem. Thanks to advances in state-of-the-art SMT solvers such as Z3 [25], our approach is usually efficient in practice.

4 Decision Procedure for the Scheduling Problem

4.1 Transformation from CCSL into SMT

Let us fix a set of CCSL constraints Φ defined over a set C of clocks. Each clock $c \in C$ is interpreted as a predicate $t_c : \mathbb{N}^+ \to \mathsf{Bool}$ such that for all $i \in \mathbb{N}^+$, $t_c(i)$ is true iff the clock c ticks at i, where Bool denotes Boolean sort. A schedule δ of Φ is encoded as a set of predicates $\mathcal{T}_C = \{t_c | c \in C\}$ such that the following condition holds: for all $t_c \in \mathcal{T}_C$,

$$\forall i \in \mathbb{N}^+ . t_c(i) \Leftrightarrow c \in \delta(i).$$

Recalling that schedules forbid stuttering steps, this condition is enforced by restricting the predicates t_c in $\mathcal{T}_C$ to satisfy the following condition:

$$\forall i \in \mathbb{N}^+ . \vee_{c \in C} t_c(i) \qquad (F1)$$

Formula F1 specifies that at each step i at least one clock c ticks, i.e., $t_c(i)$ holds.

For each clock $c \in C$, we introduce an auxiliary function $h_c : \mathbb{N}^+ \to \mathbb{N}$ to encode its history. For each $i \in \mathbb{N}^+$,

$$h_c(i) := \begin{cases} 0, & \text{if } i = 1; \\ h_c(i-1), & \text{if } i > 1 \wedge \neg t_c(i-1); \\ h_c(i-1) + 1, & \text{if } i > 1 \wedge t_c(i-1). \end{cases} \qquad (F2)$$

Intuitively, $h_c(i)$ is equivalent to $\chi(c, i)$ for each $i \in \mathbb{N}^+$. The set of all the auxiliary functions is denoted by $\mathcal{H}_C$.

By replacing each occurrence of clock c in $\delta(n)$ (resp. $c \notin \delta(n)$) with $t_c(n)$ (resp. $\neg t_c(n)$) and $\chi(c, n)$ with $h_c(n)$ in the definition of each CCSL constraint, each CCSL constraint ϕ can be encoded as an SMT formula $[\![\phi]\!]$.

We use $[\![\Phi]\!]$ to denote the conjunction of Formulas F1, F2 and the SMT encodings of CCSL constraints in Φ. Formally,

$$[\![\Phi]\!] := \text{F1} \wedge \text{F2} \wedge (\wedge_{\phi \in \Phi} [\![\phi]\!]).$$

Finding a schedule for Φ amounts to finding a solution, i.e., definitions of predicates in $\mathcal{T}_C$, which satisfies $[\![\Phi]\!]$.

Proposition 1. *Φ has a schedule iff $[\![\Phi]\!]$ is satisfiable.*

The scheduling problem of Φ is transformed into the satisfiability problem of the formula $[\![\Phi]\!]$. However, according to the SMT-LIB standard [4], $[\![\Phi]\!]$ belongs to the logic of UFLIA (formulas with <u>U</u>ninterpreted <u>F</u>unctions and <u>L</u>inear <u>I</u>nteger <u>A</u>rithmetic), whose satisfiability problem is undecidable in general. Nevertheless, the SMT encoding is still useful to solve the bounded scheduling problem, which we will present in the next subsection.

4.2 Decision Procedure for the Bounded Scheduling Problem

For k-bounded scheduling problem, it suffices to consider schedules $\delta : \mathbb{N}^+_{\leq k} \to 2^C$. Moreover, the quantifiers in $[\![\Phi]\!]$ can be eliminated once the bound k is fixed. Hence, we can resort to state-of-the-art SMT solvers. Formally, let $[\![\Phi]\!]_k$ be the formula obtained from $[\![\Phi]\!] = F1 \wedge F2 \wedge (\bigwedge_{\phi \in \Phi} [\![\phi]\!])$ by

- restricting the domain of predicates $t_c \in \mathcal{T}_C$ and functions $h_c \in \mathcal{H}_C$ to $\mathbb{N}^+_{\leq k}$;
- replacing quantifications $\forall n \in \mathbb{N}^+$ and $\exists m \in \mathbb{N}^+$ with $\forall n \in \mathbb{N}^+_{\leq k}$ and $\exists m \in \mathbb{N}^+_{\leq k}$ in $(\bigwedge_{\phi \in \Phi} [\![\phi]\!])$.

Proposition 2. *Φ is k-bounded schedulable iff $[\![\Phi]\!]_k$ is satisfiable.*
Moreover, if $[\![\Phi]\!]_k$ is satisfiable, then $[\![\Phi]\!]_{k'}$ is satisfiable for all $k' \leq k$.

4.3 A Sound Algorithm for the Scheduling Problem

According to Theorem 1, Propositions 1 and 2, (1) if $[\![\Phi]\!]$ is satisfiable, then Φ is schedulable, and (2) if $[\![\Phi]\!]_k$ for some $k \in \mathbb{N}^+$ is unsatisfiable, then Φ is unschedulable. We can deduce a sound algorithm for checking the general scheduling problem. However, randomly choosing a bound k and checking whether or not $[\![\Phi]\!]_k$ is unsatisfiable may be inefficient, as the k-bounded scheduling problem is NP-hard (cf. Theorem 2), and larger bound k may result in time out, but smaller bound k may result in that $[\![\Phi]\!]_k$ is satisfiable. Indeed, if we consider the maximal bound B, then the random approach may have to call SMT solving $\mathbf{O}(B)$ times. Alternatively, we propose a binary-search based approach as shown in Algorithm 1 for a given maximal bound B, which invokes SMT solving at most $\mathbf{O}(|\log_2 B|)$ times.

Algorithm 1: A sound algorithm for the scheduling problem

    Input : a set of constraints Φ, a timeout threshold T, a maximal bound B
    Output: $\{\texttt{SAT}, \texttt{UNSAT}, \texttt{Timeout}\} \times \mathbb{N}^+$
1 $\texttt{result}_1 \leftarrow \texttt{SMTSolver}([\![\Phi]\!], T)$;
2   **if** $\texttt{result}_1 = \texttt{SAT}$ **then**   /* Schedulable */
3 $\lfloor$ **return** $(\texttt{SAT}, 0)$
4 $l \leftarrow 0; u \leftarrow B$;
5   **while** $l \leq u$ **do**   /* Binary search */
6 $k \leftarrow \lfloor \frac{l+u}{2} \rfloor$;
7 $\texttt{result}_2 \leftarrow \texttt{SMTSolver}([\![\Phi]\!]_k, T)$;
8   **if** $\texttt{result}_2 = \texttt{SAT}$ **then** $l \leftarrow k + 1$;   /* Upper half */
9   **else**   /* Lower half */
10 $u \leftarrow k - 1$;
11   **if** $\texttt{result}_1 = \texttt{UNSAT} \vee \texttt{result}_2 = \texttt{UNSAT}$ **then**
12 $\lfloor$ $\texttt{result}_1 \leftarrow \texttt{UNSAT}$;
13 **if** $\texttt{result}_2 \neq \texttt{SAT}$ **then** $k \leftarrow k - 1$;
14 **return** $(\texttt{result}_1, k)$;

Given a set Φ of constraints in CCSL, a timeout threshold T and a maximal bound B, Algorithm 1 first invokes an SMTSolver to decide whether $[\![\Phi]\!]$ is satisfiable or not within T time. If $[\![\Phi]\!]$ is satisfiable, then Algorithm 1 returns (SAT, 0), meaning that Φ is schedulable. Otherwise, it binary searches a bound $k \leq B$ such that $[\![\Phi]\!]_k$ is satisfiable while $[\![\Phi]\!]_{k+1}$ (if $k + 1 \leq B$) is unsatisfiable or cannot be verified in time T.

Theorem 3. *Algorithm 1 has the following three properties:*

1. *If it returns* (SAT, 0), *then Φ is schedulable.*
2. *If it returns* (UNSAT, k), *then Φ is unschedulable. If $k \neq 0$, then Φ has k-bounded schedulable, otherwise does not have any bounded schedulable.*
3. *If it returns* (Timeout, k), *then Φ is k-bounded schedulable if $k \neq 0$, otherwise no bounded schedule is found for Φ.*

5 Case Study and Performance Evaluation

We implemented our approach in a prototype tool with Z3 [25] as its underlying SMT solver. We conduct a case study on expressing requirements of an interlocking system in CCSL constraints and analyzing its schedulability. Then, we prove 12 algebraic properties of CCSL constraints using the tool. Finally, we evaluate the performance of the tool using 9 sets of CCSL constraints.

5.1 Schedulability of an Interlocking System

The interlocking system is a subsystem of a rail transit system. It is used to prevent trains from collisions and derailments when they are moving under the control of signal lights. As shown in Fig. 3, the interlocking system monitors the occupancy status of the individual track section, and sends signals to inform drivers whether they are allowed to enter the route or not. The railway tracks are divided into sections. Each section is associated with a track circuit for detecting whether it is occupied by a train or not. Signal lights are placed between track sections. They can be red and green to indicate proceeding and stopping, respectively.

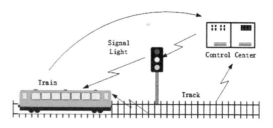

Fig. 3. Interlocking system

The mechanism and operation procedure of the interlocking system are summarized as follows.

1. To enter a track, a train first sends a request to the control center.
2. On receiving the request, the control center sends an inquiry to the track circuit to detect the status of the track.

Table 2. CCSL constraints of the interlocking system

request $\prec$ inquiry	responseOfTrack $\triangleq$ checkSucc + checkFail
checkFail $\prec$ redPulse	responseOfTrain $\triangleq$ enter + wait
redPulse $\preccurlyeq$ showRed	inquiry $\prec$ responseOfTrack
showRed $\prec$ wait	getOccupied $\sim$ getUnoccupied
checkSucc $\prec$ greenPulse	getOccupied $\#$ getUnoccupied
greenPulse $\preccurlyeq$ showGreen	request $\sim$ responseOfTrain
showGreen $\prec$ enter	inquiry $-$ responseOfTrack ≤ 40
enter $\prec$ leave	greenPulse $-$ showGreen ≤ 30
enter $\subseteq$ getOccupied	redPulse $-$ showRed ≤ 30
leave $\subseteq$ getUnoccupied	request $-$ responseOfTrain ≤ 50
getOccupied $\sim$ tmp$_1$	checkFail $-$ showRed ≤ 40
getUnoccupied $\sim$ tmp$_1$	checkSucc $-$ showGreen ≤ 40
checkFail $\subseteq$ tmp$_1$	getUnoccupied $\prec$ tmp$_2$
tmp$_2$ $\prec$ getOccupied	checkSucc $\subseteq$ tmp$_2$

3. If the track is occupied, it sends *checkFail* to the control center, and otherwise *checkSucc*.
4. On receiving the message *checkFail* (*resp. checkSucc*), the control center sends a red (*resp.* green) signal pulse to the signal light.
5. The signal light turns red (*resp.* green) on receiving the red (*resp.* green) signal pulse.
6. The train will enter after seeing the light is green, and the track becomes occupied. In case of the red light, the train must stop and wait.
7. The track becomes unoccupied after the train leaves. If the train is waiting, it must send a request again after some time.

There are time constraints on the above operations. For instance, the control center needs to get a response from the track circuit within 30 ms after sending an inquiry to it. The train must make decision within 50 ms after it sends a request to the control center. The light should turn to the corresponding color within 30 ms after it receives a pulse. After the track becomes occupied (*resp.* unoccupied), the light must turn red (*resp.* green) within 40 ms.

Table 2 shows the main logical constraints on the operations in the system and their timing constraints. We use some non-standard constraint expressions for the sake of compactness. Constraint $a - b \leq n$ denotes that b must tick within n steps after a ticks. It equals the set of the following three constraints:

$$a \prec b, \quad t \triangleq a \ \$ \ n \ on \ \mathbf{1}, \quad b \preccurlyeq t.$$

Note that in this example the unit of time is millisecond (ms). Thus, there is an implicit assumption in the constraints that every tick of a logic clock means the elapse of one millisecond.

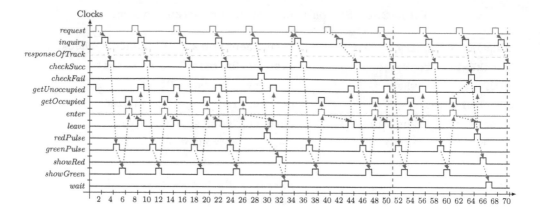

Fig. 4. A bounded schedule for the CCSL constraints in the case study

Most constraints in Table 2 are straightforward, except the six constraints marked with waved underlines. The first three constraints specify that checkFail only can occur between the occurrences of getUnoccupied and getOccupied. The others specify the following two requirements:

1. checkSucc only can occur after getUnoccupied and before getOccupied;
2. getUnoccupied precedes getOccupied.

Given these constraints, our tool found a bounded schedule as depicted in Fig. 4. From step 1 to step 7, one complete process is finished. Initially, the track gets unoccupied. At step 2, a request is made, which causes subsequent operations to occur from step 3 to step 7. At step 29, a fail case occurs because another train enters (step 26) but has not left (step 31). The train that made the request has to wait (step 33).

If we extend the bounded schedule by infinitely repeating the behaviors of all the clocks between step 51 and 69 from step 70, we obtain an infinite schedule. The extended schedule satisfies all the constraints, and thus it is a witness of the schedulability of designed mechanism for the interlocking system.

In this paper, we are only concerned with the schedulability of the constraints in the example. Some other kinds of temporal properties also need to verify. For instance, we must guarantee that whenever a train requests to enter the station, it must eventually enter. We also need to verify the system is deadlock-free. Such temporal properties can be verified by LTL model checking of CCSL constraints using SMT technique [40]. We omit it because it is beyond the scope of this paper.

5.2   Automatic Proof of CCSL Algebraic Properties

Using the proposed approach, we can also prove automatically algebraic properties of CCSL constraints such as the commutativity of exclusion and transitivity of causality. Algebraic properties of CCSL constraints can be represented as $\Phi \Rightarrow \phi$, where Φ is a set of CCSL constraints and ϕ is a constraint derived from Φ. Proving $\Phi \Rightarrow \phi$ is valid equals proving the unsatisfiability of $[\![\Phi]\!] \wedge \neg[\![\phi]\!]$, which can be solved by Algorithm 1.

Table 3. Proved algebraic properties of CCSL constraints

Algebraic property	Definition
Commutativity of exclusion	$c1 \# c2 \Rightarrow c2 \# c1$
Transitivity of causality	$c_1 \preccurlyeq c_2 \,,\, c_2 \preccurlyeq c_3 \Rightarrow c_1 \preccurlyeq c_3$
Antisymmetry of causality	$c_1 \preccurlyeq c_2 \,,\, c_2 \preccurlyeq c_1 \Rightarrow c_1 = c_2$
Fastness of infimum	$c_1 \triangleq c_2 \wedge c_3 \Rightarrow c_1 \preccurlyeq c_2, c_1 \preccurlyeq c_3$
Slowestness of infimum	$c_1 \triangleq c_2 \wedge c_3, c_4 \preccurlyeq c_2, c_4 \preccurlyeq c_3 \Rightarrow c_4 \preccurlyeq c_1$
Slowness of supremum	$c_1 \triangleq c_2 \vee c_3 \Rightarrow c_2 \preccurlyeq c_1, c_3 \preccurlyeq c_1$
Fastestness of supremum	$c_1 \triangleq c_2 \vee c_3, c_2 \preccurlyeq c_4, c_3 \preccurlyeq c_4 \Rightarrow c_1 \preccurlyeq c_4$
Causality of subclock	$c_1 \subseteq c_2 \Rightarrow c_2 \preccurlyeq c_1$
Causality of union	$c_1 \triangleq c_2 + c_3 \Rightarrow c_1 \preccurlyeq c_2, c_1 \preccurlyeq c_3$
Causality of intersection	$c_1 \triangleq c_2 * c_3 \Rightarrow c_2 \preccurlyeq c_1, c_3 \preccurlyeq c_1$
Subclocking of sampling	$c_1 \triangleq c_2 \wr c_3 \Rightarrow c_1 \subseteq c_3$
Subclocking of union	$c_1 \triangleq c_2 + c_3 \Rightarrow c_2 \subseteq c_1, c_3 \subseteq c_1$
Subclocking of intersection	$c_1 \triangleq c_2 * c_3 \Rightarrow c_1 \subseteq c_2, c_1 \subseteq c_3$

Let us consider the proof of the slowestness of infimum as an example. The slowestness of infimum means that an infimum constraint $c_1 \triangleq c_2 \wedge c_3$ defines the slowest clock c_1 among those that are faster than both c_2 and c_3.

Proposition 3 (Slowestness of infimum). *Given two clocks c_2, c_3, let $c_1 \triangleq c_2 \wedge c_3$ and c_4 be an arbitrary clock such that $c_4 \preccurlyeq c_2$ and $c_4 \preccurlyeq c_3$, then $c_4 \preccurlyeq c_1$.*

This is proved by transforming CCSL constraints into the following SMT formula according the SMT encoding method:

$$[\![c_1 \triangleq c_2 \wedge c_3]\!] \wedge [\![c_4 \preccurlyeq c_2]\!] \wedge [\![c_4 \preccurlyeq c_3]\!] \wedge \neg [\![c_4 \preccurlyeq c_1]\!].$$

Algorithm 1 returns (UNSAT, 0), which means that the formula is proved unsatisfiable. The proposition is proved.

Table 3 lists the algebraic properties that have been successfully proved in our approach. Algebraic properties are useful to help understand the relation among CCSL constraints. Using them we can also verify whether some CCSL constraints are redundant or inconsistent for a given set of CCSL constraints.

5.3 Performance Evaluation

To evaluate the performance our tool, we collected 9 sets of CCSL constraints from the literature and real-world applications, and analyzed their schedulability using our tool. Under different time thresholds, we calculate the maximal bounds under which the constraints are schedulable.

Table 4 shows all the experimental results including the corresponding execution time. All the experiments were conducted on a Win 10 running on an i7 CPU with 2.70 GHz and 16 GB memory. The numbers followed by asterisks

Table 4. Experimental results of bounded schedulability analysis

CS	Clks.	Cons.	THD: 10 s		THD: 20 s		THD: 30 s		THD: 40 s	
			BD	TM	BD	TM	BD	TM	BD	TM
CS1	3	3	8	0.06	8	0.06	8	0.06	8	0.06
CS2	3	4	2^*	0.06	2^*	0.06	2^*	0.06	2^*	0.06
CS3	8	9	48	6.20	59	15.88	70	28.72	75	39.82
CS4	8	7	70	7.12	70	7.12	70	7.12	70	7.12
CS5	9	9	80	8.29	90	19.95	110	26.81	111	39.84
CS6	10	6	95	9.40	113	14.26	113	14.26	113	14.26
CS7	12	9	69	8.80	76	19.42	89	27.69	95	40.00
CS8	17	20	16	0.81	16	0.81	16^*	27.36	16^*	27.36
CS9	27	51	30	9.94	41	17.19	45	29.78	45	29.78

Remarks: CS: constraint set, Cons: the number of constraints, Clks: the number of clocks, THD: timeout threshold, TM: Time (second), BD: upper bound.

are the maximal bounds such that the corresponding constraints are bounded schedulable, but unschedulable in the next step. It is interesting to observe from Table 4 that time cost is loosely related to size (the number of clocks and constraints), thanks to efficient search strategies of SMT solvers. This is in striking contrasts to automata-based [29, 35] and the rewriting-based approaches [38], whose scalability suffers from both the numbers of clocks and constraints.

6   Related Work

CCSL is directly derived from the family of synchronous languages, such as Lustre [9], Esterel [6] and Signal [5], and its the scheduling problem of CCSL is akin to what synchronous languages call clock calculus. The main differences are: CCSL is a specification language, while others are programming languages; and CCSL partially describes what is expected to happen in a declarative way and does not give a direct operational deterministic description of what must happen. Furthermore, CCSL only deals with pure clocks while the others deal with signals and extract the clocks when needed.

The Esterel compiler [31] applies a constructive approach to decide when a signal must occur (compute its clock) and what its value should be. This requires a detection of *causality cycles*, or intra-cycle data dependencies, which are also naturally addressed by our approach. However, the Esterel compiler compiles an imperative program into a Boolean circuit, or equivalently a finite state machine. Consequently, it cannot deal with CCSL unbounded schedules.

The clock calculus in Signal attempts to detect whether the specification is endochronous [30], in which case it can generate some efficient code. This analysis is mainly based on the subclock relationship that also exists in CCSL. In CCSL, we consider the problem whether there is at least one possible schedule or not.

In Lustre and its extensions, clocks are regarded as abstract types [13] and the clock calculus computes the relative rates of clocks while rejecting the program when computing the rates is not possible. In most cases, the compiler attempts to build bounded buffers and to ensure that the functional determinism can be preserved with a finite memory. In our case, we do not seek to reach a finite representation, as in the first specification steps this is not a primary goal for the designers. Indeed, this might lead to an over-specification of the problem.

Classical real-time scheduling problem [32] usually relies on task models, arrival patterns and constraints (e.g., precedence, resources) to propose algorithms for the scheduling problem with analytical results [19] or heuristics depending on the specific model (e.g., priorities, preemptive). Other solutions, based on timed automata [1,2,17] or timed Petri nets [8,18], propose a general framework for describing all the relevant aspects without assuming a specific task model. CCSL offers an alternative method based on logical time. It is believed that logical time and multiform time bases offer some flexibility to unify functional requirements and performance constraints. We rely on CCSL and we claim that after encoding a task model in CCSL, finding a schedule for the CCSL model also gives a schedule for the encoded task model [24].

There have been many efforts made towards the scheduling problem of CCSL, though no conclusion is drawn on its decidability. TimeSquare [14] is a simulation tool for CCSL which can produce a possible schedule for a given set of CCSL, up to a given user-defined bound. It also supports different simulation strategies for producing desired execution traces. Some earlier work [20] define the notion of *safe* CCSL specifications that can be encoded with a finite-state machine. The scheduling problem is decidable for safe specifications, as one can merely enumerate all the (finite) solutions. A semi-algorithm can build the finite representation when the specification is safe [21]. In [37], Zhang et al. proposed a state-based approach and a sufficient condition to decide whether safe and unsafe specifications accept a so-called *periodic schedule* [39]. This allows to build a finite solution for unsafe specifications, while there may also exist infinite solutions. Xu et al. proposed a notion of *divergence* of CCSL to study the schedulability of CCSL, and proved that a set of CCSL constraints is schedulable if all the constraints are divergent [34]. They resorted to the theorem prover PVS [27] to assist the divergence proof.

The scheduling problem of CCSL constraints in this work resorts to SMT solving to deal with the bounded and unbounded schedules. Using SMT solving has two advantages: (1) it is usually efficient in practice, and (2) it can deal with unsafe CCSL constraints such as infimum and supremum [21].

Some basic algebraic properties on CCSL relations have been established manually before [23] but we provide here an automatic framework to do so.

7   Conclusion and Future Work

In this work, we proved that the bounded scheduling problem of CCSL is NP-complete, and proposed an SMT-based decision procedure for the bounded scheduling problem. The procedure is sound and complete. The experimental results also show its efficiency in practice. Based on this decision procedure, we devised a sound algorithm for the general scheduling problem. We evaluated the effectiveness of the proposed approach on an interlocking system. We also showed our approach can be used to prove algebraic properties of CCSL constraints.

Our approach to the bounded scheduling problem of CCSL makes us one step closer to tackling the general (i.e. unbounded) scheduling problem. As the case study demonstrates, one may find an infinite schedule by extending a bounded one such that the extended infinite schedule still satisfies the constraints. This observation inspires future work to investigate mechanisms of finding such bounded schedules, hopefully with SMT solvers by extending our algorithm. In our earlier work [37], we proposed a similar approach to search for periodical schedules in bounded steps. In that approach, CCSL constraints are transformed into finite state machine and consequently suffers from the state explosion problem. We believe our SMT-based approach can be extended to their work while still avoiding state explosion. We leave it to future work.

References

1. Abdeddaïm, Y., Asarin, E., Maler, O.: Scheduling with timed automata. Theor. Comput. Sci. **354**(2), 272–300 (2006)
2. Amnell, T., Fersman, E., Mokrushin, L., Pettersson, P., Yi, W.: TIMES: a tool for schedulability analysis and code generation of real-time systems. In: Larsen, K.G., Niebert, P. (eds.) FORMATS 2003. LNCS, vol. 2791, pp. 60–72. Springer, Heidelberg (2004). https://doi.org/10.1007/978-3-540-40903-8_6
3. André, C., Mallet, F., de Simone, R.: Modeling time(s). In: Engels, G., Opdyke, B., Schmidt, D.C., Weil, F. (eds.) MODELS 2007. LNCS, vol. 4735, pp. 559–573. Springer, Heidelberg (2007). https://doi.org/10.1007/978-3-540-75209-7_38
4. Barrett, C., Fontaine, P., Tinelli, C.: The SMT-LIB standard (2016)
5. Benveniste, A., Guernic, P.L., Jacquemot, C.: Synchronous programming with events and relations: the SIGNAL language and its semantics. Sci. Comput. Program. **16**(2), 103–149 (1991)
6. Berry, G., Gonthier, G.: The esterel synchronous programming language: design, semantics, implementation. Sci. Comput. Program. **19**(2), 87–152 (1992)
7. Boehm, B., Basili, V.R.: Software defect reduction top 10 list. Computer **34**(1), 135–137 (2001)
8. Bucci, G., Fedeli, A., Sassoli, L., Vicario, E.: Modeling flexible real time systems with preemptive time petri nets. In: Proceedings of the 15th ECRTS, Porto, Portugal, pp. 279–286. IEEE (2003)
9. Caspi, P., Pilaud, D., Halbwachs, N., Plaice, J.: LUSTRE: a declarative language for programming synchronous systems. In: Proceedings of 14th POPL, Tucson, USA, pp. 178–188. ACM Press (1987)
10. Chen, X., Yin, L., Yu, Y., Jin, Z.: Transforming timing requirements into CCSL constraints to verify cyber-physical systems. In: Duan, Z., Ong, L. (eds.) ICFEM 2017. LNCS, vol. 10610, pp. 54–70. Springer, Cham (2017). https://doi.org/10.1007/978-3-319-68690-5_4
11. Chen, Y., Chen, Y., Madelaine, E.: Timed-pNets: a communication behavioural semantic model for distributed systems. Front. Comput. Sci. **9**(1), 87–110 (2015)

12. Colaço, J., Pagano, B., Pouzet, M.: SCADE 6: a formal language for embedded critical software development. In: Proceedings of the 11th TASE, Sophia Antipolis, France, pp. 1–11. IEEE (2017)

13. Colaço, J.-L., Pouzet, M.: Clocks as first class abstract types. In: Alur, R., Lee, I. (eds.) EMSOFT 2003. LNCS, vol. 2855, pp. 134–155. Springer, Heidelberg (2003). https://doi.org/10.1007/978-3-540-45212-6_10

14. Deantoni, J., Mallet, F.: TimeSquare: treat your models with logical time. In: Proceedings of the 50th TOOLS, Prague, Czech Republic, pp. 34–41. IEEE (2012)

15. Feiler, P.H., Gluch, D.P.: Model-based engineering with AADL - an introduction to the SAE architecture analysis and design language. SEI, Addison-Wesley (2012)

16. Kang, E., Schobbens, P.: Schedulability analysis support for automotive systems: from requirement to implementation. In: Proceedings of the 29th SAC, Gyeongju, Korea, pp. 1080–1085. ACM (2014)

17. Krčál, P., Yi, W.: Decidable and undecidable problems in schedulability analysis using timed automata. In: Jensen, K., Podelski, A. (eds.) TACAS 2004. LNCS, vol. 2988, pp. 236–250. Springer, Heidelberg (2004). https://doi.org/10.1007/978-3-540-24730-2_20

18. Lime, D., Roux, O.: A translation based method for the timed analysis of scheduling extended time petri nets. In: Proceedings of the 25th RTSS, pp. 187–196. IEEE (2004)

19. Liu, C.L., Layland, J.W.: Scheduling algorithms for multiprogramming in a hard-real-time environment. J. ACM **20**(1), 46–61 (1973)

20. Mallet, F., Millo, J.-V.: Boundness issues in CCSL specifications. In: Groves, L., Sun, J. (eds.) ICFEM 2013. LNCS, vol. 8144, pp. 20–35. Springer, Heidelberg (2013). https://doi.org/10.1007/978-3-642-41202-8_3

21. Mallet, F., de Simone, R.: Correctness issues on MARTE/CCSL constraints. Sci. Comput. Program. **106**, 78–92 (2015)

22. Mallet, F., Villar, E., Herrera, F.: MARTE for CPS and CPSoS. In: Nakajima, S., Talpin, J.-P., Toyoshima, M., Yu, H. (eds.) Cyber-Physical System Design from an Architecture Analysis Viewpoint, pp. 81–108. Springer, Singapore (2017). https://doi.org/10.1007/978-981-10-4436-6_4

23. Mallet, F., Millo, J., de Simone, R.: Safe CCSL specifications and marked graphs. In: Proceedings of the 11th MEMOCODE, Portland, OR, USA, pp. 157–166. IEEE (2013)

24. Mallet, F., Zhang, M.: Work-in-progress: from logical time scheduling to real-time scheduling. In: Proceedings of the 39th RTSS, Nashville, USA, pp. 143–146. IEEE (2018)

25. de Moura, L., Bjørner, N.: Z3: an efficient SMT solver. In: Ramakrishnan, C.R., Rehof, J. (eds.) TACAS 2008. LNCS, vol. 4963, pp. 337–340. Springer, Heidelberg (2008). https://doi.org/10.1007/978-3-540-78800-3_24

26. OMG: UML profile for MARTE: modeling and analysis of real-time embedded systems (2015)

27. Owre, S., Rushby, J.M., Shankar, N.: PVS: a prototype verification system. In: Kapur, D. (ed.) CADE 1992. LNCS, vol. 607, pp. 748–752. Springer, Heidelberg (1992). https://doi.org/10.1007/3-540-55602-8_217

28. Peters, J., Przigoda, N., Wille, R., Drechsler, R.: Clocks vs. instants relations: verifying CCSL time constraints in UML/MARTE models. In: Proceedings of the 14th MEMOCODE, Kanpur, India, pp. 78–84. IEEE (2016)

29. Peters, J., Wille, R., Przigoda, N., Kühne, U., Drechsler, R.: A generic representation of CCSL time constraints for UML/MARTE models. In: Proceedings of the 52nd DAC, pp. 122:1–122:6. ACM (2015)

30. Potop-Butucaru, D., Caillaud, B., Benveniste, A.: Concurrency in synchronous systems. Formal Methods Syst. Des. **28**(2), 111–130 (2006)
31. Potop-Butucaru, D., Edwards, S.A., Berry, G.: Compiling Esterel. Springer, Boston (2007). https://doi.org/10.1007/978-0-387-70628-3
32. Sha, L., et al.: Real time scheduling theory: a historical perspective. Real-Time Syst. **28**(2–3), 101–155 (2004)
33. Suryadevara, J., Seceleanu, C., Mallet, F., Pettersson, P.: Verifying MARTE/CCSL mode behaviors using UPPAAL. In: Hierons, R.M., Merayo, M.G., Bravetti, M. (eds.) SEFM 2013. LNCS, vol. 8137, pp. 1–15. Springer, Heidelberg (2013). https://doi.org/10.1007/978-3-642-40561-7_1
34. Xu, Q., de Simone, R., DeAntoni, J.: Divergence detection for CCSL specification via clock causality chain. In: Fränzle, M., Kapur, D., Zhan, N. (eds.) SETTA 2016. LNCS, vol. 9984, pp. 18–37. Springer, Cham (2016). https://doi.org/10.1007/978-3-319-47677-3_2
35. Yin, L., Mallet, F., Liu, J.: Verification of MARTE/CCSL time requirements in Promela/SPIN. In: Proceedings of the 16th ICECCS, USA, pp. 65–74. IEEE (2011)
36. Yu, H., Talpin, J., Besnard, L., et al.: Polychronous controller synthesis from MARTE/CCSL timing specifications. In: Proceedings of the 9th MEMOCODE, Cambridge, UK, pp. 21–30. IEEE (2011)
37. Zhang, M., Dai, F., Mallet, F.: Periodic scheduling for MARTE/CCSL: theory and practice. Sci. Comput. Program. **154**, 42–60 (2018)
38. Zhang, M., Mallet, F.: An executable semantics of clock constraint specification language and its applications. In: Artho, C., Ölveczky, P.C. (eds.) FTSCS 2015. CCIS, vol. 596, pp. 37–51. Springer, Cham (2016). https://doi.org/10.1007/978-3-319-29510-7_2
39. Zhang, M., Mallet, F., Zhu, H.: An SMT-based approach to the formal analysis of MARTE/CCSL. In: Ogata, K., Lawford, M., Liu, S. (eds.) ICFEM 2016. LNCS, vol. 10009, pp. 433–449. Springer, Cham (2016). https://doi.org/10.1007/978-3-319-47846-3_27
40. Zhang, M., Ying, Y.: Towards SMT-based LTL model checking of clock constraint specification language for real-time and embedded systems. In: Proceedings of the 18th LCTES, Barcelona, Spain, pp. 61–70. ACM (2017)

A Logic-Based Incremental Approach to Graph Repair

Sven Schneider[1]([✉]), Leen Lambers[1], and Fernando Orejas[2]

[1] Hasso Plattner Institut, University of Potsdam, Potsdam, Germany
Sven.Schneider@HPI.de
[2] Universitat Politècnica de Catalunya, Barcelona, Spain

Abstract. Graph repair, restoring consistency of a graph, plays a prominent role in several areas of computer science and beyond: For example, in model-driven engineering, the abstract syntax of models is usually encoded using graphs. Flexible edit operations temporarily create inconsistent graphs not representing a valid model, thus requiring graph repair. Similarly, in graph databases—managing the storage and manipulation of graph data—updates may cause that a given database does not satisfy some integrity constraints, requiring also graph repair.

We present a logic-based incremental approach to graph repair, generating a sound and complete (upon termination) overview of least-changing repairs. In our context, we formalize consistency by so-called graph conditions being equivalent to first-order logic on graphs. We present two kind of repair algorithms: State-based repair restores consistency independent of the graph update history, whereas delta-based (or incremental) repair takes this history explicitly into account. Technically, our algorithms rely on an existing model generation algorithm for graph conditions implemented in AUTOGRAPH. Moreover, the delta-based approach uses the new concept of satisfaction (ST) trees for encoding if and how a graph satisfies a graph condition. We then demonstrate how to manipulate these STs incrementally with respect to a graph update.

1 Introduction

Graph repair, restoring consistency of a graph, plays a prominent role in several areas of computer science and beyond. For example, in model-driven engineering, models are typically represented using graphs and the use of flexible edit operations may temporarily create inconsistent graphs not representing a valid model, thus requiring graph repair. This includes the situation where different views of an artifact are represented by a different model, i.e., the artifact is described by a multi-model, see, e.g. [6], and updates in some models may cause a global inconsistency in the multimodel. Similarly, in graph databases—managing the storage and manipulation of graph data—updates may cause that a given database does not satisfy some integrity constraints [1], requiring also graph repair.

Numerous approaches on model inconsistency and repair (see [12] for an excellent recent survey) operate in varying frameworks with diverse assumptions. In our framework, we consider a typed directed graph (cf. [7]) to be inconsistent if it does not satisfy a given finite set of constraints, which are expressed by graph conditions [8], a formalism with the expressive power of first-order logic on graphs. A graph repair is, then, a description of an update that, if applied to the given graph, makes it consistent. Our algorithms do not just provide one repair, but a set of them from which the user must select the right repair to be applied. Moreover, we derive only least changing repairs, which do not include other smaller viable repairs. Our approach uses techniques (and the tool AUTOGRAPH) [17] designed for model generation of graph conditions.

We consider two scenarios: In the first one, the aim is to repair a given graph (state-based repair). In the second one, a consistent graph is given together with an update that may make it inconsistent. In this case, the aim is to repair the graph in an incremental way (delta-based repair).

The main contributions of the paper are the following ones:

- A precise definition of what an update is, together with the definition of some properties, like e.g. least changing, that a repair update may satisfy.
- Two kind of graph repair algorithms: state-based and incremental (for the delta-based case). Moreover, we demonstrate for all algorithms *soundness* (the repair result provided by the algorithms is consistent) and *completeness* (upon termination, our algorithms will find all possible desired repairs)[1].

Summarizing, most repair techniques do not provide guarantees for the functional semantics of the repair and suffer from lack of information for the deployment of the techniques (see conclusion of the survey [12]). With our logic-based graph repair approach we aim at alleviating this weakness by presenting formally its functional semantics and describing the details of the underlying algorithms.

The paper is organized as follows: After introducing preliminaries in Sect. 2, we proceed in Sect. 3 with defining graph updates and repairs. In Sect. 4, we present the state-based scenario. We continue with introducing satisfaction trees in Sect. 5 that are needed for the delta-based scenario in Sect. 6. We close with a comparison with related work in Sect. 7 and conclusion with outlook in Sect. 8. For proofs of theorems and example details we refer to our technical report [18].

2   Preliminaries on Graph Conditions

We recall graph conditions (GCs), defined here over typed directed graphs, used for representing properties on such graphs. In our running example[2], we employ

---

[1] Note that completeness implies totality (if the given set of constraints is satisfiable by a finite graph, then the algorithms will find a repair for any inconsistent graph).

[2] We refer to Sect. 1 with pointers to related work including diverse use cases in Software Engineering for graph repair with more complex and motivating examples.

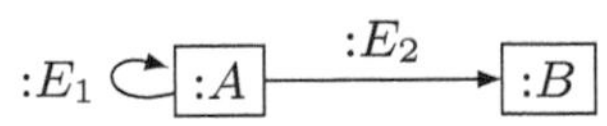

$$:E_1 \hookleftarrow \boxed{:A} \xrightarrow{\ :E_2\ } \boxed{:B} \qquad \neg\exists(\,a\,, \neg(\exists(\,a\xrightarrow{\ e\ }b\,, true) \wedge \neg\exists(\,a\,\rotatebox{180}{$\circlearrowleft$}\,e\,, true)))$$

Fig. 1. The type graph TG (left) and the GC ψ (right) for our running example

the type graph TG from Fig. 1 and we use nodes with names a_i and b_i to indicate that they are of type $:A$ and $:B$, respectively.

GCs state facts about the existence of graph patterns in a given graph, called a host graph. For example, in the syntax used in our running example, the GC $\exists(a, true)$ means that the host graph must include a node of type $:A$. Also, $\exists(a\longrightarrow b, true)$ means that the host graph must include a node of type $:A$, another node of type $:B$, and an edge from the $:A$-node to the $:B$-node.

In general, in the syntax that we use in our running example, an atomic GC is of the form $\exists(H, \phi)$ (or $\neg\exists(H, \phi)$) where H is a graph that must be (or must not be) included in the host graph and where ϕ is a condition expressing more restrictions on how this graph is found (or not found) in the host graph. For instance, $\exists(a, \neg\exists(a\xrightarrow{e}b, true))$ states that the host graph must include an $:A$-node such that it has no outgoing edge e to a $:B$-node. Moreover, we use the standard boolean operators to combine atomic GCs to form more complex ones. For instance, $\exists(a, \neg(\exists(a\xrightarrow{e}b, true) \wedge \neg\exists(a\rotatebox{180}{$\circlearrowleft$}e, true)))$ states that the host graph must include an $:A$-node, such that it does not hold that there is an outgoing edge e to a $:B$-node and node a has no loop. In addition, as an abbreviation for readability, we may use the universal quantifier with the meaning $\forall(H, \phi) = \neg\exists(H, \neg\phi)$. In this sense, the condition ϕ from Fig. 1, used in our running example, states that every node of type $:A$ must have an outgoing edge to a node of type $:B$ and that such an $:A$-node must have no loop.

Formally, the syntax of GCs [8], expressively equivalent to first-order logic on graphs [5], is given subsequently. This logic encodes properties of graph extensions, which must be explicitly mentioned as graph inclusions. For instance, the GC $\exists(a, \neg\exists(a\xrightarrow{e}b, true))$ in simplified notation is formally given in the syntax of GCs as $\exists(i_H, \neg\exists(a \hookrightarrow (a\xrightarrow{e}b), true))$, where i_H denotes the inclusion $\emptyset \hookrightarrow H$ with H the graph consisting of node a. This is because it expresses a property of the extension i_H. Moreover, therein the GC $\neg\exists(a \hookrightarrow (a\xrightarrow{e}b), true)$ is actually a property of the extension $a \hookrightarrow (a\xrightarrow{e}b)$.

Definition 1 (Graph Conditions (GCs)) [8]. *The class of graph conditions Φ_H^{GC} for the graph H is defined inductively:*

- $\wedge S \in \Phi_H^{\mathrm{GC}}$ *if* $S \subseteq_{\mathrm{fin}} \Phi_H^{\mathrm{GC}}$.
- $\neg\phi \in \Phi_H^{\mathrm{GC}}$ *if* $\phi \in \Phi_H^{\mathrm{GC}}$.
- $\exists(a : H \hookrightarrow H', \phi) \in \Phi_H^{\mathrm{GC}}$ *if* $\phi \in \Phi_{H'}^{\mathrm{GC}}$.

In addition true, false, $\vee S$, $\phi_1 \Rightarrow \phi_2$, and $\forall(a, \phi)$ can be used as abbreviations, with their obvious replacement.

A mono $m : H \hookrightarrow G$ satisfies a GC $\psi \in \Phi_H^{\mathrm{GC}}$, written $m \models_{\mathrm{GC}} \psi$, if one of the following cases applies.

- $\psi = \wedge S$ and $m \models_{\mathrm{GC}} \phi$ for each $\phi \in S$.
- $\psi = \neg \phi$ and not $m \models_{\mathrm{GC}} \phi$.
- $\psi = \exists(a : H \hookrightarrow H', \phi)$ and $\exists q : H' \hookrightarrow G.\ q \circ a = m \wedge q \models_{\mathrm{GC}} \phi$.

A graph G satisfies a GC $\psi \in \Phi_{\emptyset}^{\mathrm{GC}}$, written $G \models_{\mathrm{GC}} \psi$ or $G \in [\![\psi]\!]$, if $i_G \models_{\mathrm{GC}} \psi$.

3   Graph Updates and Repairs

In this section, we define graph updates to formalize arbitrary modifications of graphs, graph repairs as the desired graph updates resulting in repaired graphs, as well as further desireable properties of graph updates.

In particular, it is well known that a modification or update of G_1 resulting in a graph G_2 can be represented by two inclusions or, in general two monos, which we denote by $(l : I \hookrightarrow G_1, r : I \hookrightarrow G_2)$, where I represents the part of G_1 that is preserved by this update. Intuitively, $l : I \hookrightarrow G_1$ describes the deletion of elements from G_1 (i.e., all elements in $G_1 \setminus l(I)$ are deleted) and $r : I \hookrightarrow G_2$ describes the addition of elements to I to obtain G_2 (i.e., all elements in $G_2 \setminus r(I)$ are added).

Definition 2 (Graph Update). A (graph) update u is a pair $(l : I \hookrightarrow G_1, r : I \hookrightarrow G_2)$ of monos. The class of all updates is denoted by $\mathcal{U}$.

Graph updates such as $(i_G : \emptyset \hookrightarrow G, i_G : \emptyset \hookrightarrow G)$ where G is not the empty graph delete all the elements in G that are added by r afterwards. To rule out such updates, we define an update $(l : I \hookrightarrow G_1, r : I \hookrightarrow G_2)$ to be *canonical* when the graph I is as large as possible, i.e. intuitively $I = G_1 \cap G_2$. Formally:

Definition 3 (Canonical Graph Update). If $(l : I \hookrightarrow G_1, r : I \hookrightarrow G_2) \in \mathcal{U}$ and every $(l' : I' \hookrightarrow G_1, r' : I' \hookrightarrow G_2) \in \mathcal{U}$ and mono $i : I \hookrightarrow I'$ with $l' \circ i = l$ and $r' \circ i = r$ satisfies that i is an isomorphism then (l, r) is canonical, written $(l, r) \in \mathcal{U}_{\mathrm{can}}$.

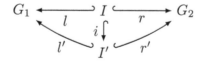

An update u_1 is a sub-update (see [14]) of u whenever the modifications defined by u_1 are fully contained in the modifications defined by u. Intuitively, this is the case when u_1 can be composed with another update u_2 such that (a) the resulting update has the same effect as u and (b) u_2 does not delete any element that was added before by u_1. This is stated, informally speaking, by requiring that I is the intersection (pullback) of I_1 and I_2 and that G_2 is its union (pushout).

Definition 4 (Sub-update [14]). If $u = (l : I \hookrightarrow G_1, r : I \hookrightarrow G_2) \in \mathcal{U}$, $u_1 = (l_1 : I_1 \hookrightarrow G_1, r_1 : I_1 \hookrightarrow G_3) \in \mathcal{U}$, $u_2 = (l_2 : I_2 \hookrightarrow G_3, r_2 : I_2 \hookrightarrow G_2) \in \mathcal{U}$,

$(r'_1 : I \hookrightarrow I_1, l'_2 : I \hookrightarrow I_2)$ *is the pullback of* (r_1, l_2), *and* (r_1, l_2) *is the pushout of* (r'_1, l'_2) *then* u_1 *is a* sub-update *of* u, *written* $u_1 \leq^{u_2} u$ *or simply* $u_1 \leq u$.

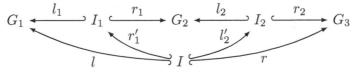

Moreover, we write $u_1 <^{u_2} u$ *or* $u_1 < u$ *when* $u_1 \leq^{u_2} u$ *and not* $u \leq u_1$.

We now define graph repairs as graph updates where the result graph satisfies the given consistency constraint ψ.

Definition 5 (Graph Repair). *If* $u = (l : I \hookrightarrow G_1, r : I \hookrightarrow G_2) \in \mathcal{U}$, $\psi \in \Phi_{\emptyset}^{\mathrm{GC}}$, *and* $G_2 \models_{\mathrm{GC}} \psi$ *then* u *is a* graph repair *or simply* repair *of* G_1 *with respect to* ψ, *written* $u \in \mathcal{U}(G_1, \psi)$.

To define a finite set of desirable repairs, we introduce the notion of least changing repairs that are repairs for which no sub-updates exist that are also repairs.

Definition 6 (Least Changing Graph Repair). *If* $\psi \in \Phi_{\emptyset}^{\mathrm{GC}}$, $u = (l : I \hookrightarrow G_1, r : I \hookrightarrow G_2) \in \mathcal{U}(G_1, \psi)$, *and there is no* $u' \in \mathcal{U}(G_1, \psi)$ *such that* $u' < u$ *then* u *is a* least changing graph repair *of* G_1 *with respect to* ψ, *written* $u \in \mathcal{U}_{\mathrm{lc}}(G_1, \psi)$.

Note that every least changing repair is canonical according to this definition. Moreover, the notion of least changing repairs is unrelated to other notions of repairs such as the set of all repairs that require a smallest amount of atomic modifications of the graph at hand to result in a graph satisfying the consistency constraint. For instance, a repair u_1 adding two nodes of type $:A$ may be a least changing repair even if there is a repair u_2 adding only one node of type $:B$.

A graph repair algorithm is *stable* [12], if the repair procedure returns the identity update $(\mathrm{id}_G : G \hookrightarrow G, \mathrm{id}_G : G \hookrightarrow G)$ when graph G is already consistent. Obviously, a graph repair algorithm that only returns least changing repairs is stable, since the identity update is a sub-update of any other repair.

4   State-Based Repair

In this section, we introduce two state-based graph repair algorithms (see [18] for additional technical detail), which compute a set of graph repairs restoring consistency for a given graph.

Definition 7 (State-Based Graph Repair Algorithm). *A state-based graph repair algorithm takes a graph* G *and a GC* $\psi \in \Phi_{\emptyset}^{\mathrm{GC}}$ *as inputs and returns a set of graph repairs in* $\mathcal{U}(G, \psi)$.

Note that the tool AUTOGRAPH [17] can be used to verify this condition as follows: It determines the operation $\mathcal{A}$ that constructs a finite set of all minimal graphs satisfying a given GC ψ. Formally, $\mathcal{A}(\psi) = \cap\{S \subseteq \llbracket \psi \rrbracket \mid \forall G' \in \llbracket \psi \rrbracket. \exists G \in$

$S. \exists m : G \hookrightarrow G'.true\}$. While AUTOGRAPH may not terminate when computing this operation due to the inherent expressiveness of GCs, it is known that AUTOGRAPH terminates whenever ψ is not satisfied by any graph.

The state-based algorithm $\mathcal{Repair}_{\mathrm{sb},1}$ uses $\mathcal{A}$ to obtain repairs. $\mathcal{Repair}_{\mathrm{sb},1}$ computes the set $\mathcal{A}(\psi \wedge \exists(i_G, true))$ that contains all minimal graphs that (a) satisfy ψ and (b) include a copy of G. All these extensions of G correspond to a graph repair. For our running example, we do not obtain any repair for graph $\mathbf{G'_u}$ from Fig. 2 and GC ψ from Fig. 1 because the loop on node a_2 would invalidate any graph including $\mathbf{G'_u}$. We state that $\mathcal{Repair}_{\mathrm{sb},1}$ indeed computes the non-deleting least changing graph repairs.

Theorem 1 (Functional Semantics of $\mathcal{Repair}_{\mathrm{sb},1}$). $\mathcal{Repair}_{\mathrm{sb},1}$ *is* sound, *i.e.,* $\mathcal{Repair}_{\mathrm{sb},1}(G, \psi) \subseteq \mathcal{U}_{\mathrm{lc}}(G, \psi)$, *and* complete (upon termination) *with respect to non-deleting repairs in* $\mathcal{U}_{\mathrm{lc}}(G, \psi)$.

The second state-based algorithm $\mathcal{Repair}_{\mathrm{sb},2}$ computes *all* least changing graph repairs. In this algorithm we use the approach of $\mathcal{Repair}_{\mathrm{sb},1}$ but compute $\mathcal{A}(\psi \wedge \exists(i_{G_c}, true))$ whenever an inclusion $l : G_c \hookrightarrow G$ describes how G can be restricted to one of its subgraphs G_c. Every graph G' obtained from the application of $\mathcal{A}$ for one of these graphs G_c then results in one graph repair returned by $\mathcal{Repair}_{\mathrm{sb},2}$ except for those that are not least changing.

To this extent we introduce the notion of a restriction tree (see example in Fig. 2) having all subgraphs G_c of a given graph G as nodes as long as they include the graph G_{min}, which is the empty graph in the state-based algorithm $\mathcal{Repair}_{\mathrm{sb},2}$ but not in the algorithm $\mathcal{Repair}_{\mathrm{db}}$ in Sect. 6, and where edges are given in this tree by inclusions that add precisely one node or edge.

Definition 8 (Restriction Tree RT). *If G and G_{min} are graphs and $S = \{l : G_c \hookrightarrow G_p \mid G_{min} \subseteq G_c \subset G_p \subseteq G, l$ is an inclusion$\}$, S' is the least subset of S such that the closure of S' under $\circ$ equals S then a restriction tree $\mathrm{RT}(G, G_{min})$ is a least subset of S' such that for all two inclusions $l_1 : G \hookrightarrow G_1 \in S'$ and $l_2 : G \hookrightarrow G_2 \in S'$ one of them is in $\mathrm{RT}(G, G_{min})$.*

Considering our running example, the restriction tree in Fig. 2 is traversed entirely except for the four graphs without a border, which are not traversed as they have the supergraph marked 9 satisfying ψ and therefore traversing those would generate repairs that are not least changing. The resulting graph repairs for the condition ψ are given by the graphs marked by 3–6.

Our second state-based graph repair algorithm is indeed sound and complete whenever the calls to AUTOGRAPH using $\mathcal{A}$ terminate.

Theorem 2 (Functional Semantics of $\mathcal{Repair}_{\mathrm{sb},2}$). $\mathcal{Repair}_{\mathrm{sb},2}$ *is* sound, *i.e.,* $\mathcal{Repair}_{\mathrm{sb},2}(G, \psi) \subseteq \mathcal{U}_{\mathrm{lc}}(G, \psi)$, *and* complete, *i.e.,* $\mathcal{U}_{\mathrm{lc}}(G, \psi) \subseteq \mathcal{Repair}_{\mathrm{sb},2}(G, \psi)$, *upon termination.*

5 Satisfaction Trees

The state-based algorithms introduced in the previous section are inefficient when used in a scenario where a graph needs repair after a sequence of updates

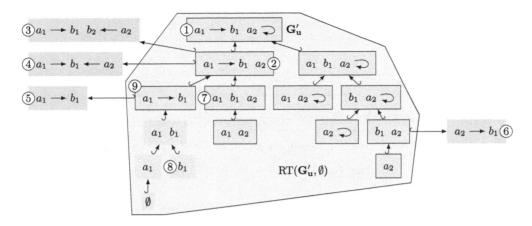

Fig. 2. The restriction tree $\text{RT}(\mathbf{G}'_\mathbf{u}, \emptyset)$ (enclosed by the polygon) and four graph repairs (marked 3–6) generated using $\mathcal{R}\text{epair}_{\text{sb},2}$

that all need repair. We thus present in Sect. 6 an incremental algorithm reducing the computational cost for a repair when an update is provided. This algorithm uses an additional data structure, called *satisfaction tree* or ST, which stores information on if and how a graph G satisfies a GC ψ (according to Definition 1). In this section, given ψ and G, we define how such an ST γ is constructed and how it is updated once the graph G is updated.

If ψ is a conjunction of conditions, its associated ST γ is a conjunction of STs and if ψ is a negation of a conditions, its associated γ is a negation of an ST. In the case when ψ is a $\exists(a : H \hookrightarrow H', \phi)$, recall that a match $m : H \hookrightarrow G$ satisfies ψ if there exists a $q : H' \hookrightarrow G$ such that $m = q \circ a$ and $q \models_{\text{GC}} \phi$. For this case, we keep in ST each q satisfying these two conditions and also each q that satisfies the first condition, but not the second. More precisely, for the case of existential quantification, the corresponding ST is of the form $\exists(a : H \hookrightarrow H', \phi, m_t, m_f)$, where m_t and m_f are partial mappings (we use $\sup(f)$ to denoted the elements actually mapped by a partial map f) that map matches $q : H' \hookrightarrow G$ that satisfy $m = q \circ a$ (for a previously known $m : H \hookrightarrow G$) to an ST for the subcondition ϕ. The difference between both partial functions is that m_t maps matches q to STs for which $q \models_{\text{GC}} \phi$ while m_f maps matches q to STs for which $q \not\models_{\text{GC}} \phi$. Consider Fig. 3b for an example of an ST $\gamma_\mathbf{u}$.

The following definition describes the syntax of STs. The STs are defined over matches into a graph G to allow for the basic well-formedness condition that every mapped match q satisfies $q \circ a = m$.

Definition 9 (Satisfaction Trees (STs)). *The class of all* Satisfaction Trees Γ^{ST}_m *for a mono* $m : H \hookrightarrow G$ *contains* γ *if one of the following cases applies.*

- $\gamma = \wedge S$ *and* $S \subseteq_{\text{fin}} \Gamma^{\text{ST}}_m$.
- $\gamma = \neg \chi$ *and* $\chi \in \Gamma^{\text{ST}}_m$.
- $\gamma = \exists(a, \phi, m_t, m_f)$, $a : H \hookrightarrow H'$, $\phi \in \Phi^{\text{GC}}_{H'}$, $m_t, m_f \subseteq_{\text{fin}} \{(q : H' \hookrightarrow G, \bar{\gamma}) \mid q \circ a = m, \bar{\gamma} \in \Gamma^{\text{ST}}_q\}$, *and* m_t, m_f *are partial maps.*

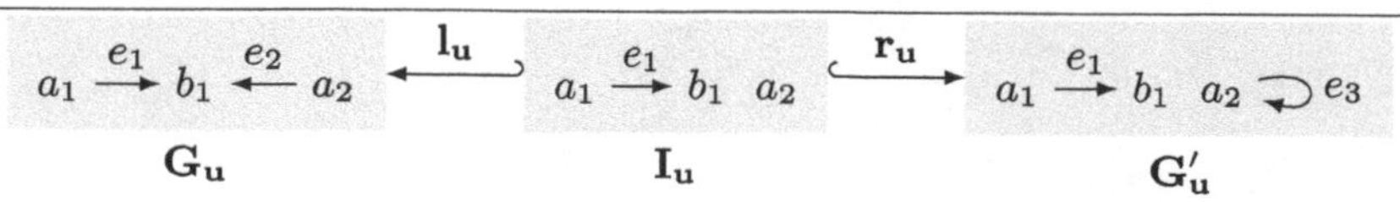

$$a_1 \xrightarrow{e_1} b_1 \xleftarrow{e_2} a_2 \quad \xleftarrow{\mathbf{l_u}} \quad a_1 \xrightarrow{e_1} b_1 \quad a_2 \quad \xhookrightarrow{\mathbf{r_u}} \quad a_1 \xrightarrow{e_1} b_1 \quad a_2 \circlearrowright e_3$$

$$\mathbf{G_u} \qquad\qquad\qquad \mathbf{I_u} \qquad\qquad\qquad \mathbf{G'_u}$$

(a)   A graph update $\mathbf{u} = (\mathbf{l_u} : \mathbf{I_u} \hookrightarrow \mathbf{G_u}, \mathbf{r_u} : \mathbf{I_u} \hookrightarrow \mathbf{G'_u})$

$$\gamma_{\mathbf{u}} = \neg\exists(a, \neg(\exists(a \xrightarrow{e} b, true) \wedge \neg\exists(a \circlearrowright e, true)), \emptyset, \{a_2 \mapsto \gamma_{\mathbf{u},1}, a_1 \mapsto \gamma_{\mathbf{u},2}\})$$

$$\gamma_{\mathbf{u},1} = \neg(\exists(a \xrightarrow{e} b, \underline{true}, \{a_2 \xrightarrow{e_2} b_1 \mapsto true\}, \emptyset) \wedge \neg\exists(a \circlearrowright e, \underline{true}, \emptyset, \emptyset))$$

$$\gamma_{\mathbf{u},2} = \neg(\exists(a \xrightarrow{e} b, \underline{true}, \{a_1 \xrightarrow{e_1} b_1 \mapsto true\}, \emptyset) \wedge \neg\exists(a \circlearrowright e, \underline{true}, \emptyset, \emptyset))$$

(b)   The ST $\gamma_{\mathbf{u}}$ for $\mathbf{G_u}$ (see Fig. 3a) and ψ (see Fig. 1).

$$\gamma_{\mathbf{u}}^{\mathbf{I}} = \neg\exists(a, \neg(\exists(a \xrightarrow{e} b, true) \wedge \neg\exists(a \circlearrowright e, true)), \{a_2 \mapsto \gamma_{\mathbf{u},1}^{\mathbf{I}}\}, \{a_1 \mapsto \gamma_{\mathbf{u},2}^{\mathbf{I}}\})$$

$$\gamma_{\mathbf{u},1}^{\mathbf{I}} = \neg(\exists(a \xrightarrow{e} b, \underline{true}, \emptyset, \emptyset) \wedge \neg\exists(a \circlearrowright e, \underline{true}, \{a_2 \circlearrowright e_3 \mapsto true\}, \emptyset))$$

$$\gamma_{\mathbf{u},2}^{\mathbf{I}} = \neg(\exists(a \xrightarrow{e} b, \underline{true}, \{a_1 \xrightarrow{e_1} b_1 \mapsto true\}, \emptyset) \wedge \neg\exists(a \circlearrowright e, \underline{true}, \emptyset, \emptyset))$$

(c) The ST $\gamma_{\mathbf{u}}^{\mathbf{I}}$ for $\mathbf{I_u}$ (see Fig. 3a) and ψ (see Fig. 1) that is obtained as the backward propagation $\mathrm{ppgB}(\gamma_{\mathbf{u}}, \mathbf{l_u})$ from $\gamma_{\mathbf{u}}$ (see Fig. 3b) and $\mathbf{l_u}$ (see Fig. 3a)

$$\gamma'_{\mathbf{u}} = \neg\exists(a, \neg(\exists(a \xrightarrow{e} b, true) \wedge \neg\exists(a \circlearrowright e, true)), \{a_2 \xmapsto{\mathrm{(R1)}} \gamma'_{\mathbf{u},1}\}, \{a_1 \mapsto \gamma'_{\mathbf{u},2}\})$$

$$\gamma'_{\mathbf{u},1} = \neg(\exists(a \xrightarrow{e} b, \underline{true}, \emptyset_{\mathrm{(R2)}}, \emptyset) \wedge \neg\exists(a \circlearrowright e, \underline{true}, \{a_2 \circlearrowright e_3 \xmapsto{\mathrm{(R3)}} true\}, \emptyset))$$

$$\gamma'_{\mathbf{u},2} = \neg(\exists(a \xrightarrow{e} b, \underline{true}, \{a_1 \xrightarrow{e_1} b_1 \mapsto true\}, \emptyset) \wedge \neg\exists(a \circlearrowright e, \underline{true}, \emptyset, \emptyset))$$

(d)   The ST $\gamma'_{\mathbf{u}}$ for $\mathbf{G'_u}$ (see Fig. 3a) and ψ (see Fig. 1) that is obtained as the forward propagation $\mathrm{ppgF}(\gamma_{\mathbf{u}}^{\mathbf{I}}, \mathbf{r_u})$ from $\gamma_{\mathbf{u}}^{\mathbf{I}}$ (see Fig. 3b) and $\mathbf{r_u}$ (see Fig. 3a). Also $\gamma'_{\mathbf{u}}$ is the result of $\mathrm{ppgU}(\gamma_{\mathbf{u}}, \mathbf{u})$ that applies backward and forward propagation. The viable points for the delta-based repair discussed in Sec. 6 are indicated by (R1)–(R3).

Fig. 3. A graph update and an ST with its propagation over the graph update where GCs are underlined in STs for readability

The following satisfaction predicate $\models_{\mathrm{GC}}$ for STs defines when an ST γ for a mono m states that the contained GC ψ is satisfied by the morphism m.

Definition 10 (ST Satisfaction). *An ST* $\gamma \in \Gamma_{m:H \hookrightarrow G}^{\mathrm{ST}}$ *is satisfied, written* $\models_{\mathrm{ST}} \gamma$, *if one of the following cases applies.*

- $\gamma = \wedge S$ *and* $\models_{\mathrm{ST}} \chi$ *(for each* $\chi \in S$*)*
- $\gamma = \neg\chi$ *and* $\not\models_{\mathrm{ST}} \chi$.
- $\gamma = \exists(a, \phi, m_t, m_f)$ *and* $m_t \neq \emptyset$.

The following recursive operation constructs an ST γ for a graph G and a condition ψ so that γ represents how G satisfies (or not satisfies) ψ. Note that the match m in the definition of STs above and the construction of an ST below corresponds to the match $m : H \hookrightarrow G$ from Definition 1 that we operationalize in the following definition. For conjunction and negation, we construct the STs from the STs for the subconditions. For the case of existential quantification, we consider all morphisms $q : H' \hookrightarrow G$ for which the triangle $q \circ a = m$ commutes and construct the STs for the subcondition ϕ under this extended match q. The resulting STs are inserted into m_t and m_f according to whether they are satisfied.

Definition 11 (Construct ST (cst)). *Given* $m : H \hookrightarrow G$ *and* $\psi \in \Phi_H^{GC}$, *we define* $\mathrm{cst}(\psi, m) = \gamma$, *with* $\gamma \in \Gamma_m^{ST}$ *as follows.*

- *If* $\psi = \wedge S$ *then* $\gamma = \wedge \{\mathrm{cst}(\phi, m) \mid \phi \in S\}$.
- *If* $\psi = \neg \phi$ *then* $\gamma = \neg \, \mathrm{cst}(\phi, m)$.
- *If* $\psi = \exists(a : H \hookrightarrow H', \phi)$, $m_{all} = \{(q : H' \hookrightarrow G, \chi) \mid q \circ a = m, \mathrm{cst}(\phi, q) = \chi\}$, $m_t = \{(q, \chi) \in m_{all} \mid \models_{ST} \chi\}$, $m_f = m_{all} \setminus m_t$, *then* $\gamma = \exists(a, \phi, m_t, m_f)$.

If G is a graph and $\psi \in \Phi_\emptyset^{GC}$, *then* $\mathrm{cst}(\psi, G) = \mathrm{cst}(\psi, i_G)$.

This construction of STs then ensures that $\models_{ST} \gamma$ if and only if $G \models_{GC} \psi$. Note that $\models_{ST} \gamma_\mathbf{u}$ holds for the ST $\gamma_\mathbf{u}$ from Fig. 3b, the GC ψ from Fig. 1, and the graph $\mathbf{G_u}$ from Fig. 3.

Theorem 3 (Sound Construction of STs). *Given* $m : H \hookrightarrow G$, $\psi \in \Phi_H^{GC}$, *and* $\mathrm{cst}(\psi, m) = \gamma$ *then* $\models_{ST} \gamma$ *iff* $m \models_{GC} \psi$.

Subsequently, we define a propagation operation ppgU of an ST γ for a graph update $u = (l : I \hookrightarrow G, r : I \hookrightarrow G')$ to obtain an ST γ' such that $\gamma' = \mathrm{cst}(\psi, G')$ whenever $\gamma = \mathrm{cst}(\psi, G)$. This overall propagation is performed by a backward propagation of γ for l using the operation ppgB followed by a forward propagation of the resulting ST for r using the operation ppgF.

For backward propagation, we describe how the deletion of elements in G by $l : I \hookrightarrow G$ affect its associated ST γ. To this end, we preserve those matches $q : H \hookrightarrow G$ for which no matched elements are deleted. This is formalized by requiring a mono $q' : H \hookrightarrow I$ such that $l \circ q' = q$. The matches q with deleted matched elements can not be preserved and are therefore removed.

Definition 12 (Propagate Match (ppgMatch)). *If* $q : H \hookrightarrow G$ *and* $l : I \hookrightarrow G$ *are monos, then* $\mathrm{ppgMatch}(q, l)$ *is the unique* $q' : H \hookrightarrow I$ *such that* $l \circ q' = q$ *if it exists and* $\bot$ *otherwise.*

The following recursive backward propagation defines how deletions affect the maps m_t and m_f of the given ST. That is, when $\gamma = \exists(a, \phi, m_t, m_f)$, we (a) entirely remove a mapping (m, χ) from m_t or m_f if $\mathrm{ppgMatch}(q, l) = \bot$ and (b) construct for a mapping (m, χ) from m_t or m_f the pair $(\mathrm{ppgMatch}(q, l), \chi')$ where χ' is obtained from recursively applying the backward propagation on χ when $\mathrm{ppgMatch}(q, l) \neq \bot$. The updated pair $(\mathrm{ppgMatch}(q, l), \chi')$ must be rechecked to decide to which partial map this pair must be added to ensure that the resulting ST corresponds to the ST that would be constructed for G' directly.

Definition 13 (Backward Propagation (ppgB)**).** *If* $m : H \hookrightarrow G$, $\gamma \in \Gamma_m^{ST}$, $l : I \hookrightarrow G$, $\mathrm{ppgMatch}(m, l) = m' : H \hookrightarrow I$, *and* $\gamma' \in \Gamma_{m'}^{ST}$ *then* $\mathrm{ppgB}(\gamma, l) = \gamma'$ *if one of the following cases applies.*

- $\gamma = \wedge S$ *and* $\gamma' = \wedge\{\mathrm{ppgB}(\chi, l) \mid \chi \in S\}$.
- $\gamma = \neg\chi$ *and* $\gamma' = \neg\,\mathrm{ppgB}(\chi, l)$.
- $\gamma = \exists(a, \phi, m_t, m_f)$, $m_{all} = \{(q', \chi') \mid (q, \chi) \in m_t \cup m_f \wedge \mathrm{ppgMatch}(q, l) = q' \neq \perp \wedge \mathrm{ppgB}(\chi, l) = \chi'\}$, $m'_t = \{(q, \chi) \in m_{all} \mid\models_{ST} \chi\}$, $m'_f = m_{all} \setminus m'_t$, *and* $\gamma' = \exists(a, \phi, m'_t, m'_f)$.

Note that $\mathrm{ppgMatch}(i_G, l) = i_G$ and, hence, the operation ppgB is applicable for all ST $\gamma \in \Gamma_{i_G}^{ST}$, which is sufficient as we define consistency constraints using GCs over the empty graph as well.

In the case of forward propagation where additions are given by $r : I \hookrightarrow G'$ we can preserve all matches using an adaptation. But the addition of further elements may result in additional matches as well that may satisfy the conditions to be included in the corresponding m_t and m_f from the ST at hand.

Definition 14 (Forward Propagation (ppgF)**).** *If* $\gamma \in \Gamma_{m:H \hookrightarrow I}^{ST}$, $r : I \hookrightarrow G'$, *and* $\gamma' \in \Gamma_{r \circ m}^{ST}$ *then* $\mathrm{ppgF}(\gamma, r) = \gamma'$ *if one of the following cases applies.*

- $\gamma = \wedge S$ *and* $\gamma' = \wedge\{\mathrm{ppgF}(\chi, r) \mid \chi \in S\}$.
- $\gamma = \neg\chi$ *and* $\gamma' = \neg\,\mathrm{ppgF}(\chi, r)$.
- $\gamma = \exists(a, \phi, m_t, m_f)$, $m_{all} = \{(r \circ q, \gamma') \mid (q, \chi) \in m_t \cup m_f \wedge \mathrm{ppgF}(\chi, r) = \gamma'\} \cup \{(q, \gamma_q) \mid q \circ a = r \circ m, (\nexists q' \in \sup(m_t) \cup \sup(m_f).\ r \circ q' = q), \mathrm{cst}(\phi, q) = \gamma_q\}$, $m'_t = \{(q, \chi) \in m_{all} \mid\models_{ST} \chi\}$, $m'_f = m_{all} \setminus m'_t$, *and* $\gamma' = \exists(a, \phi, m'_t, m'_f)$.

We now define the composition of both propagations to obtain the operation ppgU that updates an ST for an entire graph update.

Definition 15 (Update Propagation (ppgU)**).** *If* $m : H \hookrightarrow G$, $\gamma \in \Gamma_m^{ST}$, $l : I \hookrightarrow G$, $\mathrm{ppgMatch}(m, l) = m' : H \hookrightarrow G'$, *and* $r : I \hookrightarrow G'$ *then* $\mathrm{ppgU}(\gamma, (l, r)) = \mathrm{ppgF}(\mathrm{ppgB}(\gamma, l), r) \in \Gamma_{m'}^{ST}$.

The overall propagation given by this operation is *incremental*, in the sense that the operation cst is only used in the forward propagation on parts of the graph G', where the addition of graph elements by r from the graph update results in additional matches q according to the satisfaction relation for GCs. Finally, we state that ppgU incrementally computes the ST obtained using cst. The proof of this theorem relies on the fact that this property also holds for ppgB and ppgF.

Theorem 4 (ppgU is Compatible with cst**).** *If* G *is a graph,* $\psi \in \Phi_\emptyset^{GC}$, $l : I \hookrightarrow G$, *and* $r : I \hookrightarrow G'$ *then* $\mathrm{ppgU}(\mathrm{cst}(\psi, G), (l, r)) = \mathrm{cst}(\psi, G')$.

6   Delta-Based Repair

The local states of delta-based graph repair algorithms may contain, besides the current graph as in state-based graph repair algorithms, an additional value. In our delta-based graph repair algorithm this will be an ST.

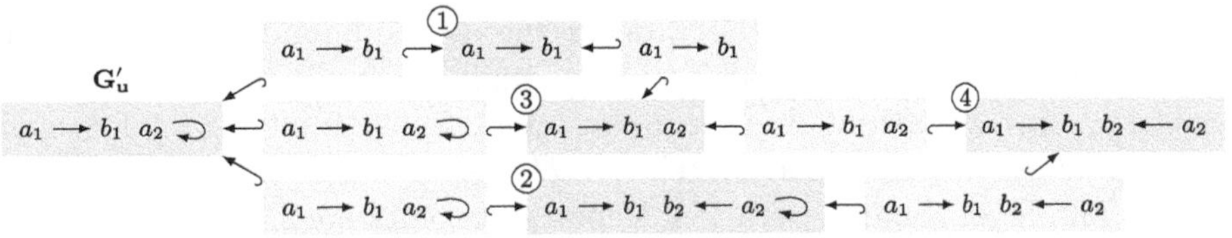

Fig. 4. An example for delta-based graph repair using $\mathcal{R}epair_{db}$

Definition 16 (Delta-Based Graph Repair Algorithm). *Delta-based graph repair algorithms take a graph G, a GC $\psi \in \Phi_\emptyset^{GC}$, and a value q as inputs and return a set of pairs (u, q') where $u \in \mathcal{U}(G, \psi)$ is a graph repair and q' is a value.*

Our delta-based graph repair algorithm $\mathcal{R}epair_{db}$ will be based on the single step operation $\mathcal{R}epair_{db1}$. Given a graph G, a GC $\psi \in \Phi_\emptyset^{GC}$, the ST γ that equals $cst(\psi, G)$, and a graph update $u = (l : I \hookrightarrow G, r : I \hookrightarrow G')$, the single step operation $\mathcal{R}epair_{db}$ first updates γ using ppgU for the graph update u and then determines using $\mathcal{R}epair_{db1}$, if necessary, graph repairs for the resulting ST γ' according to the repair rules described in the following. The algorithm $\mathcal{R}epair_{db}$ then uses $\mathcal{R}epair_{db1}$ in a breadth first manner to obtain multi-step repairs.

For our example from Fig. 3a, such a multi-step repair of $\mathbf{G'_u}$ is given in Fig. 4 where the graph updates are obtained resulting in the graphs marked 1–3, of which only the graph marked 1 satisfies ψ. The algorithm $\mathcal{R}epair_{db}$ then computes further graph updates resulting in the graph marked 4 also satisfying ψ.

The operation $\mathcal{R}epair_{db1}$ for deriving single-step repairs depends on two local modifications. Firstly, a GC $\exists(a : H \hookrightarrow H', \phi)$ occurring as a subcondition in the consistency constraint ψ may be violated because, for the match $m : H \hookrightarrow G$ that locates a copy of H in the graph G under repair, no suitable match $q : H' \hookrightarrow G$ can be found for which $q \circ a = m$ and $q \models_{GC} \phi$ are satisfied. The operation $\mathcal{R}epair_{add}$ resolves this violation by (a) using AUTOGRAPH to construct a suitable graph H_s and by (b) integrating this graph H_s into G resulting in G' such that a suitable match $q : H' \hookrightarrow G'$ can be found.

Definition 17 (Local Addition Operation $\mathcal{R}epair_{add}$). *If $a : H \hookrightarrow H'$, $\phi \in \Phi_{H'}^{GC}$, $m : H \hookrightarrow G$, $H_s \in \mathcal{A}(\exists(i_H, \exists(a, \phi)))$, $k : H \hookrightarrow H_s$, and $(\bar{m} : H_s \hookrightarrow G', r : G \hookrightarrow G')$ is the pushout of (m, k) then $r \in \mathcal{R}epair_{add}(a, \phi, m)$.*

$$
\begin{array}{ccc}
H' \stackrel{a}{\longleftarrow\!\!\!\shortmid} H & \stackrel{k}{\longmapsto} & H_s \\
{\scriptstyle m}\downarrow & & \downarrow{\scriptstyle \bar{m}} \\
G & \stackrel{r}{\longmapsto} & G'
\end{array}
$$

In our running example, $\mathcal{R}epair_{add}$ determines a graph repair resulting in the graph marked 2 in Fig. 4. For this repair, we considered the sub-ST marked by (R2) in Fig. 3d, where the morphism m matches the node a from ψ to the node a_2 in $\mathbf{G'_u}$, but where no extension of m can also match a node $:B$ and an edge between these two nodes. The repair performed then uses $a \stackrel{e}{\longrightarrow} b$ for the graph H_s, resulting in the addition of the node b_2 and the edge from a_2 to b_2.

Secondly, a GC $\exists(a : H \hookrightarrow H', \phi)$ occurring as a subcondition in the consistency constraint ψ may be satisfied even though it should not when occurring underneath some negation. Such a violation is determined, again for a given match $m : H \hookrightarrow G$, by some match $q : H' \hookrightarrow G$ satisfying $q \circ a = m$ and $q \models_{GC} \phi$. The local repair operation $\mathcal{R}\text{epair}_{del}$ repairs such an undesired satisfaction by selecting a graph H_p such that $H \subseteq H_p \subset H'$ using a restriction tree (see Definition 8) and deleting $G_{del} = q(H') \setminus q(H_p)$ from G. Technically, we can not use the pushout complement of a' and q as it does not exists when edges from $G \setminus G_{del}$ are attached to nodes in G_{del}. Hence, we determine the pushout complement of a'' and k', which must be constructed for this purpose suitably.

Definition 18 (Local Deletion Operation $\mathcal{R}\text{epair}_{del}$). *If $a : H \hookrightarrow H'$, $q : H' \hookrightarrow G$, $a' : H_p \hookrightarrow H' \in \text{RT}(H', H)$, $m_1 : H' \hookrightarrow X_2$ where X_2 is obtained from $q(H')$ by adding all edges (with their nodes) that are connected to nodes in $q(H') \setminus q(a'(H_p))$, $k' : X_2 \hookrightarrow G$ is obtained such that $k' \circ m_1 = q$, $m_2 : H_p \hookrightarrow X_1$ where X_1 is obtained from H_p by adding all nodes in $X_2 \setminus q(H')$, $a'' : X_1 \hookrightarrow X_2$ is obtained such that $a'' \circ m_2 = m_1 \circ a'$, and $(l : G' \hookrightarrow G, m' : X_1 \hookrightarrow G')$ is the pushout complement of (a'', k') then $l \in \mathcal{R}\text{epair}_{del}(a, q)$.*

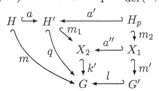

In our example, $\mathcal{R}\text{epair}_{del}$ determines a repair resulting in the graph marked 1 in Fig. 4. For this repair, we considered the sub-ST marked by (R1) in Fig. 3d where the mono m matches the node a from ψ to the node a_2 in $\mathbf{G'_u}$. The repair performed then uses $H_p = \emptyset$ for the removal of the node a_2 along with its adjacent loop (for which the technical handling in $\mathcal{R}\text{epair}_{del}$ is required).

The recursive operation $\mathcal{R}\text{epair}_{db1}$ below derives updates from an ST γ that corresponds to the current graph G (for our running example, these are $\gamma'_\mathbf{u}$ and $\mathbf{G'_u}$ from Fig. 3d). In the algorithm $\mathcal{R}\text{epair}_{db}$, we apply $\mathcal{R}\text{epair}_{db1}$ for the initial match i_G, γ, and *true* where this boolean indicates that we want γ to be satisfied. This boolean is changed in Rule 3 whenever the recursion is applied to an ST $\neg\gamma'$ because we expect that γ' is not to be satisfied iff we expect that $\neg\gamma'$ is to be satisfied. For conjunction, we either attempt to repair a sub-ST for $b = true$ in Rule 1 or we attempt to break one sub-ST for $b = false$. For existential quantification and $b = true$, we use $\mathcal{R}\text{epair}_{add}$ as discussed before in Rule 4 or we attempt to repair one existing match contained in m_f in Rule 5. Also, for existential quantification and $b = false$, we use $\mathcal{R}\text{epair}_{del}$ as discussed before in Rule 6 or we attempt to break one existing match contained in m_t in Rule 7.

Definition 19 (Single-Step Delta-Based Repair Algorithm $\mathcal{R}\text{epair}_{db1}$). *If $m : H \hookrightarrow G$, $\gamma \in \Gamma^{ST}_m$, and $b \in \mathbf{B}$ then $(l : I \hookrightarrow G, r : I \hookrightarrow G') \in \mathcal{R}\text{epair}_{db1}(m, \gamma, b)$ if one of the following cases applies.*

- Rule 1 (repair one subcondition of a conjunction):
  $b = true, \gamma = \wedge S, \chi \in S, \not\models_{ST} \chi, (l, r) \in \mathcal{R}epair_{db1}(m, \chi, b)$.
- Rule 2 (break one subcondition of a conjunction):
  $b = false, \gamma = \wedge S, \chi \in S, \models_{ST} \chi, (l, r) \in \mathcal{R}epair_{db1}(m, \chi, b)$.
- Rule 3 (repair/break the subcondition of a negation):
  $\gamma = \neg \chi, (l, r) \in \mathcal{R}epair_{db1}(m, \chi, \neg b)$.
- Rule 4 (repair an existential quantification by local extension):
  $b = true, \gamma = \exists(a, \phi, m_t, m_f), m_t = \emptyset, r \in \mathcal{R}epair_{add}(a, \phi, m), l = \mathrm{id}_G$.
- Rule 5 (repair an existential quantification recursively):
  $b = true, \gamma = \exists(a, \phi, m_t, m_f), m_t = \emptyset, m_f(k) = \chi, (l, r) \in \mathcal{R}epair_{db1}(k, \chi, b)$.
- Rule 6 (break an existential quantification by local removal):
  $b = false, \gamma = \exists(a, \phi, m_t, m_f), m_t(k) \neq \bot, l \in \mathcal{R}epair_{del}(a, k), r = \mathrm{id}_{G'}$.
- Rule 7 (break an existential quantification recursively):
  $b = false, \gamma = \exists(a, \phi, m_t, m_f), m_t(k) = \chi, (l, r) \in \mathcal{R}epair_{db1}(k, \chi, b)$.

We define the recursive algorithm $\mathcal{R}epair_{db}$ to apply $\mathcal{R}epair_{db1}$ to obtain repairs as iterated applications of single-step repairs computed by $\mathcal{R}epair_{db1}$.

Definition 20 (Delta-Based Repair Algorithm $\mathcal{R}epair_{db}$). *If* $u = (l : I \hookrightarrow G, r : I \hookrightarrow G') \in \mathcal{U}$, $\gamma \in \Gamma_{i_G}^{ST}$, *and* $\gamma' = \mathrm{ppgU}(\gamma, u)$ *then* $\mathcal{R}epair_{db}(u, \gamma) = S$ *if one of the following cases applies.*

- $\models_{ST} \gamma'$ *and* $S = \{((\mathrm{id}_{G'}, \mathrm{id}_{G'}), \gamma')\}$.
- $\not\models_{ST} \gamma'$, $S' = \{(u', \mathrm{ppgU}(\gamma', u')) \mid u' \in \mathcal{R}epair_{db1}(i_G, \gamma', true)\}$, *and*
  $S = \{(u', \gamma') \in S' \mid \models_{ST} \gamma'\} \cup \bigcup \{(u'' \circ u', \gamma'') \mid (u', \gamma') \in S', \not\models_{ST} \gamma', (u'', \gamma'') \in \mathcal{R}epair_{db}(u', \gamma'), u'' \circ u' \neq \bot\}$.[3]

This computation does not terminate when repairs trigger each other ad infinitum. However, a breadth-first-computation of $\mathcal{R}epair_{db}$ gradually computes a set of sound repairs. Obviously, GCs that trigger such nonterminating computations should be avoided but machinery for detecting such GCs is called for.

Note that the algorithm $\mathcal{R}epair_{db}$ computes fewer graph repairs compared to $\mathcal{R}epair_{sb,2}$ because repairs are applied locally in the scope defined by the GC ψ. For example, no repair would be constructed resulting in the graph marked 4 in Fig. 2. In general, explicitly also using bigger contexts in ψ results in the additional computation of less–local graph repairs. For example, the condition ψ may be rephrased into $\psi' = \psi \wedge \neg \exists(a \; b, \neg \exists(a \xrightarrow{e} b, true))$ to also obtain the graph repair marked 4 in Fig. 2. We now define the updates, which we expect to be computed by $\mathcal{R}epair_{db1}$, as those that repair a single violation of the GC ψ by defining a local update to be embeddable into the resulting update via a double pushout diagram as in the DPO approach to graph transformation [16].

Definition 21 (Locally Least Changing Graph Update). *If* G_1 *is a graph,* $\psi \in \Phi_{\emptyset}^{GC}$, $G_1 \not\models_{GC} \psi$, $(l : I \hookrightarrow G_1, r : I \hookrightarrow G_2) \in \mathcal{U}_{lc}(G_1, \psi)$, $G_2 \models_{GC} \psi$, X_1 *is a minimal subgraph of* G_1 *with a violation of* ψ *that is also a violation of* ψ *in*

---

[3] If u_1 and u_2 are updates then $u_1 \circ u_2 = u$ if $u_1 \leq^{u_2} u$ or $u = \bot$ otherwise (see Definition 4).

G, and the diagram below exists and the right part of it is a DPO diagram then
(l, r) *is a* locally least changing graph update.

$$X_1 \hookleftarrow I' \hookrightarrow X_2$$
$$\downarrow \quad \uparrow \downarrow \uparrow \quad \downarrow$$
$$G_1 \xleftarrow{l} I \xhookrightarrow{r} G_2$$

$\mathcal{R}\text{epair}_{db1}$ indeed generates such locally least changing graph updates because the graph X_1 in this definition corresponds to the H_1 and the H_2 from an ST $\exists(a : H_1 \hookrightarrow H_2, \phi, m_t, m_f)$ that is subject to $\mathcal{R}\text{epair}_{add}$ and $\mathcal{R}\text{epair}_{del}$, respectively. For example, for $\mathcal{R}\text{epair}_{add}$, the graph H_1 in the ST determines a subgraph in G_1 that is a violation of the overall consistency condition given by a GC ψ as its match can not be extended to the graph H_2.

We now define the locally least changing graph repairs (which are to be computed by $\mathcal{R}\text{epair}_{db}$ such as for example the graphs marked 1 and 4 in Fig. 4) as the composition of a sequence of locally least changing updates where precisely the last graph update results in a graph satisfying the GC ψ.

Definition 22 (Locally Least Changing Graph Repair). *If G_1 is a graph, $\psi \in \Phi_{\emptyset}^{GC}$, $\pi = (l_1 : I_1 \hookrightarrow G_1, r_1 : I_1 \hookrightarrow G_2) \ldots (l_n : I_n \hookrightarrow G_n, r_n : I_n \hookrightarrow G_{n+1})$ is a sequence of locally least changing graph updates, $G_1 \in \llbracket \psi \rrbracket$ implies $n = 0$ and $l_1 = r_1 = \text{id}_{G_1}$, $G_i \notin \llbracket \psi \rrbracket$ (for each $2 \leq i \leq n$), $G_{n+1} \in \llbracket \psi \rrbracket$, (l, r) is the iterated composition of the updates in π, and $(l, r) \in \mathcal{U}(G_1, \psi)$ is a least changing graph repair then (l, r) is a* locally least changing graph repair.

We now state that our delta-based graph repair algorithm $\mathcal{R}\text{epair}_{db}$ returns all desired locally least changing graph repairs upon termination.

Theorem 5 (Functional Semantics of $\mathcal{R}\text{epair}_{db}$). *$\mathcal{R}\text{epair}_{db}$ is sound (i.e., it generates only locally least changing graph repairs) and complete (upon termination) with respect to locally least changing graph repairs.*

The state-based algorithms $\mathcal{R}\text{epair}_{sb,1}$ and $\mathcal{R}\text{epair}_{sb,2}$ are inappropriate in environments where numerous updates that may invalidate consistency are applied to a large graph because the procedure of AUTOGRAPH has exponential cost. The incremental delta-based algorithm $\mathcal{R}\text{epair}_{db}$ is a viable alternative when additional memory requirements for storing the ST are acceptable. The AUTOGRAPH applications for this algorithm have negligible costs because they may be performed a priori and must only be performed for subconditions of the consistency constraint, which can be assumed to feature reasonably small graphs only.

Finally, a classification of locally least changing repairs is useful for user-based repair selection. Delta preserving repairs defined below represent such a basic class, containing only those repairs that preserve the update resulting in a graph not satisfying GC ψ, i.e., it may be desirable to avoid repairs that revert additions or deletions of this update. In our example, the repair related to the graph marked 4 in Fig. 4 is not delta preserving w.r.t. **u** from Fig. 3a.

Definition 23 (Delta Preserving Graph Repair). *If $\psi \in \Phi_{\emptyset}^{GC}$, $u_2 = (l_2 : I_2 \hookrightarrow G_2, r_2 : I_2 \hookrightarrow G_3) \in \mathcal{U}(G_2, \psi)$ is a graph repair, $u_1 = (l_1 : I_1 \hookrightarrow G_1, r_1 :*

$I_1 \hookrightarrow G_2$) *is a graph update, and there exists a graph update u such that $u_1 <^{u_2} u$ then u_2 is a* delta preserving graph repair *with respect to u_1.*

7   Related Work

According to the recent survey on *model repair* [12], and the corresponding exhaustive classification of primary studies selected in the literature review, published online [11], we can see that the amount and wide variety of existing approaches makes a detailed comparison with all of them infeasible.

We consider our approach to be innovative, not only because of the proposed solutions, but because it addresses the issues of *completeness* and *least changing* for incremental graph repair in a precise and formal way. From the survey [11,12] we can see that only two other approaches [10,19] address completeness and least changing, relying also on constraint-solving technology. The main difference with our approach is that they are not incremental. In particular, the work of Schoenboeck et al. [19] proposes a logic programming approach allowing the exploration of model repair solutions ranked according to some quality criteria, re-establishing conformance of a model with its metamodel. Soundness and completeness of these repair actions is not formally proven. Moreover, the least changing bidirectional model transformation approach of Macedo et al. [10] has only a bounded search for repairs, relying on a bounded constraint solver.

Some *recent work* on rule-based *graph repair* [9] (not covered by the survey) addresses the least-changing principle by developing so-called maximally preserving (items are preserved whenever possible) repair programs. This state-based approach considers a subset of consistency constraints (up to nesting depth 2) handled by our approach, and is not complete, since it produces repairs including only a minimal amount of deletions. Some other recent rule-based graph repair approach [13,20] (also not covered by the survey) proposes so-called change preserving repairs (similar to what we define as delta-preserving). The main difference with our work is that we do not require the user to specify consistency-preserving operations from which repairs are generated, since we derive repairs using constraint solving techniques directly from the consistency constraints.

Finally, there is a variety of work on *incremental evaluation of graph queries* (see e.g. [2,4]), developed with the aim of efficiently re-evaluating a graph query after an update has been performed. Although not employed with the specific aim of complete and least changing graph repair, this work is related to our newly introduced concept of satisfaction trees, also using specific data structures to record with some detail the set of answers to a given query (as described for graph conditions, for example, also in [3]). It is part of ongoing work to evaluate how STs can be employed similarly in this field of incremental query evaluation.

8   Conclusion and Future Work

We presented a logic-based incremental approach to graph repair. It is the first approach to graph repair returning a sound and complete overview of least changing repairs with respect to graph conditions equivalent to first-order logic on graphs. Technically, it relies on an existing model generation procedure for graph conditions together with the newly introduced concept of satisfaction trees, encoding if and how a graph satisfies a graph condition.

As future work, we aim at supporting partial consistency and gradually improving it. We are confident that we can extend our work to support attributes, since our underlying model generation procedure supports it. Ongoing work is the support of more expressive consistency constraints, allowing path-related properties. Moreover, we are in the process of implementing the algorithms presented here and evaluating them on a variety of case studies. The evaluation also pertains to the overall efficiency (for which we employ techniques for localized pattern matching) and includes a comparison with other approaches for graph repair. Finally, we aim at presenting new and refined properties distinguishing between all possible repairs supporting the implementation of interactive repair selection procedures.

References

1. Angles, R., Gutiérrez, C.: Survey of graph database models. ACM Comput. Surv. **40**(1), 1:1–1:39 (2008). https://doi.org/10.1145/1322432.1322433
2. Bergmann, G., Ökrös, A., Ráth, I., Varró, D., Varró, G.: Incremental pattern matching in the viatra model transformation system. In: GRaMoT, pp. 25–32. ACM (2008). https://doi.org/10.1145/1402947.1402953
3. Beyhl, T., Blouin, D., Giese, H., Lambers, L.: On the operationalization of graph queries with generalized discrimination networks. In: Echahed, R., Minas, M. (eds.) ICGT 2016. LNCS, vol. 9761, pp. 170–186. Springer, Cham (2016). https://doi.org/10.1007/978-3-319-40530-8_11
4. Beyhl, T., Giese, H.: Incremental view maintenance for deductive graph databases using generalized discrimination networks. In: GaM@ETAPS, EPTCS, vol. 231, pp. 57–71 (2016). https://doi.org/10.4204/EPTCS.231.5
5. Courcelle, B.: The expression of graph properties and graph transformations in monadic second-order logic. In: Rozenberg [16], pp. 313–400
6. Diskin, Z., König, H., Lawford, M.: Multiple model synchronization with multiary delta lenses. In: Russo, A., Schürr, A. (eds.) FASE 2018. LNCS, vol. 10802, pp. 21–37. Springer, Cham (2018). https://doi.org/10.1007/978-3-319-89363-1_2
7. Ehrig, H., Ehrig, K., Prange, U., Taentzer, G.: Fundamentals of Algebraic Graph Transformation. Springer, Heidelberg (2006). https://doi.org/10.1007/3-540-31188-2
8. Habel, A., Pennemann, K.: Correctness of high-level transformation systems relative to nested conditions. MSCS **19**(2), 245–296 (2009). https://doi.org/10.1017/S0960129508007202
9. Habel, A., Sandmann, C.: Graph repair by graph programs. In: Mazzara, M., Ober, I., Salaün, G. (eds.) STAF 2018. LNCS, vol. 11176, pp. 431–446. Springer, Cham (2018). https://doi.org/10.1007/978-3-030-04771-9_31
10. Macedo, N., Cunha, A.: Least-change bidirectional model transformation with QVT-R and ATL. Softw. Syst. Model. **15**(3), 783–810 (2016). https://doi.org/10.1007/s10270-014-0437-x

11. Macedo, N., Tiago, J., Cunha, A.: Systematic literature review of model repair approaches. http://tinyurl.com/hv7eh6h. Accessed 14 Nov 2018
12. Macedo, N., Tiago, J., Cunha, A.: A feature-based classification of model repair approaches. IEEE Trans. Softw. Eng. **43**(7), 615–640 (2017). https://doi.org/10.1109/TSE.2016.2620145
13. Ohrndorf, M., Pietsch, C., Kelter, U., Kehrer, T.: Revision: a tool for history-based model repair recommendations. In: ICSE, pp. 105–108. ACM (2018). https://doi.org/10.1145/3183440.3183498
14. Orejas, F., Boronat, A., Ehrig, H., Hermann, F., Schölzel, H.: On propagation-based concurrent model synchronization. ECEASST **57** (2013). http://journal.ub.tu-berlin.de/eceasst/article/view/871
15. Rensink, A.: Representing first-order logic using graphs. In: Ehrig, H., Engels, G., Parisi-Presicce, F., Rozenberg, G. (eds.) ICGT 2004. LNCS, vol. 3256, pp. 319–335. Springer, Heidelberg (2004). https://doi.org/10.1007/978-3-540-30203-2_23
16. Rozenberg, G. (ed.): Handbook of Graph Grammars and Computing by Graph Transformations, Volume 1: Foundations. World Scientific (1997)
17. Schneider, S., Lambers, L., Orejas, F.: Automated reasoning for attributed graph properties. STTT **20**(6), 705–737 (2018). https://doi.org/10.1007/s10009-018-0496-3
18. Schneider, S., Lambers, L., Orejas, F.: A logic-based incremental approach to graph repair. Technical report, 126, Hasso Plattner Institute at the University of Potsdam, Potsdam, Germany (2019)
19. Schoenboeck, J., et al.: CARE - A constraint-based approach for re-establishing conformance-relationships. In: APCCM 2014, vol. 154, pp. 19–28. Australian Computer Society (2014). http://crpit.com/abstracts/CRPITV154Schoenboeck.html
20. Taentzer, G., Ohrndorf, M., Lamo, Y., Rutle, A.: Change-preserving model repair. In: Huisman, M., Rubin, J. (eds.) FASE 2017. LNCS, vol. 10202, pp. 283–299. Springer, Heidelberg (2017). https://doi.org/10.1007/978-3-662-54494-5_16

Tool Support
for Correctness-by-Construction

Tobias Runge[1(✉)], Ina Schaefer[1], Loek Cleophas[2,3], Thomas Thüm[1],
Derrick Kourie[3,4], and Bruce W. Watson[3,4]

[1] Software Engineering, TU Braunschweig, Braunschweig, Germany
{tobias.runge,i.schaefer,t.thuem}@tu-bs.de
[2] Software Engineering Technology, TU Eindhoven, Eindhoven, The Netherlands
[3] Information Science, Stellenbosch University, Stellenbosch, South Africa
{loek,derrick,bruce}@fastar.org
[4] Centre for Artificial Intelligence Research, CSIR, Pretoria, South Africa

Abstract. Correctness-by-Construction (CbC) is an approach to incrementally create formally correct programs guided by pre- and postcondition specifications. A program is created using refinement rules that guarantee the resulting implementation is correct with respect to the specification. Although CbC is supposed to lead to code with a low defect rate, it is not prevalent, especially because appropriate tool support is missing. To promote CbC, we provide tool support for CbC-based program development. We present CorC, a graphical and textual IDE to create programs in a simple while-language following the CbC approach. Starting with a specification, our open source tool supports CbC developers in refining a program by a sequence of refinement steps and in verifying the correctness of these refinement steps using the theorem prover KeY. We evaluated the tool with a set of standard examples on CbC where we reveal errors in the provided specification. The evaluation shows that our tool reduces the verification time in comparison to post-hoc verification.

1 Introduction

Correctness-by-Construction (CbC) [12,13,19,23] is a methodology to construct formally correct programs guided by a specification. CbC can improve program development because every part of the program is designed to meet the corresponding specification. With the CbC approach, source code is incrementally constructed with a low defect rate [19] mainly based on three reasons. First, introducing defects is hard because of the structured reasoning discipline that is enforced by the refinement rules. Second, if defects occur, they can be tracked through the refinement structure of specifications. Third, the trust in the program is increased because the program is developed following a formal process [14].

Despite these benefits, CbC is still not prevalent and not applied for large-scale program development. We argue that one reason for this is missing tool support for a CbC-style development process. Another issue is that the programmer mindset is often tailored to the prevalent post-hoc verification approach. CbC has been shown to be beneficial even in domains where post-hoc verification is required [29]. In post-hoc verification, a method is verified against pre- and postconditions. In the CbC approach, we refine the method stepwise, and we can check the method partially after each step since every statement is surrounded by a pair of pre- and postconditions. The verification of refinement steps and Hoare triples reduces the proof complexity since the proof task is split into smaller problems. The specifications and code developed using the CbC approach can be used to bootstrap the post-hoc verification process and allow for an easier post-hoc verification as the method constructed using CbC generally is of a structure that is more amenable to verification [29].

In this paper, we present CorC,[1] a tool designed to develop programs following the CbC approach. We deliberately built our tool on the well-known post-hoc verifier KeY [4] to profit from the KeY ecosystem and future extensions of the verifier. We also add CbC as another application area to KeY, which opens the possibility for KeY users to adopt the CbC approach. This could spread the constructive CbC approach to areas where post-hoc verification is prevalent.

Our tool CorC offers a hybrid textual-graphical editor to develop programs using CbC. The textual editor resembles a normal programming editor, but is enriched with support for pre- and postcondition specifications. The graphical editor visualizes the code, its specification, and the program refinements in a tree-like structure. The developers can switch back and forth between both views. In order to support the correct application of the refinement rules, the tool is integrated with KeY [4] such that proof obligations can be immediately discharged during program development. In a preliminary evaluation, we found benefits of CorC compared to paper-and-pencil-based application of CbC and compared to post-hoc verification.

2 Foundations of Correctness-by-Construction

Classically, CbC [19] starts with the specification of a program as a Hoare triple comprising a precondition, an abstract statement, and a postcondition. Such a triple, say T, should be read as a total correctness assertion: if T is in a state where the precondition holds and its abstract statement is executed, then the execution will terminate and the postcondition will hold. T will be true for a certain set of concrete program instantiations of the abstract program and false for other instantiations. A refinement of T is a triple, say T', which is true for a subset of concrete programs that render T to be true.

In our work, pre-/post-condition specifications for programs are written in *first-order logic* (FOL). A formula in FOL consists of atomic formulas which are logically connected. An atomic formula is a predicate which evaluates to true or

---

[1] https://github.com/TUBS-ISF/CorC, CorC is an acronym for Correctness-by-Construction.

{P} S {Q}	*can be refined to*
1. *Skip* :	{P} *skip* {Q} *iff* P *implies* Q
2. *Assignment* :	{P} $x := E$ {Q} *iff* P *implies* Q$[x := E]$
3. *Composition* :	{P} S1 ; S2 {Q} *iff there is an intermediate condition* M *such that* {P} S1 {M} *and* {M} S2 {Q}
4. *Selection* :	{P} **if** $G_1 \rightarrow S_1$ **elseif** ... $G_n \rightarrow S_n$ **fi** {Q} *iff* (P *implies* $G_1 \vee G_2 \vee \ldots \vee G_n$) *and* {P $\wedge G_i$} S_i {Q} *holds for all i.*
5. *Repetition* :	{P} **do** $[I, V]$ $G \rightarrow S$ **od** {Q} *iff* (P *implies* I) *and* (I $\wedge \neg G$ *implies* Q) *and* {I $\wedge$ G} S {I} *and* {I $\wedge$ G $\wedge V{=}V_0$} S {I $\wedge 0{\leq}V \wedge V{<}V_0$}
6. *Weaken pre* :	{P′} S {Q} *iff* P *implies* P′
7. *Strengthen post* :	{P} S {Q′} *iff* Q′ *implies* Q
8. *Subroutine* :	{P} *Sub* {Q} *with subroutine* {P′} *Sub* {Q′} *iff* P *is equal to* P′ *and* Q′ *is equal to* Q

Fig. 1. Refinement rules in CbC [19]

false. Programs in this work are written in the CorC language, which is inspired by the *Guarded Command Language* (GCL) [11] and presented below.

For the concrete instantiation of conditions and assignments, our tool uses a host language. We decided for Java, but other languages are also possible.

To create programs using CbC, we use refinement rules. A Hoare triple is refined by applying rules, which introduce CorC language statements, so that a concrete program is created. The concrete program obtained by refinement is guaranteed to be correct by construction, provided that the correctness-preserving refinement steps have been accurately applied. In Fig. 1, we present the statements and refinement rules used in CbC and our tool.

Skip. A skip or empty statement is a statement that does not alter the state of the program (i.e., it does nothing) [11,19]. This means a Hoare triple with a skip statement evaluates to true if the precondition implies the postcondition.

Assignment. An assignment statement assigns an expression of type T to a variable, also of type T. In the tool, we use a Java-like assignment $(x = y)$. To refine a Hoare triple {P} S {Q} with an assignment statement, the assignment rule is used. This rule replaces the abstract statement S by an assignment {P} $x = E$ {Q} iff P implies Q$[x := E]$.

Composition. A composition statement is a statement which splits one abstract statement into two. A Hoare triple {P} S {Q} is split to {P} S_1 {M} and {M} S_2 {Q} in which S is refined to S1 and S2. M is an intermediate condition which evaluates to true after S1 and before S2 is executed [11].

Selection. Selection in our CorC language works as a switch statement. It refines a Hoare triple {P} S {Q} to {P} **if** $G_1 \rightarrow S_1$ **elseif** ... $G_n \rightarrow S_n$ **fi** {Q}. The guards G_i are evaluated, and the sub-statement S_i of the *first* satisfied guard is executed.

We use a switch-like statement so that every sub-statement has an associated guard for further reasoning. The selection refinement rule can only be used if the precondition P implies the disjunction of all guards so that at least one sub-statement could be executed.

Repetition. The repetition statement $\{P\}$ **do** $[I, V]$ $G \rightarrow$ S **od** $\{Q\}$ works like a while loop in other languages. If the loop guard G evaluates to true, the associated loop statement S is executed. The repetition statement is specified with an invariant I and a variant V. To refine a Hoare triple $\{P\}$ S $\{Q\}$ with a repetition statement, (1) the precondition P has to imply the invariant I of the repetition statement, (2) the conjunction of invariant and the negation of the loop guard G have to imply the postcondition Q, and (3) the loop body has to preserve the invariant by showing that $\{I \wedge G\}$ S $\{I\}$ holds. To verify termination, we have to show that the variant V monotonically decreases in each loop iteration and has 0 as a lower bound.

Weaken precondition. The precondition of a Hoare triple can be weakened if necessary. The weaken precondition rule replaces the precondition P with a new one P' only if P implies P' [12].

Strengthen postcondition. To strengthen a postcondition, the strengthen postcondition rule can be used. A postcondition Q is replaced by a new one Q' only if Q' implies Q [12].

Subroutine. A subroutine can be used to split a program into smaller parts. We use a simple subroutine call where we prohibit side effects and parameters. A triple $\{P\}$ S $\{Q\}$ can be refined to a subroutine $\{P'\}$ *Sub* $\{Q'\}$, if the precondition P' of the subroutine is equal to the precondition P of the refined statement and the postcondition Q' of the subroutine is equal to the postcondition Q of the refined statement. The subroutine can be constructed as a separate CbC program to verify that it satisfies the specification. The Hoare triple $\{P'\}$ *Sub* $\{Q'\}$ is the starting point to construct a program using CbC.

3 Correctness-by-Construction by Example

To introduce the programming style of CbC, we demonstrate the construction of a linear search algorithm using CbC [19]. The linear search problem is defined as follows: We have an integer array a of some length, and an integer variable x. We try to find an element in the array a which has the same value as the variable x, and we return the index i where the (last) element x was found, or -1 if the element is not in the array.

To construct the algorithm, we start with concretizing the pre- and postcondition of the algorithm. Before the algorithm is executed, we know that we have an integer array. Therefore, we specify a$\neq$null $\wedge$ a.length$\geq$0 as precondition P. The postcondition forces that if the index i is greater than or equal to zero, the element is found on the returned index i ($Q := (i{\geq}0 \implies a[i]{=}x)$).

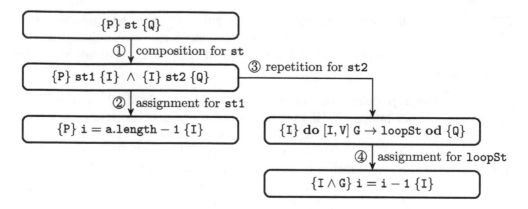

Fig. 2. Refinement steps for the linear search algorithm

Our algorithm traverses the array in reverse order and checks for each index whether the value is equal to x. In this case, the index is returned. To create this algorithm, we construct an invariant I for the loop:

$$I := \neg\texttt{appears}(\texttt{a}, \texttt{x}, \texttt{i} + 1, \texttt{a.length}) \wedge \texttt{i} \geq -1 \wedge \texttt{i} < \texttt{a.length}$$

The invariant is used to split the array into two parts. A part from i + 1 to a.length where x is not contained, and a part from zero to i which is not checked yet. In every iteration, the next index of the array is checked. The predicate appears(a, x, l, h) asserts that x occurs in array a inside the range from l (included) to h (excluded). The predicate can be translated to FOL as $\exists\texttt{i} : (\texttt{i} \geq \texttt{l} \wedge \texttt{i} < \texttt{h} \wedge \texttt{a[i]} = \texttt{x})$.

We can use the CbC refinement rules to implement linear search. The refinement steps for the example are shown in Fig. 2 and numbered from ① to ④. To create a loop in the program, we need to initialize a loop counter variable to establish the invariant. Therefore, we split the program by introducing a composition statement (① in Fig. 2). The invariant I is used as intermediate condition (i.e., M := I), because it has to be true after the initialization, and before the first loop step. The statement st1 is refined to an assignment statement ②. We initialize i with a.length − 1 to start at the end of the array. This assignment satisfies the intermediate condition I where i is replaced by a.length − 1. The range of appears is empty, and therefore the predicate evaluates to true. To refine the second statement (st2), we use the repetition refinement rule ③. As long as x is not found, we iterate through the array. As guard of the repetition, we use (i≥0 ∧ a[i]≠x). The invariant of the repetition is the invariant I introduced above. The variant V is i + 1. To verify that this refinement is valid, we have to verify that the precondition of the repetition statement implies the invariant, and that the invariant and the negated guard imply the postcondition of the repetition (cf. Rule 5). Both are valid because the precondition is equal to the invariant and the postcondition of the repetition statement (in this case it is Q) is equal to the negated guard. The last step is to refine the abstract loop statement (loopSt) ④. We use an assignment to decrease i and get the final program. We can verify that the invariant holds after each loop iteration. The program terminates because the variant decreases in every step and it is always greater than or equal to zero.

4 Tool Support in CorC

CorC extends KeY's application area by enabling CbC to spread the constructive engineering to areas where post-hoc verification is prevalent. KeY programmers can use both approaches to construct formally correct programs. By using CorC, they develop specification and code that can bootstrap the post-hoc verification. The CorC tool[2] is realized as an Eclipse plug-in in Java. We use the Eclipse Modeling Framework (EMF)[3] to specify a CbC meta model. This meta model is used by two editor views, a textual and a graphical editor. The Hoare triple verification is implemented by the deductive program verification tool KeY [4]. In the following list, we summarize the features of CorC.

- Programs are written as Hoare triple specifications, including pre-/postcondition specifications and abstract statements or assignment/skip statements in concrete triples.
- CorC has eight rules to construct programs: skip, assignment, composition, selection, repetition, weakening precondition, strengthening postcondition, and subroutine (cf. Sect. 2).
- Pre-/postconditions and invariant specification are automatically propagated through the program.
- CorC comprises a graphical and a textual editor that can be used interchangeably.
- Up to now, CorC supports integers, chars, strings, arrays, and subroutine calls without side effects, I/O, and library calls.
- Hoare triples are typically verified by KeY automatically. If the proof cannot be closed automatically, the user can interact with KeY.
- Helper methods written in Java 1.5 can be used in a specification.
- CorC comprises content assist and an automatic generation of intermediate conditions.

4.1 Graphical Editor

The graphical editor represents CbC-based program refinement by a tree structure. A node represents the Hoare triple of a specific CorC language statement. Figure 3 presents the linear search algorithm of Sect. 3 in the graphical editor. The structure of the tree is the same as in Fig. 2. The additional nodes on the right specify used program variables including their type and global invariant

---

[2] https://github.com/TUBS-ISF/CorC.
[3] https://eclipse.org/emf/.

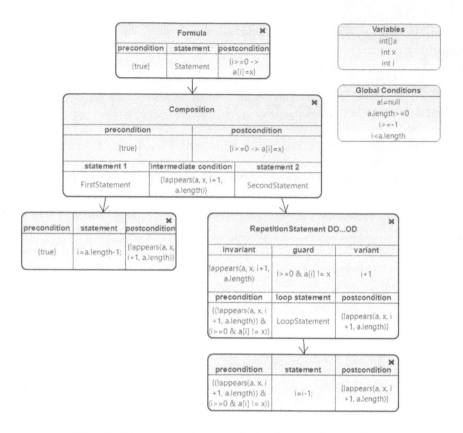

Fig. 3. Linear search example in the graphical editor

conditions. The global invariant conditions are added to every pre- and post-condition of Hoare triples to simplify the construction of the program. In the example, we specify the array `a` and the range of variable `i` to support the verification, as KeY requires this range to be explicit for verification.

The root node of the tree shows the abstract Hoare triple for the overall program with a symbolic name for the abstract statement. In every node, the pre- and postcondition are specified on the left and right of the node under the corresponding header. A composition statement node, the second statement of the tree, contains the pre- and postcondition and additionally defines an intermediate condition. The intermediate condition is the middle term in the bottom line. Both abstract sub-statements of the composition have a symbolic name and can be further refined by adding a connection to another node (i.e., creating a parent-child relation). The repetition node contains fields to specify the invariant, the guard and the variant of the repetition. These fields are in the middle row. The pre- and postcondition are associated to the inner loop statement. An assignment node (cf. both leaf nodes of the figure) contains the precondition, the assignment, and the postcondition. The representations of the nodes for the refinements not illustrated in this example are similar.

Refinement steps are represented by edges. The pre- and postconditions are propagated from parents to their children on drawing the parent/child relation. We explicitly show the propagated conditions in a node to improve readability. The propagated conditions from the parent are unmodifiable because refinement rules determine explicitly how conditions are propagated. An exception are the rules to weaken the precondition or strengthen the postcondition. Here, the conditions can be overridden. At the repetition statement, we only depict the pre-/postconditions of the inner loop statement to reduce the size of this node. The pre-/postconditions of the parent node (in our example the composition statement) are not shown explicitly, but they are propagated internally to verify that the repetition refinement rule is satisfied. To visualize the verification status, the nodes have a green border if proven, a red one otherwise.

By showing the Hoare triples explicitly, problems in the program can be localized. If some leaf node cannot be proven, the user has to check the assignment and the corresponding pre-/postcondition. If an error occurred, the conditions on the refinement path up to pre-/postcondition of the starting Hoare triple can be altered. Other paths do not need to be checked. To prove the program correct, we have to prove that the refinement is correct. Aside from the side conditions of refinement rules (cf. iff conditions in refinement rules), only the leaf nodes of the refinement tree which contain basic Hoare triples with skip or assignment statements need to be verified by a prover, while all composite statements are correct by construction of their conditions.

To support the user in developing intermediate conditions for composition statements, our tool can compute the weakest precondition from a postcondition and a concrete assignment by using the KeY theorem prover. So, the user can create a specific assignment statement and generate the intermediate conditions afterwards. We also support modularization, to cover cases where algorithms become too large. Sub-algorithms can be created using CbC in other CorC programs. We introduce a simple subroutine rule which can be used as a leaf node in the editor. The subroutine has a name and it is connected to a second diagram with the same name as the subroutine. This subroutine call is similar to a classic method call. It can be used to decompose larger CbC developments to multiple smaller programs.

4.2 Textual Editor

The textual editor is an editor for the CorC programming language described above. The user writes code by using keywords for the specific statements and enriches the code with conditions, such as invariants or intermediate conditions, and assignments in our CorC syntax. The syntax of the composed statements in the textual editor is shown in Fig. 4. In the GlobalConditions declaration, we enumerate the needed global conditions separated with a comma. The used variables are enumerated after the JavaVariables keyword.

The linear search example program presented in Sect. 3 is shown in the syntax of CorC in Listing 1. The program starts with keyword Formula. The pre- and postcondition of the abstract Hoare triple are written after the pre: and post:

Selection statement

if ("guard") **then** {statement}

elseif ("guard") **then** {statement}

...

fi

Repetition statement

while ("guard")

inv: ["invariant"] **var**: ["variant"]

do {statement} **od**

Fig. 4. Syntax of statements in textual editor

```
1   Formula "linearSearch"
2   pre: {"true"}
3   {
4     {
5       i=a.length-1;
6     }
7     intm: ["!appears(a, x, i+1, a.length)"]
8     {
9       while ("i>=0 & a[i]!=x")
10      inv: ["!appears(a, x, i+1, a.length)"]
11      var: ["i+1"] do
12      {
13        i=i-1;
14      } od
15    }
16  }
17  post: {"i>=0 -> a[i]=x"}
18
19  GlobalConditions
20    conditions {"a!=null", "a.length>=0",
21      "i>=-1", "i<a.length"}
22
23  JavaVariables
24    variables {"int[] a", "int x", "int i"}
```

Listing 1. Linear search example in the textual editor

keywords. The abstract statement of the Hoare triple is refined to a composition statement in lines 3–16. The statements are surrounded by curly brackets to establish the refinement structure. We have the first statement in lines 4–6, the intermediate condition in line 7 and the second statement in lines 8–15. The first statement is refined to an assignment (Line 5). The refinement is done by introducing an assignment in Java syntax ($i = a.length - 1;$). The second statement is refined to a repetition statement (cf. the syntax of a repetition statement in Fig. 4). We specify the guard, the invariant, and the variant. Finally, the single statement of the loop body is refined to an assignment in Line 13.

As in the graphical editor, pre-/postconditions are propagated top-down from a parent to a child statement. For example, the intermediate condition of a

```
1  \javaSource "src";
2  \include "helper.key";
3  \programVariables {int x;}
4  \problem {
5    (x = 0) -> \<{x=x+1;}\> (x = 1)
6  }
```

Listing 2. KeY problem file

composition statement which is the postcondition of the first sub-statement and the precondition of the second, appears only once in the editor (e.g., Line 7). To support the user, we implemented syntax highlighting and a content assist. When starting to write a statement, a user may employ auto-completion where the statements are inserted following the syntax in Fig. 4. The user can specify the conditions, then the next statement can be refined. The editor also automatically checks the syntax and highlights syntax errors. Information markers are used to indicate statements which are not proven yet. For example, the Hoare triple of the assignment statement ($i = $ a.length $- 1$) in Listing 1 has to be verified, and CorC marks the statement according to the proof completion results.

4.3 Verification of CorC Programs

To prove the refined program is correct, we have to prove side conditions of refinements correct (e.g., prove that an assignment satiesfies the pre-/postcondition specification). This reduces the proof complexity because the challenge to prove a complete program is decomposed into smaller verification tasks. The intermediate Hoare triples are verified indirectly through the soundness of the refinement rules and the propagation of the specifications from parent nodes to child nodes [19]. Side conditions occur in all refinements (cf. iff conditions in refinement rules). These side conditions, such as the termination of repetition statements or that at least one guard in a selection has to evaluate to true, are proven in separate KeY files.

For the proof of concrete Hoare triples, we use the deductive program verifier KeY [4]. Hoare triples are transformed to KeY's dynamic logic syntax. The syntax of KeY problem files is shown in Listing 2. Using the keyword javaSource, we specify the path to Java helper methods which are called in the specifications. These methods have to be verified independently with KeY. A KeY helper file, where the users can define their own FOL predicates for the specification, is included with the keyword include. For example, in CorC a predicate $appears(a, x, l, h)$ (cf. the linear search example) can be used which is specified in the helper file as a FOL formula. The variables used in the program are listed after the keyword programVariables. After problem, we define the Hoare triple to be proven, which is translated to dynamic logic as used by KeY. KeY problem files are verified by KeY. As we are only verifying simple Hoare triples with skip or assignment statements, KeY is usually able to close the proofs automatically if the Hoare triple is valid.

To verify total correctness of the program, we have to prove that all repetition statements terminate. The termination of repetition statements is shown by proving that the variants in the program monotonically decrease and are bounded. Without loss of generality, we assume this bound to equal 0, as this is what KeY requires. This is done by specifying the problem in the KeY file in the following way: `(invariant & guard) -> {var0:=var} \<{std}\>` `(invariant & var<var0 & var>=0)`. The code of the loop body is specified at `std` to verify that after one iteration of the loop body the variant `var` is smaller than before but greater than or equal to zero.

To verify Hoare triples in the graphical editor, we implemented a menu entry. The user can right-click on a statement and start the automatic proof. If the proof is not closed, the user can interact with the opened KeY interface. To prove Hoare triples in the textual editor, we automatically generate all needed problem files for KeY whenever the user saves the editor file. The proof of the files is started using a menu button. The user gets feedback which triples are not proven by means of markers in the editor.

4.4   Implementation as Eclipse Plugin

We extended the Eclipse modeling framework with plugins to implement the two editors. We have created a meta model of the CbC language to represent the required constructs (i.e., statements with specification). The statements can be nested to create the CbC refinement hierarchy. The graphical and the textual editor are projections on the same meta model. The graphical editor is implemented using the framework Graphiti.[4] It provides functionality to create nodes and to associate them to domain elements, such as statements and specifications. The nodes can be added from a palette at the side of the editor, so no incorrect statement with its associated specification can be created. We implemented editing functionality to change the text in the node; the background model is changed simultaneously. Graphiti also provides the possibility to update nodes (e.g., to propagate pre- and postconditions), if we connect those nodes by refinement edges. The refinement is checked for compliance with the CbC rules.

The textual editor is implemented using XText.[5] We created a grammar covering every statement and the associated specification. If the user writes a program, the text is parsed and translated to an instance of the meta model. If a program is created in one editor, a model (an instance of our meta model) of the program is created in the background. We can easily transform one view into the other. The transformation is a generation step and not a live synchronization between both views, but it is carried out invisibly for the user when changing the views.

---

[4] https://eclipse.org/graphiti/.
[5] https://eclipse.org/Xtext/.

Table 1. Evaluation of the example programs

Algo-rithm	#Nodes in GE	#Lines in TE	#Lines with JML	#Verified CorC triples	CbC Total Proof-Nodes	CbC Total Proof-Time	PhV Total Proof-Nodes	PhV Total Proof-Time
Linear Search	5	12	10	5/5	285	0.4 s	589	1.2 s
Max. Element	9	21	15	9/9	1023	1.2 s	993	1.8 s
Pattern Matching	14	23	20	13/13	21131	54.9 s	201619	1479.3 s
Exponen-tiation	7	21	17	7/7	6588	15.2 s	7303	20.4 s
Log. Approx.	5	16	12	5/5	13756	42.7 s	18835	68.5 s
Dutch Flag	8	26	24	8/8	4107	5.7 s	4993	13.4 s
Factorial	5	15	13	4/4	1554	3.6 s	1598	4.4 s

(GE) Grahical Editor, (TE) Textual Editor, (PhV) Post-hoc Verification

In implementing CorC, we considered the exchangeability of the host language. The specifications and assignments are saved as strings in the meta model. They are checked by a parser to comply with Java. This parser could be exchanged to support a different language. The verification is done by generating KeY files which are then evaluated by KeY. Here, we have to exchange the generation of the files if another theorem prover should be integrated. The information of the meta model may have to be adopted to fit the needs of the other prover. We also have to implement a programmatic call to the other prover.

5 Evaluation

The tool support offers new chances to evaluate CbC versus post-hoc verification. We quantitatively compare the development and verification of programs with CorC and with post-hoc verification. This is to check the hypothesis that the verification of algorithms is faster with CorC than with post-hoc verification. We created the first eight algorithms from the book by Kourie and Watson [19] in our graphical editor. For comparison purposes, we also wrote each example as a plain Java program with JML specifications in order to directly verify it with KeY. The specifications are the same as in CorC. We measured the verification time and the proof nodes that KeY needed to close the proofs for both approaches. The results of the evaluation are presented in Table 1 (verification time rounded).

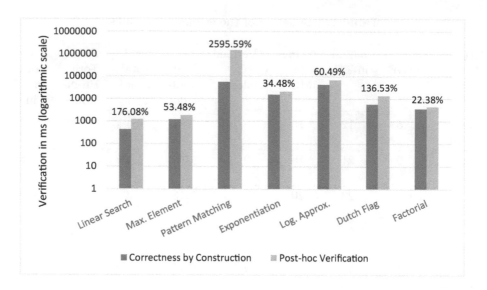

Fig. 5. Proof time of CbC and post-hoc verification in logarithmic scale

The algorithms have 5 to 14 nodes in the graphical editor and 12 to 26 lines of code in the textual editor. The Java version with a JML specification always has fewer lines (between 8% and 29% smaller). The additional specifications, such as the intermediate conditions of composition statements, and the global invariant conditions and variables cause more lines of code in the CbC program.

The verification of the eight algorithms worked nearly without problems. We verified 7 out of 8 examples within CorC. In the cases without problems, every Hoare triple and the termination of the loops could be proven. We had to prove fewer Hoare triples than nodes in the editor, as not every node has to be proven separately. Composition nodes are proven indirectly through the refinement structure. For *exponentiation, logarithm,* and *factorial,* we had to implement recursive helper methods which are used in the specification. Therefore, the programs impose upper bounds for integers to shorten the proof. The *binary search* algorithm could not be verified automatically in KeY using post-hoc verification or CorC. In each step, when the element is not found, the algorithm halves the array. KeY could not prove that the searched element is in the new boundaries because verification problems with arithmetic division are hard to prove for KeY automatically.

In the case of measured proof nodes, *maximum element* needs slightly fewer nodes proved with post-hoc verification than with CbC. In the other cases, the proofs for the algorithms constructed with CbC are 3% to 854% smaller. The largest difference was measured for the *pattern matching* algorithm. The proof is reduced to a ninth of the nodes.

The verification time is visualized in Fig. 5. The time is measured in milliseconds and scaled logarithmically. The proofs for the CbC approach are always faster showing lower proof complexity. For *maximum element, exponentiation, logarithm* and *factorial*, the post-hoc verification time requires between 22% and 60% more time. The difference increases for *Dutch flag* and *linear search* to 137% and 176%, respectively. Algorithm *pattern matching* has the biggest difference. Here, the CbC approach needs nearly a minute, but the post-hoc approach needs over 24 min. To verify our hypothesis, we apply the non-parametric paired Wilcoxon-Test [30] with a significance level of 5%. We can reject the null hypothesis that CbC verification and post-hoc verification have no significant difference in verification time (p-value = 0.007813). This rejection of the null hypothesis in an empirical evidence for our hypothesis that verification is faster with CorC than with post-hoc verification.

With our tool support, we were able to compare the CbC approach with post-hoc verification. For our examples, we evaluated that the verification effort is reduced significantly which indicates a reduced proof complexity. It is worthwhile to further investigate the CbC approach, also to profit from synergistic effects in combination with post-hoc verification. As we built CorC on top of KeY, the post-hoc verification of programs constructed with CorC is feasible.

An advantage of CorC is the overview on all Hoare triples during development. In this way, we found some specifications where descriptions in the book by Kourie and Watson [19] were not precise enough to verify the problem in KeY. For example, in the *pattern matching* algorithm, we had to verify two nested loops. At one point, we had to verify that the invariant of the inner loop implies the invariant of the outer loop. This was not possible, so we extended the invariant of the inner loop to be the conjunction of both invariants. In the book of Kourie and Watson [19], this conjunction of both invariants was not explicitly used.

6   Related Work

We compare CorC to other programming languages and tools using specification or refinements. The programming language Eiffel is an object-oriented programming language with a focus on design-by-contract [21, 22]. Classes and methods are annotated with pre-/postconditions and invariants. Programs written in Eiffel can be verified using AutoProof [18, 28]. The verification tool translates the program with assertions to a logic formula. An SMT-solver proves the correctness and returns the result. Spec# is a similar tool for specifying C# programs with pre-/postcondition contracts. These programs can be verified using Boogie. The code and specification is translated to an intermediate language (BoogiePL) and verified [5, 6]. VCC [8] is a tool to annotate and verify C code. For this purpose, it reuses the Spec# tool chain. VeriFast [16] is another tool to verify C and Java programs with the help of contracts. The contracts are written in separation logic (a variant of Hoare logic). As in Eiffel, the focus of Spec#, VCC, and VeriFast is on post-hoc verification and debugging failed proof attempts.

The Event-B framework [2] is a related CbC approach. Automata-based systems including a specification are refined to a concrete implementation.

Atelier B [1] implements the B method by providing an automatic and inter-active prover. Rodin [3] is another tool implementing the Event-B method. The main difference to CorC is that CorC works on code and specifications rather than on automata-based systems.

ArcAngel [25] is a tool supporting Morgan's refinement calculus. Rules are applied to an initial specification to produce a correct implementation. The tool implements a tactic language for refinements to apply a sequence of rules. In comparison to our tool, ArcAngel does not offer a graphical editor to visualize the refinement steps. Another difference is that ArcAngel creates a list of proof obligations which have to be proven separately. CRefine [26] is a related tool for the Circus refinement calculus, a calculus for state-rich reactive systems. Like our tool, CRefine provides a GUI for the refinement process. The difference is that we specify and implement source code, but they use a state-based language. ArcAngelC [10] is an extension to CRefine which adds refinement tactics.

The tools iContract [20] and OpenJML [9] apply design-by-contract. They use a special comment tag to insert conditions into Java code. These conditions are translated to assertions and checked at runtime which is a difference to our tool because no formal verification is done. DBC-Python is a similar approach for the Python language which also checks assertions at runtime [27].

To verify the CbC program, we need a theorem prover for Hoare triples, such as KeY [4]. There are other theorem provers which could be used (e.g., Coq [7] or Isabelle/HOL [24]). The Tecton Proof System [17] is a related tool to structure and interactively prove Hoare logic specification. The proofs are represented graphically as a set of linked trees. These interactive provers do not fit our needs because we want to automate the verification process. KeY provides a symbolic execution debugger (SED) that represents all execution paths with specifications of the code to the verification [15]. This visualization is similar to our tree representation of the graphical editor. The SED can be used to debug a program if an error occur during the post-hoc verification process.

7   Conclusion and Future Work

We implemented CorC to support the Correctness-by-Construction process of program development. We created a textual and a graphical editor that can be used interchangeably to enable different styles of CbC-based program develop-ment. The program and its specification are written in one of the editors and can be verified using KeY. This reduces the proof complexity with respect to post-hoc verification. We extended the KeY ecosystem with CorC. CorC opens the possibility to utilize CbC in areas where post-hoc verification is used as pro-grammers could benefit from synergistic effects of both approaches. With tool support, CbC can be studied in experiments to determine the value of using CbC in industry.

For future work, we want to extend the tool support, and we want to evaluate empirically the benefits and drawbacks of CorC. To extend the expressiveness, we implement a rule for methods to use method calls in CorC. These methods have to be verified independently by CorC/KeY. We could investigate whether the method call rules of KeY can be used for our CbC approach. Another future work is the inference of conditions to reduce the manual effort. Postconditions can be generated automatically for known statements by using the strongest postcondition calculus. Invariants could be generated by incorporating external tools. As mentioned earlier, other host languages and other theorem provers can be integrated in our IDE.

The second work package for future work comprise the evaluation with a user study. We could compare the effort of creating and verifying algorithms with post-hoc verification and with our tool support. The feedback can be used to improve the usability of the tool.

References

1. Abrial, J.R.: The B-Book: Assigning Programs to Meanings. Cambridge University Press, Cambridge (2005)
2. Abrial, J.R.: Modeling in Event-B: System and Software Engineering. Cambridge University Press, Cambridge (2010)
3. Abrial, J.R., Butler, M., Hallerstede, S., Hoang, T.S., Mehta, F., Voisin, L.: Rodin: an open toolset for modelling and reasoning in Event-B. Int. J. Softw. Tools Technol. Transfer **12**(6), 447–466 (2010)
4. Ahrendt, W., Beckert, B., Bubel, R., Hähnle, R., Schmitt, P.H., Ulbrich, M.: Deductive Software Verification - The KeY Book: From Theory to Practice, vol. 10001. Springer, Heidelberg (2016). https://doi.org/10.1007/978-3-319-49812-6
5. Barnett, M., Fähndrich, M., Leino, K.R.M., Müller, P., Schulte, W., Venter, H.: Specification and verification: the Spec# experience. Commun. ACM **54**(6), 81–91 (2011)
6. Barnett, M., Leino, K.R.M., Schulte, W.: The Spec# programming system: an overview. In: Barthe, G., Burdy, L., Huisman, M., Lanet, J.-L., Muntean, T. (eds.) CASSIS 2004. LNCS, vol. 3362, pp. 49–69. Springer, Heidelberg (2005). https://doi.org/10.1007/978-3-540-30569-9_3
7. Bertot, Y., Castéran, P.: Interactive Theorem Proving and Program Development: Coq'Art: The Calculus of Inductive Constructions. Springer, Heidelberg (2013). https://doi.org/10.1007/978-3-662-07964-5
8. Cohen, E., et al.: VCC: a practical system for verifying concurrent C. In: Berghofer, S., Nipkow, T., Urban, C., Wenzel, M. (eds.) TPHOLs 2009. LNCS, vol. 5674, pp. 23–42. Springer, Heidelberg (2009). https://doi.org/10.1007/978-3-642-03359-9_2
9. Cok, D.R.: OpenJML: JML for Java 7 by extending OpenJDK. In: Bobaru, M., Havelund, K., Holzmann, G.J., Joshi, R. (eds.) NFM 2011. LNCS, vol. 6617, pp. 472–479. Springer, Heidelberg (2011). https://doi.org/10.1007/978-3-642-20398-5_35
10. Conserva Filho, M., Oliveira, M.V.M.: Implementing tactics of refinement in CRefine. In: Eleftherakis, G., Hinchey, M., Holcombe, M. (eds.) SEFM 2012. LNCS, vol. 7504, pp. 342–351. Springer, Heidelberg (2012). https://doi.org/10.1007/978-3-642-33826-7_24

11. Dijkstra, E.W.: Guarded commands, nondeterminacy and formal derivation of programs. Commun. ACM **18**(8), 453–457 (1975)
12. Dijkstra, E.W.: A Discipline of Programming. Prentice Hall, Upper Saddle River (1976)
13. Gries, D.: The Science of Programming. Springer, Heidelberg (1987). https://doi.org/10.1007/978-1-4612-5983-1
14. Hall, A., Chapman, R.: Correctness by construction: developing a commercial secure system. IEEE Softw. **19**(1), 18–25 (2002)
15. Hentschel, M.: Integrating symbolic execution, debugging and verification. Ph.D. thesis, Technische Universität Darmstadt (2016)
16. Jacobs, B., Smans, J., Piessens, F.: A quick tour of the verifast program verifier. In: Ueda, K. (ed.) APLAS 2010. LNCS, vol. 6461, pp. 304–311. Springer, Heidelberg (2010). https://doi.org/10.1007/978-3-642-17164-2_21
17. Kapur, D., Nie, X., Musser, D.R.: An overview of the Tecton proof system. Theoret. Comput. Sci. **133**(2), 307–339 (1994)
18. Khazeev, M., Rivera, V., Mazzara, M., Johard, L.: Initial steps towards assessing the usability of a verification tool. In: Ciancarini, P., Litvinov, S., Messina, A., Sillitti, A., Succi, G. (eds.) SEDA 2016. AISC, vol. 717, pp. 31–40. Springer, Cham (2018). https://doi.org/10.1007/978-3-319-70578-1_4
19. Kourie, D.G., Watson, B.W.: The Correctness-by-Construction Approach to Programming. Springer, Heidelberg (2012). https://doi.org/10.1007/978-3-642-27919-5
20. Kramer, R.: iContract - the Java design by contract tool. In: Proceedings, Technology of Object-Oriented Languages. TOOLS 26 (Cat. No. 98EX176), pp. 295–307. IEEE, August 1998
21. Meyer, B.: Eiffel: a language and environment for software engineering. J. Syst. Softw. **8**(3), 199–246 (1988)
22. Meyer, B.: Applying "design by contract". Computer **25**(10), 40–51 (1992)
23. Morgan, C.: Programming from Specifications, 2nd edn. Prentice Hall, Upper Saddle River (1994)
24. Nipkow, T., Paulson, L.C., Wenzel, M. (eds.): Isabelle/HOL. LNCS, vol. 2283. Springer, Heidelberg (2002). https://doi.org/10.1007/3-540-45949-9
25. Oliveira, M.V.M., Cavalcanti, A., Woodcock, J.: ArcAngel: a tactic language for refinement. Formal Aspects Comput. **15**(1), 28–47 (2003)
26. Oliveira, M.V.M., Gurgel, A.C., Castro, C.G.: CRefine: support for the circus refinement calculus. In: 2008 Sixth IEEE International Conference on Software Engineering and Formal Methods, pp. 281–290. IEEE, November 2008
27. Plosch, R.: Tool support for design by contract. In: Proceedings, Technology of Object-Oriented Languages. TOOLS 26 (Cat. No. 98EX176), pp. 282–294. IEEE, August 1998
28. Tschannen, J., Furia, C.A., Nordio, M., Polikarpova, N.: AutoProof: auto-active functional verification of object-oriented programs. In: Baier, C., Tinelli, C. (eds.) TACAS 2015. LNCS, vol. 9035, pp. 566–580. Springer, Heidelberg (2015). https://doi.org/10.1007/978-3-662-46681-0_53
29. Watson, B.W., Kourie, D.G., Schaefer, I., Cleophas, L.: Correctness-by-construction and post-hoc verification: a marriage of convenience? In: Margaria, T., Steffen, B. (eds.) ISoLA 2016. LNCS, vol. 9952, pp. 730–748. Springer, Cham (2016). https://doi.org/10.1007/978-3-319-47166-2_52
30. Wohlin, C., Runeson, P., Höst, M., Ohlsson, M.C., Regnell, B., Wesslén, A.: Experimentation in Software Engineering. Springer, Heidelberg (2012). https://doi.org/10.1007/978-3-642-29044-2

4

Pyro: Generating Domain-Specific Collaborative Online Modeling Environments

Philip Zweihoff[(✉)], Stefan Naujokat, and Bernhard Steffen

Chair for Programming Systems, TU Dortmund University, Dortmund, Germany
{philip.zweihoff,stefan.naujokat,bernhard.steffen}@tu-dortmund.de

Abstract. We present Pyro, a framework for enabling domain-specific modeling via the internet. Provided with an adequate metamodel specification, Pyro turns your browser into a collaborative, domain-specific, graphical development environment with features reminiscent of desktop IDEs for textual programming languages. The required metamodeling is supported in a high-level, simplicity-driven fashion, and the entire ready-to-run browser-based domain-specific development environment is generated fully automatically. We will illustrate the steps of this development along the realization of a graphical IDE for the Architecture Analysis and Design Language (AADL).

1 Introduction

Domain-specific languages (DSLs) aim at closing the gap between domain knowledge and software development by explicitly supporting the required domain concepts. Graphical domain-specific languages have turned out to be particularly suitable for domain experts without any programming background. The bottleneck in practice is the enormous effort to develop the required domain-specific graphical modeling tools. The CINCO *SCCE Meta Tooling Suite* [26] has been designed to overcome this bottleneck by providing a holistic, simplicity-driven [22] approach for the creation of such domain-specific graphical modeling tools. A key feature of CINCO is that it generates the entire graphical modeling environment (referred to as 'CINCO Products' in the remainder of the paper) from high-level specifications of the defined model structures and functionalities. The (translational) semantics of the specified modeling language is defined in terms of code generation, model transformation, evaluation, and/or interpretation [20]. CINCO Products are Eclipse-based, graphical modeling tools that are realized via a number of Eclipse plug-ins [13]. Thus, setting up a CINCO Product involves some technical aspects that are beyond the competence of typical domain experts, and it becomes even more tedious when one wants to enable a cooperative development.

In this paper, we present *Pyro*, a tool that enables one to generate CINCO Products for collaborative modeling that run in a web browser. Conceptually, Pyro borrows from modern online editors for collaborative work, like Google

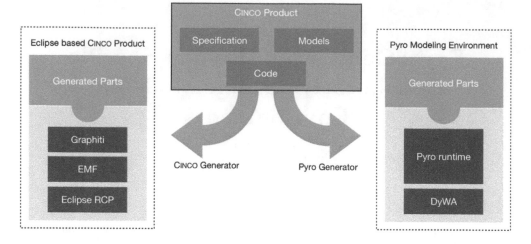

Fig. 1. Cinco generation architecture.

Docs, Microsoft Office 365, or solutions like ShareLaTeX/Overleaf that even free one from maintaining a corresponding build and runtime environment.

Key to the realization of Pyro is that CINCO follows a fully generative approach on the meta level, which allows one to modularly 'retarget' the CINCO Product Generation for the web (cf. Fig. 1). Technically, Pyro web modeling environments utilize *DyWA* [27] (Dynamic Web Application) for data modeling, empowering prototype-driven application development.

In order to achieve this retargeting and to enable collaborative work, Pyro needs to, in particular, compensate for all the required functionality provided by the Eclipse platform, like the EMF framework with GMF or Graphiti for graphical editors. Altogether, this poses the following three key challenges:

- Developing an adequate web solution for the metamodel-based model handling (API, persistence, event system, etc.) that in the Eclipse world is provided by the EMF framework [33] (see *Architecture Backend*, Sect. 3.1).
- Developing a frontend on top of these model structures that feels like a modern integrated development environment with a graphical editor for the models, which in the Eclipse world is provided by the Rich Client Platform (RCP) [24] and the Graphiti editor framework [2] (see *Architecture Frontend*, Sect. 3.2).
- Enabling real-time live collaborative working on models, which is not foreseen in an offline client like Eclipse (see *Collaborative Editing*, Sect. 4).

In the course of this tool paper, Pyro is illustrated along the development of a graphical modeling environment for the *Architecture Analysis and Design Language* (AADL), an SAE standard for modeling the architecture of embedded real-time systems [29]. CINCO was used to develop a graphical AADL modeling tool supporting a subset of AADL's features tailored to be used in teaching [28],

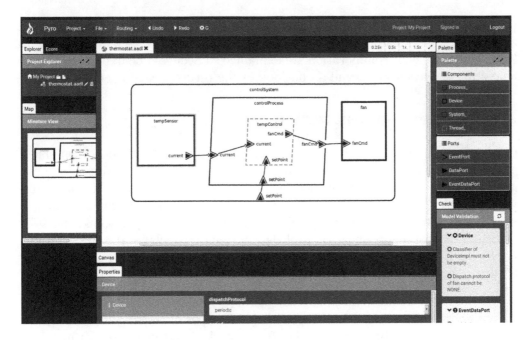

Fig. 2. Pyro web-based modeling environment for the AADL language.

where it replaces the graphical editor of the OSATE tool [8] (AADL's reference implementation). Furthermore, a dedicated code generator was developed to support verification with behavior specified with the BLESS language [17]. Another example for Pyro realizing a DSL for point and click adventures can be found in [21].

Figure 2 shows the web-based graphical AADL editor in Pyro[1]. We will use this editor in the remainder of this paper to illustrate CINCO's and Pyro's core ideas and concepts. The user interface is designed after commonly known concepts from integrated development environments, like Eclipse or IntelliJ. The main area in the center is covered by the *modeling canvas* showing the currently edited model. On the right, there is the *palette* showing the available types of modeling elements. They can be placed onto the canvas just by drag&drop. The attributes of the currently selected element in the editor can be set via the *properties* view at the bottom. The *validation* view (bottom right corner) constantly checks for the syntax and static semantics of the model in the canvas and provides appropriate error or warning messages. Finally, a *project explorer* and a *menu bar* complete the IDE-like appearance.

The remainder of the paper is organized as follows: While Sect. 2 briefly describes the use of CINCO's specification languages to define a sophisticated graphical

---

[1] The editor is available for experimentation on the Pyro website: https://pyro.scce.info.

modeling language, the generation to a web-based environment and the resulting architecture is explained in Sect. 3. The mechanisms and techniques used to enable simultaneous collaboration are explained in Sect. 4. The paper closes with a summary, related work, and an outlook of the future development in Sect. 5.

2   DSL Development with Cinco

CINCO is a language workbench [11] for the simplicity-driven development of graphical modeling environments that are domain-specific [12], support full code generation [10,15], and easily integrate existing solutions in the form of services [23]. As CINCO is itself a meta-level application of these principles [25], it is specialized to the domain of 'graph-based graphical modeling tools' and fully generates such tools from meta-level descriptions (models) – the key enabling factor for the whole Pyro approach. Primarily relevant in this regard are two CINCO metamodeling languages:[2]

1. The *Meta Graph Language* (MGL) allows for the definition of the abstract syntax of the developed language, i.e., which types of language elements exist and how they can be related. In the context of AADL, this means, for instance, that a *system* model consists of *devices*, *processes* and *threads*, and that all of them have *ports* (of different types) that can be connected with *data/information flow* edges.
2. The *Meta Style Language* (MSL) is used to specify the concrete graphical syntax of those MGL-defined concepts by means of simple hierarchical shapes and their appearance (such as color, line type/width, etc.). As can be seen in Fig. 2, for instance, *devices* are depicted by a black thick line rectangle, while *threads* appear as a grey dashed line parallelogram.

With these meta-level specification files, the CINCO Product Generator (which is part of CINCO) generates plug-ins for the Eclipse Rich Client Platform (RCP) that realize the editor based on the Eclipse Modeling Framework (EMF) and the Graphiti graphical editor framework. Further additions to the editor, which are not covered by these two specification files, can be injected in an aspect-oriented fashion [16]: CINCO provides a so-called mechanism of *hooks* that are triggered on the occurrence of certain events, for instance, when a node is created, moved, or deleted. Hooks are inserted into the MGL file with *annotations* on the model elements defined therein. The effect of a hook can either be modeled in a transformation language [20] or directly be written as Java code using the generated model API. In the context of the AADL editor, e.g., a `postMoveHook` is used to move a port to the nearest border within its container after it has been moved by the user. This results in a very natural 'snapping to the border' effect during modeling.

As CINCO follows a fully generative approach, the very same specification files are utilized by Pyro to generate a web-based modeling editor that runs in

---

[2] For a more elaborate introduction on how to define a graphical editor with CINCO, as well as other case studies and exemplary modeling languages, please refer to [26].

the browser (cf. Fig. 1). Of course, in this context, the running platform won't be based on Eclipse anymore, but based on common web frameworks like Angular for the frontend and Java EE for the backend. The aspects of a CINCO Product included in a service-oriented fashion via native components written in Java (for instance a code generator or editor-assisting features like the hooks discussed above) can thus directly be run also in the backend of the Pyro editor.

In the following, we will focus on two particularly important aspects of Pyro: After discussing the frontend/backend architecture of the generated Pyro modeling environments in Sect. 3, we will take a deeper look at the communication pattern between the involved components that facilitates synchronous collaborative modeling (cf. Sect. 4).

3   Architecture

In contrast to developing an Eclipse-based modeling environment, for the realization of a web-based solution one nearly has to start from scratch. Eclipse itself is built on a huge amount of plug-ins, developed over the past seventeen years. In particular, the Eclipse Modeling Project provides many frameworks for developing modeling languages based on metamodels and bundling them into a rich IDE. In the context of the web, development of integrated environments has just started, so that only a few best practices, plug-ins, and frameworks are available. This means, even fundamental features often have to be implemented to enable basic functionalities. The main difference between local desktop IDEs and a web-based environment like Pyro is the opportunity to provide distributed access to a centralized instance by multiple users at the same time. This results in new challenges and requirements regarding the synchronization between multiple users and conflict resolution for oppositional modifications.

Thus, the Pyro architecture must be built in a way that adequately substitutes what Eclipse already provides in the desktop application context, but also be prepared for the distributed setting with multiple users – in particular for supporting live collaborative editing on the same models. In this section, the generation of Pyro web-based modeling environments is described in a way that shows how the needed information is collected from CINCO's high-level specification metamodels and where the generated code is placed and distributed in the overall context to build the Pyro architecture.

The previously introduced specification of the AADL modeling language constitutes the source for the tool generation step. After the Pyro generator is triggered, all MGL and MSL files for a CINCO-based modeling tool are collected to gather the required information. At this point, all modeling languages, including their available node and edge types, are visible for the generator.

In the next step, a template of the modeling environment web application is created. The gray parts with dotted borders in Fig. 3 show the static elements independent of the given language specification, whereas the blue parts with solid borders are specifically generated from this specification. The template consists of a *DyWA*-based backend, extended by a specific *Domain Layer*

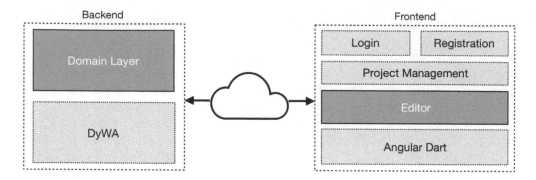

Fig. 3. Overall architecture of the generated web-based modeling environment.

for communication. On the client side, some general parts provide *Registration*, *Login*, and *Project Management*, but the main component is the specific *Editor* generated to handle instances of the graphical modeling language. The underlying single-page web application framework *Angular Dart* [1] is utilized to enable the required features of a rich internet application, like versatile user interaction and asynchronous communication.

Essentially, in the backend, the challenge of providing the metamodel-based model handling (persistence, API, event handling, etc.) is solved, which in the CINCO desktop client world is provided by the EMF framework. The frontend, on the other hand, realizes the rich IDE-like frame application with the graphical editor for the models. In the following, these two parts are explained in more detail to show how the different layers are connected and which parts are generated to establish the entire integrated environment.

3.1   Backend

The backend of a modeling environment generated using Pyro consists of two main layers: One is responsible for the centralized persistence of model instances, the other for receiving and distributing modifications. The lowest level of the web application is the database to store information in a centralized fashion. This layer handles the representation of predefined metamodels for the given domain-specific languages. Pyro modeling environments utilize the *DyWA* as an abstraction layer of a database to store types and objects in a dynamic and loosely coupled fashion [27]. Based on the specified languages' node and edge types, a *Domain Data Plug-in* (see Fig. 4) is generated by Pyro which declares types, associations, attributes, and inheritance. The main reason for using the *DyWA* as model layer is its *Domain Generator*, which generates a specific *DyWA API* providing entities and controllers for the previously given types to handle their instances on a simplified layer above the database. This closely resembles the APIs generated by EMF in the Eclipse world, so that the effort of generating the required *CINCO API* adapters is greatly reduced, which provides functionalities with identical signatures as EMF, so that already

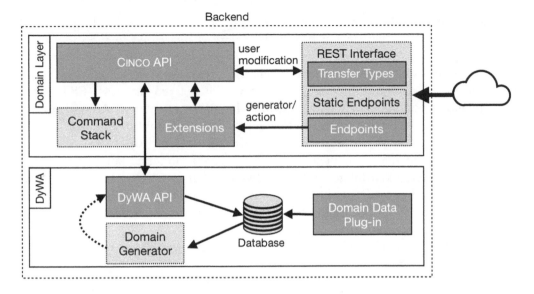

Fig. 4. Backend component architecture and interaction.

existing code can directly be applied (see below). Beyond that, DyWA is prepared for dynamic change of the metamodel, which becomes necessary during modeling language evolution (see [19]).

Since CINCO supports to extend the definition of graphical modeling languages by user-written Java code for hooks, actions, validation checks, and code generators, a holistic reuse mechanism has to be provided in the context of Pyro. To meet this goal, the same CINCO interfaces are rebuilt in the generated web-based modeling environment, providing the same structure and identical signatures. As a result of this, the domain-specific interfaces (see Fig. 4, *CINCO API*) generated by Pyro are compatible to the one CINCO generates for Eclipse and EMF to be used identically by these extensions. In contrast to the desktop-based CINCO Product, a Pyro graph model instance is not persisted in a file on the local system. The Pyro web modeling environment as a distributed system utilizes the DyWA database for storage and centralized access as a server. Thus, the *CINCO API* is internally connected to the corresponding generated *DyWA API* to persist changes in the database, which is hidden from the extensions.

Multi-user collaborative editing with the generated domain-specific modeling languages is one of the main challenges for Pyro. All changes to a centrally held instance of a graph model have to be shared with all participants. For the distribution of the changes performed on a graph model by calling the *CINCO API*) methods, a *Command Stack* is used, to store each individual modification. Since CINCO provides hooks for aspect-oriented extensions, a single action like the movement of a node on the canvas can result in multiple successive commands. As a result, all modifications on a model or any of their elements at runtime are encoded in commands and sequentially stored in the stack. The recorded commands during the *CINCO API* usage are used to synchronize between different clients looking at the same model as well as the realization of redo and undo functionalities. This synchronization mechanism is described in more detail in Sect. 4.

To use the web modeling environment in a desktop application fashion, an uninterruptible user interaction is necessary. Thus, Pyro utilizes REST-based asynchronous communication for non-blocking data exchange. As a result of this, the outermost component of the generated web application is a *REST Interface*. The interface consists of *Static Endpoints* for project, file, and user management, which are independent from the given modeling languages. These parts are supplemented by generated *Endpoints*, which are based on the CINCO specification and provide methods to create, read, update, and delete (CRUD) a single graph model. In addition to this, the interface contains the central endpoint for commands sent from a client's frontend to the backend. Depending on the used *Extensions*, additional *Endpoints* are generated to fetch and trigger user-written actions or a generator.

3.2   Frontend

To mimic the look and feel of a local desktop modeling environment, the web-based variant generated by Pyro has to provide versatile user interactions. As a result of this, the *Frontend* of the generated web application (see Fig. 5), which realizes the interface for the user, is focused on quick responses and familiar input behavior. To achieve this goal, the frontend part of a web modeling environment is built upon the *Angular Dart* [1] framework, which is used to realize single-page web applications with built-in cross-platform support and comprises an architecture focused on reusable components. In addition to this, it is tailored to asynchronous user interaction and client-side routing, so that it can be used to build rich internet applications, like, for instance, ones resembling integrated development environments (IDEs).

In contrast to a local desktop application, a web application requires additional multi-user focused interfaces. Therefore, the template for the frontend, which is initially created, consists of static user interfaces for *Registration* and *Login* as well as a *Project Management* area to create, edit, and share projects. The specifically generated parts are used by the *Editor*, which comprises domain-specific components. Its user interface is similar to the known Eclipse IDE used by regular CINCO Products (see Fig. 2).

The challenge of preventing delays in the system's response on a user input to enable fluent interaction can be met by avoiding synchronized communication with the backend. The *editor* facilitates this frontend-side computation by two layers used to interact with instances of the graph models. The *Mirror Layer* stores a snapshot of the model present in the database, whereas the *Interaction Layer* is a direct representation of a visible graph which can be modified by the user. This separation enables a delta between the last valid graph, stored in the *Mirror Layer* and the currently visible graph. Thanks to this, generated syntactical validators (e.g., for ensuring lower bounds of given cardinalities) can

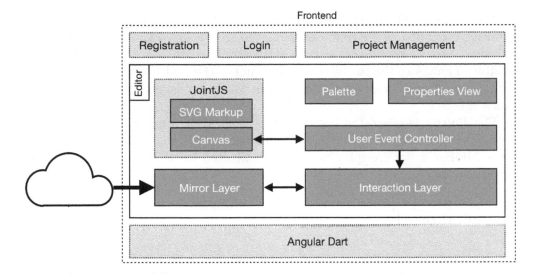

Fig. 5. Front end architecture.

raise errors and the appropriate rollback operation works immediately on the client side without additional communication with the backend.

Pyro specifically aims at supporting users switching from already existing CINCO Products to the web-based modeling environment. Thus, the *Editor*, which is the main part of the frontend, provides multiple components similar to the Eclipse IDE. To not confuse users, functions, behavior and arrangement are recreated. Besides common user interface parts like a project explorer and a menu, specific components for the modeling environment are generated, like the *Canvas*, a *Properties View*, and the *Palette*.

The *Canvas* is based on the *JointJS* framework [9], which in general renders SVGs and adds versatile user interaction for manipulation of nodes and edges via drag&drop functionalities. Using this, it was possible that the web modeling environment running in a browser provides very similar handling to the Eclipse-based desktop application with its Graphiti editor. The exact replication of the node and edge appearance is a central goal of the generated *Canvas*. Ideally, a user cannot distinguish between a Pyro and CINCO visualization of a graph model. This requires the same hierarchical shape structure for the web as in the Graphiti editor, which can be realized by scalable vector graphics (SVGs). The *SVG Markup*, which defines the shapes and styling information of the nodes and edges, is generated based on the concrete syntax specified in the MSL files of CINCO. The *JointJS* framework and *SVG Markup* files are observed by a domain-specific *User Event Controller*, which realizes the listeners and stream handling mechanisms for a single graph model to modify the underlying layers.

Besides the distinct and visible modifications available directly in the *Canvas*, attributes of an edge, node or the graph model (as defined in the MGL metamodel) can be modified using the *Properties View*. It has a generic frame based on a tree view to recursively walk through associated types of the currently selected element. For every type present in an MGL file, a form for editing the primitive attributes (e.g string, Boolean or integer) is generated. The single fields are tailored to the specified data type of the attribute, to give as much support as possible. Thanks to the two-way data binding of the underlying Angular framework, every change to an attribute is immediately propagated to the underlying layer.

The *Palette* is generated based on the given MGL specifications. It lists all node types available for modeling. In addition to this, the optional annotations of the MGL, e.g. for grouping nodes and dedicated icons for visual support, are considered as well.

4   Collaborative Editing

One of the main features of modeling environments generated by Pyro is the simultaneous editing of graph models by multiple clients at the same time. The continuous synchronization between clients avoids classical revision control repositories for distributed access and instead enables immediate collaboration. To reach the goal of simultaneous synchronization, different aspects have been considered to maintain consistency, scalability and achieve a real-time effect.

In this section, the mechanism used for Pyro web-based modeling environments to communicate is presented and explained. The first part discusses the different challenges of a distributed system with respect to the domain of graphical modeling environments, whereas the second part describes the realization of the command pattern used to exchange modifications on a graph model.

4.1   Simultaneous Synchronization Mechanism

The main communication concept of a generated modeling environment by Pyro as a distributed system is the *optimistic replication strategy* [30]. This concept replicates data and allows the single replicas to diverge, which in the context of Pyro is realized by the separated graph model replicas held in each client. The optimistic replication belongs to the *eventually consistent* consistency model and is furthermore classified as *basically available, soft state and eventually consistent* (BASE) [36]. It benefits from high availability, since it only exchanges updates on given items. In the context of a web-based modeling environment, the updates are based on the modifications a client can do to a node or edge. To enable conflict resolution and maintain consistency regarding commutativity and idempotency, *conflict-free replicated data types* (CRDTs) are represented by commands. CRDT was originally used for text-based synchronization as a simplification of *operational transformation* [34]. It utilizes an additional data structure, based on an identifier of the client, the changed value and the position to create a unique identifier for each changed character of the text. Regarding the graph models handled by Pyro, CRDTs are realized by commands for each type of possible model element modification, which store a unique identifier and the changed properties of the relevant element. In addition to this, the previous values of the updated properties are stored as well, to enable rollback, undo, and redo functionalities. Thus, Pyro uses operation-based and state-based CRDTs. Thanks to the CRDTs, conflicts of simultaneously editing the same model element at the same time can be detected. In the context of graphical DSLs, conflicts can arise by violating the given static semantics defined in the metamodel. If a conflict is detected, the corresponding command is flagged for rollback and returned to its sender. The client then inverts the modification encoded by the command and applies it to revert the conflicting change.

4.2 Distributed Command Pattern

The distribution of modifications made to a graph model in the Pyro web modeling environment is realized by a *command pattern* [14]. It belongs to the behavioral design pattern, which is used to encapsulate all information needed to perform an update on an object. The commands are sent as HTTP POST requests, combining the graph model and client identifier. An exemplified collaboration of two clients (red and green) modifying the same graph model simultaneously is presented in Fig. 6.

After the initial read from the database, a client only calculates, exchanges and receives commands when a modification is done (see Fig. 6(1)). For every possible change on nodes and edges (e.g., moving a node or bending an edge), a dedicated command encoding the modification is created and sent to the server, extended with a unique identifier of the sender. Thanks to this assignment, all commands can be differentiated (see red commands by client A and green commands by client B in Fig. 6). As an example, the command for the creation of a node consists of the node type, the position and an identifier of the container where it should be instantiated. Other commands, e.g., the move node commands, contain information of the previous as well as the new position, so that they store the delta of the modification.

The *Serializer* (see Fig. 6(2)) is used to parse the received payload and assign the commands to the associated *Command Applier*. Thanks to additional reflective *type* annotations, the received payload can be parsed to recreate the correct command type. The assignment depends on the given graph model type the command belongs to.

The *Command Applier* (see Fig. 6(3)) is the main component of the web server, since it receives, validates and executes the commands. Every modification encoded by a command is initially validated against the syntactical constraints defined by the graph model type. In the case of a constraint violation, the command is inverted based on the given delta, and returned to undo the invalid operation sent from a client. After a successful validation, the modification encoded by the command is applied to the generated domain-specific API, which also triggers the annotated hooks and finally modify the node or edge instances in the central database. Modifications performed on the API itself (e.g., performed by a hook implementation) are again internally encoded as commands for further distribution to other clients. The updates resulting from the hook execution inside the API are combined with the initial command to be

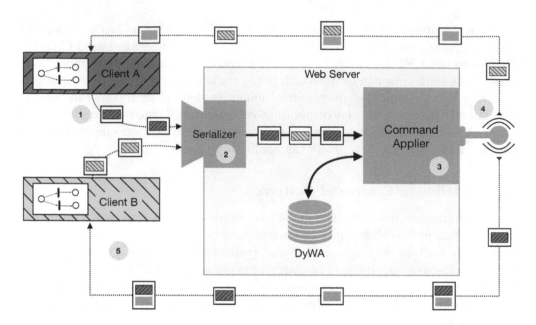

Fig. 6. Concept of the distributed command pattern. (Color figure online)

interpreted as a single transaction shown by the packages of Fig. 6. To ensure the consistency between the sender of a command and the other clients, the initiator is also informed about internally arisen modification based on hook execution. All commands, collected during the execution of the initial modification, are broadcast to other listening clients (see Fig. 6(4)). This mechanism uses bidirectional ongoing connections, so that clients can request to listen on changes made to their currently open graph model.

The commands received by a client (see Fig. 6(5)) are parsed and inspected, to ensure that commands initiated by the client itself are neglected. New changes from other clients are applied to all layers and displayed on the canvas. In addition to this, the client is notified about received changes. Updates caused as a result of self-sent commands (e.g., a modification performed during a hook execution), are only partially applied to guarantee that nodes and edges will not be modified twice.

The command pattern applied to the generated modeling environments is tailored to enable real-time collaborative editing. The main design decisions are focused on scalability and high availability by BASE and CRDT. The operational approach realized with this command pattern is more suitable than a textual language protocol like the *Language Server Protocol* (LSP) [3]. The main difference between the command pattern and the LSP is the way of distributing modifications on the model. In contrast to the presented communication protocol of Pyro, the LSP uses changed regions of a text document for propagation. The intention of the modification has to be evaluated afterwards, whereas in graphical DSLs the commands are used for a direct representation of the occurred change.

5   Conclusion and Perspectives

We have presented Pyro, a framework for enabling domain-specific modeling via the internet. Provided with an adequate metamodel specification, Pyro turns a browser into a collaborative, domain-specific, graphical development environment with features reminiscent of desktop IDEs for programming textual languages. The required metamodeling is supported in a high-level, simplicity-driven fashion: The MGL describes the available node types, edge types, and syntactical constraints, whereas the MSL defines the visual appearance of the modeling artifacts defined in the MGL. Based on these specifications, the entire ready-to-run browser-based domain-specific development environment is generated fully automatically, as has been illustrated along the construction of a graphical development environment for the Architecture Analysis and Design Language (AADL).

The field of web-based development environments is still quite young, so that not many related solutions exist yet. There are the aforementioned collaborative online text editors like Google Docs, Microsoft Office 365 and ShareLaTeX/Overleaf, but in the area of DSLs and modeling, so far we only encountered WebGME [5], an (early stage) online adaption of Vanderbilt University's Generic Modeling Environment [18] and Theia [4], a cross-platform web and desktop IDE for textual DSLs. In addition, itemis (the German company who significantly contributed to the well-known Xtext [6] DSL framework) is currently working on a platform called 'Convecton', which aims at bringing modeling with and execution of domain-specific languages online into the cloud [35]. However, none of these solutions provide a Pyro-like, graphical, collaborative modeling support.

Pyro is still in an early stage of development, and there is a lot of room for improvement, like further enhancing and easing the graphical modeling features, or improving the performance of collaborative modeling by taking advantage of peer-to-peer communication. Pyro is envisioned to enable cross-competence collaboration on a single project in a domain/purpose-specific fashion according to the Language-Driven Engineering (LDE) paradigm [31]. LDE aims at allowing the different stakeholders to formulate their intents in they way they are used to, i.e., in their domain language, and restricted in a fashion that the efforts of the other involved stakeholders are maintained, or as we say, constitute Archimedean points [32] of the considered domain-specific language. Currently, we are starting to explore the impact of the Pyro technology on a larger scale for DIME [7], our framework for developing Web applications.

References

1. About AngularDart. https://webdev.dartlang.org/angular. Accessed 13 Feb 2019
2. Graphiti - A Graphical Tooling Infrastructure. http://www.eclipse.org/graphiti/. Accessed 13 Feb 2019
3. Official page for Language Server Protocol. https://microsoft.github.io/language-server-protocol/. Accessed 12 Feb 2019
4. Theia - Cloud and Desktop IDE. https://www.theia-ide.org. Accessed 12 Feb 2019

5. WebGME. https://webgme.org/. Accessed 13 Feb 2019
6. Xtext - Language Engineering Made Easy! http://www.eclipse.org/Xtext/. Accessed 13 Feb 2019
7. Boßelmann, S., et al.: DIME: a programming-less modeling environment for web applications. In: Margaria, T., Steffen, B. (eds.) ISoLA 2016. LNCS, vol. 9953, pp. 809–832. Springer, Cham (2016). https://doi.org/10.1007/978-3-319-47169-3_60
8. Carnegie Mellon University: Welcome to OSATE. http://osate.org/. Accessed 13 Feb 2019
9. client IO: Joint API. http://www.jointjs.com/api. Accessed 13 Feb 2019
10. Czarnecki, K., Eisenecker, U.W.: Generative Programming: Methods, Tools, and Applications. ACM Press/Addison-Wesley Publishing Co., New York (2000)
11. Fowler, M.: Language Workbenches: The Killer-App for Domain Specific Languages? June 2005. http://martinfowler.com/articles/languageWorkbench.html. Accessed 13 Feb 2019
12. Fowler, M., Parsons, R.: Domain-Specific Languages. Addison-Wesley/ACM Press (2011). http://books.google.de/books?id=ri1muolw_YwC
13. Gronback, R.C.: Eclipse Modeling Project: A Domain-Specific Language (DSL) Toolkit. Addison-Wesley, Boston (2008)
14. Hannemann, J., Kiczales, G.: Design pattern implementation in Java and AspectJ. In: Proceedings of the 17th ACM SIGPLAN Conference on Object-Oriented Programming, Systems, Languages, and Applications (OOPSLA 2002). ACM SIGPLAN Notices, vol. 37, pp. 161–173. ACM (2002)
15. Kelly, S., Tolvanen, J.P.: Domain-Specific Modeling: Enabling Full Code Generation. Wiley/IEEE Computer Society Press, Hoboken (2008)
16. Kiczales, G., et al.: Aspect-oriented programming. In: Akşit, M., Matsuoka, S. (eds.) ECOOP 1997. LNCS, vol. 1241, pp. 220–242. Springer, Heidelberg (1997). https://doi.org/10.1007/BFb0053381
17. Larson, B.R., Chalin, P., Hatcliff, J.: BLESS: formal specification and verification of behaviors for embedded systems with software. In: Brat, G., Rungta, N., Venet, A. (eds.) NFM 2013. LNCS, vol. 7871, pp. 276–290. Springer, Heidelberg (2013). https://doi.org/10.1007/978-3-642-38088-4_19
18. Ledeczi, A., et al.: The generic modeling environment. In: Workshop on Intelligent Signal Processing (WISP 2001) (2001)
19. Lybecait, M., Kopetzki, D., Naujokat, S., Steffen, B.: Towards Language-to-Language Transformation (2019, to appear)
20. Lybecait, M., Kopetzki, D., Steffen, B.: Design for 'X' through model transformation. In: Margaria, T., Steffen, B. (eds.) ISoLA 2018. LNCS, vol. 11244, pp. 381–398. Springer, Cham (2018). https://doi.org/10.1007/978-3-030-03418-4_23
21. Lybecait, M., Kopetzki, D., Zweihoff, P., Fuhge, A., Naujokat, S., Steffen, B.: A tutorial introduction to graphical modeling and metamodeling with CINCO. In: Margaria, T., Steffen, B. (eds.) ISoLA 2018. LNCS, vol. 11244, pp. 519–538. Springer, Cham (2018). https://doi.org/10.1007/978-3-030-03418-4_31
22. Margaria, T., Steffen, B.: Simplicity as a driver for agile innovation. Computer 43(6), 90–92 (2010)
23. Margaria, T., Steffen, B.: Service-orientation: conquering complexity with XMDD. In: Hinchey, M., Coyle, L. (eds.) Conquering Complexity, pp. 217–236. Springer, London (2012). https://doi.org/10.1007/978-1-4471-2297-5_10
24. McAffer, J., Lemieux, J.M., Aniszczyk, C.: Eclipse Rich Client Platform, 2nd edn. Addison-Wesley Professional (2010)

25. Naujokat, S.: Heavy Meta. Model-Driven Domain-Specific Generation of Generative Domain-Specific Modeling Tools. Dissertation, TU Dortmund, Dortmund, Germany, August 2017. http://hdl.handle.net/2003/36060
26. Naujokat, S., Lybecait, M., Kopetzki, D., Steffen, B.: CINCO: a simplicity-driven approach to full generation of domain-specific graphical modeling tools. Softw. Tools Technol. Transf. **20**(3), 327–354 (2017)
27. Neubauer, J., Frohme, M., Steffen, B., Margaria, T.: Prototype-driven development of web applications with DyWA. In: Margaria, T., Steffen, B. (eds.) ISoLA 2014. LNCS, vol. 8802, pp. 56–72. Springer, Heidelberg (2014). https://doi.org/10.1007/978-3-662-45234-9_5
28. Robby, Hatcliff, J., Belt, J.: Model-based development for high-assurance embedded systems. In: Margaria, T., Steffen, B. (eds.) ISoLA 2018. LNCS, vol. 11244, pp. 539–545. Springer, Cham (2018). https://doi.org/10.1007/978-3-030-03418-4_32
29. SAE International: Architecture Analysis & Design Language (AADL), January 2017. https://www.sae.org/standards/content/as5506c/. SAE Standard AS5506C
30. Saito, Y., Shapiro, M.: Optimistic replication. ACM Comput. Surv. (CSUR) **37**(1), 42–81 (2005)
31. Steffen, B., Gossen, F., Naujokat, S., Margaria, T.: Language-driven engineering: from general-purpose to purpose-specific languages. In: Steffen, B., Woeginger, G. (eds.) Computing and Software Science: State of the Art and Perspectives. LNCS, vol. 10000. Springer, Heidelberg (2019, to appear)
32. Steffen, B., Naujokat, S.: Archimedean points: the essence for mastering change. LNCS Trans. Found. Mastering Change (FoMaC) **1**(1), 22–46 (2016)
33. Steinberg, D., Budinsky, F., Paternostro, M., Merks, E.: EMF: Eclipse Modeling Framework, 2nd edn. Addison-Wesley, Boston (2008)
34. Sun, C., Ellis, C.: Operational transformation in real-time group editors: issues, algorithms, and achievements. In: Proceedings of the 1998 ACM Conference on Computer Supported Cooperative Work (CSCW 1998), pp. 59–68. ACM (1998)
35. Voelter, M.: Convecton Presentation at LangDev Meetup at CWI 8–9 March 2018. https://github.com/cwi-swat/langdev/blob/gh-pages/slides/Convecton@LangDev.pdf. Accessed 13 Feb 2019
36. Vogels, W.: Eventually consistent. Commun. ACM **52**(1), 40–44 (2009)

5

Variability Abstraction and Refinement for Game-Based Lifted Model Checking of Full CTL

Aleksandar S. Dimovski[1]([⊠]) [iD], Axel Legay[2], and Andrzej Wasowski[3] [iD]

[1] Mother Teresa University, 12 Udarna Brigada 2a, 1000 Skopje, Macedonia
aleksandar.dimovski@unt.edu.mk
[2] UCLouvain, Belgium and IRISA/Inria Rennes, Rennes, France
[3] IT University of Copenhagen, Rued Langgaards Vej 7, 2300 Copenhagen, Denmark

Abstract. Variability models allow effective building of many custom model variants for various configurations. Lifted model checking for a variability model is capable of verifying all its variants simultaneously in a single run by exploiting the similarities between the variants. The computational cost of lifted model checking still greatly depends on the number of variants (the size of configuration space), which is often huge. One of the most promising approaches to fighting the configuration space explosion problem in lifted model checking are *variability abstractions*. In this work, we define a novel game-based approach for variability-specific abstraction and refinement for lifted model checking of the full CTL, interpreted over 3-valued semantics. We propose a direct algorithm for solving a 3-valued (abstract) lifted model checking game. In case the result of model checking an abstract variability model is indefinite, we suggest a new notion of refinement, which eliminates indefinite results. This provides an iterative incremental variability-specific abstraction and refinement framework, where refinement is applied only where indefinite results exist and definite results from previous iterations are reused.

1 Introduction

Software Product Line (SPL) [6] is an efficient method for systematic development of a family of related models, known as *variants* (*valid products*), from a common code base. Each variant is specified in terms of *features* (static configuration options) selected for that particular variant. SPLs are particularly popular in the embedded and critical system domains (e.g. cars, phones, avionics, healthcare).

Lifted model checking [4,5] is a useful approach for verifying properties of variability models (SPLs). Given a variability model and a specification, the lifted model checking algorithm, unlike the standard non-lifted one, returns precise conclusive results for all individual variants, that is, for each variant it reports whether it satisfies or violates the specification. The main disadvantage of lifted model checking is the *configuration space explosion problem*, which refers to the high number of variants in the variability model. In fact, exponentially many variants can be derived from only few configuration options (features). One of the most successful approaches to fighting the configuration space explosion are so-called *variability abstractions* [12,14,15,17]. They hide some of the configuration details, so that many of the concrete configurations become indistinguishable and can be collapsed into a single abstract configuration (variant). This results in smaller abstract variability models with a smaller number of abstract configurations. In order to be conservative w.r.t. the full CTL temporal logic, abstract variability models have two types of transitions: *may-transitions* which represent possible transitions in the concrete model, and *must-transitions* which represent the definite transitions in the concrete model. May and must transitions correspond to over and under approximations, and are needed in order to preserve universal and existential CTL properties, respectively.

Here we consider the 3-valued semantics for interpreting CTL formulae over abstract variability models. This semantics evaluates a formula on an abstract model to either *true*, *false*, or *indefinite*. Abstract variability models are designed to be conservative for both *true* and *false*. However, the *indefinite* answer gives no information on the value of the formula on the concrete model. In this case, a refinement is needed in order to make the abstract models more precise.

The technique proposed here significantly extends the scope of existing automatic variability-specific abstraction refinement procedures [8,18], which currently support the verification of universal LTL properties only. They use conservative variability abstractions to construct over-approximated abstract variability models, which preserve LTL properties. If a spurious counterexample (introduced due to the abstraction) is found in the abstract model, the procedures [8,18] use Craig interpolation to extract relevant information from it in order to define the refinement of abstract models. Variability abstractions that preserve all (universal and existential) CTL properties have been previously introduced [12], but without an automatic mechanism for constructing them and no notion of refinement. The abstractions [12] has to be constructed manually by an engineer before verification. In order to make the entire verification procedure automatic, we need to develop an abstraction and refinement framework for CTL properties.

In this work, we propose the first variability-specific abstraction refinement procedure for automatically verifying arbitrary formulae of CTL. To achieve this aim, model checking *games* [24–26] represent the most suitable framework for defining the refinement. In this way, we establish a brand new connection between games and family-based (SPL) model checking. The refinement is defined by finding the reason for the indefinite result of an algorithm that solves the corresponding model checking game, which is played by two players: Player $\forall$ (trying to refute the formula Φ on an abstract model $\mathcal{M}$) and Player $\exists$ (trying to verify Φ on $\mathcal{M}$). The game is played on a *game board*, which consists of configurations of the form (s, Φ') where s is a state of the abstract model $\mathcal{M}$ and Φ' is a subformula of Φ, such that the value of Φ' in s is relevant for determining the final model checking result. The players make moves between configurations in which they try to verify or refute Φ' in s. All possible plays of a game are captured in the game-graph, whose nodes are the elements of the game board and whose edges are the possible moves of the players. The model checking game is solved via a coloring algorithm which colors each node (s, Φ') in the game-graph by T, F, or ? iff the value of Φ' in s is *true*, *false*, or indefinite, respectively. Player $\forall$ has a winning strategy at the node (s, Φ') iff the node is colored by F iff Φ' does not hold in s, and Player $\exists$ has a winning strategy at (s, Φ') iff the node is colored by T iff Φ' holds in s. In addition, it is also possible that neither of players has a winning strategy, in which case the node is colored by ? and the value of Φ' in s is indefinite. In this case, we want to refine the abstract model. We can find the reason for the tie by examining the game-graph. We choose a refinement criterion, which splits abstract configurations so that the new, refined abstract configurations represent smaller subsets of concrete configurations.

2 Background

Variability Models. Let $\mathbb{F} = \{A_1, \ldots, A_n\}$ be a finite set of Boolean variables representing the features available in a variability model. A specific subset of features, $k \subseteq \mathbb{F}$, known as *configuration*, specifies a *variant* (valid product) of a variability model. We assume that only a subset $\mathbb{K} \subseteq 2^{\mathbb{F}}$ of configurations are *valid*. An alternative representation of configurations is based upon propositional formulae. Each configuration $k \in \mathbb{K}$ can be represented by a formula: $k(A_1) \wedge \ldots \wedge k(A_n)$, where $k(A_i) = A_i$ if $A_i \in k$, and $k(A_i) = \neg A_i$ if $A_i \notin k$ for $1 \le i \le n$.

We use *transition systems* (TS) to describe behaviors of single-systems.

Definition 1. *A transition system (TS) is a tuple $\mathcal{T} = (S, Act, trans, I, AP, L)$, where S is a set of states; Act is a set of actions; $trans \subseteq S \times Act \times S$ is a transition relation which is* total, *so that for each state there is an outgoing transition; $I \subseteq S$ is a set of initial states; AP is a set of atomic propositions; and $L : S \to 2^{AP}$ is a labelling function specifying which propositions hold in a state. We write $s_1 \xrightarrow{\lambda} s_2$ whenever $(s_1, \lambda, s_2) \in trans$.*

An *execution* (behaviour) of a TS $\mathcal{T}$ is an *infinite* sequence $\rho = s_0 \lambda_1 s_1 \lambda_2 \ldots$ with $s_0 \in I$ such that $s_i \xrightarrow{\lambda_{i+1}} s_{i+1}$ for all $i \ge 0$. The *semantics* of the TS $\mathcal{T}$, denoted as $[\![\mathcal{T}]\!]_{TS}$, is the set of its executions.

A *featured transition system* (FTS) is a particular instance of a variability model, which describes the behavior of a whole family of systems in a single monolithic description, where the transitions are guarded by a *presence condition* that identifies the variants they belong to. The presence conditions ψ are drawn from the set of feature expressions, *FeatExp*($\mathbb{F}$), which are propositional logic formulae over $\mathbb{F}$: $\psi ::= true \mid A \in \mathbb{F} \mid \neg\psi \mid \psi_1 \wedge \psi_2$. We write $[\![\psi]\!]$ to denote the set of configurations from $\mathbb{K}$ that satisfy ψ, i.e. $k \in [\![\psi]\!]$ iff $k \models \psi$.

Definition 2. *A featured transition system (FTS) represents a tuple $\mathcal{F} = (S, Act, trans, I, AP, L, \mathbb{F}, \mathbb{K}, \delta)$, where $S, Act, trans, I, AP,$ and L form a TS; $\mathbb{F}$ is the set of available features; $\mathbb{K}$ is a set of valid configurations; and $\delta : trans \to FeatExp(\mathbb{F})$ is a total function decorating transitions with presence conditions.*

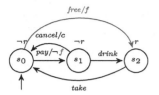

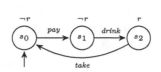

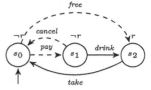

Fig. 1. VENDMACH   **Fig. 2.** $\pi_\emptyset$(VENDMACH)   **Fig. 3.** α^{join}(VENDMACH)

The *projection* of an FTS $\mathcal{F}$ to a configuration $k \in \mathbb{K}$, denoted as $\pi_k(\mathcal{F})$, is the TS $(S, Act, trans', I, AP, L)$, where $trans' = \{t \in trans \mid k \models \delta(t)\}$. We lift the definition of *projection* to sets of configurations $\mathbb{K}' \subseteq \mathbb{K}$, denoted as $\pi_{\mathbb{K}'}(\mathcal{F})$, by keeping the transitions admitted by at least one of the configurations in $\mathbb{K}'$. That is, $\pi_{\mathbb{K}'}(\mathcal{F})$, is the FTS $(S, Act, trans', I, AP, L, \mathbb{F}, \mathbb{K}', \delta')$, where $trans' = \{t \in trans \mid \exists k \in \mathbb{K}'.k \models \delta(t)\}$ and $\delta' = \delta|_{trans'}$ is the restriction of δ to $trans'$. The *semantics* of an FTS $\mathcal{F}$, denoted as $[\![\mathcal{F}]\!]_{FTS}$, is the union of behaviours of the projections on all valid variants $k \in \mathbb{K}$, i.e. $[\![\mathcal{F}]\!]_{FTS} = \cup_{k \in \mathbb{K}}[\![\pi_k(\mathcal{F})]\!]_{TS}$.

Modal transition systems (MTSs) [22] are a generalization of transition systems equipped with two transition relations: *must* and *may*. The former (must) is used to specify the required behavior, while the latter (may) to specify the allowed behavior of a system. We will use MTSs for representing abstractions of FTSs.

Definition 3. *A modal transition system (MTS) is represented by a tuple* $\mathcal{M} = (S, Act, trans^{may}, trans^{must}, I, AP, L)$, *where* $trans^{may} \subseteq S \times Act \times S$ *describe may transitions of* $\mathcal{M}$; $trans^{must} \subseteq S \times Act \times S$ *describe must transitions of* $\mathcal{M}$, *such that* $trans^{may}$ *is total and* $trans^{must} \subseteq trans^{may}$.

A *may-execution* in $\mathcal{M}$ is an execution (infinite sequence) with all its transitions in $trans^{may}$; whereas a *must-execution* in $\mathcal{M}$ is a maximal sequence with all its transitions in $trans^{must}$, which cannot be extended with any other transition from $trans^{must}$. Note that since $trans^{must}$ is not necessarily total, must-executions can be finite. We use $[\![\mathcal{M}]\!]_{MTS}^{may}$ (resp., $[\![\mathcal{M}]\!]_{MTS}^{must}$) to denote the set of all may-executions (resp., must-executions) in $\mathcal{M}$ starting in an initial state.

Example 1. Throughout this paper, we will use a beverage vending machine as a running example [4]. Figure 1 shows the FTS of a VENDMACH family. It has two features, and each of them is assigned an identifying letter and a color. The features are: CancelPurchase (c, in brown), for canceling a purchase after a coin is entered; and FreeDrinks (f, in blue) for offering free drinks. Each transition is labeled by an *action* followed by a *feature expression*. For instance, the transition $s_0 \xrightarrow{free/f} s_2$ is included in variants where the feature f is enabled. For clarity, we omit to write the presence condition *true* in transitions. There is only one atomic proposition served $\in AP$, which is abbreviated as r. Note that $r \in L(s_2)$, whereas $r \notin L(s_0)$ and $r \notin L(s_1)$.

By combining various features, a number of variants of this VENDMACH can be obtained. The set of valid configurations is: $\mathbb{K}^{\text{VM}} = \{\emptyset, \{c\}, \{f\}, \{c, f\}\}$ (or, equivalently $\mathbb{K}^{\text{VM}} = \{\neg c \wedge \neg f, c \wedge \neg f, \neg c \wedge f, c \wedge f\}$). Figure 2 shows a basic version of VENDMACH that only serves a drink, described by the configuration: $\emptyset$ (or, as formula $\neg c \wedge \neg f$). It takes a coin, serves a drink, opens a compartment so the customer can take the drink. Figure 3 shows an MTS, where must transitions are denoted by solid lines, while may transitions by dashed lines.   □

CTL Properties. We present Computation Tree Logic (CTL) [1] for specifying system properties. CTL state formulae Φ are given by:

$$\Phi ::= true \mid false \mid l \mid \Phi_1 \wedge \Phi_2 \mid \Phi_1 \vee \Phi_2 \mid A\phi \mid E\phi, \qquad \phi ::= \bigcirc\Phi \mid \Phi_1 U \Phi_2 \mid \Phi_1 V \Phi_2$$

where $l \in Lit = AP \cup \{\neg a \mid a \in AP\}$ and ϕ represent CTL path formulae. Note that the CTL state formulae Φ are given in negation normal form ($\neg$ is applied only to atomic propositions). The path formula $\bigcirc\Phi$ can be read as "in the next state Φ", $\Phi_1 U \Phi_2$ can be read as "Φ_1 until Φ_2", and its dual $\Phi_1 V \Phi_2$ can be read as "Φ_2 while not Φ_1" (where Φ_1 may never hold).

We assume the standard CTL semantics over TSs is given [1] (see also [16, Appendix A]). We write $[\mathcal{T} \models \Phi] = tt$ to denote that $\mathcal{T}$ satisfies the formula Φ, whereas $[\mathcal{T} \models \Phi] = ff$ to denote that $\mathcal{T}$ does not satisfy Φ.

We say that an FTS $\mathcal{F}$ satisfies a CTL formula Φ, written $[\mathcal{F} \models \Phi] = tt$, iff all its valid variants satisfy the formula, i.e. $\forall k \in \mathbb{K}. [\pi_k(\mathcal{F}) \models \Phi] = tt$. Otherwise, we say $\mathcal{F}$ does not satisfy Φ, written $[\mathcal{F} \models \Phi] = ff$. In this case, we also want to determine a non-empty set of violating variants $\mathbb{K}' \subseteq \mathbb{K}$, such that $\forall k' \in \mathbb{K}'. [\pi_{k'}(\mathcal{F}) \models \Phi] = ff$ and $\forall k \in \mathbb{K} \setminus \mathbb{K}'. [\pi_k(\mathcal{F}) \models \Phi] = tt$.

We define the 3-valued semantics of CTL over an MTS $\mathcal{M}$ slightly differently from the semantics for TSs. A CTL state formula Φ is satisfied in a state s of an MTS $\mathcal{M}$, denoted $[\mathcal{M}, s \models^3 \Phi]$, iff ($\mathcal{M}$ is omitted when clear from context):[1]

$$(1)\ [s \models^3 a] = \begin{cases} tt, & \text{if } a \in L(s) \\ ff, & \text{if } a \notin L(s) \end{cases}, \qquad [s \models^3 \neg a] = \begin{cases} tt, & \text{if } a \notin L(s) \\ ff, & \text{if } a \in L(s) \end{cases}$$

$$(2)\ [s \models^3 \Phi_1 \wedge \Phi_2] = \begin{cases} tt, & \text{if } [s \models^3 \Phi_1] = tt \text{ and } [s \models^3 \Phi_2] = tt \\ ff, & \text{if } [s \models^3 \Phi_1] = ff \text{ or } [s \models^3 \Phi_2] = ff \\ \bot, & \text{otherwise} \end{cases}$$

$$(3)\ [s \models^3 A\phi] = \begin{cases} tt, & \text{if } \forall \rho \in [\![\mathcal{M}]\!]_{MTS}^{\text{may},s}. [\rho \models^3 \phi] = tt \\ ff, & \text{if } \exists \rho \in [\![\mathcal{M}]\!]_{MTS}^{\text{must},s}. [\rho \models^3 \phi] = ff \\ \bot, & \text{otherwise} \end{cases}$$

$$[s \models^3 E\phi] = \begin{cases} tt, & \text{if } \exists \rho \in [\![\mathcal{M}]\!]_{MTS}^{\text{must},s}. [\rho \models^3 \phi] = tt \\ ff, & \text{if } \forall \rho \in [\![\mathcal{M}]\!]_{MTS}^{\text{may},s}. [\rho \models^3 \phi] = ff \\ \bot, & \text{otherwise} \end{cases}$$

where $[\![\mathcal{M}]\!]_{MTS}^{\text{may},s}$ (resp., $[\![\mathcal{M}]\!]_{MTS}^{\text{must},s}$) denotes the set of all may-executions (must-executions) starting in the state s of $\mathcal{M}$. Satisfaction of a path formula ϕ for a may- or must-execution $\rho = s_0 \lambda_1 s_1 \lambda_2 \ldots$ of an MTS $\mathcal{M}$ (we write $\rho_i = s_i$ to

---

[1] See [16, Appendix A] for definitions of $[s \models^3 \Phi_1 \vee \Phi_2]$, $[\rho \models^3 \bigcirc\Phi]$, and $[\rho \models^3 (\Phi_1 V \Phi_2)]$.

denote the i-th state of ρ, and $|\rho|$ to denote the number of states in ρ), denoted $[\mathcal{M}, \rho \models^3 \phi]$, is defined as ($\mathcal{M}$ is omitted when clear from context):

$$(4)\ [\rho \models^3 (\Phi_1 U \Phi_2)] = \begin{cases} tt, & \text{if } \exists 0 \le i \le |\rho|. ([\rho_i \models^3 \Phi_2] = tt \wedge (\forall j < i.[\rho_j \models^3 \Phi_1] = tt)) \\ ff, & \text{if } \begin{array}{l} \forall 0 \le i \le |\rho|. (\forall j < i.[\rho_j \models^3 \Phi_1] \ne ff \Longrightarrow [\rho_i \models^3 \Phi_2] = ff) \\ \wedge\ \forall i \ge 0.[\rho_i \models^3 \Phi_1] \ne ff \Longrightarrow |\rho| = \infty \end{array} \\ \perp, & \text{otherwise} \end{cases}$$

A MTS $\mathcal{M}$ satisfies a formula Φ, written $[\mathcal{M} \models^3 \Phi] = tt$, iff $\forall s_0 \in I. [s_0 \models^3 \Phi] = tt$. We say that $[\mathcal{M} \models^3 \Phi] = ff$ if $\exists s_0 \in I. [s_0 \models^3 \Phi] = ff$. Otherwise, $[\mathcal{M} \models^3 \Phi] = \perp$.

Example 2. Consider the FTS VENDMACH and MTS $\alpha^{\text{join}}(\text{VENDMACH})$ in Figs. 1 and 3. The property $\Phi_1 = A(\neg r U r)$ states that in the initial state along every execution will eventually reach the state where r holds. Note that $[\text{VENDMACH} \models \Phi_1] = ff$. E.g., if the feature c is enabled, a counter-example where the state s_2 that satisfies r is never reached is: $s_0 \rightarrow s_1 \rightarrow s_0 \rightarrow \ldots$. The set of violating products is $[\![c]\!] = \{\{c\}, \{f, c\}\} \subseteq \mathbb{K}^{VM}$. However, $[\pi_{[\![\neg c]\!]}(\text{VENDMACH}) \models \Phi_1] = tt$. We also have that $[\alpha^{\text{join}}(\text{VENDMACH}) \models^3 \Phi_1] = \perp$, since (1) there is a may-execution in $\alpha^{\text{join}}(\text{VENDMACH})$ where s_2 is never reached: $s_0 \rightarrow s_1 \rightarrow s_0 \rightarrow \ldots$, and (2) there is no must-execution that violates Φ_1.

Consider the property $\Phi_2 = E(\neg r U r)$, which describes a situation where in the initial state there exists an execution that will eventually reach s_2 that satisfies r. Note that $[\text{VENDMACH} \models \Phi_2] = tt$, since even for variants with the feature c there is a continuation from the state s_1 to s_2. But, $[\alpha^{\text{join}}(\text{VENDMACH}) \models \Phi_2] = \perp$ since (1) there is no a must-execution in $\alpha^{\text{join}}(\text{VENDMACH})$ that reaches s_2 from s_0, and (2) there is a may-execution that satisfies Φ_2. □

3 Abstraction of FTSs

We now introduce the variability abstractions [12] which preserve full CTL. We start working with Galois connections[2] between Boolean complete lattices of feature expressions, and then induce a notion of abstraction of FTSs.

The Boolean complete lattice of feature expressions (propositional formulae over $\mathbb{F}$) is: $(FeatExp(\mathbb{F})_{/\equiv}, \models, \vee, \wedge, true, false, \neg)$. The elements of the domain $FeatExp(\mathbb{F})_{/\equiv}$ are equivalence classes of propositional formulae $\psi \in FeatExp(\mathbb{F})$ obtained by quotienting by the semantic equivalence $\equiv$. The ordering $\models$ is the standard entailment between propositional logics formulae, whereas the least upper bound and the greatest lower bound are just logical disjunction and conjunction respectively. Finally, the constant *false* is the least, *true* is the greatest element, and negation is the complement operator.

---

[2] $\langle L, \le_L \rangle \xleftrightarrow[\alpha]{\gamma} \langle M, \le_M \rangle$ is a *Galois connection* between complete lattices L (concrete domain) and M (abstract domain) iff $\alpha : L \rightarrow M$ and $\gamma : M \rightarrow L$ are total functions that satisfy: $\alpha(l) \le_M m \iff l \le_L \gamma(m)$, for all $l \in L, m \in M$.

Over-approximating abstractions. The *join abstraction*, $\boldsymbol{\alpha}^{\mathrm{join}}$, replaces each feature expression ψ with *true* if there exists at least one configuration from $\mathbb{K}$ that satisfies ψ. The abstract set of features is empty: $\boldsymbol{\alpha}^{\mathrm{join}}(\mathbb{F}) = \emptyset$, and abstract set of configurations is a singleton: $\boldsymbol{\alpha}^{\mathrm{join}}(\mathbb{K}) = \{true\}$. The abstraction and concretization functions between $FeatExp(\mathbb{F})$ and $FeatExp(\emptyset)$ are:

$$\boldsymbol{\alpha}^{\mathrm{join}}(\psi) = \begin{cases} true & \text{if } \exists k \in \mathbb{K}.k \models \psi \\ false & \text{otherwise} \end{cases} \qquad \boldsymbol{\gamma}^{\mathrm{join}}(\psi) = \begin{cases} true & \text{if } \psi \text{ is } true \\ \bigvee_{k \in 2^{\mathbb{F}} \setminus \mathbb{K}} k & \text{if } \psi \text{ is } false \end{cases}$$

which form a Galois connection [15]. In this way, we obtain a single abstract variant that includes all transitions occurring in any variant.

Under-approximating abstractions. The *dual join abstraction*, $\widetilde{\boldsymbol{\alpha}^{\mathrm{join}}}$, replaces each feature expression ψ with *true* if all configurations from $\mathbb{K}$ satisfy ψ. The abstraction and concretization functions between $FeatExp(\mathbb{F})$ and $FeatExp(\emptyset)$, forming a Galois connection [12], are defined as [9]: $\widetilde{\boldsymbol{\alpha}^{\mathrm{join}}} = \neg \circ \boldsymbol{\alpha}^{\mathrm{join}} \circ \neg$ and $\widetilde{\boldsymbol{\gamma}^{\mathrm{join}}} = \neg \circ \boldsymbol{\gamma}^{\mathrm{join}} \circ \neg$, that is:

$$\widetilde{\boldsymbol{\alpha}^{\mathrm{join}}}(\psi) = \begin{cases} true & \text{if } \forall k \in \mathbb{K}.k \models \psi \\ false & \text{otherwise} \end{cases} \qquad \widetilde{\boldsymbol{\gamma}^{\mathrm{join}}}(\psi) = \begin{cases} \bigwedge_{k \in 2^{\mathbb{F}} \setminus \mathbb{K}}(\neg k) & \text{if } \psi \text{ is } true \\ false & \text{if } \psi \text{ is } false \end{cases}$$

In this way, we obtain a single abstract variant that includes only those transitions that occur in all variants.

Abstract MTS and Preservation of CTL. Given a Galois connection $(\boldsymbol{\alpha}^{\mathrm{join}}, \boldsymbol{\gamma}^{\mathrm{join}})$ defined on the level of feature expressions, we now define the abstraction of an FTS as an MTS with two transition relations: one (may) preserving universal properties, and the other (must) preserving existential properties. The may transitions describe the behaviour that is possible in some variant of the concrete FTS, but not need be realized in the other variants; whereas the must transitions describe behaviour that has to be present in all variants of the FTS.

Definition 4. *Given the FTS* $\mathcal{F} = (S, Act, trans, I, AP, L, \mathbb{F}, \mathbb{K}, \delta)$, *define MTS* $\boldsymbol{\alpha}^{\mathrm{join}}(\mathcal{F}) = (S, Act, trans^{may}, trans^{must}, I, AP, L)$ *to be its* abstraction, *where* $trans^{may} = \{t \in trans \mid \boldsymbol{\alpha}^{\mathrm{join}}(\delta(t)) = true\}$, *and* $trans^{must} = \{t \in trans \mid \widetilde{\boldsymbol{\alpha}^{\mathrm{join}}}(\delta(t)) = true\}$.

Note that the abstract model $\boldsymbol{\alpha}^{\mathrm{join}}(\mathcal{F})$ has no variability in it, i.e. it contains only one abstract configuration. We now show that the 3-valued semantics of the MTS $\boldsymbol{\alpha}^{\mathrm{join}}(\mathcal{F})$ is designed to be *sound* in the sense that it preserves both satisfaction (*tt*) and refutation (*ff*) of a formula from the abstract model to the concrete one. However, if the truth value of a formula in the abstract model is $\bot$, then its value over the concrete model is not known. We prove [16, Appendix B]:

Theorem 1 (Preservation results). *For every $\Phi \in CTL$, we have:*

(1) $[\alpha^{\mathrm{join}}(\mathcal{F}) \models^3 \Phi] = tt \implies [\mathcal{F} \models \Phi] = tt.$

(2) $[\alpha^{\mathrm{join}}(\mathcal{F}) \models^3 \Phi] = ff \implies [\mathcal{F} \models \Phi] = ff$ *and* $[\pi_k(\mathcal{F}) \models \Phi] = ff$ *for all* $k \in \mathbb{K}.$

Divide-and-conquer strategy. The problem of evaluating $[\mathcal{F} \models \Phi]$ can be reduced to a number of smaller problems by partitioning the configuration space $\mathbb{K}$. Let the subsets $\mathbb{K}_1, \mathbb{K}_2, \ldots, \mathbb{K}_n$ form a *partition* of the set $\mathbb{K}$. Then, $[\mathcal{F} \models \Phi] = tt$ iff $[\pi_{\mathbb{K}_i}(\mathcal{F}) \models \Phi] = tt$ for all $i = 1, \ldots, n$. Also, $[\mathcal{F} \models \Phi] = ff$ iff $[\pi_{\mathbb{K}_j}(\mathcal{F}) \models \Phi] = ff$ for some $1 \leq j \leq n$. By using Theorem 1, we obtain the following result.

Corollary 1. *Let* $\mathbb{K}_1, \mathbb{K}_2, \ldots, \mathbb{K}_n$ *form a* partition *of* $\mathbb{K}$.

(1) *If* $[\alpha^{\mathrm{join}}(\pi_{\mathbb{K}_1}(\mathcal{F})) \models \Phi] = tt \wedge \ldots \wedge [\alpha^{\mathrm{join}}(\pi_{\mathbb{K}_n}(\mathcal{F})) \models \Phi] = tt$, *then* $[\mathcal{F} \models \Phi] = tt.$

(2) *If* $[\alpha^{\mathrm{join}}(\pi_{\mathbb{K}_j}(\mathcal{F})) \models \Phi] = ff$ *for some* $1 \leq j \leq n$, *then* $[\mathcal{F} \models \Phi] = ff$ *and* $[\pi_k(\mathcal{F}) \models \Phi] = ff$ *for all* $k \in \mathbb{K}_j$.

Example 3. Recall the FTS VENDMACH of Fig. 1. Figure 3 shows the MTS $\alpha^{\mathrm{join}}(\mathrm{VENDMACH})$, where the allowed (may) part of the behavior includes the transitions that are associated with the optional features c and f in VEND-MACH, and the required (must) part includes transitions with the presence condition *true*. Consider the properties introduced in Example 2. We have $[\alpha^{\mathrm{join}}(\mathrm{VENDMACH}) \models^3 \Phi_1] = \bot$ and $[\alpha^{\mathrm{join}}(\mathrm{VENDMACH}) \models^3 \Phi_2] = \bot$, so we cannot conclude whether Φ_1 and Φ_2 are satisfied by VENDMACH or not. □

4   Game-Based Abstract Lifted Model Checking

The 3-valued model checking game [24, 25] on an MTS $\mathcal{M}$ with state set S, a state $s \in S$, and a CTL formula Φ is played by Player $\forall$ and Player $\exists$ in order to evaluate Φ in s of $\mathcal{M}$. The goal of Player $\forall$ is either to refute Φ on $\mathcal{M}$ or to prevent Player $\exists$ from verifying it. The goal of Player $\exists$ is either to verify Φ on $\mathcal{M}$ or to prevent Player $\forall$ from refuting it. The *game board* is the Cartesian product $S \times sub(\Phi)$, where $sub(\Phi)$ is defined as:

if $\Phi = true, false, l$, then $sub(\Phi) = \{\Phi\}$; if $\Phi = \text{Æ} \bigcirc \Phi_1$, then $sub(\Phi) = \{\Phi\} \cup sub(\Phi_1)$
if $\Phi = \Phi_1 \wedge \Phi_2, \Phi_1 \vee \Phi_2$, then $sub(\Phi) = \{\Phi\} \cup sub(\Phi_1) \cup sub(\Phi_2)$
if $\Phi = \text{Æ}(\Phi_1 \mathsf{U} \Phi_2), \text{Æ}(\Phi_1 \mathsf{V} \Phi_2)$, then $sub(\Phi) = exp(\Phi) \cup sub(\Phi_1) \cup sub(\Phi_2)$

where Æ ranges over both A and E. The expansion $exp(\Phi)$ is defined as:

$$\Phi = \text{Æ}(\Phi_1 \mathsf{U} \Phi_2) : exp(\Phi) = \{\Phi, \Phi_2 \vee (\Phi_1 \wedge \text{Æ} \bigcirc \Phi), \Phi_1 \wedge \text{Æ} \bigcirc \Phi, \text{Æ} \bigcirc \Phi\}$$
$$\Phi = \text{Æ}(\Phi_1 \mathsf{V} \Phi_2) : exp(\Phi) = \{\Phi, \Phi_2 \wedge (\Phi_1 \vee \text{Æ} \bigcirc \Phi), \Phi_1 \vee \text{Æ} \bigcirc \Phi, \text{Æ} \bigcirc \Phi\}$$

A *single play* from (s, Φ) is a possibly infinite sequence of configurations $C_0 \to_{p_0} C_1 \to_{p_1} C_2 \to_{p_2} \ldots$, where $C_0 = (s, \Phi)$, $C_i \in S \times sub(\Phi)$, and $p_i \in \{\text{Player } \forall, \text{Player } \exists\}$. The subformula in C_i determines which player p_i makes the next move. The possible moves at each configuration are:

(1) $C_i = (s, \mathit{false})$, $C_i = (s, \mathit{true})$, $C_i = (s, l)$: the play is finished. Such configurations are called *terminal*.

(2) if $C_i = (s, A \bigcirc \Phi)$, Player $\forall$ chooses a must-transition $s \to s'$ (for refutation) or a may-transition $s \to s'$ of $\mathcal{M}$ (to prevent satisfaction), and $C_{i+1} = (s', \Phi)$.

(3) if $C_i = (s, E \bigcirc \Phi)$, Player $\exists$ chooses a must-transition $s \to s'$ (for satisfaction) or a may-transition $s \to s'$ of $\mathcal{M}$ (to prevent refutation), and $C_{i+1} = (s', \Phi)$.

(4) if $C_i = (s, \Phi_1 \wedge \Phi_2)$, then Player $\forall$ chooses $j \in \{1, 2\}$ and $C_{i+1} = (s, \Phi_j)$.

(5) if $C_i = (s, \Phi_1 \vee \Phi_2)$, then Player $\exists$ chooses $j \in \{1, 2\}$ and $C_{i+1} = (s, \Phi_j)$.

(6), (7) if $C_i = (s, \text{Æ}(\Phi_1 \mathsf{U} \Phi_2))$, then $C_{i+1} = (s, \Phi_2 \vee (\Phi_1 \wedge \text{Æ} \bigcirc \text{Æ}(\Phi_1 \mathsf{U} \Phi_2)))$.

(8), (9) if $C_i = (s, \text{Æ}(\Phi_1 \mathsf{V} \Phi_2))$, then $C_{i+1} = (s, \Phi_2 \wedge (\Phi_1 \vee \text{Æ} \bigcirc \text{Æ}(\Phi_1 \mathsf{V} \Phi_2)))$.

The moves (6)–(9) are deterministic, thus any player can make them.

A play is a *maximal play* iff it is infinite or ends in a terminal configuration. A play is infinite [26] iff there is exactly one subformula of the form $A\mathsf{U}$, $A\mathsf{V}$, $E\mathsf{U}$, or $E\mathsf{V}$ that occurs infinitely often in the play. Such a subformula is called a *witness*. We have the following *winning criteria*:

- Player $\forall$ *wins* a (maximal) play iff in each configuration of the form $C_i = (s, A \bigcirc \Phi)$, Player $\forall$ chooses a move based on must-transitions and one of the following holds: (1) the play is finite and ends in a terminal configuration of the form $C_i = (s, \mathit{false})$ or $C_i = (s, a)$ where $a \notin L(s)$ or $C_i = (s, \neg a)$ where $a \in L(s)$; (2) the play is infinite and the witness is of the form $A\mathsf{U}$ or $E\mathsf{U}$.
- Player $\exists$ *wins* a (maximal) play iff in each configuration of the form $C_i = (s, E \bigcirc \Phi)$, Player $\exists$ chooses a move based on must-transitions and one of the following holds: (1) the play is finite and ends in a terminal configuration of the form $C_i = (s, \mathit{true})$ or $C_i = (s, a)$ where $a \in L(s)$ or $C_i = (s, \neg a)$ where $a \notin L(s)$; (2) the play is infinite and the witness is of the form $A\mathsf{V}$ or $E\mathsf{V}$.
- Otherwise, the play ends in a *tie*.

A *strategy* is a set of rules for a player, telling the player which move to choose in the current configuration. A *winning strategy* from (s, Φ) is a set of rules allowing the player to win every play that starts at (s, Φ) if he plays by the rules. It was shown in [24, 25] that the model checking problem of evaluating $[\mathcal{M}, s \models^3 \Phi]$ can be reduced to the problem of finding which player has a winning strategy from (s, Φ) (i.e. to solving the given 3-valued model checking game).

The algorithm proposed in [24, 25] for solving the given 3-valued model checking game consists of two parts. First, it constructs a *game-graph*, then it runs an *algorithm for coloring* the game-graph. The game-graph is $G_{\mathcal{M} \times \Phi} = (N, E)$ where $N \subseteq S \times sub(\Phi)$ is the set of nodes and $E \subseteq N \times N$ is the set of edges. N contains a node for each configuration that was reached during the construction of the game-graph that starts from initial configurations $I \times \{\Phi\}$ in a BFS manner, and E contains an edge for each possible move that was applied. The nodes of the game-graph can be classified as: terminal nodes, $\wedge$-nodes, $\vee$-nodes, $A\bigcirc$-nodes, and $E\bigcirc$-nodes. Similarly, the edges can be classified as: progress edges, which originate in $A\bigcirc$ or $E\bigcirc$ nodes and reflect real transitions of the MTS $\mathcal{M}$, and auxiliary nodes, which are all other edges. We distinguish two types of progress edges, two types of children, and two types of SCCs

(Strongly Connected Components). *Must-edges* (*may-edges*) are edges based on must-transitions (may-transitions) of MTSs. A node n' is a *must-child* (*may-child*) of the node n if there exists a must-edge (may-edge) (n, n'). A *must-SCC* (*may-SCC*) is an SCC in which all progress edges are must-edges (may-edges).

The game-graph is partitioned into its may-Maximal SCCs (may-MSCCs), denoted Q_i's. This partition induces a partial order $\leq$ on the Q_i's, such that edges go out of a set Q_i only to itself or to a smaller set Q_j. The partial order is extended to a total order $\leq$ arbitrarily. The *coloring algorithm* processes the Q_i's according to $\leq$, bottom-up. Let Q_i be the smallest set that is not fully colored. The nodes of Q_i are colored in two phases, as follows.

Phase 1. Apply these rules to all nodes in Q_i until none of them is applicable.

- A terminal node C is colored: by T if Player $\exists$ wins in it (when $C = (s, \textit{true})$ or $C = (s, a)$ with $a \in L(s)$ or $C = (s, \neg a)$ with $a \notin L(s)$); and by F if Player $\forall$ wins in it (when $C = (s, \textit{false})$ or $C = (s, a)$ with $a \notin L(s)$ or $C = (s, \neg a)$ with $a \in L(s)$).
- An $A\bigcirc$ node is colored: by T if all its may-children are colored by T; by F if it has a must-child colored by F; by $?$ if all its must-children are colored by T or $?$, and it has a may-child colored by F or $?$.
- An $E\bigcirc$ node is colored: by T if it has a must-child colored by T; by F if all its may-children are colored by F; by $?$ if it has a may-child colored by T or $?$, and all its must-children are colored by F or $?$.
- An $\wedge$-node ($\vee$-node) is colored: by T (F) if both its children are colored by T (F); by F (T) if it has a child that is colored by F (T); by $?$ if it has a child colored by $?$ and the other child is colored by $?$ or T (F).

Phase 2. If after propagation of the rules of Phase 1, there are still nodes in Q_i that remain uncolored, then Q_i must be a non-trivial may-MSCC that has exactly one witness. We consider two cases.

Case U. The witness is of the form $A(\Phi_1 \mathsf{U} \Phi_2)$ or $E(\Phi_1 \mathsf{U} \Phi_2)$.

Phase 2a. Repeatedly color by $?$ each node in Q_i that satisfies one of the following conditions, until there is no change:

(1) An $A\bigcirc$ node that all its must-children are colored by T or $?$; (2) An $E\bigcirc$ node that has a may-child colored by T or $?$; (3) An $\wedge$ node that both its children are colored T or $?$; (4) An $\vee$ node that has a child colored by T or $?$. In fact, each node for which the F option is no longer possible according to the rules of Phase 1 is colored by $?$.

Phase 2b. Color the remaining nodes in Q_i by F.

Case V. The witness is of the form $A(\Phi_1 \mathsf{V} \Phi_2)$ or $E(\Phi_1 \mathsf{V} \Phi_2)$ (see [16, Appendix B]).

The result of the coloring is a *3-valued coloring function* $\chi : N \to \{T, F, ?\}$.

Theorem 2 ([24]). *For each* $n = (s, \Phi') \in G_{\mathcal{M} \times \Phi}$:

(1) $[(\mathcal{M}, s) \models^3 \Phi'] = \textit{tt}$ *iff* $\chi(n) = T$ *iff Player* $\exists$ *has a winning strategy at* n.
(2) $[(\mathcal{M}, s) \models^3 \Phi'] = \textit{ff}$ *iff* $\chi(n) = F$ *iff Player* $\forall$ *has a winning strategy at* n.

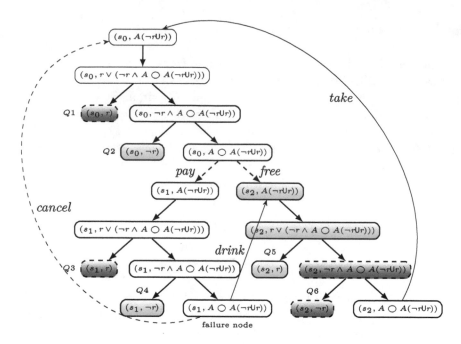

Fig. 4. The colored game-graph for $\alpha^{\text{join}}(\text{VENDMACH})$ and $\Phi_1 = A(\neg r \mathsf{U} r)$. (Color figure online)

(3) $[(\mathcal{M}, s) \models^3 \Phi'] = \bot$ *iff* $\chi(n) = ?$ *iff none of players has a winning strategy at* n.

Using Theorems 1 and 2, given the colored game-graph of the MTS $\alpha^{\text{join}}(\mathcal{F})$, if all its initial nodes are colored by T then $[\mathcal{F} \models \Phi] = tt$, if at least one of them is colored by F then $[\mathcal{F} \models \Phi] = ff$. Otherwise, we do not know.

Example 4. The colored game-graph for the MTS $\alpha^{\text{join}}(\text{VENDMACH})$ and $\Phi_1 = A(\neg r \mathsf{U} r)$ is shown in Fig. 4. Green, red (with dashed borders), and white nodes denote nodes colored by T, F, and ?, respectively. The partitions from Q_1 to Q_6 consist of a single node shown in Fig. 4, while Q_7 contains all the other nodes. The initial node (s_0, Φ_1) is colored by ?, so we obtain an indefinite answer.   □

5   Incremental Refinement Framework

Given an FTS $\pi_{\mathbb{K}'}(\mathcal{F})$ with a configuration set $\mathbb{K}' \subseteq \mathbb{K}$, we show how to exploit the game-graph of the abstract MTS $\mathcal{M} = \alpha^{\text{join}}(\pi_{\mathbb{K}'}(\mathcal{F}))$ in order to do refinement in case that the model checking resulted in an indefinite answer. The refinement consists of two parts. First, we use the information gained by the coloring algorithm of $G_{\mathcal{M} \times \Phi}$ in order to split the single abstract configuration $true \in \alpha^{\text{join}}(\mathbb{K}')$ that represents the whole concrete configuration set $\mathbb{K}'$. We then construct the refined abstract models, using the refined abstract configurations.

Algorithm. `Verify(`$\mathcal{F}, \mathbb{K}, \Phi$`)`

1 Check by game-based model checking algorithm $[\alpha^{\mathrm{join}}(\mathcal{F}) \models^3 \Phi]$?

2 If the result is tt, then return that Φ is satisfied for all variants in $\mathbb{K}$. If the result is ff, then return that Φ is violated for all variants in $\mathbb{K}$.

3 Otherwise, an indefinite result is returned. Let the may-edge from $n = (s, \Phi_1)$ to $n' = (s', \Phi_1')$ be the reason for failure, and let ψ be the feature expression guarding the transition from s to s' in $\mathcal{F}$. We generate $\mathcal{F}_1 = \pi_{[\![\psi]\!]}(\mathcal{F})$ and $\mathcal{F}_2 = \pi_{[\![\neg\psi]\!]}(\mathcal{F})$, and call `Verify(`$\mathcal{F}_1, \mathbb{K} \cap [\![\psi]\!], \Phi$`)` and `Verify(`$\mathcal{F}_2, \mathbb{K} \cap [\![\neg\psi]\!], \Phi$`)`.

Fig. 5. The refinement procedure that checks $[\mathcal{F} \models \Phi]$.

There are a failure node and a failure reason associated with an indefinite answer. The goal in the refinement is to find and eliminate at least one of the failure reasons.

Definition 5. *A node n is a* failure node *if it is colored by ?, whereas none of its children was colored by ? at the time n got colored by the coloring algorithm.*

Such failure node can be seen as the point where the loss of information occurred, so we can use it in the refinement step to change the final model checking result.

Lemma 1 ([24]). *A failure node is one of the following.*

- *An $A\bigcirc$-node ($E\bigcirc$-node) that has a may-child colored by F (T).*
- *An $A\bigcirc$-node ($E\bigcirc$-node) that was colored during Phase 2a based on an AU (AV) witness, and has a may-child colored by ?.*

Given a failure node $n = (s, \Phi)$, suppose that its may-child is $n' = (s', \Phi_1')$ as identified in Lemma 1. Then the may-edge from n to n' is considered as *the failure reason*. Since the failure reason is a may-transition in the abstract MTS $\alpha^{\mathrm{join}}(\pi_{\mathbb{K}'}(\mathcal{F}))$, it needs to be refined in order to result either in a must transition or no transition at all. Let $s \xrightarrow{\alpha/\psi} s'$ be the transition in the concrete model $\pi_{\mathbb{K}'}(\mathcal{F})$ corresponding to the above (failure) may-transition. We split the configuration space $\mathbb{K}'$ into $[\![\psi]\!]$ and $[\![\neg\psi]\!]$ subsets, and we partition $\pi_{\mathbb{K}'}(\mathcal{F})$ in $\pi_{[\![\psi]\!]\cap\mathbb{K}'}(\mathcal{F})$ and $\pi_{[\![\neg\psi]\!]\cap\mathbb{K}'}(\mathcal{F})$. Then, we repeat the verification process based on abstract models $\alpha^{\mathrm{join}}(\pi_{[\![\psi]\!]\cap\mathbb{K}'}(\mathcal{F}))$ and $\alpha^{\mathrm{join}}(\pi_{[\![\neg\psi]\!]\cap\mathbb{K}'}(\mathcal{F}))$. Note that, in the former, $\alpha^{\mathrm{join}}(\pi_{[\![\psi]\!]\cap\mathbb{K}'}(\mathcal{F}))$, $s \xrightarrow{\alpha} s'$ becomes a must-transition, while in the latter, $\alpha^{\mathrm{join}}(\pi_{[\![\neg\psi]\!]\cap\mathbb{K}'}(\mathcal{F}))$, $s \xrightarrow{\alpha} s'$ is removed. The complete refinement procedure is shown in Fig. 5. We prove that (see [16, Appendix A]):

Theorem 3. *The procedure* `Verify(`$\mathcal{F}, \mathbb{K}, \Phi$`)` *terminates and is correct.*

Example 5. We can do a failure analysis on the game-graph of $\alpha^{\mathrm{join}}(\textsc{VendMach})$ in Fig. 4. The failure node is $(s_1, A \bigcirc A(\neg r \mathsf{U} r))$ and the reason is the may-edge $(s_1, A \bigcirc A(\neg r \mathsf{U} r)) \xrightarrow{cancel} (s_0, A(\neg r \mathsf{U} r))$. The corresponding concrete transition in $\textsc{VendMach}$ is $s_1 \xrightarrow{cancel/c} s_0$. So, we partition the configuration space $\mathbb{K}^{\mathrm{VM}}$ into subsets $[\![c]\!]$ and $[\![\neg c]\!]$, and in the next second iteration we consider FTSs $\pi_{[\![c]\!]}(\textsc{VendMach})$ and $\pi_{[\![\neg c]\!]}(\textsc{VendMach})$. $\square$

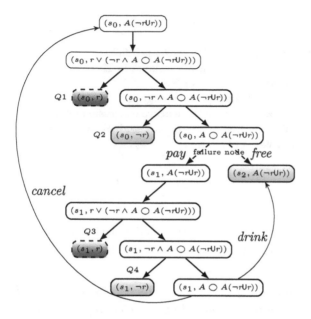

Fig. 6. $G_{\alpha^{\text{join}}(\pi_{[\![c]\!]}(\text{VendMach}))\times\Phi_1}$.

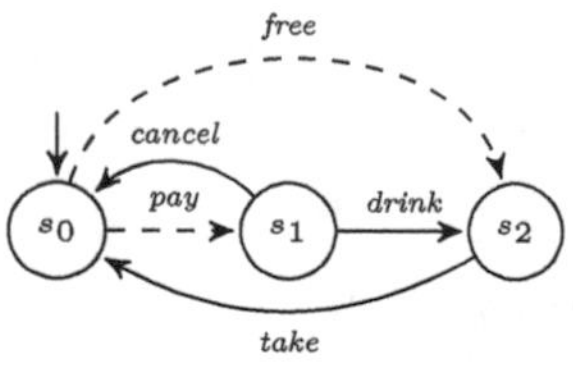

Fig. 7. $\alpha^{\text{join}}(\pi_{[\![c]\!]}(\text{VendMach}))$

The game-based model checking algorithm provides us with a convenient framework to use results from previous iterations and avoid unnecessary calculations. At the end of the i-th iteration of abstraction-refinement, we remember those nodes that were colored by definite colors. Let D denote the set of such nodes. Let $\chi_D : D \to \{T, F\}$ be the coloring function that maps each node in D to its definite color. The incremental approach uses this information both in the construction of the game-graph and its coloring. During the construction of a new refined game-graph performed in a BFS manner in the next $i + 1$-th iteration, we prune the game-graph in nodes that are from D. When a node $n \in D$ is encountered, we add n to the game-graph and do not continue to construct the game-graph from n onwards. That is, $n \in D$ is considered as terminal node and colored by its previous color. As a result of this pruning, only the reachable sub-graph that was previously colored by ? is refined.

Example 6. The property Φ_1 holds for $\pi_{[\![\neg c]\!]}(\text{VendMach})$. The initial node of the game-graph $G_{\alpha^{\text{join}}(\pi_{[\![\neg c]\!]}(\text{VendMach}))\times\Phi_1}$ (see [16, Fig. 13, Appendix C]), is colored by T. On the other hand, we obtain an indefinite answer for $\pi_{[\![c]\!]}(\text{VendMach})$. The model $\alpha^{\text{join}}(\pi_{[\![c]\!]}(\text{VendMach}))$ is shown in Fig. 7, whereas the final colored game-graph $G_{\alpha^{\text{join}}(\pi_{[\![c]\!]}(\text{VendMach}))\times\Phi_1}$ is given in Fig. 6. The failure node is $(s_0, A \bigcirc A(\neg r\mathsf{U}r))$, and the reason is the may-edge $(s_0, A \bigcirc A(\neg r\mathsf{U}r)) \xrightarrow{pay} (s_1, A(\neg r\mathsf{U}r))$. The corresponding concrete transition in $\pi_{[\![c]\!]}(\text{VendMach})$ is $s_0 \xrightarrow{pay/\neg f} s_1$. So, in the next third iteration we consider FTSs $\pi_{[\![c\wedge\neg f]\!]}(\text{VendMach})$ and $\pi_{[\![c\wedge f]\!]}(\text{VendMach})$.

The initial node of the graph $G_{\alpha^{\text{join}}(\pi_{[\![c\wedge\neg f]\!]}(\text{VendMach}))\times\Phi_1}$ (see [16, Fig. 16, Appendix C]) is colored by F in Phase 2b. The initial node of $G_{\alpha^{\text{join}}(\pi_{[\![c\wedge f]\!]}(\text{VendMach}))\times\Phi_1}$ (see [16, Fig. 17, Appendix C]) is colored by T.

In the end, we conclude that Φ_1 is satisfied by the variants $\{\neg c \wedge \neg f, \neg c \wedge f, c \wedge f\}$, and Φ is violated by the variant $\{c \wedge \neg f\}$.

On the other hand, we need two iterations to conclude that $\Phi_2 = E(\neg r \mathsf{U} r)$ is satisfied by all variants in $\mathbb{K}^{\mathrm{VM}}$ (see [16, Appendix D] for details). $\square$

6   Evaluation

To evaluate our approach, we use a synthetic example to demonstrate specific characteristics of our approach, and the ELEVATOR model which is often used as benchmark in SPL community [4,12,15,20,23]. We compare (1) our abstraction-refinement procedure Verify with the game-based model checking algorithm implemented in Java from scratch vs. (2) family-based version of the NuSMV model checker, denoted fNuSMV, which implements the standard lifted model checking algorithm [5]. For each experiment, we measure T(IME) to perform an analysis task, and CALL which is the number of times an approach calls the model checking engine. All experiments were executed on a 64-bit Intel®Core^{TM} i5-3337U CPU running at 1.80 GHz with 8 GB memory. All experimental data is available from: https://aleksdimovski.github.io/automatic-ctl.html.

Synthetic example. The FTS M_n (where $n > 0$) consists of n features $A_1, \ldots, A_n$ and an integer data variable x, such that the set AP consists of all evaluations of x which assign nonnegative integer values to x. The set of valid configurations is $\mathbb{K}_n = 2^{\{A_1, \ldots, A_n\}}$. M_n has a tree-like structure, where in the root is the initial state with $x = 0$. In each level k ($k \geq 1$), there are two states that can be reached with two transitions leading from a state from a previous level. One transition is allowable for variants with the feature A_k enabled, so that in the target state the variable's value is $x + 2^{k-1}$ where x is its value in the source state, whereas the other transition is allowable for variants with A_k disabled, so that the value of x does not change. For example, M_2 is shown in Fig. 8, where in each state we show the current value of x and all transitions have the silent action τ.

We consider two properties: $\Phi = A(true \, \mathsf{U}(x \geq 0))$ and $\Phi' = A(true \, \mathsf{U}(x \geq 1))$. The property Φ is satisfied by all variants in $\mathbb{K}$, whereas Φ' is violated only by one configuration $\neg A_1 \wedge \ldots \wedge \neg A_n$ (where all features are disabled). We have verified M_n against Φ and Φ' using fNuSMV (e.g. see fNuSMV models for M_1 and M_2 in [16, Fig. 23, Appendix E]). We have also checked M_n using our Verify procedure. For Φ, Verify terminates in one iteration since $\alpha^{\mathrm{join}}(M_n)$ satisfies Φ (see $G_{\alpha^{\mathrm{join}}(M_1) \times \Phi}$ in [16, Fig. 24, Appendix E]). For Φ', Verify needs $n + 1$ iterations. First, an indefinite result is reported for $\alpha^{\mathrm{join}}(M_n)$ (e.g. see $G_{\alpha^{\mathrm{join}}(M_1) \times \Phi'}$ in [16, Fig. 27, Appendix E]), and the configuration space is split into $[\![\neg A_1]\!]$ and $[\![A_1]\!]$ subsets. The refinement procedure proceeds in this way until we obtain definite results for all variants. The performance results are shown in Fig. 9. Notice that, fNuSMV reports all results in only one iteration. As n grows, Verify becomes faster than fNuSMV. For $n = 11$ ($|\mathbb{K}| = 2^{11}$), fNuSMV timeouts after 2 h. In contrast, Verify is feasible even for large values of n.

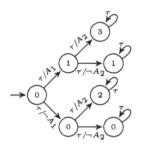

n	Φ				Φ'			
	fNuSMV		Verify		fNuSMV		Verify	
	CALL	T	CALL	T	CALL	T	CALL	T
2	1	0.08	1	0.07	1	0.08	5	0.83
7	1	1.64	1	0.16	1	1.68	15	2.68
10	1	992.80	1	0.68	1	1019.27	21	4.57
11	1	infeasible	1	1.42	1	infeasible	23	5.98
15	1	infeasible	1	26.55	1	infeasible	31	41.64

Fig. 8. The model M_2.   **Fig. 9.** Verification of M_n (T in seconds).

prop-erty	fNuSMV		Verify		Improvement TIME
	CALL	T	CALL	T	
Φ_1	1	15.22 s	1	0.55 s	28 $\times$
Φ_2	1	1.59 s	1	0.59 s	2.7 $\times$
Φ_3	1	1.76 s	1	0.67 s	2.6 $\times$

Fig. 10. Verification of ELEVATOR properties (T in seconds).

ELEVATOR. We have experimented with the ELEVATOR model with four floors, designed by Plath and Ryan [23]. It contains about 300 LOC of fNuSMV code and 9 independent optional features that modify the basic behaviour of the elevator, thus yielding $2^9 = 512$ variants. To use our `Verify` procedure, we have manually translated the fNuSMV model into an FTS and then we have called `Verify` on it. The basic ELEVATOR system consists of a single lift that travels between four floors. There are four platform buttons and a single lift, which declares variables $floor, door, direction$, and a further four cabin buttons. When serving a floor, the lift door opens and closes again. We consider three properties "$\Phi_1 = E(tt \, \mathsf{U}(floor = 1 \wedge idle \wedge door = closed))$", "$\Phi_2 = A(tt \, \mathsf{U}(floor = 1 \wedge idle \wedge door = closed))$", and "$\Phi_3 = E(tt \, \mathsf{U}((floor = 3 \wedge \neg liftBut3.pressed \wedge direction = up) \implies door = closed))$". The performance results are shown in Fig. 10. The properties Φ_1 and Φ_2 are satisfied by all variants, so `Verify` achieves speed-ups of 28 times for Φ_1 and 2.7 times for Φ_2 compared to the fNuSMV approach. fNuSMV takes 1.76 sec to check Φ_3, whereas `Verify` ends in 0.67 sec thus giving 2.6 times performance speed-up.

7   Related Work and Conclusion

There are different formalisms for representing variability models [2, 21]. Classen et al. [4] present Featured Transition Systems (FTSs). They show how specifically designed lifted model checking algorithms [5, 7] can be used for verifying FTSs against LTL and CTL properties. The variability abstractions that preserve LTL are introduced in [14, 15, 17], and subsequently automatic abstraction refinement procedures [8,18] for lifted model checking of LTL are proposed, by using Craig interpolation to define the refinement. The variability abstractions that preserve the full CTL are introduced in [12], but they are constructed manually and no notion of refinement is defined there. In this paper, we define an automatic abstraction refinement procedure for lifted model checking of full CTL by using games to define the refinement. To the best of our knowledge, this is the first such procedure in lifted model checking.

One of the earliest attempts for using games for CTL model checking has been proposed by Stirling [26]. Shoham and Grumberg [3,19,24,25] have extended this game-based approach for CTL over 3-valued semantics. In this work, we exploit and apply the game-based approach in a completely new direction, for automatic CTL verification of variability models.

The works [11,13] present an approach for software lifted model checking of #ifdef-based program families using symbolic game semantics models [10].

To conclude, in this work we present a game-based lifted model checking for abstract variability models with respect to the full CTL. We also suggest an automatic refinement procedure, in case the model checking result is indefinite.

References

1. Baier, C., Katoen, J.: Principles of Model Checking. MIT Press, Cambridge (2008)
2. ter Beek, M.H., Fantechi, A., Gnesi, S., Mazzanti, F.: Modelling and analysing variability in product families: model checking of modal transition systems with variability constraints. J. Log. Algebr. Methods Program. **85**(2), 287–315 (2016). https://doi.org/10.1016/j.jlamp.2015.09.004
3. Campetelli, A., Gruler, A., Leucker, M., Thoma, D.: *Don't Know* for multi-valued systems. In: Liu, Z., Ravn, A.P. (eds.) ATVA 2009. LNCS, vol. 5799, pp. 289–305. Springer, Heidelberg (2009). https://doi.org/10.1007/978-3-642-04761-9_22
4. Classen, A., Cordy, M., Schobbens, P., Heymans, P., Legay, A., Raskin, J.: Featured transition systems: foundations for verifying variability-intensive systems and their application to LTL model checking. IEEE Trans. Softw. Eng. **39**(8), 1069–1089 (2013). http://doi.ieeecomputersociety.org/10.1109/TSE.2012.86
5. Classen, A., Heymans, P., Schobbens, P.Y., Legay, A.: Symbolic model checking of software product lines. In: Proceedings of the 33rd International Conference on Software Engineering, ICSE 2011, pp. 321–330. ACM (2011). http://doi.acm.org/10.1145/1985793.1985838
6. Clements, P., Northrop, L.: Software Product Lines: Practices and Patterns. Addison-Wesley, Boston (2001)
7. Cordy, M., Classen, A., Heymans, P., Schobbens, P., Legay, A.: Provelines: a product line of verifiers for software product lines. In: 17th International SPLC 2013 Workshops, pp. 141–146. ACM (2013). http://doi.acm.org/10.1145/2499777.2499781
8. Cordy, M., Heymans, P., Legay, A., Schobbens, P., Dawagne, B., Leucker, M.: Counterexample guided abstraction refinement of product-line behavioural models. In: Proceedings of the 22nd ACM SIGSOFT International Symposium on Foundations of Software Engineering, (FSE-22), pp. 190–201. ACM (2014). http://doi.acm.org/10.1145/2635868.2635919

9. Cousot, P.: Partial completeness of abstract fixpoint checking. In: Choueiry, B.Y., Walsh, T. (eds.) SARA 2000. LNCS (LNAI), vol. 1864, pp. 1–25. Springer, Heidelberg (2000). https://doi.org/10.1007/3-540-44914-0_1

10. Dimovski, A.S.: Program verification using symbolic game semantics. Theor. Comput. Sci. **560**, 364–379 (2014). https://doi.org/10.1016/j.tcs.2014.01.016

11. Dimovski, A.S.: Symbolic game semantics for model checking program families. In: Bošnački, D., Wijs, A. (eds.) SPIN 2016. LNCS, vol. 9641, pp. 19–37. Springer, Cham (2016). https://doi.org/10.1007/978-3-319-32582-8_2

12. Dimovski, A.S.: Abstract family-based model checking using modal featured transition systems: preservation of CTL*. In: Russo, A., Schürr, A. (eds.) FASE 2018. LNCS, vol. 10802, pp. 301–318. Springer, Cham (2018). https://doi.org/10.1007/978-3-319-89363-1_17

13. Dimovski, A.S.: Verifying annotated program families using symbolic game semantics. Theor. Comput. Sci. **706**, 35–53 (2018). https://doi.org/10.1016/j.tcs.2017.09.029

14. Dimovski, A.S., Al-Sibahi, A.S., Brabrand, C., Wąsowski, A.: Family-based model checking without a family-based model checker. In: Fischer, B., Geldenhuys, J. (eds.) SPIN 2015. LNCS, vol. 9232, pp. 282–299. Springer, Cham (2015). https://doi.org/10.1007/978-3-319-23404-5_18

15. Dimovski, A.S., Al-Sibahi, A.S., Brabrand, C., Wasowski, A.: Efficient family-based model checking via variability abstractions. STTT **19**(5), 585–603 (2017). https://doi.org/10.1007/s10009-016-0425-2

16. Dimovski, A.S., Legay, A., Wasowski, A.: Variability abstraction and refinement for game-based lifted model checking of full CTL (extended version). CoRR (2019). http://arxiv.org/

17. Dimovski, A.S., Wąsowski, A.: From transition systems to variability models and from lifted model checking back to UPPAAL. In: Aceto, L., Bacci, G., Bacci, G., Ingólfsdóttir, A., Legay, A., Mardare, R. (eds.) Models, Algorithms, Logics and Tools. LNCS, vol. 10460, pp. 249–268. Springer, Cham (2017). https://doi.org/10.1007/978-3-319-63121-9_13

18. Dimovski, A.S., Wąsowski, A.: Variability-specific abstraction refinement for family-based model checking. In: Huisman, M., Rubin, J. (eds.) FASE 2017. LNCS, vol. 10202, pp. 406–423. Springer, Heidelberg (2017). https://doi.org/10.1007/978-3-662-54494-5_24

19. Grumberg, O., Lange, M., Leucker, M., Shoham, S.: When not losing is better than winning: abstraction and refinement for the full mu-calculus. Inf. Comput. **205**(8), 1130–1148 (2007). https://doi.org/10.1016/j.ic.2006.10.009

20. Iosif-Lazar, A.F., Melo, J., Dimovski, A.S., Brabrand, C., Wasowski, A.: Effective analysis of c programs by rewriting variability. Program. J. **1**(1), 1 (2017). https://doi.org/10.22152/programming-journal.org/2017/1/1

21. Larsen, K.G., Nyman, U., Wąsowski, A.: Modal I/O automata for interface and product line theories. In: De Nicola, R. (ed.) ESOP 2007. LNCS, vol. 4421, pp. 64–79. Springer, Heidelberg (2007). https://doi.org/10.1007/978-3-540-71316-6_6

22. Larsen, K.G., Thomsen, B.: A modal process logic. In: Proceedings of the Third Annual Symposium on Logic in Computer Science (LICS 1988), pp. 203–210. IEEE Computer Society (1988). http://dx.doi.org/10.1109/LICS.1988.5119

23. Plath, M., Ryan, M.: Feature integration using a feature construct. Sci. Comput. Program. **41**(1), 53–84 (2001). https://doi.org/10.1016/S0167-6423(00)00018-6

24. Shoham, S., Grumberg, O.: A game-based framework for CTL counterexamples and 3-valued abstraction-refinement. ACM Trans. Comput. Log. **9**(1), 1 (2007). https://doi.org/10.1145/1297658.1297659

25. Shoham, S., Grumberg, O.: Compositional verification and 3-valued abstractions join forces. Inf. Comput. **208**(2), 178–202 (2010). https://doi.org/10.1016/j.ic.2009.10.002
26. Stirling, C.: Modal and Temporal Properties of Processes. Texts in Computer Science. Springer, New York (2001). https://doi.org/10.1007/978-1-4757-3550-5

6

Software Assurance in an Uncertain World

Marsha Chechik[✉]![ORCID], Rick Salay, Torin Viger,
Sahar Kokaly, and Mona Rahimi

University of Toronto, Toronto, Canada
chechik@cs.toronto.edu

Abstract. From financial services platforms to social networks to vehicle control, software has come to mediate many activities of daily life. Governing bodies and standards organizations have responded to this trend by creating regulations and standards to address issues such as safety, security and privacy. In this environment, the compliance of software development to standards and regulations has emerged as a key requirement. Compliance claims and arguments are often captured in assurance cases, with linked evidence of compliance. Evidence can come from testcases, verification proofs, human judgment, or a combination of these. That is, experts try to build (safety-critical) systems carefully according to well justified methods and articulate these justifications in an assurance case that is ultimately judged by a human. Yet software is deeply rooted in uncertainty; most complex open-world functionality (e.g., perception of the state of the world by a self-driving vehicle), is either not completely specifiable or it is not cost-effective to do so; software systems are often to be placed into uncertain environments, and there can be uncertainties that need to be We argue that the role of assurance cases is to be the grand unifier for software development, focusing on capturing and managing uncertainty. We discuss three approaches for arguing about safety and security of software under uncertainty, in the absence of fully sound and complete methods: assurance argument rigor, semantic evidence composition and applicability to new kinds of systems, specifically those relying on ML.

1 Introduction

From financial services platforms to social networks to vehicle control, software has come to mediate many activities of daily life. Governing bodies and standards organizations have responded to this trend by creating regulations and standards to address issues such as safety, security and privacy. In this environment, the compliance of software development to standards and regulations has emerged as a key requirement.

Development of safety-critical systems begins with *hazard analysis*, aimed to identify possible causes of harm. It uses severity, probability and controllability of a hazard's occurrence to assign the Safety Integrity Levels (in the automotive industry, these are referred to as ASILs [35]) – the higher the ASIL level, the more rigor is expected to be put into identifying and mitigating the hazard. Mitigating hazards therefore becomes the main requirement of the system, with system safety requirements being directly linked to the hazards. These requirements are then refined along the LHS of the V until individual modules and their implementation can be built. The RHS includes appropriate testing and validation, used as supporting evidence in developing an argument that the system adequately handles its hazards, with the expectation that the higher the ASIL level, the stronger the required justification of safety is.

Assurance claims and arguments are often captured by *assurance cases*, with linked evidence supporting it. Evidence can come from testcases, verification proofs, human judgment, or a combination of these. Assurance cases organize information allowing argument unfolding in a comprehensive way and ultimately allowing safety engineers to determine whether they trust that the system was adequately designed to avoid systematic faults (before delivery) and adequately detect and react to failures at runtime [35].

Yet software is deeply rooted in uncertainty; most complex open-world functionality (e.g., perception of the state of the world by a self-driving vehicle), is either not completely specifiableor it is not cost-effective to do so [12]. Software systems are often to be placed into uncertain environments [48], and there can be uncertainties that need to be considered at the design phase [20]. Thus, we believe that the role of assurance cases is to *explicitly capture and manage uncertainty coming from different sources, assess it and ultimately reduce it to an acceptable level, either with respect to a standard, company processes, or assessor judgment.* The various software development steps are currently not well integrated, and uncertainty is not expressed or managed explicitly in a uniform manner. Our claim in this paper is that *an assurance case is the unifier among the different software development steps, and can be used to make uncertainties explicit, which also makes them manageable. This provides a well-founded basis for modeling confidence about satisfaction of a critical system quality (security, safety, etc.) in an assurance case, making assurance cases play a crucial role in software development.* Specifically, we enumerate sources of uncertainty in software development. We also argue that organizing software development and analysis activities around the assurance case as a *living document* allows all parts of the software development to explicitly articulate uncertainty, steps taken to manage it, and the degree of confidence that artifacts acting as evidence have been performed correctly. This information can then help potential assessors in checking that the development outcome adequately satisfies the software desired quality (e.g., safety).

The area of system dependability has produced a significant body of work describing how to model assurance cases (e.g., [4,5,14,38]), and how to assess reviewer's confidence in the argument being made (e.g., [16,31,45,59,60]). There is also early work on assessing the impact of change on the assurance argument when the system undergoes change [39]. A recent survey [43] provides a comprehensive list of assurance case tools developed over the past 20 years and an analysis of their functionalities including support for assurance case creation, assessment and maintenance. We believe that the road to truly making assurance cases the grand unifier for software development for complex high-assurance systems has many challenges. One is to be able to successfully argue about safety and security of software under uncertainty, without fully sound and complete methods. For that, we believe that *assurance arguments must be rigorous* and that we need to properly understand how to perform *evidence composition* for traditional systems, but also for *new kinds of systems*, specifically those relying on ML. We discuss these issues below.

Rigor. To be validated or reused, assurance case structures must be as rigorous as possible [51]. Of course, assurance arguments ultimately depend on human judgment (with some facts treated as "obvious" and "generally acceptable"), but the structure of the argument should be fully formal so as to allow to assess its completeness. Bandur and McDermid called this approach "formal modulo engineering expertise" [1].

Evidence Composition. We need to effectively combine the top-down process of uncertainty reduction with the bottom-up process of composing evidence, specifically, evidence obtained from applying testing and verification techniques.

Applicability to "new" kinds of systems. We believe that our view – rigorous, uncertainty-reduction focused and evidence composing – is directly applicable to systems developed using machine learning, e.g., self-driving cars.

This paper is organized as follows: In Sect. 2, we briefly describe syntax of assurance cases. In Sect. 3, we outline possible sources of uncertainty encountered as part of system development. In Sect. 4, we describe the benefits of a rigorous language for assurance cases by way of example. In Sect. 5, we describe, again by way of example, a possible method of composing evidence. In Sect. 6, we develop a high-level assurance case for a pedestrian detection subsystem. We conclude in Sect. 7 with a discussion of possible challenges and opportunities.

2   Background on Assurance Case Modeling Notation

The most commonly used representation for safety cases is the graphical Goal Structuring Notation (GSN) [30], which is intended to support the assurance of critical properties of systems (including safety). GSN is comprised of six core elements – see Fig. 1. Arguments in GSN are typically organized into a tree of the core elements shown in Fig. 1[1]. The root is the overall goal to be satisfied by the system, and it is gradually decomposed (possibly via strategies) into sub-goals and finally into solutions, which are the leaves of the safety case. Connections between goals, strategies and solutions represent *supported-by* relations, which indicate inferential or evidential relationships between elements. Goals and strategies may be optionally associated with some contexts, assumptions and/or justifications by means of *in-context-of* relations, which declare a contextual relationship between the connected elements.

---

[1] In this paper, we use both diamond and triangle shapes interchangeably to depict an "undeveloped" element.

Fig. 1. Core GSN elements from [30].

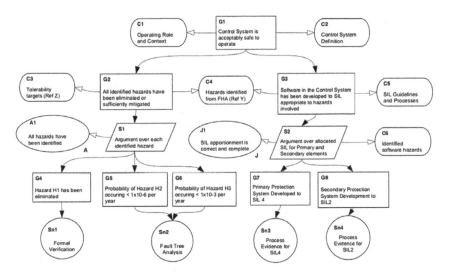

Fig. 2. Example safety case in GSN (from [30]).

For example, consider the safety case in Fig. 2. The overall goal **G1** is that the "Control System is acceptably safe to operate" given its role, context and definition, and it is decomposed into two sub-goals: **G2**, for eliminating and mitigating all identified hazards, and **G3**, for ensuring that the system software is developed to an appropriate ASIL. Assuming that all hazards have been identified, **G2** can in turn be decomposed into three sub-goals by considering each hazard separately (**S1**), and each separate hazard is shown to be satisfied using evidence from formal verification (**Sn1**) or fault tree analysis (**Sn2**). Similarly, under some specific context and justification, **G3** can be decomposed into two sub-goals, each of which is shown to be satisfied by the associated evidence.

3 Sources of Uncertainty in Software Development

In this section, we briefly survey uncertainty in software development, broadly split into the categories of uncertainties about the specifications, about the environment, about the system itself, and about the argument of its safety. For each part, we aim to address how building an assurance case is related to understanding and mitigating such uncertainties.

Uncertainty in Specifications. Software specifications tend to suffer from incompleteness, inconsistency and ambiguity [42,46]. Specification uncertainty stems from a misunderstanding or an incomplete understanding of how the system is supposed to function in early phases of development; e.g., miscommunication and inability of stakeholders to transfer knowledge due to differing concepts and vocabularies [2,13]; unknown values for sets of known events (a.k.a. the *known unknowns*); and the unknown and unidentifiable events (a.k.a. the *unknown unknowns*) [57].

Recently, machine-learning approaches for interactively learning the software specifications have become popular; we discuss one such example, of pedestrian detection, in Sect. 6. Other mitigations of specification uncertainties, suggested by various standards and research, are identification of edge cases [36], hazard and obstacle analysis [55] to help identify unknown unknowns [35], step-wise refinement to handle partiality in specifications, ontology- [9] and information retrieval-driven requirements engineering approaches [21], as well as generally building arguments about addressing specification uncertainties.

Environmental Uncertainty. The system's environment can refer to adjacent agents interacting with the system, a human operator using the system, or physical conditions of the environment. Sources of environmental uncertainties have been thoroughly investigated [19,48]. One source originates from unpredictable and changing properties of the environment, e.g., assumptions about actions of other vehicles in the autonomous vehicle domain or assuming that a plane is on the runway if its wheels are turning. Another uncertainty source is input errors from broken sensors, missing, noisy and inaccurate input data, imprecise measurements, or disruptive control signals from adjacent systems. Yet another source might be when changes in the environment affect the specification. For example, consider a robotic arm that moves with the expected precision but the target has moved from its estimated position.

A number of techniques have been developed to mitigate environmental uncertainties, e.g., runtime monitoring systems such as RESIST [10], or machine-learning approaches such as FUSION [18] which self-tune the adaptive behavior of systems to unanticipated changes in the environment. More broadly, environmental uncertainties are mitigated by a careful requirements engineering process, by principled system design and, in assurance cases, by an argument that they had been adequately identified and adequately handled.

System Uncertainties. One important source of uncertainty is faced by developers who do not have sufficient information to make decisions about their system during development. For example, a developer may have insufficient information to choose a particular implementation platform. In [19,48], this source of uncertainty is referred to as *design-time uncertainty*, and some approaches to handling it are offered in [20]. Decisions made while resolving such uncertainties are crucial to put into an assurance argument, to capture the context, i.e., a particular platform is selected because of its performance, at the expense of memory requirements.

Another uncertainty refers to correctness of the implementation [7]. This uncertainty lays in the V&V procedure and is caused by whether the implementation of the tool can be trusted, whether the tool is used appropriately (that is, its assumptions are satisfied), and in general, whether a particular verification technique is the right one for verifying the fulfillment of the system requirements [15]. We address some of these uncertainties in Sect. 5.

Argument Uncertainty. The use of safety arguments to demonstrate safety of software-intensive systems raises questions such as the extent to which these arguments can be trusted. That is, how confident are we that a verified, validated software is actually safe? How much evidence and how thorough of an argument do we require for that?

To assess uncertainties which may affect the system's safety, researchers have proposed techniques to estimate confidence in structured assurance cases, either through qualitative or quantitative approaches [27,44]. The majority of these are based on the Dempster-Shafer Theory [31,60], Josang's Opinion Triangle [17], Bayesian Belief Networks (BNNs) [16,61], Evidential Reasoning (ER) [45] and weighted averages [59]. The approaches which use BBNs treat safety goals as nodes in the network and try to compute their conditional probability based on given probabilities for the leaf nodes of the network. Dempster-Shafer Theory is similar to BBNs but is based on the *belief function* and its *plausibility* which is used to combine separate pieces of information to calculate the probability. The ER approach [45] allows the assessors to provide individual judgments concerning the trustworthiness and appropriateness of the evidence, building a separate argument from the assurance case.

These approaches focus on assigning and propagating confidence measures but do not specifically address uncertainty in the argument. They also focus on aggregating evidence coming from multiple sources but treat it as a "black box", instead of how a piece of evidence from one source might compose with another. We look at these questions in Sects. 4 and 5, respectively.

4 Formality in Assurance Cases

As discussed in Sect. 1, we believe that the ultimate goal of an assurance case is to explicitly capture and manage uncertainty, and ultimately reduce it to an acceptable level. Even informal arguments improve safety, e.g., by making people decompose the top level goal case-wise, and examine the decomposed parts critically. But the decomposed cases tend to have an ad hoc structure dictated by experience and preference, with under-explored completeness claims, giving both developers and regulators a false sense of confidence, no matter how confidence is measured, since they feel that their reasoning is rigorous even though it is not [58]. Moreover, as assurance cases are produced and judged by humans, they are typically based on *inductive arguments*. Such arguments are susceptible to fallacies (e.g., arguing through circular reasoning, using justification based

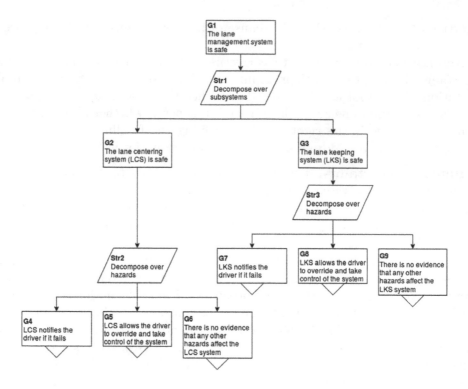

Fig. 3. A fragment of the Lane Management (LMS) Safety case.

on false dichotomies), and evaluations by different reviewers may lead to the discovery of different fallacies [28].

There have been several attempts to improve credibility of an argument by making the argument structure more formal. [25] introduces the notion of confidence maps as an explicit way of reasoning about sources of doubt in an argument, and proposes justifying confidence in assurance arguments through *eliminative induction* (i.e., an argument by eliminating sources of doubt). [29] highlights the need to model both evidential and argumentation uncertainties when evaluating assurance arguments, and considers applications of the formally evaluatable extension of Toulmin's argument style proposed by [56]. [11] details VAA – a method for assessing assurance arguments based on Dempster-Shafer theory. [51] is a proponent of completely deductive reasoning, narrowing the scope of the argument so that it can be formalized and potentially formally checked, using automated theorem provers, arguing that this would give a modular framework for assessing (and, we presume, reusing) assurance cases. [1] relaxes Rushby's position a bit, aiming instead at formal assurance argumentation "modulo engineering expertise", and proof obligations about consistency of arguments remain valid even for not fully formal assurance arguments. To this end, they provided a specific formalization of goal validity given validity of subgoals and contexts/context assumptions, resulting in such rules as

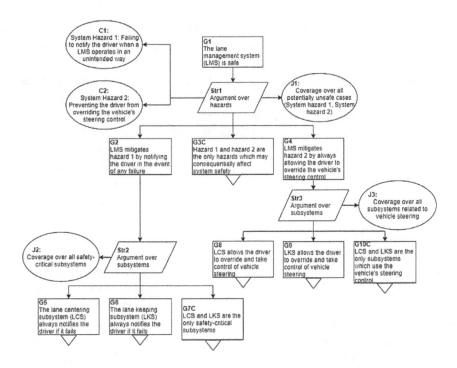

Fig. 4. An alternative representation of the same LMS fragment.

"assumptions on any given element must not be contradictory nor contradict the context assumed for that goal" [1].

Our Position. We believe that a degree of formality in assurance cases can go a long way not only towards establishing its validity, identifying and framing implicit uncertainties and avoiding fallacies, but also supporting assurance case modularity, refactoring and reuse. We illustrate this position on an example.

Example. Consider two partially developed assurance cases that argue that the lane management system (LMS) of a vehicle is safe (Figs. 3 and 4). The top-level safety goal **G1** in Fig. 3 is first decomposed by the strategy **Str1** into a set of subgoals which assert the safety of the LMS subsystems. An assessor can only trust that goals **G2** and **G3** imply **G1** by making an implicit assumption that the system safety is completely determined by the safety of its individual subsystems. Neither the need for this assumption nor the credibility of the assumption itself are made explicit in the assurance case, which weakens the argument and complicates the assessment process. The argument is further weakened by the absence of a completeness claim that all subsystems have been covered by this decomposition.

Strategies **Str2** and **Str3** in Fig. 3 decompose the safety claims about each subsystem into arguments over the relevant hazards. Yet the hazards themselves are never explicitly stated in the assurance case, making the direct relevance of each decomposed goal to its corresponding parent goal, and thus to the argument as a whole, unclear. While goals **G6** and **G9** attempt to provide completeness claims for their respective decompositions, they do so by citing lack of negative evidence without describing efforts to uncover such evidence. This justification is fallacious and can be categorized as "an argument from ignorance" [28].

Now consider the assurance case in Fig. 4 which presents a variant of the argument in Fig. 3, refined with context nodes, justification nodes and completeness claims. The top-level goal **G1** is decomposed into a set of subgoals asserting that particular hazards have been mitigated, as well as a completeness claim **G3C** stating that hazards **H1** and **H2** are the only ones that may be prevalent enough to defeat claim **G1**. Context nodes **C1** and **C2** define the hazards themselves, which clarifies the relevance of each hazard-mitigating goal. The node **J1** provides a justification for the validity of **Str1** by framing the decomposition as a proof by (exhaustive) cases. That is, **Str1** is justified by the statement that if **H1** and **H2** are the only hazards that could potentially make the system unsafe, then the system is safe if **H1** and **H2** have been adequately mitigated. This rigorous argument can be represented by the logical expression $\mathbf{G3C} \implies ((\mathbf{G2} \wedge \mathbf{G4}) \implies \mathbf{G1})$, and if completeness holds then **G2** and **G4** are sufficient to show **G1**. We now have a rigorous argument step that our confidence in **G1** is a direct consequence of confidence in its decomposed goals **G2**, **G3C** and **G4**, even though there may still be uncertainty in the evidential evaluation of **G2**, **G3C** and **G4**. That is, uncertainty has been made explicit and can be reasoned about at the evidential level. By removing argumentation uncertainty and explicating implicit assumptions, we get a more comprehensive framework for assurance case evaluation, where the relation between all reasoning steps is formally clear. Note that if the justification provides an inference rule, then the argument becomes deductive. Otherwise, it is weaker (the justification node can be used to quantify just *how* weaker) but still rigorous.

While the completeness claim **G3C** in Fig. 4 may be directly supported by evidence, the goals **G2** and **G4** are further decomposed by the strategies **Str2** and **Str3**, respectively, which represent decompositions over subsystems. These strategies are structured similarly to **Str1**, and can be expressed by the logical expressions $\mathbf{G7C} \implies ((\mathbf{G5} \wedge \mathbf{G6}) \implies \mathbf{G2})$ and $\mathbf{G10C} \implies ((\mathbf{G8} \wedge \mathbf{G9}) \implies \mathbf{G4})$, respectively. In Fig. 3, a decomposition by subsystems was applied directly to the top-level safety goal which necessitated a completeness claim that the safety of all individual subsystems implied safety of the entire system. Instead, the argument in Fig. 4 only needs to show that the set of subsystems in each decomposition is complete w.r.t. a particular hazard, which may be a more feasible claim to argue. This ability to transform an argument into a more easily justifiable form is another benefit of arguing via rigorous reasoning steps.

5   Combining Evidence

Evidence for assurance cases can come from a variety of sources: results from different testing and verification techniques, human judgment, or their combination. Multiple testing and verification techniques may be used to make the evidence more complete. A verification technique *complements* another if it is able

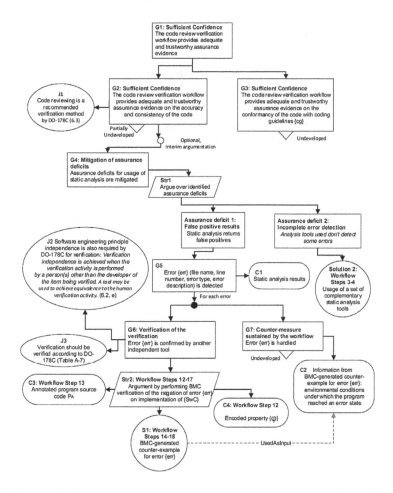

Fig. 5. Confidence argument for code review workflow (from [6]).

to verify types of requirements which cannot be verified by the other technique. For example, results of verification of properties via a bounded model checker (BMC) are complemented by additional test cases [8]. A verification technique *supports* another if it is used to detect faults in the other's verification results, thus providing backing evidence [33]. For example, a model checking technique may support a static analysis technique by verifying the faults detected [6]. Note that these approaches are principally different from just aggregating evidence treating it as a blackbox!

Habli and Kelly [32] and Denney and Pai [15] present safety case patterns for the use of formal method results for certification. Bennion et al. [3] present a safety case for arguing the compliance of a particular model checker, namely, the Simulink Design Verifier for DO-178C. Gallina and Andrews [23] argue about adequacy of a model-based testing process, and Carlan et al. [7] provide a safety pattern for choosing and composing verification techniques based on how they contribute to the identification or mitigation of systematic faults known to affect system safety.

Our Position. We, as a community, need to figure out the precise conditions under which particular testing and verification techniques "work" (e.g., modeling floating-point numbers as reals, making a small model hypothesis to justify sufficiency of a particular loop unrolling, etc.), and how they are intended to be composed in order to reduce uncertainty about whether software satisfies its specification. We illustrate a particular composition here.

Example. In this example, taken from [6], a model checker supports static analysis tools (that produce false negatives) by verifying the detected faults [6]. The assurance case is based on a workflow (not shown here) where an initial review report is constructed, by running static analysis tools and possibly peer code reviews. Then the program is annotated with the negation of each potential erroneous behavior as a desirable property for the program, and given to a model-checker. If the model-checker is able to verify the property, it is removed from the initial review report and not considered as an error. If the model-checker finds a violation, the alleged error is confirmed. In this case, a weakest-precondition generation mechanism is applied to find out the environmental conditions (external parameters that are not under the control of the program) under which the program shows the erroneous behavior. These conditions and the error trace are then added to the error description.

The paper [6] presents both the assurance case and the confidence argument for the code review workflow. We reproduce only the latter here (see Fig. 5), focusing on reducing uncertainty about the accuracy and consistency of the code property (goal **G2**). False positives generated by static analysis are mitigated using BMC – a method with a completely different verification rationale, thus implementing the safety engineering principle of independence (**J2**). Strategy (**Str2**) explains how errors can be confirmed or dismissed using BMC (goal **G6**). The additional information given by BMC can be used for the mitigation of the error (**C2**).

This approach takes good steps towards mitigating particular assurance deficits using a composition of verification techniques but leaves open several problems: how to ensure that BMC runs under the same environmental conditions as the static analysis tools? how deeply should the loops be unrolled? what to do with cases when the model-checker runs out of resources without giving a conclusive answer? and in general, what are the conditions under which it is safe to trust the "yes" answers of the model-checker.

6 Assurance Cases for ML Systems

Academia and industry are actively building systems using AI and machine learning, including a rapid push for ML in safety-critical domains such as medical devices and self-driving cars. For their successful adoption in society, we need to ensure that they are trustworthy, including obtaining confidence in their behavior and robustness.

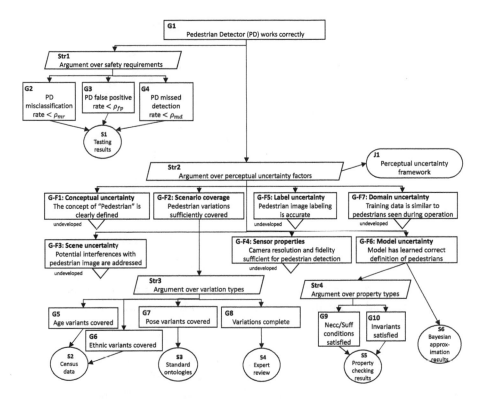

Fig. 6. A partially developed GSN safety case of pedestrian detector example.

Significant strides have already been made in this space, from extending mature testing and verification techniques to reasoning about neural networks [24,37,47,54] for properties such as safety, robustness and adequate handling of adversarial examples [26,34]. There is active work in designing systems that balance learning under uncertainty and acting safely, e.g., [52] as well as the broad notion of fairness and explainability in AI, e.g., [49].

Our Position. We believe that assurance cases remain a unifying view for ML-based systems just as much as for more conventional systems, allowing us to understand how the individual approaches fit into the overall goal of assuring safety and reliability and where there are gaps.

Example. We illustrate this idea with an example of a simple pedestrian detector (PD) component used as part of an autonomous driving system. The functions that PD supports consist of detection of objects in the environment ahead of the vehicle, classification of an object as a *pedestrian* or *other*, and localization of the position and extent of the pedestrian (indicated by bounding box). We assume that PD is implemented as a convolutional deep neural network with various stages to perform feature extraction, proposing regions containing objects and classification of the proposed objects. This is a typical approach for two-stage object detectors (e.g., see [50]).

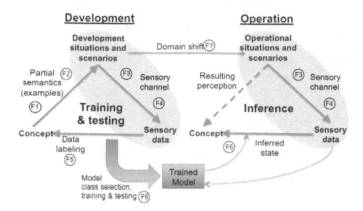

Fig. 7. A framework for factors affecting perceptual uncertainty (source: [12]).

As part of a safety critical system, PD contributes to the satisfaction of a top-level safety goal requiring that the vehicle always maintain a safe distance from all pedestrians. Specific safety requirements for PD can be derived from this goal, such as (RQ1) PD misclassification rate (i.e., classifying a pedestrian as "other") must be less than ρ_{mc}, (RQ2) PD false positive rate (i.e., classifying any non-pedestrian object or non-object as "pedestrian") must be less than ρ_{fp}, and (RQ3) PD missed detection rate (i.e., missing the presence of pedestrian) must be less than ρ_{md}. Here, the parameters ρ_{mc}, ρ_{fp} and ρ_{md} must be derived in conjunction with the control system that uses the output from PD to plan the vehicle trajectory.

The partially developed safety case for PD is shown in Fig. 6. The three safety requirements are addressed via the strategy **Str1** and, as expected, testing results are given as evidence of their satisfaction. However, since testing can only provide limited assurance about the behaviour of PD in operation, we use an additional strategy, **Str2**, to argue that a rigorous method was followed to develop PD. Specifically, we follow the framework of [12] for identifying the factors that lead to uncertainty in ML-based perceptual software such as PD.

The framework is defined at a high level in Fig. 7. The left "perception triangle" shows how the perceptual concept (in the case of PD, the concept "pedestrian") can occur in various scenarios in the world, how it is detected using sensors such as cameras, and how this can be used to collect and label examples in order to train an ML component to learn the concept. The perception triangle on the right is similar but shows how the trained ML component can be used during the system operation to make inferences (e.g., perform the pedestrian detection). The framework identifies seven factors that could contribute to uncertainty in the behaviour of the perceptual component. A safety case demonstrating a rigorous development process should provide evidence that each factor has been addressed.

In Fig. 6, strategy **Str2** uses the framework to argue that the seven factors are adequately addressed for PD. We illustrate development of two of these factors here. Scenario coverage (Goal **G-F2**) deals with the fact that the training data must represent the concept in a sufficient variety of scenarios in which it could occur in order for the training to be effective. The argument here first decomposes this goal into different types of variation (**Str3**) and provides appropriate evidence for each. The adequacy of age and ethnicity variation in the data set is supported by census data (**S2**) about the range of these dimensions of variation in the population. The variation in the pedestrian pose (i.e., standing, leaning, crouching, etc.) is supplied by a standard ontology of human postures (**S3**). Finally, evidence that the types are adequate to provide sufficient coverage of variation (completeness) is provided by an expert review (**S4**).

Another contributing factor developed in Fig. 6 is model uncertainty (Goal **G-F6**). Since there is only finite training data, there can be many possible models that are equally consistent with the training data, and the training process could produce any one of them, i.e., there is residual uncertainty whether the produced model is in fact correct. The presence of model uncertainty means that while the trained model may perform well on inputs similar to the training data, there is no guarantee that it will produce the right output for other inputs. Some evidence of good behaviour here can be gathered if there are known properties that partially characterize the concept and can be checked. For example, a reasonable necessary condition for PD is that the object being classified as a pedestrian should be less than 9 ft tall. Another useful property type is an invariant, e.g., a rotated pedestrian image is still a pedestrian. Tools for property checking of neural networks (e.g., [37]) can provide this kind of evidence (**S5**). Another way to deal with model uncertainty is to estimate it directly. Bayesian deep learning approaches [22] can do this by measuring the degree of disagreement between multiple trained models that are equally consistent with the training data. The more the models are in agreement are about how to classify a new input, the less model uncertainty is present and the more confident one can be in the prediction. Using this approach on a test data set can provide evidence (**S6**) about the degree of model uncertainty in the model. This approach can also be used during the operation to generate a confidence score in each prediction and use a fault tolerance strategy that takes a conservative action when the confidence falls below a threshold.

7   Summary and Future Outlook

In this paper, we tried to argue that an assurance case view on establishing system correctness provides a way to unify different components of the software development process and to explicitly manage uncertainty. Furthermore, although our examples came from the world of safety-critical automotive systems, the assurance case view is broadly applicable to a variety of systems, not just those in the safety-critical domain and includes those constructed by non-traditional means such as ML. This view is especially relevant to much of the research activity being conducted by the ETAPS community since it allows, in principle, to understand how each method contributes to the overall problem of system assurance.

Most traditional assurance methods aim to build an informal argument, ultimately judged by a human. However, while these are useful for showing compliance to standards and are relatively easy to construct and read, such arguments may not be rigorous, missing essential properties such as completeness, independence, relevance, or a clear statement of assumptions [51]. As a result, fallacies in existing assurance cases are present in abundance [28]. To address this weakness, we argued that building assurance cases should adhere to systematic principles that ensure rigor. Of course, not all arguments can be fully deductive since relevance and admissibility of evidence is often based on human judgment. Yet, an explicit modeling and management of uncertainty in evidence, specifications and, assumptions as well as the clear justification of each step can go a long way toward making such arguments valid, reusable, and generally useful in helping produce high quality software systems.

Challenges and Opportunities. Achieving this vision has a number of challenges and opportunities. In our work on impact assessment of model change on assurance cases [39,40], we note that even small changes to the system may have significant impact on the assurance case. Because creation of an assurance case is costly, this brittleness must be addressed. One opportunity here is to recognize that assurance cases can be refactored to improve their qualities without affecting their semantics. For example, in Sect. 4, we showed that the LMS safety claim could either be decomposed first by hazards and then by subsystems or vice versa. Thus, we may want to choose the order of decomposition based on other goals, e.g., to minimize the impact of change on the assurance case by pushing the affected subgoals lower in the tree. Another issue is that complex systems yield correspondingly complex assurance cases. Since these must ultimately be judged by humans, we must manage the cognitive load the assurance case puts on the assessor. This creates opportunities for mechanized support, both in terms of querying, navigating and analyzing assurance cases as well as in terms of modularization and reuse of assurance cases.

Evidence composition discussed in Sect. 5 also presents significant challenges. While standards such as DO-178C and ISO26262 give recommendations on the use of testing and verification, it is not clear how to compose partial evidence or how to use results of one analysis to support another. Focusing on how each technique reduces potential faults in the program, clearly documenting their context of applicability (e.g., the small model hypothesis justifying partial unrolling of loops, properties not affected by approximations of complex program operations and datatypes often done by model-checkers, connections between the modeled and the actual environment, etc.) and ultimately connecting them to reducing uncertainties about whether the system satisfies the essential property are keys to making tangible progress in this area.

Finally, in Sect. 6, we showed how the assurance case view could apply to new development approaches such as ML. Although such new approaches provide benefits over traditional software development, they also create challenges for assurance. One challenge is that analysis techniques used for verification may be immature. For example, while neural networks have been studied since the

1950's, pragmatic approaches to their verification have been investigated only recently [53]. Another issue is that prerequisites for assurance may not be met by the development approach. For example, although they are expressive, neural networks suffer from uninterpretability [41] – that is, it is not feasible for a human to examine a trained network and understand what it is doing. This is a serious obstacle to assurance because formal and automated methods account for only part of the verification process, augmented by reviews. As a result, increasing the interpretability of ML models is an active area of current research.

While all these challenges are significant, the benefit of addressing them is worth the effort. As our world moves towards increasing automation, we must develop approaches for assuring the dependability of the complex systems we build. Without this, we either stall progress or run the risk of endangering ourselves – neither alternative seems desirable.

References

1. Bandur, V., McDermid, J.: Informing assurance case review through a formal interpretation of GSN core logic. In: Koornneef, F., van Gulijk, C. (eds.) SAFECOMP 2015. LNCS, vol. 9338, pp. 3–14. Springer, Cham (2015). https://doi.org/10.1007/978-3-319-24249-1_1
2. Bell, T.E., Thayer, T.A.: Software requirements: are they really a problem? In: Proceedings of the 2nd International Conference on Software Engineering, pp. 61–68. IEEE Computer Society Press (1976)
3. Bennion, M., Habli, I.: A candid industrial evaluation of formal software verification using model checking. In: Companion Proceedings of ICSE 2014, pp. 175–184 (2014)
4. Bloomfield, R., Bishop, P.: Safety and assurance cases: past, present and possible future - an Adelard perspective. In: Dale, C., Anderson, T. (eds.) Safety-Critical Systems: Problems, Process and Practice, pp. 51–67. Springer, London (2010). https://doi.org/10.1007/978-1-84996-086-1_4
5. Brunel, J., Cazin, J.: Formal verification of a safety argumentation and application to a complex UAV system. In: Ortmeier, F., Daniel, P. (eds.) SAFECOMP 2012. LNCS, vol. 7613, pp. 307–318. Springer, Heidelberg (2012). https://doi.org/10.1007/978-3-642-33675-1_27
6. Carlan, C., Beyene, T.A., Ruess, H.: Integrated formal methods for constructing assurance cases. In: Proceedings of ISSRE 2016 Workshops (2016)
7. Cârlan, C., Gallina, B., Kacianka, S., Breu, R.: Arguing on software-level verification techniques appropriateness. In: Tonetta, S., Schoitsch, E., Bitsch, F. (eds.) SAFECOMP 2017. LNCS, vol. 10488, pp. 39–54. Springer, Cham (2017). https://doi.org/10.1007/978-3-319-66266-4_3
8. Cârlan, C., Ratiu, D., Schätz, B.: On using results of code-level bounded model checking in assurance cases. In: Skavhaug, A., Guiochet, J., Schoitsch, E., Bitsch, F. (eds.) SAFECOMP 2016. LNCS, vol. 9923, pp. 30–42. Springer, Cham (2016). https://doi.org/10.1007/978-3-319-45480-1_3
9. Castaameda, V., Ballejos, L., Caliusco, M.L., Galli, M.R.: The use of ontologies in requirements engineering. Glob. J. Res. Eng. **10**(6) (2010)
10. Cooray, D., Malek, S., Roshandel, R., Kilgore, D.: RESISTing reliability degradation through proactive reconfiguration. In: Proceedings of ASE 2010, pp. 83–92. ACM (2010)

11. Cyra, L., Gorski, J.: Support for argument structures review and assessment. J. Reliab. Eng. Syst. Saf. **96**, 26–37 (2011)
12. Czarnecki, K., Salay, R.: Towards a framework to manage perceptual uncertainty for safe automated driving. In: Gallina, B., Skavhaug, A., Schoitsch, E., Bitsch, F. (eds.) SAFECOMP 2018. LNCS, vol. 11094, pp. 439–445. Springer, Cham (2018). https://doi.org/10.1007/978-3-319-99229-7_37
13. Davis, A., et al.: Identifying and measuring quality in a software requirements specification. In: 1993 Proceedings First International Software Metrics Symposium, pp. 141–152. IEEE (1993)
14. de la Vara, J.L.: Current and necessary insights into SACM: an analysis based on past publications. In: Proceedings of RELAW 2014, pp. 10–13. IEEE (2014)
15. Denney, E., Pai, G.: Evidence arguments for using formal methods in software verification. In: Proceedings of ISSRE 2013 Workshops (2013)
16. Denney, E., Pai, G., Habli, I.: Towards measurement of confidence in safety cases. In: Proceedings of ESEM 2011 (2011)
17. Duan, L., Rayadurgam, S., Heimdahl, M.P.E., Sokolsky, O., Lee, I.: Representing confidence in assurance case evidence. In: Koornneef, F., van Gulijk, C. (eds.) SAFECOMP 2015. LNCS, vol. 9338, pp. 15–26. Springer, Cham (2015). https://doi.org/10.1007/978-3-319-24249-1_2
18. Elkhodary, A., Esfahani, N., Malek, S.: FUSION: a framework for engineering self-tuning self-adaptive software systems. In: Proceedings of FSE 2010, pp. 7–16. ACM (2010)
19. Esfahani, N., Malek, S.: Uncertainty in self-adaptive software systems. In: de Lemos, R., Giese, H., Müller, H.A., Shaw, M. (eds.) Software Engineering for Self-Adaptive Systems II. LNCS, vol. 7475, pp. 214–238. Springer, Heidelberg (2013). https://doi.org/10.1007/978-3-642-35813-5_9
20. Famelis, M., Chechik, M.: Managing design-time uncertainty. J. Softw. Syst. Model. (2017)
21. Fanmuy, G., Fraga, A., Llorens, J.: Requirements verification in the industry. In: Hammami, O., Krob, D., Voirin, J.L. (eds.) Complex Systems Design & Management, pp. 145–160. Springer, Heidelberg (2012). https://doi.org/10.1007/978-3-642-25203-7_10
22. Gal, Y., Ghahramani, Z.: Dropout as a Bayesian approximation: representing model uncertainty in deep learning. In: Proceedings of ICML 2016, pp. 1050–1059 (2016)
23. Gallina, B., Andrews, A.: Deriving verification-related means of compliance for a model-based testing process. In: Proceedings of DASC 2016 (2016)
24. Gehr, T., Milman, M., Drachsler-Cohen, D., Tsankov, P., Chaudhuri, S., Vechev, M.: AI2: safety and robustness certification of neural networks with abstract interpretation. In: Proceedings of IEEE S&P 2018 (2018)
25. Goodenough, J., Weinstock, C., Klein, A.: Eliminative induction: a basis for arguing system confidence. In: Proceedings of ICSE 2013 (2013)
26. Gopinath, D., Wang, K., Zhang, M., Pasareanu, C., Khunshid, S.: Symbolic execution for deep neural networks. arXiv:1807.10439v1 (2018)
27. Graydon, P.J., Holloway, C.M.: An investigation of proposed techniques for quantifying confidence in assurance arguments. J. Saf. Sci. **92**, 53–65 (2017)
28. Greenwell, W.S., Knight, J.C., Holloway, C.M., Pease, J.J.: A taxonomy of fallacies in system safety arguments. In: Proceedings of ISSC 2006 (2006)
29. Grigorova, S., Maibaum, T.: Argument evaluation in the context of assurance case confidence modeling. In: Proceedings of ISSRE Workshops (2014)

30. GSN: Goal Structuring Notation Working Group, "GSN Community Standard Version 1", November 2011. http://www.goalstructuringnotation.info/
31. Guiochet, J., Hoang, Q.A.D., Kaaniche, M.: A model for safety case confidence assessment. In: Koornneef, F., van Gulijk, C. (eds.) SAFECOMP 2015. LNCS, vol. 9337, pp. 313–327. Springer, Cham (2015). https://doi.org/10.1007/978-3-319-24255-2_23
32. Habli, I., Kelly, T.: A generic goal-based certification argument for the justification of formal analysis. ENTCS **238**(4), 27–39 (2009)
33. Hawkins, R., Kelly, T.: A structured approach to selecting and justifying software safety evidence. In: Proceedings of SAFECOMP 2010 (2010)
34. Huang, X., Kwiatkowska, M., Wang, S., Wu, M.: Safety verification of deep neural networks. In: Majumdar, R., Kunčak, V. (eds.) CAV 2017. LNCS, vol. 10426, pp. 3–29. Springer, Cham (2017). https://doi.org/10.1007/978-3-319-63387-9_1
35. International Organization for Standardization: ISO 26262: Road Vehicles – Functional Safety, 1st version (2011)
36. International Organization for Standardization: ISO/AWI PAS 21448: Road Vehicles – Safety of the Intended Functionality (2019)
37. Katz, G., Barrett, C., Dill, D.L., Julian, K., Kochenderfer, M.J.: Reluplex: an efficient SMT solver for verifying deep neural networks. In: Majumdar, R., Kunčak, V. (eds.) CAV 2017. LNCS, vol. 10426, pp. 97–117. Springer, Cham (2017). https://doi.org/10.1007/978-3-319-63387-9_5
38. Kelly, T., Weaver, R.: The goal structuring notation – a safety argument notation. In: Proceedings of Dependable Systems and Networks Workshop on Assurance Cases (2004)
39. Kokaly, S., Salay, R., Cassano, V., Maibaum, T., Chechik, M.: A model management approach for assurance case reuse due to system evolution. In: Proceedings of MODELS 2016, pp. 196–206. ACM (2016)
40. Kokaly, S., Salay, R., Chechik, M., Lawford, M., Maibaum, T.: Safety case impact assessment in automotive software systems: an improved model-based approach. In: Tonetta, S., Schoitsch, E., Bitsch, F. (eds.) SAFECOMP 2017. LNCS, vol. 10488, pp. 69–85. Springer, Cham (2017). https://doi.org/10.1007/978-3-319-66266-4_5
41. Lipton, Z.C.: The mythos of model interpretability. Commun. ACM **61**(10), 36–43 (2018)
42. Lutz, R.R.: Analyzing software requirements errors in safety-critical, embedded systems. In: Proceedings of IEEE International Symposium on Requirements Engineering, pp. 126–133. IEEE (1993)
43. Maksimov, M., Fung, N.L.S., Kokaly, S., Chechik, M.: Two decades of assurance case tools: a survey. In: Gallina, B., Skavhaug, A., Schoitsch, E., Bitsch, F. (eds.) SAFECOMP 2018. LNCS, vol. 11094, pp. 49–59. Springer, Cham (2018). https://doi.org/10.1007/978-3-319-99229-7_6
44. Nair, S., de la Vara, J.L., Sabetzadeh, M., Falessic, D.: Evidence management for compliance of critical systems with safety standards: a survey on the state of practice. Inf. Softw. Technol. **60**, 1–15 (2015)
45. Nair, S., Walkinshaw, N., Kelly, T., de la Vara, J.L.: An evidential reasoning approach for assessing confidence in safety evidence. In: Proceedings of ISSRE 2015 (2015)
46. Nikora, A., Hayes, J., Holbrook, E.: Experiments in automated identification of ambiguous natural-language requirements. In: Proceedings 21st IEEE International Symposium on Software Reliability Engineering. IEEE Computer Society, San Jose (2010, to appear)

47. Pei, K., Cao, Y., Yang, J., Jana, S.: DeepXplore: automated whitebox testing of deep learning systems. In: Proceedings of SOSP 2017 (2017)
48. Ramirez, A.J., Jensen, A.C., Cheng, B.H.: A taxonomy of uncertainty for dynamically adaptive systems. In: Proceedings of SEAMS 2012 (2012)
49. Ras, G., van Gerven, M., Haselager, P.: Explanation methods in deep learning: users, values, concerns and challenges. In: Escalante, H.J., et al. (eds.) Explainable and Interpretable Models in Computer Vision and Machine Learning. TSSCML, pp. 19–36. Springer, Cham (2018). https://doi.org/10.1007/978-3-319-98131-4_2
50. Ren, S., He, K., Girshick, R., Sun, J.: Faster R-CNN: towards real-time object detection with region proposal networks. In: Advances in Neural Information Processing Systems, pp. 91–99 (2015)
51. Rushby, J., Xu, X., Rangarajan, M., Weaver, T.L.: Understanding and evaluating assurance cases. Technical report CR-2015-218802, NASA (2015)
52. Sadigh, D., Kapoor, A.: Safe control under uncertainty with probabilistic signal temporal logic. In: Proceedings of RSS 2016 (2016)
53. Seshia, S.A., Sadigh, D.: Towards verified artificial intelligence. CoRR, abs/1606.08514 (2016)
54. Tian, Y., Pei, K., Jana, S., Ray, B.: DeepTest: automated testing of deep-neural-network-driven autonomous cars. In: Proceedings of ICSE 2018 (2018)
55. Van Lamsweerde, A.: Goal-oriented requirements engineering: a guided tour. In: Proceedings of RE 2001, pp. 249–262. IEEE (2001)
56. Verheij, B.: Evaluating arguments based on Toulmin's scheme. Argumentation 19(3), 347–371 (2005)
57. Ward, S., Chapman, C.: Transforming project risk management into project uncertainty management. Int. J. Proj. Manag. 21(2), 97–105 (2003)
58. Wassyng, A.: Private Communication (2019)
59. Yamamoto, S.: Assuring security through attribute GSN. In: Proceedings of ICITCS 2015 (2015)
60. Zeng, F., Lu, M., Zhong, D.: Using DS evidence theory to evaluation of confidence in safety case. J. Theoret. Appl. Inf. Technol. 47(1) (2013)
61. Zhao, X., Zhang, D., Lu, M., Zeng, F.: A new approach to assessment of confidence in assurance cases. In: Ortmeier, F., Daniel, P. (eds.) SAFECOMP 2012. LNCS, vol. 7613, pp. 79–91. Springer, Heidelberg (2012). https://doi.org/10.1007/978-3-642-33675-1_7

A Hybrid Dynamic Logic
for Event/Data-Based Systems

Rolf Hennicker[1], Alexandre Madeira[2,3]([⊠]), and Alexander Knapp[4]

[1] Ludwig-Maximilians-Universität München, Munich, Germany
`hennicke@pst.ifi.lmu.de`
[2] CIDMA, University of Aveiro, Aveiro, Portugal
`madeira@ua.pt`
[3] QuantaLab, University of Minho, Braga, Portugal
[4] Universität Augsburg, Augsburg, Germany
`knapp@informatik.uni-augsburg.de`

Abstract. We propose $\mathcal{E}^{\downarrow}$-logic as a formal foundation for the specification and development of event-based systems with local data states. The logic is intended to cover a broad range of abstraction levels from abstract requirements specifications up to constructive specifications. Our logic uses diamond and box modalities over structured actions adopted from dynamic logic. Atomic actions are pairs $e /\!\!/ \psi$ where e is an event and ψ a state transition predicate capturing the allowed reactions to the event. To write concrete specifications of recursive process structures we integrate (control) state variables and binders of hybrid logic. The semantic interpretation relies on event/data transition systems; specification refinement is defined by model class inclusion. For the presentation of constructive specifications we propose operational event/data specifications allowing for familiar, diagrammatic representations by state transition graphs. We show that $\mathcal{E}^{\downarrow}$-logic is powerful enough to characterise the semantics of an operational specification by a single $\mathcal{E}^{\downarrow}$-sentence. Thus the whole development process can rely on $\mathcal{E}^{\downarrow}$-logic and its semantics as a common basis. This includes also a variety of implementation constructors to support, among others, event refinement and parallel composition.

1 Introduction

Event-based systems are an important kind of software systems which are open to the environment to react to certain events. A crucial characteristics of such systems is that not any event can (or should) be expected at any time. Hence the control flow of the system is significant and should be modelled by appropriate means. On the other hand components administrate data which may change upon the occurrence of an event. Thus also the specification of admissible data changes caused by events plays a major role.

There is quite a lot of literature on modelling and specification of event-based systems. Many approaches, often underpinned by graphical notations, provide formalisms aiming at being constructive enough to suggest particular designs or implementations, like e.g., Event-B [1,7], symbolic transition systems [17], and UML behavioural and protocol state machines [12,16]. On the other hand, there are logical formalisms to express desired properties of event-based systems. Among them are temporal logics integrating state and event-based styles [4], and various kinds of modal logics involving data, like first-order dynamic logic [10] or the modal μ-calculus with data and time [9]. The gap between logics and constructive specification is usually filled by checking whether *the* model of a constructive specification satisfies certain logical formulae.

In this paper we are interested in investigating a logic which is capable to express properties of event/data-based systems on various abstraction levels in a common formalism. For this purpose we follow ideas of [15], but there data states, effects of events on them and constructive operational specifications (see below) were not considered. The advantage of an expressive logic is that we can split the transition from system requirements to system implementation into a series of gradual refinement steps which are more easy to understand, to verify, and to adjust when certain aspects of the system are to be changed or when a product line of similar products has to be developed.

To that end we propose $\mathcal{E}^{\downarrow}$-logic, a dynamic logic enriched with features of hybrid logic. The dynamic part uses diamond and box modalities over structured actions. Atomic actions are of the form $e/\!\!/\psi$ with e an event and ψ a state transition predicate specifying the admissible effects of e on the data. Using sequential composition, union, and iteration we obtain complex actions that, in connection with the modalities, can be used to specify required and forbidden behaviour. In particular, if E is a finite set of events, though data is infinite we are able to capture all reachable states of the system and to express safety and liveness properties. But $\mathcal{E}^{\downarrow}$-logic is also powerful enough to specify concrete, recursive process structures by integrating state variables and binders from hybrid logic [6] with the subtle difference that our state variables are used to denote control states only. We show that the dynamic part of the logic is bisimulation invariant while the hybrid part, due to the ability to bind names to states, is not.

An axiomatic specification $Sp = (\Sigma, Ax)$ in $\mathcal{E}^{\downarrow}$ is given by an event/data signature $\Sigma = (E, A)$, with a set E of events and a set A of attributes to model local data states, and a set of $\mathcal{E}^{\downarrow}$-sentences Ax, called axioms, expressing requirements. For the semantic interpretation we use event/data transition systems (edts). Their states are reachable configurations $\gamma = (c, \omega)$ where c is a control state, recording the current state of execution, and ω is a local data state, i.e., a valuation of the attributes. Transitions between configurations are labelled by events. The semantics of a specification Sp is "loose" in the sense that it consists of *all* edts satisfying the axioms of the specification. Such structures are called models of Sp. Loose semantics allows us to define a simple refinement notion: Sp_1 refines to Sp_2 if the model class of Sp_2 is included in the model class of Sp_1. We may also say that Sp_2 is an implementation of Sp_1.

Our refinement process starts typically with axiomatic specifications whose axioms involve only the dynamic part of the logic. Hybrid features will successively be added in refinements when specifying more concrete behaviours, like loops. Aiming at a concrete design, the use of an axiomatic specification style may, however, become cumbersome since we have to state explicitly also all negative cases, what the system should not do. For a convenient presentation of constructive specifications we propose operational event/data specifications, which are a kind of symbolic transition systems equipped again with a model class semantics in terms of edts. We will show that $\mathcal{E}^{\downarrow}$-logic, by use of the hybrid binder, is powerful enough to characterise the semantics of an operational specification. Therefore we have not really left $\mathcal{E}^{\downarrow}$-logic when refining axiomatic by operational specifications. Moreover, since several constructive notations in the literature, including (essential parts of) Event-B, symbolic transition systems, and UML protocol state machines, can be expressed as operational specifications, $\mathcal{E}^{\downarrow}$-logic provides a logical umbrella under which event/data-based systems can be developed.

In order to consider more complex refinements we take up an idea of Sannella and Tarlecki [18,19] who have proposed the notion of constructor implementation. This is a generic notion applicable to specification formalisms based on signatures and semantic structures for signatures. As both are available in the context of $\mathcal{E}^{\downarrow}$-logic, we complement our approach by introducing a couple of constructors, among them event refinement and parallel composition. For the latter we provide a useful refinement criterion relying on a relationship between syntactic and semantic parallel composition. The logic and the use of the implementation constructors will be illustrated by a running example.

Hereafter, in Sect. 2, we introduce syntax and semantics of $\mathcal{E}^{\downarrow}$-logic. In Sect. 3, we consider axiomatic as well as operational specifications and demonstrate the expressiveness of $\mathcal{E}^{\downarrow}$-logic. Refinement of both types of specifications using several implementation constructors is considered in Sect. 4. Section 5 provides some concluding remarks. Proofs of theorems and facts can be found in [11].

2 A Hybrid Dynamic Logic for Event/Data Systems

We propose the logic $\mathcal{E}^{\downarrow}$ to specify and reason about event/data-based systems. $\mathcal{E}^{\downarrow}$-logic is an extension of the hybrid dynamic logic considered in [15] by taking into account changing data. Therefore, we first summarise our underlying notions used for the treatment of data. We then introduce the syntax and semantics of $\mathcal{E}^{\downarrow}$ with its hybrid and dynamic logic features applied to events and data.

2.1 Data States

We assume given a universe $\mathcal{D}$ of *data values*. A *data signature* is given by a set A of *attributes*. An A-*data state* ω is a function $\omega : A \to \mathcal{D}$. We denote by $\Omega(A)$ the set of all A-data states. For any data signature A, we assume given a set $\Phi(A)$ of *state predicates* to be interpreted over single A-data states, and a set

$\Psi(A)$ of *transition predicates* to be interpreted over pairs of pre- and post-A-data states. The concrete syntax of state and transition predicates is of no particular importance for the following. For an attribute $a \in A$, a state predicate may be $a > 0$; and a transition predicate e.g. $a' = a + 1$, where a refers to the value of attribute a in the pre-data state and a' to its value in the post-data state. Still, both types of predicates are assumed to contain true and to be closed under negation (written $\neg$) and disjunction (written $\vee$); as usual, we will then also use false, $\wedge$, etc. Furthermore, we assume for each $A_0 \subseteq A$ a transition predicate $\mathrm{id}_{A_0} \in \Psi(A)$ expressing that the values of attributes in A_0 are the same in pre- and post-A-data states.

We write $\omega \models^{\mathcal{D}}_A \varphi$ if $\varphi \in \Phi(A)$ is satisfied in data state ω; and $(\omega_1, \omega_2) \models^{\mathcal{D}}_A \psi$ if $\psi \in \Psi(A)$ is satisfied in the pre-data state ω_1 and post-data state ω_2. In particular, $(\omega_1, \omega_2) \models^{\mathcal{D}}_A \mathrm{id}_{A_0}$ if, and only if, $\omega_1(a_0) = \omega_2(a_0)$ for all $a_0 \in A_0$.

2.2 $\mathcal{E}^{\downarrow}$-Logic

Definition 1. *An* event/data signature *(ed signature, for short)* $\Sigma = (E, A)$ *consists of a finite set of* events E *and a data signature* A. *We write* $E(\Sigma)$ *for* E *and* $A(\Sigma)$ *for* A. *We also write* $\Omega(\Sigma)$ *for* $\Omega(A(\Sigma))$, $\Phi(\Sigma)$ *for* $\Phi(A(\Sigma))$, *and* $\Psi(\Sigma)$ *for* $\Psi(A(\Sigma))$. *The class of ed signatures is denoted by* $Sig^{\mathcal{E}^{\downarrow}}$.

Any ed signature Σ determines a class of semantic structures, the *event/data transition systems* which are reachable transition systems with sets of initial states and events as labels on transitions. The states are pairs $\gamma = (c, \omega)$, called *configurations*, where c is a *control state* recording the current execution state and ω is an $A(\Sigma)$-data state; we write $c(\gamma)$ for c and $\omega(\gamma)$ for ω.

Definition 2. *A* Σ-event/data transition system *(Σ-edts, for short)* $M = (\Gamma, R, \Gamma_0)$ *over an ed signature* Σ *consists of a set of* configurations $\Gamma \subseteq C \times \Omega(\Sigma)$ *for a set of* control states C; *a family of* transition relations $R = (R_e \subseteq \Gamma \times \Gamma)_{e \in E(\Sigma)}$; *and a non-empty set of* initial configurations $\Gamma_0 \subseteq \{c_0\} \times \Omega_0$ *for an initial control state* $c_0 \in C$ *and a set of* initial data states $\Omega_0 \subseteq \Omega(\Sigma)$ *such that* Γ *is reachable via* R, *i.e., for all* $\gamma \in \Gamma$ *there are* $\gamma_0 \in \Gamma_0$, $n \geq 0$, $e_1, \ldots, e_n \in E(\Sigma)$, *and* $(\gamma_i, \gamma_{i+1}) \in R_{e_{i+1}}$ *for all* $0 \leq i < n$ *with* $\gamma_n = \gamma$. *We write* $\Gamma(M)$ *for* Γ, $C(M)$ *for* C, $R(M)$ *for* R, $c_0(M)$ *for* c_0, $\Omega_0(M)$ *for* Ω_0, *and* $\Gamma_0(M)$ *for* Γ_0. *The class of* Σ-edts *is denoted by* $Edts^{\mathcal{E}^{\downarrow}}(\Sigma)$.

Atomic actions are given by expressions of the form $e /\!\!/ \psi$ with e an event and ψ a state transition predicate. The intuition is that the occurrence of the event e causes a state transition in accordance with ψ, i.e., the pre- and post-data states satisfy ψ, and ψ specifies the possible effects of e. Following the ideas of dynamic logic we also use complex, structured actions formed over atomic actions by union, sequential composition and iteration. All kinds of actions over an ed signature Σ are called Σ-*event/data actions* (Σ-ed actions, for short). The set $\Lambda(\Sigma)$ of Σ-ed actions is defined by the grammar

$$\lambda ::= e /\!\!/ \psi \mid \lambda_1 + \lambda_2 \mid \lambda_1; \lambda_2 \mid \lambda^*$$

where $e \in E(\Sigma)$ and $\psi \in \Psi(\Sigma)$. We use the following shorthand notations for actions: For a subset $F = \{e_1, \ldots, e_k\} \subseteq E(\Sigma)$, we use the notation F to denote the complex action $e_1 /\!/ \text{true} + \ldots + e_k /\!/ \text{true}$ and $-F$ to denote the action $E(\Sigma) \setminus F$. For the action $E(\Sigma)$ we will write $\boldsymbol{E}$. For $e \in E(\Sigma)$, we use the notation e to denote the action $e /\!/ \text{true}$ and $-e$ to denote the action $\boldsymbol{E} \setminus \{e\}$. Hence, if $E(\Sigma) = \{e_1, \ldots, e_n\}$ and $e_i \in E(\Sigma)$, the action $-e_i$ stands for $e_1 /\!/ \text{true} + \ldots + e_{i-1} /\!/ \text{true} + e_{i+1} /\!/ \text{true} + \ldots + e_n /\!/ \text{true}$.

The actions $\Lambda(\Sigma)$ are *interpreted* over a Σ-edts M as the family of relations $(R(M)_\lambda \subseteq \Gamma(M) \times \Gamma(M))_{\lambda \in \Lambda(\Sigma)}$ defined by

- $R(M)_{e /\!/ \psi} = \{(\gamma, \gamma') \in R(M)_e \mid (\omega(\gamma), \omega(\gamma')) \models^{\mathcal{D}}_{A(\Sigma)} \psi\}$,
- $R(M)_{\lambda_1 + \lambda_2} = R(M)_{\lambda_1} \cup R(M)_{\lambda_2}$, i.e., union of relations,
- $R(M)_{\lambda_1;\lambda_2} = R(M)_{\lambda_1}; R(M)_{\lambda_2}$, i.e., sequential composition of relations,
- $R(M)_{\lambda*} = (R(M)_\lambda)^*$, i.e., reflexive-transitive closure of relations.

To define the event/data formulae of $\mathcal{E}^\downarrow$ we assume given a countably infinite set X of control state variables which are used in formulae to denote the control part of a configuration. They can be bound by the binder operator $\downarrow x$ and accessed by the jump operator $@x$ of hybrid logic. The dynamic part of our logic is due to the modalities which can be formed over any ed action over a given ed signature. $\mathcal{E}^\downarrow$ thus retains from hybrid logic the use of binders, but omits free nominals. Thus sentences of the logic become restricted to express properties of configurations reachable from the initial ones.

Definition 3. *The set* $\mathrm{Frm}^{\mathcal{E}^\downarrow}(\Sigma)$ *of* Σ-ed formulae *over an ed signature* Σ *is given by*

$$\varrho ::= \varphi \mid x \mid \downarrow x . \varrho \mid @x . \varrho \mid \langle \lambda \rangle \varrho \mid \text{true} \mid \neg \varrho \mid \varrho_1 \vee \varrho_2$$

where $\varphi \in \Phi(\Sigma)$, $x \in X$, *and* $\lambda \in \Lambda(\Sigma)$. *We write* $[\lambda]\varrho$ *for* $\neg\langle\lambda\rangle\neg\varrho$ *and we use the usual boolean connectives as well as the constant* false *to denote* $\neg$true.[1] *The set* $\mathrm{Sen}^{\mathcal{E}^\downarrow}(\Sigma)$ *of* Σ-ed sentences *consists of all* Σ-ed formulae *without free variables, where the free variables are defined as usual with* $\downarrow x$ *being the unique operator binding variables.*

Given an ed signature Σ and a Σ-edts M, the satisfaction of a Σ-ed formula ϱ is inductively defined w.r.t. valuations $v : X \to C(M)$, mapping variables to control states, and configurations $\gamma \in \Gamma(M)$:

- $M, v, \gamma \models^{\mathcal{E}^\downarrow}_\Sigma \varphi$ iff $\omega(\gamma) \models^{\mathcal{D}}_{A(\Sigma)} \varphi$;
- $M, v, \gamma \models^{\mathcal{E}^\downarrow}_\Sigma x$ iff $c(\gamma) = v(x)$;
- $M, v, \gamma \models^{\mathcal{E}^\downarrow}_\Sigma \downarrow x . \varrho$ iff $M, v\{x \mapsto c(\gamma)\}, \gamma \models^{\mathcal{E}^\downarrow}_\Sigma \varrho$;
- $M, v, \gamma \models^{\mathcal{E}^\downarrow}_\Sigma @x . \varrho$ iff $M, v, \gamma' \models^{\mathcal{E}^\downarrow}_\Sigma \varrho$ for all $\gamma' \in \Gamma(M)$ with $c(\gamma') = v(x)$;
- $M, v, \gamma \models^{\mathcal{E}^\downarrow}_\Sigma \langle\lambda\rangle\varrho$ iff $M, v, \gamma' \models^{\mathcal{E}^\downarrow}_\Sigma \varrho$ for some $\gamma' \in \Gamma(M)$ with $(\gamma, \gamma') \in R(M)_\lambda$;

---

[1] We use true and false for predicates and formulae; their meaning will always be clear from the context. For boolean values we will use instead the notations *tt* and *ff*.

- $M, v, \gamma \models^{\mathcal{E}^{\downarrow}}_{\Sigma}$ true always holds;
- $M, v, \gamma \models^{\mathcal{E}^{\downarrow}}_{\Sigma} \neg\varrho$ iff $M, v, \gamma \not\models^{\mathcal{E}^{\downarrow}}_{\Sigma} \varrho$;
- $M, v, \gamma \models^{\mathcal{E}^{\downarrow}}_{\Sigma} \varrho_1 \vee \varrho_2$ iff $M, v, \gamma \models^{\mathcal{E}^{\downarrow}}_{\Sigma} \varrho_1$ or $M, v, \gamma \models^{\mathcal{E}^{\downarrow}}_{\Sigma} \varrho_2$.

If ϱ is a sentence then the valuation is irrelevant. M *satisfies* a sentence $\varrho \in$ $\text{Sen}^{\mathcal{E}^{\downarrow}}(\Sigma)$, denoted by $M \models^{\mathcal{E}^{\downarrow}}_{\Sigma} \varrho$, if $M, \gamma_0 \models^{\mathcal{E}^{\downarrow}}_{\Sigma} \varrho$ for all $\gamma_0 \in \Gamma_0(M)$.

By borrowing the modalities from dynamic logic [9,10], $\mathcal{E}^{\downarrow}$ is able to express liveness and safety requirements as illustrated in our running ATM example below. There we use the fact that we can state properties over all reachable states by sentences of the form $[\boldsymbol{E}^*]\varphi$. In particular, deadlock-freedom can be expressed by $[\boldsymbol{E}^*]\langle\boldsymbol{E}\rangle$true. The logic $\mathcal{E}^{\downarrow}$, however, is also suited to directly express process structures and, thus, the implementation of abstract requirements. The binder operator is essential for this. For example, we can specify a process which switches a boolean value, denoted by the attribute val, from tt to ff and back by the following sentence:

$$\downarrow x_0 \,.\, \mathsf{val} = tt \wedge \langle\mathsf{switch}/\!\!/\mathsf{val}' = ff\rangle\langle\mathsf{switch}/\!\!/\mathsf{val}' = tt\rangle x_0.$$

2.3   Bisimulation and Invariance

Bisimulation is a crucial notion in both behavioural systems specification and in modal logics. On the specification side, it provides a standard way to identify systems with the same behaviour by abstracting the internal specifics of the systems; this is also reflected at the logic side, where bisimulation frequently relates states that satisfy the same formulae. We explore some properties of $\mathcal{E}^{\downarrow}$ w.r.t. bisimilarity. Let us first introduce the notion of bisimilarity in the context of $\mathcal{E}^{\downarrow}$:

Definition 4. *Let M_1, M_2 be Σ-edts. A relation $B \subseteq \Gamma(M_1) \times \Gamma(M_2)$ is a* bisimulation relation *between M_1 and M_2 if for all $(\gamma_1, \gamma_2) \in B$ the following conditions hold:*

(atom) for all $\varphi \in \Phi(\Sigma)$, $\omega(\gamma_1) \models^{\mathcal{D}}_{A(\Sigma)} \varphi$ iff $\omega(\gamma_2) \models^{\mathcal{D}}_{A(\Sigma)} \varphi$;

(zig)   for all $e/\!\!/\psi \in \Lambda(\Sigma)$ and for all $\gamma_1' \in \Gamma(M_1)$ with $(\gamma_1, \gamma_1') \in R(M_1)_{e/\!\!/\psi}$, there is a $\gamma_2' \in \Gamma(M_2)$ such that $(\gamma_2, \gamma_2') \in R(M_2)_{e/\!\!/\psi}$ and $(\gamma_1', \gamma_2') \in B$;

(zag)   for all $e/\!\!/\psi \in \Lambda(\Sigma)$ and for all $\gamma_2' \in \Gamma(M_2)$ with $(\gamma_2, \gamma_2') \in R(M_2)_{e/\!\!/\psi}$, there is a $\gamma_1' \in \Gamma(M_1)$ such that $(\gamma_1, \gamma_1') \in R(M_1)_{e/\!\!/\psi}$ and $(\gamma_1', \gamma_2') \in B$.

M_1 *and M_2 are* bisimilar, *in symbols $M_1 \sim M_2$, if there exists a bisimulation relation $B \subseteq \Gamma(M_1) \times \Gamma(M_2)$ between M_1 and M_2 such that*

(init) for any $\gamma_1 \in \Gamma_0(M_1)$, there is a $\gamma_2 \in \Gamma_0(M_2)$ such that $(\gamma_1, \gamma_2) \in B$ and for any $\gamma_2 \in \Gamma_0(M_2)$, there is a $\gamma_1 \in \Gamma_0(M_1)$ such that $(\gamma_1, \gamma_2) \in B$.

Now we are able to establish a Hennessy-Milner like correspondence for a fragment of $\mathcal{E}^{\downarrow}$. Let us call *hybrid-free sentences of* $\mathcal{E}^{\downarrow}$ the formulae obtained by the grammar

$$\varrho ::= \varphi \mid \langle\lambda\rangle\varrho \mid \text{true} \mid \neg\varrho \mid \varrho_1 \vee \varrho_2.$$

Theorem 1. *Let M_1, M_2 be bisimilar Σ-edts. Then $M_1 \models_\Sigma^{\mathcal{E}^\downarrow} \varrho$ iff $M_2 \models_\Sigma^{\mathcal{E}^\downarrow} \varrho$ for all hybrid-free sentences ϱ.*

The converse of Theorem 1 does not hold, in general, and the usual image-finiteness assumption has to be imposed: A Σ-edts M is *image-finite* if, for all $\gamma \in \Gamma(M)$ and all $e \in E(\Sigma)$, the set $\{\gamma' \mid (\gamma, \gamma') \in R(M)_e\}$ is finite. Then:

Theorem 2. *Let M_1, M_2 be image-finite Σ-edts and $\gamma_1 \in \Gamma(M_1)$, $\gamma_2 \in \Gamma(M_2)$ such that $M_1, \gamma_1 \models_\Sigma^{\mathcal{E}^\downarrow} \varrho$ iff $M_2, \gamma_2 \models_\Sigma^{\mathcal{E}^\downarrow} \varrho$ for all hybrid-free sentences ϱ. Then there exists a bisimulation B between M_1 and M_2 such that $(\gamma_1, \gamma_2) \in B$.*

3 Specifications of Event/Data Systems

3.1 Axiomatic Specifications

Sentences of $\mathcal{E}^\downarrow$-logic can be used to specify properties of event/data systems and thus to write system specifications in an axiomatic way.

Definition 5. *An axiomatic ed specification $Sp = (\Sigma(Sp), Ax(Sp))$ in $\mathcal{E}^\downarrow$ consists of an ed signature $\Sigma(Sp) \in Sig^{\mathcal{E}^\downarrow}$ and a set of axioms $Ax(Sp) \subseteq \mathrm{Sen}^{\mathcal{E}^\downarrow}(\Sigma(Sp))$.*

The semantics of Sp is given by the pair $(\Sigma(Sp), \mathrm{Mod}(Sp))$ where $\mathrm{Mod}(Sp) = \{M \in Edts^{\mathcal{E}^\downarrow}(\Sigma(Sp)) \mid M \models_{\Sigma(Sp)}^{\mathcal{E}^\downarrow} Ax(Sp)\}$. The edts in $\mathrm{Mod}(Sp)$ are called models *of Sp and $\mathrm{Mod}(Sp)$ is the* model class *of Sp.*

As a direct consequence of Theorem 1 we have:

Corollary 1. *The model class of an axiomatic ed specification exclusively expressed by hybrid-free sentences is closed under bisimulation.*

This result does not hold for sentences with hybrid features. For instance, consider the specification $Sp = ((\{e\}, \{a\}), \{\downarrow x . \langle e /\!\!/ a' = a \rangle x\})$: An edts with a single control state c_0 and a loop transition $R_e = \{(\gamma_0, \gamma_0)\}$ for $c(\gamma_0) = c_0$ is a model of Sp. However, this is obviously not the case for its bisimilar edts with two control states c_0 and c and the relation $R'_e = \{(\gamma_0, \gamma), (\gamma, \gamma_0)\}$ with $c(\gamma_0) = c_0$, $c(\gamma) = c$ and $\omega(\gamma_0) = \omega(\gamma)$.

Example 1. As a running example we consider an ATM. We start with an abstract specification Sp_0 of fundamental requirements for its interaction behaviour based on the set of events $E_0 = \{\mathsf{insertCard}, \mathsf{enterPIN}, \mathsf{ejectCard}, \mathsf{cancel}\}$[2] and on the singleton set of attributes $A_0 = \{\mathsf{chk}\}$ where chk is boolean valued and records the correctness of an entered PIN. Hence our first ed signature is $\Sigma_0 = (E_0, A_0)$ and $Sp_0 = (\Sigma_0, Ax_0)$ where Ax_0 requires the following properties expressed by corresponding axioms (0.1–0.3):

---

[2] For shortening the presentation we omit further events like withdrawing money, etc.

- "Whenever a card has been inserted, a correct PIN can eventually be entered and also the transaction can eventually be cancelled."

$$[\boldsymbol{E}^*; \mathsf{insertCard}](\langle \boldsymbol{E}^*; \mathsf{enterPIN} /\!/ \mathsf{chk}' = tt\rangle \mathsf{true} \wedge \langle \boldsymbol{E}^*; \mathsf{cancel}\rangle \mathsf{true}) \qquad (0.1)$$

- "Whenever either a correct PIN has been entered or the transaction has been cancelled, the card can eventually be ejected."

$$[\boldsymbol{E}^*; (\mathsf{enterPIN} /\!/ \mathsf{chk}' = tt) + \mathsf{cancel}]\langle \boldsymbol{E}^*; \mathsf{ejectCard}\rangle \mathsf{true} \qquad (0.2)$$

- "Whenever an incorrect PIN has been entered three times in a row, the current card is not returned." This means that the card is kept by the ATM which is not modelled by an extra event. It may, however, still be possible that another card is inserted afterwards. So an ejectCard can only be forbidden as long as no next card is inserted.

$$[\boldsymbol{E}^*; (\mathsf{enterPIN} /\!/ \mathsf{chk}' = f\!f)^3; (-\mathsf{insertCard})^*; \mathsf{ejectCard}]\mathsf{false} \qquad (0.3)$$

where λ^n abbreviates the n-fold sequential composition $\lambda; \ldots; \lambda$.

The semantics of an axiomatic ed specification is loose allowing usually for many different realisations. A refinement step is therefore understood as a restriction of the model class of an abstract specification. Following the terminology of Sannella and Tarlecki [18, 19], we call a specification refining another one an *implementation*. Formally, a specification Sp' is a *simple implementation* of a specification Sp over the same signature, in symbols $Sp \rightsquigarrow Sp'$, whenever $\mathrm{Mod}(Sp) \supseteq \mathrm{Mod}(Sp')$. Transitivity of the inclusion relation ensures gradual step-by-step development by a series of refinements.

Example 2. We provide a refinement $Sp_0 \rightsquigarrow Sp_1$ where $Sp_1 = (\Sigma_0, Ax_1)$ has the same signature as Sp_0 and Ax_1 are the sentences (1.1–1.4) below; the last two use binders to specify a loop. As is easily seen, all models of Sp_1 must satisfy the axioms of Sp_0.

- "At the beginning a card can be inserted with the effect that chk is set to $f\!f$; nothing else is possible at the beginning."

$$\langle \mathsf{insertCard} /\!/ \mathsf{chk}' = f\!f\rangle \mathsf{true} \wedge \qquad (1.1)$$
$$[\mathsf{insertCard} /\!/ \neg(\mathsf{chk}' = f\!f)]\mathsf{false} \wedge [-\mathsf{insertCard}]\mathsf{false}$$

- "Whenever a card has been inserted, a PIN can be entered (directly afterwards) and also the transaction can be cancelled; but nothing else."

$$[\boldsymbol{E}^*; \mathsf{insertCard}](\langle \mathsf{enterPIN}\rangle \mathsf{true} \wedge \langle \mathsf{cancel}\rangle \mathsf{true} \wedge \qquad (1.2)$$
$$[-\{\mathsf{enterPIN}, \mathsf{cancel}\}]\mathsf{false})$$

– "Whenever either a correct PIN has been entered or the transaction has been cancelled, the card can eventually be ejected and the ATM starts from the beginning."

$$\downarrow x_0 . [\boldsymbol{E}^*; (\mathsf{enterPIN}/\!\!/\mathsf{chk}' = tt) + \mathsf{cancel}]\langle \boldsymbol{E}^*; \mathsf{ejectCard}\rangle x_0 \qquad (1.3)$$

– "Whenever an incorrect PIN has been entered three times in a row the ATM starts from the beginning." Hence the current card is kept.

$$\downarrow x_0 . [\boldsymbol{E}^*; (\mathsf{enterPIN}/\!\!/\mathsf{chk}' = f\!f)^3] x_0 \qquad (1.4)$$

3.2 Operational Specifications

Operational event/data specifications are introduced as a means to specify in a more constructive style the properties of event/data systems. They are not appropriate for writing abstract requirements for which axiomatic specifications are recommended. Though $\mathcal{E}^\downarrow$-logic is able to specify concrete models, as discussed in Sect. 2, the use of operational specifications allows a graphic representation close to familiar formalisms in the literature, like UML protocol state machines, cf. [12,16]. As will be shown in Sect. 3.3, finite operational specifications can be characterised by a sentence in $\mathcal{E}^\downarrow$-logic. Therefore, $\mathcal{E}^\downarrow$-logic is still the common basis of our development approach. Transitions in an operational specification are tuples $(c, \varphi, e, \psi, c')$ with c a source control state, φ a precondition, e an event, ψ a state transition predicate specifying the possible effects of the event e, and c' a target control state. In the semantic models an event must be enabled whenever the respective source data state satisfies the precondition. Thus isolating preconditions has a semantic consequence that is not expressible by transition predicates only. The effect of the event must respect ψ; no other transitions are allowed.

Definition 6. *An* operational ed specification $O = (\Sigma, C, T, (c_0, \varphi_0))$ *is given by an ed signature Σ, a set of* control states C, *a* transition relation specification $T \subseteq C \times \Phi(\Sigma) \times E(\Sigma) \times \Psi(\Sigma) \times C$, *an* initial control state $c_0 \in C$, *and an* initial state predicate $\varphi_0 \in \Phi(\Sigma)$, *such that C is* syntactically reachable, *i.e., for every $c \in C \backslash \{c_0\}$ there are $(c_0, \varphi_1, e_1, \psi_1, c_1), \ldots, (c_{n-1}, \varphi_n, e_n, \psi_n, c_n) \in T$ with $n > 0$ such that $c_n = c$. We write $\Sigma(O)$ for Σ, etc.*

A Σ-edts M is a model *of O if $C(M) = C$ up to a bijective renaming, $c_0(M) = c_0$, $\Omega_0(M) \subseteq \{\omega \mid \omega \models^{\mathcal{D}}_{A(\Sigma)} \varphi_0\}$, and if the following conditions hold:*

– *for all $(c, \varphi, e, \psi, c') \in T$ and $\omega \in \Omega(A(\Sigma))$ with $\omega \models^{\mathcal{D}}_{A(\Sigma)} \varphi$, there is a $((c, \omega), (c', \omega')) \in R(M)_e$ with $(\omega, \omega') \models^{\mathcal{D}}_{A(\Sigma)} \psi$;*

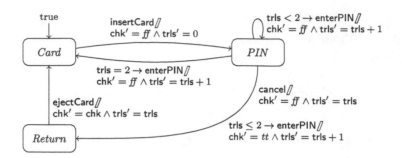

Fig. 1. Operational ed specification ATM

- for all $((c, \omega), (c', \omega')) \in R(M)_e$ there is a $(c, \varphi, e, \psi, c') \in T$ with $\omega \models^{\mathcal{D}}_{A(\Sigma)} \varphi$ and $(\omega, \omega') \models^{\mathcal{D}}_{A(\Sigma)} \psi$.

The class of all models of O is denoted by $\mathrm{Mod}(O)$. *The semantics of O is given by the pair* $(\Sigma(O), \mathrm{Mod}(O))$ *where* $\Sigma(O) = \Sigma$.

Example 3. We construct an operational ed specification, called ATM, for the ATM example. The signature of ATM extends the one of Sp_1 (and Sp_0) by an additional integer-valued attribute trls which counts the number of attempts to enter a correct PIN (with the same card). ATM is graphically presented in Fig. 1. The initial control state is $Card$, and the initial state predicate is true. Preconditions are written before the symbol $\rightarrow$. If no precondition is explicitly indicated it is assumed to be true. Due to the extended signature, ATM is not a simple implementation of Sp_1, and we will only formally justify the implementation relationship in Example 5.

Operational specifications can be composed by a syntactic parallel composition operator which synchronises shared events. Two ed signatures Σ_1 and Σ_2 are *composable* if $A(\Sigma_1) \cap A(\Sigma_2) = \emptyset$. Their parallel composition is given by $\Sigma_1 \otimes \Sigma_2 = (E(\Sigma_1) \cup E(\Sigma_2), A(\Sigma_1) \cup A(\Sigma_2))$.

Definition 7. *Let Σ_1 and Σ_2 be composable ed signatures and let O_1 and O_2 be operational ed specifications with $\Sigma(O_1) = \Sigma_1$ and $\Sigma(O_2) = \Sigma_2$. The parallel composition of O_1 and O_2 is given by the operational ed specification $O_1 \parallel O_2 = (\Sigma_1 \otimes \Sigma_2, C, T, (c_0, \varphi_0))$ with $c_0 = (c_0(O_1), c_0(O_2))$, $\varphi_0 = \varphi_0(O_1) \wedge \varphi_0(O_2)$, and C and T are inductively defined by $c_0 \in C$ and*

- *for $e_1 \in E(\Sigma_1) \setminus E(\Sigma_2)$, $c_1, c_1' \in C(O_1)$, and $c_2 \in C(O_2)$, if $(c_1, c_2) \in C$ and $(c_1, \varphi_1, e_1, \psi_1, c_1') \in T(O_1)$, then $(c_1', c_2) \in C$ and $((c_1, c_2), \varphi_1, e_1, \psi_1 \wedge \mathrm{id}_{A(\Sigma_2)}, (c_1', c_2)) \in T$;*
- *for $e_2 \in E(\Sigma_2) \setminus E(\Sigma_1)$, $c_2, c_2' \in C(O_2)$, and $c_1 \in C(O_1)$, if $(c_1, c_2) \in C$ and $(c_2, \varphi_2, e_2, \psi_2, c_2') \in T(O_2)$, then $(c_1, c_2') \in C$ and $((c_1, c_2), \varphi_2, e_2, \psi_2 \wedge \mathrm{id}_{A(\Sigma_1)}, (c_1, c_2')) \in T$;*

– *for $e \in E(\Sigma_1) \cap E(\Sigma_2)$, $c_1, c_1' \in C(O_1)$, and $c_2, c_2' \in C(O_2)$, if $(c_1, c_2) \in C$, $(c_1, \varphi_1, e, \psi_1, c_1') \in T(O_1)$, and $(c_2, \varphi_2, e, \psi_2, c_2') \in T(O_2)$, then $(c_1', c_2') \in C$ and $((c_1, c_2), \varphi_1 \wedge \varphi_2, e, \psi_1 \wedge \psi_2, (c_1', c_2')) \in T$.*[3]

3.3   Expressiveness of $\mathcal{E}^{\downarrow}$-Logic

We show that the semantics of an operational ed specification O with finitely many control states can be characterised by a single $\mathcal{E}^{\downarrow}$-sentence ϱ_O, i.e., an edts M is a model of O iff $M \models^{\mathcal{E}^{\downarrow}}_{\Sigma(O)} \varrho_O$. Using Algorithm 1, such a characterising sentence is

$$\varrho_O = \downarrow c_0 \,.\, \varphi_0 \wedge \text{sen}(c_0, Im_O(c_0), C(O), \{c_0\}) \,,$$

where $c_0 = c_0(O)$ and $\varphi_0 = \varphi_0(O)$. Algorithm 1 closely follows the procedure in [15] for characterising a finite structure by a sentence of $\mathcal{D}^{\downarrow}$-logic. A call $\text{sen}(c, I, V, B)$ performs a recursive breadth-first traversal through O starting from c, where I holds the unprocessed quadruples (φ, e, ψ, c') of transitions outgoing from c, V the remaining states to visit, and B the set of already bound states. The function first requires the existence of each outgoing transition of I, provided its precondition holds, in the resulting formula, binding any newly reached state. Then it requires that no other transitions with source state c exist using calls to fin. Having visited all states in V, it finally requires all states in $C(O)$ to be pairwise different.

Algorithm 1. Constructing a sentence from an operational ed specification

---

Require: $O \equiv$ finite operational ed specification

$\qquad Im_O(c) = \{(\varphi, e, \psi, c') \mid (c, \varphi, e, \psi, c') \in T(O)\}$ for $c \in C(O)$

$\qquad Im_O(c, e) = \{(\varphi, \psi, c') \mid (c, \varphi, e, \psi, c') \in T(O)\}$ for $c \in C(O)$, $e \in E(\Sigma(O))$

1 **function** $\text{sen}(c, I, V, B)$ $\qquad \triangleright$ c: state, I: image to visit, V: states to visit, B: bound states

2 $\quad$ **if** $I \neq \emptyset$ **then**

3 $\qquad (\varphi, e, \psi, c') \leftarrow$ **choose** I

4 $\qquad$ **if** $c' \in B$ **then**

5 $\qquad\quad$ **return** $@c \,.\, \varphi \rightarrow \langle e /\!\!/ \psi \rangle (c' \wedge \text{sen}(c, I \setminus \{(\varphi, e, \psi, c')\}, V, B))$

6 $\qquad$ **else**

7 $\qquad\quad$ **return** $@c \,.\, \varphi \rightarrow \langle e /\!\!/ \psi \rangle (\downarrow c' \,.\, \text{sen}(c, I \setminus \{(\varphi, e, \psi, c')\}, V, B \cup \{c'\}))$

8 $\quad V \leftarrow V \setminus \{c\}$

9 $\quad$ **if** $V \neq \emptyset$ **then**

10 $\qquad c' \leftarrow$ **choose** $B \cap V$

11 $\qquad$ **return** $\text{fin}(c) \wedge \text{sen}(c', Im_O(c'), V, B)$

12 $\quad$ **return** $\text{fin}(c) \wedge \bigwedge_{c_1 \in C(O), c_2 \in C(O) \setminus \{c_1\}} \neg @c_1 \,.\, c_2$

13 **function** $\text{fin}(c)$

14 $\quad$ **return** $@c \,.\, \bigwedge_{e \in E(\Sigma(O))} \bigwedge_{P \subseteq Im_O(c, e)}$
$\qquad\qquad [e /\!\!/ (\bigwedge_{(\varphi, \psi, c') \in P} (\varphi \wedge \psi)) \wedge$
$\qquad\qquad \neg(\bigvee_{(\varphi, \psi, c') \in Im_O(c, e) \setminus P} (\varphi \wedge \psi))](\bigvee_{(\varphi, \psi, c') \in P} c')$

---

[3] Note that joint moves with e cannot become inconsistent due to composability of ed signatures.

It is $\text{fin}(c)$ where this algorithm mainly deviates from [15]: To ensure that no other transitions from c exist than those specified in O, $\text{fin}(c)$ produces the requirement that at state c, for every event e and for every subset P of the transitions outgoing from c, whenever an e-transition can be done with the combined effect of P but not adhering to any of the effects of the currently not selected transitions, the e-transition must have one of the states as its target that are target states of P. The rather complicated formulation is due to possibly overlapping preconditions where for a single event e the preconditions of two different transitions may be satisfied simultaneously. For a state c, where all outgoing transitions for the same event have disjoint preconditions, the $\mathcal{E}^{\downarrow}$-formula returned by $\text{fin}(c)$ is equivalent to

$$@c \cdot \bigwedge_{e \in E(\Sigma(O))} \bigwedge_{(\varphi,\psi,c') \in Im_O(c,e)} [e /\!/ \varphi \wedge \psi] c' \wedge$$
$$[e /\!/ \neg (\bigvee_{(\varphi,\psi,c') \in Im_O(c,e)} (\varphi \wedge \psi))] \text{false}.$$

Example 4. We show the first few steps of representing the operational ed specification ATM of Fig. 1 as an $\mathcal{E}^{\downarrow}$-sentence ϱ_{ATM}. This top-level sentence is

$$\downarrow Card \,.\, \text{true} \wedge \text{sen}(Card, \{(\text{true}, \text{insertCard}, \text{chk}' = \textit{ff} \wedge \text{trls}' = 0, PIN)\},$$
$$\{Card, PIN, Return\}, \{Card\}).$$

The first call of $\text{sen}(Card, \dots)$ explores the single outgoing transition from $Card$ to PIN, adds PIN to the bound states, and hence expands to

$$@Card \,.\, \text{true} \rightarrow \langle \text{insertCard} /\!/ \text{chk}' = \textit{ff} \wedge \text{trls}' = 0 \rangle \downarrow PIN.$$
$$\text{sen}(Card, \emptyset, \{Card, PIN, Return\}, \{Card, PIN\}).$$

Now all outgoing transitions from $Card$ have been explored and the next call of $\text{sen}(Card, \emptyset, \dots)$ removes $Card$ from the set of states to be visited, resulting in

$$\text{fin}(Card) \wedge \text{sen}(PIN, \{(\text{trls} < 2, \text{enterPIN}, \dots), (\text{trls} = 2, \text{enterPIN}, \dots),$$
$$(\text{trls} \leq 2, \text{enterPIN}, \dots), (\text{true}, \text{cancel}, \dots)\},$$
$$\{PIN, Return\}, \{Card, PIN\}).$$

As there is only a single outgoing transition from $Card$, the special case of disjoint preconditions applies for the finalisation call, and $\text{fin}(Card)$ results in

$$@Card \,.\, [\text{insertCard} /\!/ \text{chk}' = \textit{ff} \wedge \text{trls}' = 0] PIN \wedge$$
$$[\text{insertCard} /\!/ \text{chk}' = \textit{tt} \vee \text{trls}' \neq 0] \text{false} \wedge$$
$$[\text{enterPIN} /\!/ \text{true}] \text{false} \wedge [\text{cancel} /\!/ \text{true}] \text{false} \wedge [\text{ejectCard} /\!/ \text{true}] \text{false}.$$

4   Constructor Implementations

The implementation notion defined in Sect. 3.1 is too simple for many practical applications. It requires the same signature for specification and implementation and does not support the process of constructing an implementation. Therefore,

Sannella and Tarlecki [18,19] have proposed the notion of constructor implementation which is a generic notion applicable to specification formalisms which are based on signatures and semantic structures for signatures. We will reuse the ideas in the context of $\mathcal{E}^{\downarrow}$-logic.

The notion of *constructor* is the basis: for signatures $\Sigma_1, \ldots, \Sigma_n, \Sigma \in Sig^{\mathcal{E}^{\downarrow}}$, a *constructor* κ from $(\Sigma_1, \ldots, \Sigma_n)$ to Σ is a (total) function $\kappa : Edts^{\mathcal{E}^{\downarrow}}(\Sigma_1) \times \ldots \times Edts^{\mathcal{E}^{\downarrow}}(\Sigma_n) \to Edts^{\mathcal{E}^{\downarrow}}(\Sigma)$. Given a constructor κ from $(\Sigma_1, \ldots, \Sigma_n)$ to Σ and a set of constructors κ_i from $(\Sigma_i^1, \ldots, \Sigma_i^{k_i})$ to Σ_i, $1 \leq i \leq n$, the constructor $(\kappa_1, \ldots, \kappa_n); \kappa$ from $(\Sigma_1^1, \ldots, \Sigma_1^{k_1}, \ldots, \Sigma_n^1, \ldots, \Sigma_n^{k_n})$ to Σ is obtained by the usual composition of functions. The following definitions apply to both axiomatic and operational ed specifications since the semantics of both is given in terms of ed signatures and model classes of edts. In particular, the implementation notion allows to implement axiomatic specifications by operational specifications.

Definition 8. *Given specifications $Sp, Sp_1, \ldots, Sp_n$ and a constructor κ from $(\Sigma(Sp_1), \ldots, \Sigma(Sp_n))$ to $\Sigma(Sp)$, the tuple $\langle Sp_1, \ldots, Sp_n \rangle$ is a constructor implementation via κ of Sp, in symbols $Sp \leadsto_\kappa \langle Sp_1, \ldots, Sp_n \rangle$, if for all $M_i \in \mathrm{Mod}(Sp_i)$ we have $\kappa(M_1, \ldots, M_n) \in \mathrm{Mod}(Sp)$. The implementation involves a decomposition if $n > 1$.*

The notion of simple implementation in Sect. 3.1 is captured by choosing the identity. We now introduce a set of more advanced constructors in the context of ed signatures and edts. Let us first consider two central notions for constructors: signature morphisms and reducts. For data signatures A, A' a *data signature morphism* $\sigma : A \to A'$ is a function from A to A'. The σ-*reduct* of an A'-data state $\omega' : A' \to \mathcal{D}$ is given by the A-data state $\omega'|\sigma : A \to \mathcal{D}$ defined by $(\omega'|\sigma)(a) = \omega'(\sigma(a))$ for every $a \in A$. If $A \subseteq A'$, the injection of A into A' is a particular data signature morphism and we denote the reduct of an A'-data state ω' to A by $\omega'{\restriction}A$. If $A = A_1 \cup A_2$ is the disjoint union of A_1 and A_2 and ω_i are A_i-data states for $i \in \{1, 2\}$ then $\omega_1 + \omega_2$ denotes the unique A-data state ω with $\omega{\restriction}A_i = \omega_i$ for $i \in \{1, 2\}$. The σ-reduct $\gamma|\sigma$ of a configuration $\gamma = (c, \omega')$ is given by $(c, \omega'|\sigma)$, and is lifted to a set of configurations Γ' by $\Gamma'|\sigma = \{\gamma'|\sigma \mid \gamma' \in \Gamma'\}$.

Definition 9. *An ed signature morphism $\sigma = (\sigma_E, \sigma_A) : \Sigma \to \Sigma'$ is given by a function $\sigma_E : E(\Sigma) \to E(\Sigma')$ and a data signature morphism $\sigma_A : A(\Sigma) \to A(\Sigma')$. We abbreviate both σ_E and σ_A by σ.*

Definition 10. *Let $\sigma : \Sigma \to \Sigma'$ be an ed signature morphism and M' a Σ'-edts. The σ-reduct of M' is the Σ-edts $M'|\sigma = (\Gamma, R, \Gamma_0)$ such that $\Gamma_0 = \Gamma_0(M')|\sigma$, and Γ and $R = (R_e)_{e \in E(\Sigma)}$ are inductively defined by $\Gamma_0 \subseteq \Gamma$ and for all $e \in E(\Sigma)$, $\gamma', \gamma'' \in \Gamma(M')$: if $\gamma'|\sigma \in \Gamma$ and $(\gamma', \gamma'') \in R(M')_{\sigma(e)}$, then $\gamma''|\sigma \in \Gamma$ and $(\gamma'|\sigma, \gamma''|\sigma) \in R_e$.*

Definition 11. *Let $\sigma : \Sigma \to \Sigma'$ be an ed signature morphism. The reduct constructor κ_σ from Σ' to Σ maps any $M' \in Edts^{\mathcal{E}^{\downarrow}}(\Sigma')$ to its reduct $\kappa_\sigma(M') = M'|\sigma$. Whenever σ_A and σ_E are bijective functions, κ_σ is a relabelling constructor. If σ_E and σ_A are injective, κ_σ is a restriction constructor.*

Example 5. The operational specification ATM is a constructor implementation of Sp_1 via the restriction constructor κ_ι determined by the inclusion signature morphism $\iota : \Sigma(Sp_1) \to \Sigma(ATM)$, i.e., $Sp_1 \rightsquigarrow_{\kappa_\iota} ATM$.

A further refinement technique for reactive systems (see, e.g., [8]), is the implementation of simple events by complex events, like their sequential composition. To formalise this as a constructor we use *composite events* $\Theta(E)$ over a given set of events E, given by the grammar $\theta ::= e \mid \theta + \theta \mid \theta; \theta \mid \theta^*$ with $e \in E$. They are *interpreted* over an (E, A)-edts M by $R(M)_{\theta_1 + \theta_2} = R(M)_{\theta_1} \cup R(M)_{\theta_2}$, $R(M)_{\theta_1; \theta_2} = R(M)_{\theta_1}; R(M)_{\theta_2}$, and $R(M)_{\theta^*} = (R(M)_\theta)^*$. Then we can introduce the intended constructor by means of reducts over signature morphisms mapping atomic to composite events:

Definition 12. *Let Σ, Σ' be ed signatures, D' a finite subset of $\Theta(E(\Sigma'))$, $\Delta' = (D', A(\Sigma'))$, and $\alpha : \Sigma \to \Delta'$ an ed signature morphism. The* event refinement constructor κ_α *from Δ' to Σ maps any $M' \in Edts^{\mathcal{E}^{\downarrow}}(\Delta')$ to its reduct $M'|\alpha \in Edts^{\mathcal{E}^{\downarrow}}(\Sigma)$.*

Finally, we consider a semantic, synchronous parallel composition constructor that allows for decomposition of implementations into components which synchronise on shared events. Given two composable signatures Σ_1 and Σ_2, the *parallel composition* $\gamma_1 \otimes \gamma_2$ of two configurations $\gamma_1 = (c_1, \omega_1)$, $\gamma_2 = (c_2, \omega_2)$ with $\omega_1 \in \Omega(A(\Sigma_1))$, $\omega_2 \in \Omega(A(\Sigma_2))$ is given by $((c_1, c_2), \omega_1 + \omega_2)$, and lifted to two sets of configurations Γ_1 and Γ_2 by $\Gamma_1 \otimes \Gamma_2 = \{\gamma_1 \otimes \gamma_2 \mid \gamma_1 \in \Gamma_1, \ \gamma_2 \in \Gamma_2\}$.

Definition 13. *Let Σ_1, Σ_2 be composable ed signatures. The* parallel composition constructor $\kappa_\otimes$ *from (Σ_1, Σ_2) to $\Sigma_1 \otimes \Sigma_2$ maps any $M_1 \in Edts^{\mathcal{E}^{\downarrow}}(\Sigma_1)$, $M_2 \in Edts^{\mathcal{E}^{\downarrow}}(\Sigma_2)$ to $M_1 \otimes M_2 = (\Gamma, R, \Gamma_0) \in Edts^{\mathcal{E}^{\downarrow}}(\Sigma_1 \otimes \Sigma_2)$, where $\Gamma_0 = \Gamma_0(M_1) \otimes \Gamma_0(M_2)$, and Γ and $R = (R_e)_{E(\Sigma_1) \cup E(\Sigma_2)}$ are inductively defined by $\Gamma_0 \subseteq \Gamma$ and*

- *for all $e_1 \in E(\Sigma_1) \setminus E(\Sigma_2)$, $\gamma_1, \gamma_1' \in \Gamma(M_1)$, and $\gamma_2 \in \Gamma(M_2)$, if $\gamma_1 \otimes \gamma_2 \in \Gamma$ and $(\gamma_1, \gamma_1') \in R(M_1)_{e_1}$, then $\gamma_1' \otimes \gamma_2 \in \Gamma$ and $(\gamma_1 \otimes \gamma_2, \gamma_1' \otimes \gamma_2) \in R_{e_1}$;*
- *for all $e_2 \in E(\Sigma_2) \setminus E(\Sigma_1)$, $\gamma_2, \gamma_2' \in \Gamma(M_2)$, and $\gamma_1 \in \Gamma(M_1)$, if $\gamma_1 \otimes \gamma_2 \in \Gamma$ and $(\gamma_2, \gamma_2') \in R(M_2)_{e_2}$, then $\gamma_1 \otimes \gamma_2' \in \Gamma$ and $(\gamma_1 \otimes \gamma_2, \gamma_1 \otimes \gamma_2') \in R_{e_2}$;*
- *for all $e \in E(\Sigma_1) \cap E(\Sigma_2)$, $\gamma_1, \gamma_1' \in \Gamma(M_1)$, and $\gamma_2, \gamma_2' \in \Gamma(M_2)$, if $\gamma_1 \otimes \gamma_2 \in \Gamma$, $(\gamma_1, \gamma_1') \in R(M_1)_{e_1}$, and $(\gamma_2, \gamma_2') \in R(M_2)_{e_2}$, then $\gamma_1' \otimes \gamma_2' \in \Gamma$ and $(\gamma_1 \otimes \gamma_2, \gamma_1' \otimes \gamma_2') \in R_e$.*

An obvious question is how the semantic parallel composition constructor is related to the syntactic parallel composition of operational ed specifications.

Proposition 1. *Let O_1, O_2 be operational ed specifications with composable signatures. Then $\mathrm{Mod}(O_1) \otimes \mathrm{Mod}(O_2) \subseteq \mathrm{Mod}(O_1 \parallel O_2)$, where $\mathrm{Mod}(O_1) \otimes \mathrm{Mod}(O_2)$ denotes $\kappa_\otimes(\mathrm{Mod}(O_1), \mathrm{Mod}(O_2))$.*

The converse $\text{Mod}(O_1 \parallel O_2) \subseteq \text{Mod}(O_1) \otimes \text{Mod}(O_2)$ does not hold: Consider the ed signature $\Sigma = (E, A)$ with $E = \{e\}$, $A = \emptyset$, and the operational ed specifications $O_i = (\Sigma, C_i, T_i, (c_{i,0}, \varphi_{i,0}))$ for $i \in \{1, 2\}$ with $C_1 = \{c_{1,0}\}$, $T_1 = \{(c_{1,0}, \text{true}, e, \text{false}, c_{1,0})\}$, $\varphi_{1,0} = \text{true}$; and $C_2 = \{c_{2,0}\}$, $T_2 = \emptyset$, $\varphi_{2,0} = \text{true}$. Then $\text{Mod}(O_1) = \emptyset$, but $\text{Mod}(O_1 \parallel O_2) = \{M\}$ with M showing just the initial configuration.

The next theorem shows the usefulness of the syntactic parallel composition operator for proving implementation correctness when a (semantic) parallel composition constructor is involved. The theorem is a direct consequence of Proposition 1 and Definition 8.

Theorem 3. *Let Sp be an (axiomatic or operational) ed specification, O_1, O_2 operational ed specifications with composable signatures, and κ an implementation constructor from $\Sigma(O_1) \otimes \Sigma(O_2)$ to $\Sigma(Sp)$: If $Sp \leadsto_\kappa O_1 \parallel O_2$, then $Sp \leadsto_{\kappa_\otimes;\kappa} \langle O_1, O_2 \rangle$.*

Example 6. We finish the refinement chain for the ATM specifications by applying a decomposition into two parallel components. The operational specification *ATM* of Example 3 (and Example 5) describes the interface behaviour of an ATM interacting with a user. For a concrete realisation, however, an ATM will also interact internally with other components, like, e.g., a clearing company which supports the ATM for verifying PINs. Our last refinement step hence realises the *ATM* specification by two parallel components, represented by the operational specification *ATM'* in Fig. 2a and the operational specification *CC* of a clearing company in Fig. 2b. Both communicate (via shared events) when an ATM sends a verification request, modelled by the event verifyPIN, to the clearing company. The clearing company may answer with correctPIN or wrongPIN and then the ATM continues following its specification. For the implementation construction we use the parallel composition constructor $\kappa_\otimes$ from $(\Sigma(ATM'), \Sigma(CC))$ to $\Sigma(ATM') \otimes \Sigma(CC)$. The signature of *CC* consists of the events shown on the transitions in Fig. 2b. Moreover, there is one integer-valued attribute cnt counting the number of verification tasks performed. The signature of *ATM'* extends $\Sigma(ATM)$ by the events verifyPIN, correctPIN and wrongPIN. To fit the signature and the behaviour of the parallel composition of *ATM'* and *CC* to the specification *ATM* we must therefore compose $\kappa_\otimes$ with an event refinement constructor κ_α such that $\alpha(\text{enterPIN}) = (\text{enterPIN}; \text{verifyPIN}; (\text{correctPIN}+\text{wrongPIN}))$; for the other events α is the identity and for the attributes the inclusion. The idea is therefore that the refinement looks like $ATM \leadsto_{\kappa_\otimes;\kappa_\alpha} \langle ATM', CC \rangle$. To prove this refinement relation we rely on the syntactic parallel composition $ATM' \parallel CC$ shown in Fig. 2c, and on Theorem 3. It is easy to see that $ATM \leadsto_{\kappa_\alpha} ATM' \parallel CC$. In fact, all transitions for event enterPIN in Fig. 1 are split into several transitions in Fig. 2c according to the event refinement defined by α. For instance, the loop transition from *PIN* to *PIN* with precondition trls < 2 in Fig. 1 is split into

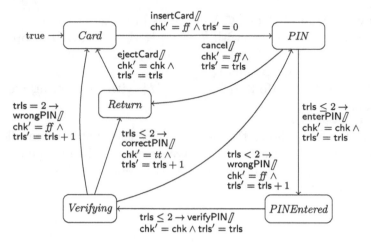

(a) Operational ed specification ATM'

(b) Operational specification CC of a clearing company

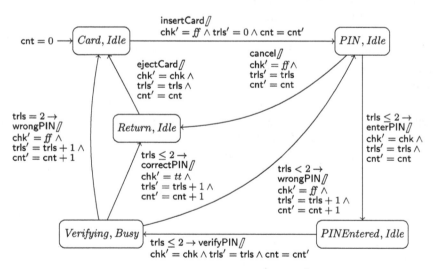

(c) Syntactic parallel composition $ATM' \parallel CC$

Fig. 2. Operational ed specifications ATM', CC and their parallel composition

the cycle from $(PIN, Idle)$ via $(PINEntered, Idle)$ and $(Verifying, Busy)$ back to $(PIN, Idle)$ in Fig. 2c. Thus, we have $ATM \rightsquigarrow_{\kappa_\alpha} ATM' \parallel CC$ and can apply Theorem 3 such that we get $ATM \rightsquigarrow_{\kappa_\otimes ; \kappa_\alpha} \langle ATM', CC \rangle$.

5 Conclusions

We have presented a novel logic, called $\mathcal{E}^{\downarrow}$-logic, for the rigorous formal development of event-based systems incorporating changing data states. To the best of our knowledge, no other logic supports the full development process for this kind of systems ranging from abstract requirements specifications, expressible by the dynamic logic features, to the concrete specification of implementations, expressible by the hybrid part of the logic.

The temporal logic of actions (TLA [13]) supports also stepwise refinement where state transition predicates are considered as actions. In contrast to TLA we model also the events which cause data state transitions. For writing concrete specifications we have proposed an operational specification format capturing (at least parts of) similar formalisms, like Event-B [1], symbolic transition systems [17], and UML protocol state machines [16]. A significant difference to Event-B machines is that we distinguish between control and data states, the former being encoded as data in Event-B. On the other hand, Event-B supports parameters of events which could be integrated in our logic as well. An institution-based semantics of Event-B has been proposed in [7] which coincides with our semantics of operational specifications for the special case of deterministic state transition predicates. Similarly, our semantics of operational specifications coincides with the unfolding of symbolic transition systems in [17] if we instantiate our generic data domain with algebraic specifications of data types (and consider again only deterministic state transition predicates). The syntax of UML protocol state machines is about the same as the one of operational event/data specifications. As a consequence, all of the aforementioned concrete specification formalisms (and several others) would be appropriate candidates for integration into a development process based on $\mathcal{E}^{\downarrow}$-logic.

There remain several interesting tasks for future research. First, our logic is not yet equipped with a proof system for deriving consequences of specifications. This would also support the proof of refinement steps which is currently achieved by purely semantic reasoning. A proof system for $\mathcal{E}^{\downarrow}$-logic must cover dynamic and hybrid logic parts at the same time, like the proof system in [15], which, however, does not consider data states, and the recent calculus of [5], which extends differential dynamic logic but does not deal with events and reactions to events. Both proof systems could be appropriate candidates for incorporating the features of $\mathcal{E}^{\downarrow}$-logic. Another issue concerns the separation of events into input and output as in I/O-automata [14]. Then also communication compatibility (see [2] for interface automata without data and [3] for interface theories with data) would become relevant when applying a parallel composition constructor.

References

1. Abrial, J.R.: Modeling in Event-B: System and Software Engineering. Cambridge University Press, Cambridge (2013)
2. de Alfaro, L., Henzinger, T.A.: Interface automata. In: Tjoa, A.M., Gruhn, V. (eds.) Proceedings 8th European Software Engineering Conference & 9th ACM SIGSOFT International Symposium Foundations of Software Engineering, pp. 109–120. ACM (2001)
3. Bauer, S.S., Hennicker, R., Wirsing, M.: Interface theories for concurrency and data. Theoret. Comput. Sci. **412**(28), 3101–3121 (2011)
4. ter Beek, M.H., Fantechi, A., Gnesi, S., Mazzanti, F.: An action/state-based model-checking approach for the analysis of communication protocols for service-oriented applications. In: Leue, S., Merino, P. (eds.) FMICS 2007. LNCS, vol. 4916, pp. 133–148. Springer, Heidelberg (2008). https://doi.org/10.1007/978-3-540-79707-4_11
5. Bohrer, B., Platzer, A.: A hybrid, dynamic logic for hybrid-dynamic information flow. In: Dawar, A., Grädel, E. (eds.) Proceedings of 33rd Annual ACM/IEEE Symposium on Logic in Computer Science, pp. 115–124. ACM (2018)
6. Braüner, T.: Hybrid Logic and its Proof-Theory. Applied Logic Series. Springer, Heidelberg (2010). https://doi.org/10.1007/978-94-007-0002-4
7. Farrell, M., Monahan, R., Power, J.F.: An institution for Event-B. In: James, P., Roggenbach, M. (eds.) WADT 2016. LNCS, vol. 10644, pp. 104–119. Springer, Cham (2017). https://doi.org/10.1007/978-3-319-72044-9_8
8. Gorrieri, R., Rensink, A.: Action refinement. In: Bergstra, J.A., Ponse, A., Smolka, S.A. (eds.) Handbook of Process Algebra, pp. 1047–1147. Elsevier, Amsterdam (2000)
9. Groote, J.F., Mousavi, M.R.: Modeling and Analysis of Communicating Systems. MIT Press, Cambridge (2014)
10. Harel, D., Kozen, D., Tiuryn, J.: Dynamic Logic. MIT Press, Cambridge (2000)
11. Hennicker, R., Madeira, A., Knapp, A.: A hybrid dynamic logic for event/data-based systems (2019). https://arxiv.org/abs/1902.03074
12. Knapp, A., Mossakowski, T., Roggenbach, M., Glauer, M.: An institution for simple UML state machines. In: Egyed, A., Schaefer, I. (eds.) FASE 2015. LNCS, vol. 9033, pp. 3–18. Springer, Heidelberg (2015). https://doi.org/10.1007/978-3-662-46675-9_1
13. Lamport, L.: Specifying Systems: The TLA+ Language and Tools for Hardware and Software Engineers. Addison-Wesley, Boston (2003)
14. Lynch, N.A.: Input/output automata: basic, timed, hybrid, probabilistic, dynamic, …. In: Amadio, R.M., Lugiez, D. (eds.) CONCUR 2003. LNCS, vol. 2761, pp. 191–192. Springer, Heidelberg (2003). https://doi.org/10.1007/978-3-540-45187-7_12
15. Madeira, A., Barbosa, L.S., Hennicker, R., Martins, M.A.: A logic for the stepwise development of reactive systems. Theoret. Comput. Sci. **744**, 78–96 (2018)
16. Object Management Group: Unified Modeling Language 2.5. Standard formal/2015-03-01, OMG (2015)
17. Poizat, P., Royer, J.C.: A formal architectural description language based on symbolic transition systems and modal logic. J. Univ. Comp. Sci. **12**(12), 1741–1782 (2006)
18. Sannella, D., Tarlecki, A.: Toward formal development of programs from algebraic specifications: implementations revisited. Acta Inf. **25**(3), 233–281 (1988)
19. Sannella, D., Tarlecki, A.: Foundations of Algebraic Specification and Formal Software Development. EATCS Monographs in Theoretical Computer Science. Springer, Heidelberg (2012). https://doi.org/10.1007/978-3-642-17336-3

8

Checking Observational Purity
of Procedures

Himanshu Arora[1], Raghavan Komondoor[1], and G. Ramalingam[2(⊠)]

[1] Indian Institute of Science, Bangalore, India
{himanshua,raghavan}@iisc.ac.in
[2] Microsoft Research, Bellevue, WA, USA
grama@microsoft.com

Abstract. Verifying whether a procedure is *observationally pure* (that is, it always returns the same result for the same input argument) is challenging when the procedure uses mutable (private) global variables, e.g., for memoization, and when the procedure is recursive.

We present a deductive verification approach for this problem. Our approach encodes the procedure's code as a logical formula, with recursive calls being modeled using a mathematical function symbol *assuming that the procedure is observationally pure*. Then, a theorem prover is invoked to check whether this logical formula agrees with the function symbol referred to above in terms of input-output behavior for all arguments. We prove the soundness of this approach.

We then present a conservative approximation of the first approach that reduces the verification problem to one of checking whether a quantifier-free formula is satisfiable and prove the soundness of the second approach.

We evaluate our approach on a set of realistic examples, using the Boogie intermediate language and theorem prover. Our evaluation shows that the invariants are easy to construct manually, and that our approach is effective at verifying observationally pure procedures.

1 Introduction

A procedure in an imperative programming language is said to be *observationally pure* (OP) if for each specific argument value it has a specific return value, across all possible sequences of calls to the procedure, irrespective of what other code runs between these calls. In other words, the input-output behavior of an OP procedure mimics a mathematical function.

A deterministic procedure that does not read any pre-existing state other than its arguments is trivially OP. However, it is common for procedures to update and read global variables, typically for performance optimization, while still being OP. In this paper, we focus on the problem of checking observational purity of procedures that read and write global variables, especially in the presence of recursion, which makes the problem harder.

```
 1
 2  int g := −1;
 3  int lastN := 0;
 4  int factCache( int n) {
 5    if(n <= 1) {
 6      result := 1;
 7    } else if (g != −1 && n == lastN) {
 8      result := g;
 9    } else {
10      g = n * factCache( n − 1 );
11      lastN = n;
12      result := g;
13    }
14    return result;
15  }
```

Listing 1.1. Procedure factCache: returns n!, and memoizes most recent result.

Motivating Example. We use procedure 'factCache' in Listing 1.1 as our running example. It returns **n**! for a given argument **n**, and caches the return value of the most recent call. It uses two *private global* variables, g and lastN, to implement the caching. g is initialized to −1. After the first call to the procedure onwards, g stores the return value of the most recent call, and lastN stores the argument of the most recent call. Clearly this procedure is OP, and mimics the input-output behavior of a factorial procedure that does not cache any results.

Proposed Approach. Our approach is based on Floyd-Hoare logic, which typically requires a specification of the procedure to be provided. One candidate specification would be a full functional specification of the procedure. If the user specifies that factCache realizes n!, then the verifier could replace Line 10 in the code with 'g = n * (n − 1)!'. This, on paper, is sufficient to assert that Line 12 always assigns n! to result. However, to establish that Line 8 also does the same, an invariant would need to be provided that describes the possible values of g before an invocation to the procedure. In our example, a suitable invariant would be '(g = −1) ∨ (g = lastN!)'. The verifier would also need to verify that at the procedure's exit the invariant is re-established. Lines 10–12, with the recursive call replaced by (n − 1)!, suffices on paper to re-establish the invariant.

The candidate approach described above, while plausible, suffers from two weaknesses. First, a mathematical specification of the function being computed may be complex and non-trivial to write. (Note, for example, that factCache is defined for negative integers while factorial is not. Thus, the previous candidate specification is actually incorrect for this edge case.) Second, the underlying theorem prover would need to prove complex arithmetic properties, e.g., that n * (n − 1)! is equal to n!. Complex proofs such as this may be beyond the scope of many existing theorem provers.

Our key insight is to sidestep the challenges mentioned by introducing a function symbol, say *factCache*, and replacing the recursive call for the purposes of verification with this function symbol. (Note that we reuse the same symbol for two purposes, which may be slightly confusing here. One denotes the procedure name, while the other denotes a function symbol for use in a logical formula. The italicized name here denotes the function symbol.) Intuitively, *factCache* represents the mathematical function that the given procedure mimics *if* the procedure is OP. In our example, Line 10 would become 'g = n * *factCache*(n − 1)'. This step needs no human involvement. The approach needs an invariant; however, in a novel manner, we allow the invariant also to refer to *factCache*. In our example, a suitable invariant would be '(g = −1) ∨ (g = lastN * *factCache*(lastN − 1))'. This sort of invariant is relatively easy to construct; e.g., a human could arrive at it just by looking at Line 2 and with a local reasoning on Lines 10 and 11. Given this invariant, (a) a theorem prover could infer that the condition in Line 7 implies that Line 8 necessarily copies the value of 'n * *factCache*(n − 1)' into 'result'. Due to the transformation to Line 10 mentioned above, (b) the theorem prover can infer that Line 12 also does the same. Note that since these two expressions are syntactically identical, a theorem prover can easily establish that they are equal in value. Finally, since Line 6 is reached under a different condition than Lines 8 and 12, the verifier has finished establishing that the procedure always returns the same expression in n for any given value of n.

Similarly, using the modified Line 10 mentioned above and from Line 11, the prover can re-establish that g is equal to 'lastN * *factCache*(lastN − 1)' when control reaches Line 12. Hence, the necessary step of proving the given invariant to be a valid invariant is also complete.

Note, the effectiveness of the approach depends on the nature of the given invariant. For instance, if the given invariant was '(g = −1) ∨ (g = lastN!)', which is also technically correct, then the theorem prover may not be able to establish that in Lines 8 and 12 the variable 'g' always stores the same expression in n. However, it is our claim that in fact it is the invariant '(g = − 1) ∨ (g = lastN * *factCache*(lastN − 1))' that is easier to infer by a human or by a potential tool, as justified by us two paragraphs above.

Salient Aspects of Our Approach. This paper makes two significant contributions. First, it tackles the circularity problem that arises due to the use of a presumed-to-be OP procedure in assertions and invariants and the use of these invariants in proving the procedure to be OP. This requires us to prove the soundness of an approach that *simultaneously* verifies observational purity as well the validity of invariants (as they cannot be decoupled).

Secondly, we show that a direct approach to this verification problem (which we call the existential approach) reduces it to a problem of verifying that a logical formula is a tautology. The structure of the generated formula, however, makes the resulting theorem prover instances hard. We show how a conservative approximation can be used to convert this hard problem into an easier problem of checking satisfiability of a quantifier-free formula, which is something within the scope of state-of-the-art theorem provers.

The most closely related previous approaches are by Barnett et al. [1,2], and by Naumann [3]. These approaches check observational purity of procedures that maintain mutable global state. However, none of these approaches use a function

```
  L ∈ Lib   ::= g̅ ̅:̅=̅ ̅c̅ P̅
  P ∈ Proc  ::= p (x) { S; return y }
  S ∈ Stmt  ::= x := e | x := p(y) | S ; S | if (e) then S else S
  e ∈ Expr  ::= c | x | e op e | unop e
 op ∈ Ops   ::= + | - | / | * | % | > | < | == | ∧ | ∨
unop ∈ UnOps ::= ¬
  x, y ∈ LocalId ∪ GlobalId, g ∈ GlobalId, c ∈ 𝒱, p ∈ ProcId
```

Fig. 1. Programming language syntax and meta-variables

symbol in place of recursive calls or within invariants. Therefore, it is not clear that these approaches can verify recursive procedures. Barnett et al., in fact, state "there is a circularity - it would take a delicate argument, and additional conditions, to avoid unsoundness in this case". To the best of our knowledge ours is the first paper to show that it is feasible to check observational purity of procedures that maintain mutable global state for optimization purposes and that make use of recursion.

Being able to verify that a procedure is OP has many potential applications. The most obvious one is that OP procedures can be memoized. That is, input-output pairs can be recorded in a table, and calls to the procedure can be elided whenever an argument is seen more than once. This would not change the semantics of the overall program that calls the procedure, because the procedure always returns the same value for the same argument (and mutates only private global variables). Another application is that if a loop contains a call to an OP procedure, then the loop can be parallelized (provided the procedure is modified to access and update its private global variables in a single atomic operation).

The rest of this paper is structured as follows. Section 2 introduces the core programming language that we address. Section 3 provides formal semantics for our language, as well as definitions of invariants and observational purity. Section 4 describes our approach formally. Section 5 discusses an approach for generating an invariant automatically in certain cases. Section 6 describes evaluation of our approach on a few realistic examples. Section 7 describes related work. More details about the proofs and the examples can be found in [4].

2   Language Syntax

In this paper, we assume that the input to the purity checker is a library consisting of one or more procedures, with shared state consisting of one or more variables that are private to the library. We refer to these variables as "global" variables to indicate that they retain their values across multiple invocations of the library procedures, but they cannot be accessed or modified by procedures outside the library (that is, the clients of the library).

In Fig. 1, we present the syntax of a simple programming language that we address in this paper. Given the foundational focus of this work, we keep the programming language very simple, but the ideas we present can be generalized. A `return` statement is required in each procedure, and is permitted only as the last statement of the procedure. The language does not contain any looping construct. Loops can be modelled as recursive procedures. The formal parameters of a procedure are readonly and cannot be modified within the procedure. We omit types from the language. We permit only variables of primitive types. In particular, the language does not allow pointers or dynamic memory allocation. Note that expressions are pure (that is, they have no side effects) in this language, and a procedure call is not allowed in an expression. Each procedure call is modelled as a separate statement.

For simplicity of presentation, without loss of conceptual generality, we assume that the library consists of a single (possibly recursive) procedure, with a single formal parameter. In the sequel, we will use the symbol P (as a metavariable) to represent this library procedure, p (as a metavariable) to represent the *name* of this procedure, and will assume that the name of the formal parameter is n. If the procedure is of the form "p (n) { S; return r }", we refer to r as the *return* variable, and refer to "S; return r" as the *procedure body* and denote it as body(P). The library also contains, outside of the procedure's code, a sequence of initializing declarations of the global variables used in the procedure, of the form "g1 := c1; ...; gN := cN". These initializations are assumed to be performed once during any execution of the client application, just before the first call to the procedure P is placed by the client application.

Throughout this paper we use the word 'procedure' to refer to the library procedure P, and use the word 'function' to refer to a mathematical function.

3 A Semantic Definition of Purity

In this section, we formalize the input-output semantics of the procedure P as a relation $\leadsto_P$, where $n \leadsto_P r$ indicates that an invocation of P with input n may return a result of r. The procedure is defined to be observationally pure if the relation $\leadsto_P$ is a (partial) function: that is, if $n \leadsto_P r_1$ and $n \leadsto_P r_2$, then $r_1 = r_2$.

The object of our analysis is a single-procedure library, not the entire (client) application. (Our approach can be generalized to handle multi-procedure libraries.) The result of our analysis is valid for any client program that uses the procedure/library. The only assumptions we make are: (a) The shared state used by the library (the global variables) are private to the library and cannot be modified by the rest of the program, and (b) The client invokes the library procedures sequentially: no concurrent or overlapping invocations of the library procedures by a concurrent client are permitted.

The following semantic formalism is motivated by the above observations. It can be seen as the semantics of the so-called "most general sequential client" of procedure P, which is the program: `while (*)  x = p (random());`. The executions (of P) produced by this program include all possible executions (of P) produced by all sequential clients.

Let G denote the set of global variables. Let L denote the set of local variables. Let $\mathcal{V}$ denote the set of numeric values (that the variables can take). An element

$$[\text{ASSIGN-LOCAL}] \ \frac{\mathbf{x} \in L \quad (\rho_\ell \uplus \rho_g, \mathbf{e}) \Downarrow v}{((\mathbf{x} := \mathbf{e}; \ \mathbf{S}, \rho_\ell)\gamma, \rho_g) \to_{\text{P}} ((\mathbf{S}, \rho_\ell[\mathbf{x} \mapsto v])\gamma, \rho_g)}$$

$$[\text{ASSIGN-GLOBAL}] \ \frac{\mathbf{x} \in G \quad (\rho_\ell \uplus \rho_g, \mathbf{e}) \Downarrow v}{((\mathbf{x} := \mathbf{e}; \ \mathbf{S}, \rho_\ell)\gamma, \rho_g) \to_{\text{P}} ((\mathbf{S}, \rho_\ell)\gamma, \rho_g[\mathbf{x} \mapsto v])}$$

$$[\text{SEQ}] \ (((\mathbf{S}_1; \mathbf{S}_2); \mathbf{S}_3, \rho_\ell)\gamma, \rho_g) \to_{\text{P}} ((\mathbf{S}_1; (\mathbf{S}_2; \mathbf{S}_3), \rho_\ell)\gamma, \rho_g)$$

$$[\text{IF-TRUE}] \ \frac{(\rho_\ell \uplus \rho_g, \mathbf{e}) \Downarrow \mathbf{true}}{(((\mathbf{if} \ (\mathbf{e}) \ \mathbf{then} \ \mathbf{S}_1 \mathbf{else} \ \mathbf{S}_2); \ \mathbf{S}_3, \rho_\ell)\gamma, \rho_g) \to_{\text{P}} ((\mathbf{S}_1; \ \mathbf{S}_3, \rho_\ell)\gamma, \rho_g)}$$

$$[\text{IF-FALSE}] \ \frac{(\rho_\ell \uplus \rho_g, \mathbf{e}) \Downarrow \mathbf{false}}{(((\mathbf{if} \ (\mathbf{e}) \ \mathbf{then} \ \mathbf{S}_1 \ \mathbf{else} \ \mathbf{S}_2); \ \mathbf{S}_3, \rho_\ell)\gamma, \rho_g) \to_{\text{P}} ((\mathbf{S}_2; \ \mathbf{S}_3, \rho_\ell)\gamma, \rho_g)}$$

$$[\text{CALL}] \ \frac{(\rho_\ell \uplus \rho_g, \mathbf{e}) \Downarrow v \quad \mathbf{P} = p(\mathbf{n}) \ \mathbf{S}_1}{((\mathbf{y} := p(\mathbf{e}); \ \mathbf{S}_2, \rho_\ell)\gamma, \rho_g) \to_{\text{P}} ((\mathbf{S}_1, [n \mapsto v])(\mathbf{y} := p(\mathbf{e}); \ \mathbf{S}_2, \rho_\ell)\gamma, \rho_g)}$$

$$[\text{RETURN}] \ \frac{(\rho_\ell \uplus \rho_g, \mathbf{r}) \Downarrow v}{((\mathbf{return} \ \mathbf{r}, \rho_\ell)(\mathbf{y} := p(\mathbf{e}); \ \mathbf{S}, \rho_\ell')\gamma, \rho_g) \to_{\text{P}} (\mathbf{S}, \rho_\ell'[\mathbf{y} \mapsto v])\gamma, \rho_g)}$$

$$[\text{TOP-LEVEL-CALL}] \ \frac{\mathbf{B} = \text{body}(\mathbf{P}) \quad v \in \mathcal{V}}{([], \rho_g) \to_{\text{P}} ([(\mathbf{B}, [n \mapsto v])], \rho_g)}$$

$$[\text{TOP-LEVEL-RETURN}] \ \frac{}{([(\mathbf{return} \ \mathbf{r}, \rho_\ell)], \rho_g) \to_{\text{P}} ([], \rho_g)}$$

Fig. 2. A small-step operational semantics for our language, represented as a relation $\sigma_1 \to_{\text{P}} \sigma_2$. A state σ_i is a configuration of the form $((\mathbf{S}, \rho_\ell)\gamma, \rho_g)$ where $\mathbf{S}$ captures statements to be executed in current procedure, ρ_ℓ assigns values to local variables, γ is the call-stack (excluding current procedure), and ρ_g assigns values to global variables.

$\rho_g \in \Sigma_G = G \hookrightarrow \mathcal{V}$ maps global variables to their values. An element $\rho_\ell \in \Sigma_L = L \hookrightarrow \mathcal{V}$ maps local variables to their values. We define a *local continuation* to be a statement sequence ending with a **return** statement. We use a local continuation to represent the part of the procedure body that still remains to be executed. Let Σ_C represent the set of local continuations. The set of runtime states (or simply, *states*) is defined to be $(\Sigma_C \times \Sigma_L)^* \times \Sigma_G$, where the first component represents a runtime stack, and the second component the values of global variables. We denote individual states using symbols $\sigma, \sigma_1, \sigma_i$, etc. The runtime stack is a sequence, each element of which is a pair $(\mathbf{S}, \rho_\ell)$ consisting of the remaining procedure fragment $\mathbf{S}$ to be executed and the values of local variables ρ_ℓ. We write $(\mathbf{S}, \rho_\ell)\gamma$ to indicate a stack where the topmost entry is $(\mathbf{S}, \rho_\ell)$ and γ represents the remaining part of the stack.

We say that a state $((\mathbf{S}, \rho_\ell)\gamma, \rho_g)$ is an *entry-state* if its location is at the procedure entry point (*i.e.*, if $\mathbf{S}$ is the entire body of the procedure), and we say that it is an *exit-state* if its location is at the procedure exit point (*i.e.*, if $\mathbf{S}$ consists of just a **return** statement).

A procedure P determines a single-step execution relation $\rightarrow_\text{P}$, where $\sigma_1 \rightarrow_\text{P}$ σ_2 indicates that execution proceeds from state σ_1 to state σ_2 in a single step. Figure 2 defines this semantics. The semantics of evaluation of a side-effect-free expression is captured by a relation $(\rho, \mathsf{e}) \Downarrow v$, indicating that the expression e evaluates to value v in an *environment* ρ (by *environment*, we mean an element of $(G \cup L) \hookrightarrow \mathcal{V}$). We omit the definition of this relation, which is straightforward. We use the notation $\rho_1 \uplus \rho_2$ to denote the union of two disjoint maps ρ_1 and ρ_2.

Note that most rules captures the usual semantics of the language constructs. The last two rules, however, capture the semantics of the most-general sequential client explained previously: when the call stack is empty, a new invocation of the procedure may be initiated (with an arbitrary parameter value).

Note that all the following definitions are parametric over a given procedure P. E.g., we will use the word "execution" as shorthand for "execution of P".

We define an *execution* (of P) to be a sequence of states $\sigma_0\sigma_1 \cdots \sigma_n$ such that $\sigma_i \rightarrow_\text{P} \sigma_{i+1}$ for all $0 \leq i < n$. Let σ_init denote the *initial state* of the library; i.e., this is the element of Σ_G that is induced by the sequence of initializing declarations of the library, namely, "$\mathsf{g1} := \mathsf{c1}; \ldots; \mathsf{gN} := \mathsf{cN}$". We say that an execution $\sigma_0\sigma_1 \cdots \sigma_n$ is a *feasible* execution if $\sigma_0 = \sigma_\text{init}$. Note, intuitively, a feasible execution corresponds to the sequence of states visited within the library across all invocations of the library procedure over the course of a single execution of the most-general client mentioned above; also, since the most-general client supplies a random parameter value to each invocation of P, in general multiple feasible executions of the library may exist.

We define a *trace* (of P) to be a substring $\pi = \sigma_0 \cdots \sigma_n$ of a feasible execution such that: (a) σ_0 is entry-state (b) σ_n is an exit-state, and (c) σ_n corresponds to the return from the invocation represented by σ_0. In other words, a trace is a state sequence corresponding to a single invocation of the procedure. A trace may contain within it nested sub-traces due to recursive calls, which are themselves traces. Given a trace $\pi = \sigma_0 \cdots \sigma_n$, we define $initial(\pi)$ to be σ_0, $final(\pi)$ to be σ_n, $input(\pi)$ to be value of the input parameter in $initial(\pi)$, and $output(\pi)$ to be the value of the return variable in $final(\pi)$.

We define the relation $\leadsto_\text{P}$ to be $\{(input(\pi), output(\pi)) \mid \pi \text{ is a trace of P}\}$.

Definition 1 (Observational Purity). *A procedure* P *is said to be observationally pure if the relation* $\leadsto_\text{P}$ *is a (partial) function: that is, if for all* n, r_1, r_2, *if* $n \leadsto_\text{P} r_1$ *and* $n \leadsto_\text{P} r_2$, *then* $r_1 = r_2$.

Logical Formula and Invariants. Our methodology makes use of *logical formulae* for different purposes, including to express a given *invariant*. Our logical formulae use the local and global variables in the library procedure as free variables, use the same operators as allowed in our language, and make use of universal as well as existential quantification. Given a formula φ, we write $\rho \models \varphi$ to denote that φ evaluates to true when its free variables are assigned values from the environment ρ.

As discussed in Sect. 1, one of our central ideas is to allow the names of the library procedures to be referred to in the invariant; *e.g.*, our running example becomes amenable to our analysis using an invariant such as '(g = −1) ∨ (g = lastN * *factCache*(lastN − 1))'. We therefore allow the use of library procedure names (in our simplified presentation, the name p) as free variables in logical formulae. Correspondingly, we let each environment ρ map each procedure name to a mathematical function in addition to mapping variables to numeric values, and extend the semantics of $\rho \models \varphi$ by substituting the values of both variables and procedure names in φ from the environment ρ.

Given an environment ρ, a procedure name p, and a mathematical function f, we will write $\rho[p \mapsto f]$ to indicate the updated environment that maps p to the value f and maps every other variable x to its original value $\rho[x]$. We will write $(\rho, f) \models \varphi$ to denote that $\rho[p \mapsto f] \models \varphi$.

Given a state $\sigma = ((\mathsf{S}, \rho_\ell)\gamma, \rho_g)$, we define env($\sigma$) to be $\rho_\ell \uplus \rho_g$, and given a state $\sigma = ([], \rho_g)$, we define env(σ) to be just ρ_g. We write $(\sigma, f) \models \varphi$ to denote that $(\mathrm{env}(\sigma), f) \models \varphi$. For any execution or trace π, we write $(\pi, f) \models \varphi$ if for every entry-state and exit-state σ in π, $(\sigma, f) \models \varphi$. We now introduce another definition of observational purity.

Definition 2 (Observational Purity wrt an Invariant). *Given an invariant φ^{inv}, a library procedure* P *is said to satisfy* pure(φ^{inv}) *if there exists a function f such that for every trace π of* P, *output(π) = f(input(π)) and $(\pi, f) \models \varphi^{inv}$.*

It is easy to see that if procedure P satisfies pure(φ^{inv}) wrt any given candidate invariant φ^{inv}, then P is observationally pure as per Definition 1.

4   Checking Purity Using a Theorem Prover

In this section we provide two different approaches that, given a procedure P and a candidate invariant φ^{inv}, use a theorem prover to check conservatively whether procedure P satisfies pure(φ^{inv}).

4.1   Verification Condition Generation

We first describe an adaptation of standard verification-condition generation techniques (*e.g.*, see [5]) that we use as a common first step in both our approaches. Given a procedure P, a candidate invariant φ^{inv}, our goal is to compute a pair $(\varphi^{post}, \varphi^{vc})$ where φ^{post} is a postcondition describing the state that exists after an execution of body(P) starting from a state that satisfies φ^{inv}, and φ^{vc} is a verification-condition that must hold true for the execution to satisfy its invariants and assertions.

We first transform the procedure body as below to create an internal representation that is input to the postcondition and verification condition generator. In the internal representation, we allow the following extra forms of statements (with their usual meaning): `havoc(x)`, `assume e`, and `assert e`.

1. For any assignment statement "x := e" where e contains x, we introduce a new temporary variable t and replace the assignment statement with "t := e; x := t".
2. For every procedure invocation "x := $p(\text{y})$", we first ensure that y is a local variable (by introducing a temporary if needed). We then replace the statement by the code fragment "assert φ^{inv}; havoc(g1); ... havoc(gN); assume $\varphi^{inv} \wedge$ x = $p(\text{y})$", where g1 to gN are the global variables.
   Note that the procedure call has been eliminated, and replaced with an "assume" expression that refers to the function symbol p. In other words, there are no procedure calls in the transformed procedure.
3. We replace the "return x" statement by "assert φ^{inv}". Note that we intentionally do *not* assert that the return value equals $p(n)$.

Let $\text{TB}(\text{P}, \varphi^{inv})$ denote the transformed body of procedure P obtained as above.

$$
\begin{aligned}
&\text{POST}(\varphi^{pre}, \text{x := e}) &&= (\exists \text{x}.\varphi^{pre}) \wedge (\text{x = e}) \ (\text{if x} \notin \text{vars(e)}) \\
&\text{POST}(\varphi^{pre}, \text{havoc(x)}) &&= \exists \text{x}.\varphi^{pre} \\
&\text{POST}(\varphi^{pre}, \text{assume e}) &&= \varphi^{pre} \wedge \text{e} \\
&\text{POST}(\varphi^{pre}, \text{assert e}) &&= \varphi^{pre} \\
&\text{POST}(\varphi^{pre}, \text{S}_1; \text{S}_2) &&= \text{POST}(\text{POST}(\varphi^{pre}, \text{S}_1), \text{S}_2) \\
&\text{POST}(\varphi^{pre}, \text{if e then S}_1 \text{ else S}_2) &&= \text{POST}(\varphi^{pre} \wedge \text{e}, \text{S}_1) \vee \text{POST}(\varphi^{pre} \wedge \neg \text{e}, \text{S}_2)
\end{aligned}
$$

$$
\begin{aligned}
&\text{VC}(\varphi^{pre}, \text{assert e}) &&= (\varphi^{pre} \Rightarrow e) \\
&\text{VC}(\varphi^{pre}, \text{S}_1; \text{S}_2) &&= \text{VC}(\varphi^{pre}, \text{S}_1) \wedge \text{VC}(\text{POST}(\varphi^{pre}, \text{S}_1), \text{S}_2) \\
&\text{VC}(\varphi^{pre}, \text{if e then S}_1 \text{ else S}_2) &&= \text{VC}(\varphi^{pre} \wedge \text{e}, \text{S}_1) \wedge \text{VC}(\varphi^{pre} \wedge \neg \text{e}, \text{S}_2) \\
&\text{VC}(\varphi^{pre}, \text{S}) &&= \text{true}(\text{for all other S})
\end{aligned}
$$

$$
\text{POSTVC}(\text{P}, \varphi^{inv}) = (\text{POST}(\varphi^{inv}, \text{TB}(\text{P}, \varphi^{inv})), \text{VC}(\varphi^{inv}, \text{TB}(\text{P}, \varphi^{inv})) \wedge (\text{INIT}(\text{P}) \Rightarrow \varphi^{inv}))
$$

Fig. 3. Generation of verification-condition and postcondition.

We then compute postconditions as formally described in Fig. 3. This lets us compute for each program point ℓ in the procedure, a condition φ_ℓ that describes what we expect to hold true when execution reaches ℓ if we start executing the procedure in a state satisfying φ^{inv} and if every recursive invocation of the procedure also terminates in a state satisfying φ^{inv}. We compute this using the standard rules for the postcondition of a statement. For an assignment statement "x := e", we use existential quantification over x to represent the value of x prior to the execution of the statement. If we rename these existentially quantified variables with unique new names, we can lift all the existential quantifiers to the outermost level. When transformed thus, the condition φ_ℓ takes the form $\exists x_1 \cdots x_n.\varphi$, where φ is quantifier-free and $x_1, \cdots, x_n$ denote intermediate values of variables along the execution path from procedure-entry to program point ℓ.

We compute a verification condition φ^{vc} that represents the conditions we must check to ensure that an execution through the procedure satisfies its obligations: namely, that the invariant holds true at every call-site and at procedure-exit. Let ℓ denote a call-site or the procedure-exit. We need to check that

```
1   g := -1;
2   lastN := 0;
3   factCache (n) {
4     if(n <= 1) {
5        result := 1;
6     } else if (g != -1 && n == lastN) {
7        result := g;
8     } else {
9        t1 := n-1;
10       // t2 := factCache(t1);
11       assert φ^{inv};
12       havoc (g); havoc (lastN);
13       assume φ^{inv}∧ (t2 = factCache(t1));
14       g := n * t2;
15       lastN := n;
16       result := g;
17     }
18     // return result;
19     assert φ^{inv};
20  }
```

Listing 1.2. Procedure factCache from Listing 1.1 transformed to incorporate a supplied candidate invariant φ^{inv}.

$\varphi_\ell \Rightarrow \varphi^{inv}$ holds. Thus, the generated verification condition essentially consists of the conjunction of this check over all call-sites and procedure-exit.

Finally, the function POSTVC computes the postcondition and verification condition for the entire procedure as shown in Fig. 3. (Thus, it returns a pair of formulae.) Note that this function also adds the check that the initial state must satisfy φ^{inv} to the verification condition (as the basis condition for induction). INIT(P) is basically the formula "g1 = c1 $\wedge \ldots$ gN = cN" (see Sect. 2).

Example. We now illustrate the postcondition and verification condition generated from our factorial example presented in Listing 1.1. Listing 1.2 shows the example expressed in our language and transformed as described earlier (using function TB), using a supplied candidate invariant φ^{inv}.

Figure 4 illustrates the computation of postcondition and verification condition from this transformed example. In this figure, we use φ_{cs}^{pre} to denote the precondition computed to hold just before the recursive callsite, and φ_{cs}^{post} to denote the postcondition computed to hold just after the recursive callsite. The postcondition φ^{post} (at the end of the procedure body) is itself a disjunction of three path-conditions representing execution through the three different paths in the program. In this illustration, we have simplified the logical conditions by omitting useless existential quantifications (that is, any quantification of the form $\exists x.\psi$ where x does not occur in ψ). Note that the existentially quantified g and lastN in φ_{cs}^{post} denote the values of these globals before the recursive call. Similarly, the existentially quantified g and lastN in φ_3^{path} denote the values of these globals when the recursive call terminates, while the free variables g and lastN denote the final values of these globals.

$$\text{INIT}(\text{P}) = (\text{g = -1}) \wedge (\text{lastN = 0})$$

$$\varphi_1^{path} = \varphi^{inv} \wedge (\text{n <= 1}) \wedge (\text{result = 1})$$

$$\varphi_2^{path} = \varphi^{inv} \wedge \neg(\text{n <= 1}) \wedge (\text{g != 1}) \wedge (\text{n = lastN}) \wedge (\text{result = g})$$

$$\varphi_{cs}^{pre} = \varphi^{inv} \wedge \neg(\text{n <= 1}) \wedge \neg((\text{g != 1}) \wedge (\text{n = lastN})) \wedge (\text{t1 = n-1})$$

$$\varphi_{cs}^{post} = (\exists\text{g}\exists\text{lastN } \varphi_{cs}^{pre}) \wedge \varphi^{inv} \wedge (\text{t2 = } factCache\,(\text{t1}))$$

$$\varphi_3^{path} = (\exists\text{g}\exists\text{lastN } \varphi_{cs}^{post}) \wedge (\text{g = n * t2}) \wedge (\text{last N = n}) \wedge (\text{result = g})$$

$$\varphi^{post} = \varphi_1^{path} \vee \varphi_2^{path} \vee \varphi_3^{path}$$

$$\varphi^{vc} = (\varphi_{cs}^{pre} \Rightarrow \varphi^{inv}) \wedge (\varphi^{post} \Rightarrow \varphi^{inv}) \wedge (\text{INIT}(\text{P}) \Rightarrow \varphi^{inv})$$

Fig. 4. The different formulae computed from the procedure in Listing 1.2 by our post-condition and verification-condition computation.

4.2 Approach 1: Existential Approach

Let P be a procedure with input parameter n and return variable r. Let $\text{POSTVC}(\text{P}, \varphi^{inv}) = (\varphi^{post}, \varphi^{vc})$. Let ψ^e denote the formula $\varphi^{vc} \wedge (\varphi^{post} \Rightarrow (r = p(n)))$. Let $\overline{x}$ denote the sequence of all free variables in ψ^e except for p. We define $\text{EA}(\text{P}, \varphi^{inv})$ to be the formula $\forall\overline{x}.\psi^e$.

In this approach, we use a theorem prover to check whether $\text{EA}(\text{P}, \varphi^{inv})$ is satisfiable. As shown by the following theorem, satisfiability of $\text{EA}(\text{P}, \varphi^{inv})$ establishes that P satisfies $\text{pure}(\varphi^{inv})$.

Theorem 1. *A procedure* P *satisfies* $\text{pure}(\varphi^{inv})$ *if* $\exists p.\text{EA}(\text{P}, \varphi^{inv})$ *is a tautology (which holds iff* $\text{EA}(\text{P}, \varphi^{inv})$ *is satisfiable).*

Proof. Note that p is the only free variable in $\text{EA}(\text{P}, \varphi^{inv})$. Assume that $[p \mapsto f]$ is a satisfying assignment for $\forall\overline{x}.\psi^e$. We show that for every feasible execution π: (P1) $(\pi, f) \vdash \varphi^{inv}$, and (P2) for every trace π' inside π, $output(\pi') = f(input(\pi'))$. This implies that P satisfies $\text{pure}(\varphi^{inv})$.

In particular, for any feasible execution π, we prove by induction over the execution steps in π that

1. For any entry state σ in π, $(\sigma, f) \vdash \varphi^{inv}$.
2. For any exit state σ in π, $(\sigma, f) \vdash \varphi^{inv}$.
3. For any exit state σ in π, if it is the exit state of a trace π', then $output(\pi') = f(input(\pi'))$.

If the above properties fail to hold, we can identify a trace π' corresponding to the first such failure. It can be shown that the sequence of states visited by this trace, when substituted for $\overline{x}$, are a witness that $[p \mapsto f]$ is not a satisfying assignment for $\forall\overline{x}.\psi^e$. This is a contradiction of our original assumption.

Please see [4] for more details of the proof. $\square$

4.3   Approach 2: Impurity Witness Approach

The existential approach presented in the previous section has a drawback. Checking satisfiability of $\text{EA}(\text{P}, \varphi^{inv})$ is hard because it contains universal quantifiers and existing theorem provers do not work well enough for this approach. We now present an approximation of the existential approach that is easier to use with existing theorem provers. This new approach, which we will refer to as the impurity witness approach, reduces the problem to that of checking whether a quantifier-free formula is unsatisfiable, which is better suited to the capabilities of state-of-the-art theorem provers. This approach focuses on finding a counterexample to show that the procedure is impure or it violates the candidate invariant.

Let P be a procedure with input parameter n and return variable r. Let $\text{POSTVC}(\text{P}, \varphi^{inv}) = (\varphi^{post}, \varphi^{vc})$. Let φ_α^{post} denote the formula obtained by replacing every free variable x other than p in φ^{post} by a new free variable x_α. Define φ_β^{post} similarly. Define $\text{IW}(\text{P}, \varphi^{inv})$ to be the formula $(\neg\varphi^{vc}) \vee (\varphi_\alpha^{post} \wedge \varphi_\beta^{post} \wedge (n_\alpha = n_\beta) \wedge (r_\alpha \neq r_\beta))$.

The impurity witness approach checks whether $\text{IW}(\text{P}, \varphi^{inv})$ is satisfiable. This can be done by separately checking whether $\neg\varphi^{vc}$ is satisfiable and whether $(\varphi_\alpha^{post} \wedge \varphi_\beta^{post} \wedge (n_\alpha = n_\beta) \wedge (r_\alpha \neq r_\beta))$ is satisfiable. As formally defined, φ^{vc} and φ^{post} contain embedded existential quantifications. As explained earlier, these existential quantifiers can be moved to the outside after variable renaming and can be omitted for a satisfiability check. (A formula of the form $\exists \overline{x}.\psi$ is satisfiable iff ψ is satisfiable.) As usual, these existential quantifiers refer to intermediate values of variables along an execution path. Finding a satisfying assignment to these variables essentially identifies a possible execution path (that satisfies some other property).

Theorem 2. *A procedure* P *satisfies* $\text{pure}(\varphi^{inv})$ *if* $\text{IW}(\text{P}, \varphi^{inv})$ *is unsatisfiable.*

Proof. We say that two traces disagree if they receive the same argument value but return different values. We say that a pair of feasible executions (π_1, π_2) is an *impurity witness* if there is a trace π_a in π_1 and a trace π_b in π_2 such that π_a and π_b disagree.

A trace is said to be compatible with a function f (and vice versa) if the trace's input-output behavior matches that of the function. An execution is said to be compatible with a function (and vice versa) if every trace in the execution is compatible with the function. We say that a feasible execution π *strongly satisfies* φ^{inv} if for every function f that is compatible with π, $(\pi, f) \models \varphi^{inv}$.

We prove the theorem using the following lemmas: if $\text{IW}(\text{P}, \varphi^{inv})$ is unsatisfiable, then Lemmas 2 and 3 imply that the preconditions of Lemma 1 hold and, hence, P satisfies $\text{pure}(\varphi^{inv})$.

1. If there exists no impurity witness, and every feasible execution strongly satisfies φ^{inv}, then P satisfies $\text{pure}(\varphi^{inv})$.
2. If a feasible execution π that does not strongly satisfy φ^{inv} exists, $\text{IW}(\text{P}, \varphi^{inv})$ is satisfiable.

3. If an impurity witness exists, then $\text{IW}(\text{P}, \varphi^{inv})$ is satisfiable.

1 is straightforward.

For 2, we use a "minimal" feasible execution π that does not strongly satisfy φ^{inv} to construct a satisfying assignment to $\neg\varphi^{vc}$.

For 3, we use a "minimal" impurity witness to construct a satisfying assignment to $(\varphi_\alpha^{post} \wedge \varphi_\beta^{post} \wedge (n_\alpha = n_\beta) \wedge (r_\alpha \neq r_\beta))$.

Please see [4] for more details of the proof.   □

5   Generating the Invariant

We now describe a simple but reasonably effective semi-algorithm for generating a candidate invariant automatically from the given procedure. Our approach of Sect. 4 can be used with a manually provided invariant or the candidate invariant generated by this semi-algorithm (whenever it terminates).

The invariant-generation approach is iterative and computes a sequence of progressively weaker candidate invariants $I_0, I_1, \cdots$ and terminates if and when $I_m \equiv I_{m+1}$, at which point I_m is returned as the candidate invariant. The initial candidate invariant I_0 captures the initial values of the global variable. In iteration k, we apply a procedure similar to the one described in Sect. 4 and compute the strongest conditions that hold true at every program point if the execution of the procedure starts in a state satisfying I_{k-1} and if every recursive invocation terminates in a state satisfying I_{k-1}. We then take the disjunction of the conditions computed at the points before the recursive call-sites and at the end of the procedure, and existentially quantify all local variables. We refer to the resulting formula as $\text{NEXT}(I_{k-1}, \text{TB}(\text{P}, I_{k-1}))$. We take the disjunction of this formula with I_{k-1} and simplify it to get I_k.

Figure 5 formalizes this semi-algorithm. Here, we exploit the fact that the `assert` statements are added precisely at every recursive callsite and end of procedure and these are the places where we take the conditions to be disjuncted.

In our running example, I_0 is '$g = -1 \wedge \text{lastN} = 0$'. Applying NEXT to I_0 yields I_0 itself as the pre-condition at the point just before the recursive call-site, and '$(g = -1 \wedge \text{lastN} = 0) \vee g = \text{lastN} * p(\text{lastN} - 1)$' (after certain simplifications) as the pre-condition at the end of the procedure. Therefore, I_1 is '$(g = -1 \wedge \text{lastN} = 0) \vee g = \text{lastN} * p(\text{lastN} - 1)$'. When we apply NEXT to I_1,

---

$I_0 = \text{INIT}(\text{P})$
$I_k = \text{SIMPLIFY}(I_{k-1} \vee \text{NEXT}(I_{k-1}, \text{TB}(\text{P}, I_{k-1})))$

$\text{NEXT}(\varphi^{pre}, \texttt{assert e}) = \exists \ell_1 \cdots \ell_m \varphi^{pre} \text{(where } \ell_1, \cdots, \ell_m \text{ are local variables in } \varphi^{pre})$
$\text{NEXT}(\varphi^{pre}, \text{S}_1; \text{S}_2) \quad = \text{NEXT}(\varphi^{pre}, \text{S}_1) \vee \text{NEXT}(\text{POST}(\varphi^{pre}, \text{S}_1), \text{S}_2)$
$\text{NEXT}(\varphi^{pre}, \texttt{if e then } \text{S}_1 \texttt{ else } \text{S}_2) = \text{NEXT}(\varphi^{pre} \wedge \texttt{e}, \text{S}_1) \vee \text{NEXT}(\varphi^{pre} \wedge \neg\texttt{e}, \text{S}_2)$
$\text{NEXT}(\varphi^{pre}, \text{S}) \quad\quad = \text{false}\text{(for all other S)}$

Fig. 5. Iterative computation of invariant.

the computed pre-conditions are I_1 itself at both the program points mentioned above. Therefore, the approach terminates with I_1 as the candidate invariant.

6 Evaluation

We have implemented our OP checking approach as a prototype using the Boogie framework [6], and have evaluated the approach using this implementation on several examples. The objective of this evaluation was primarily a sanity check, to test how our approach does on a set of OP as well as non-OP procedures.

We tried several simple non-OP programs, and our implementation terminated with a "no" answer on all of them. We also tried the approach on several OP procedures: (1) the 'factCache' running example, (2) a version of a factorial procedure that caches all arguments seen so far and their corresponding return values in an array, (3) a version of factorial that caches only the return value for argument value 19 in a scalar variable, (4) a recursive procedure that returns the nth Fibonacci number and caches all its arguments and corresponding return values seen so far in an array, and (5) a "matrix chain multiplication" (MCM) procedure. The last example is based on dynamic programming, and hence naturally uses a table to memoize results for sub-problems. Here, observational purity implies that the procedure always returns the same solution for a given sub-problem, whether a hit was found in the table or not. The appendix of a technical report associated with this paper depicts all the procedures mentioned above as created by us directly in Boogie's language, as well as the invariants that we supplied manually (in SMT2 format).

It is notable that the theorem prover was not able to handle the instances generated by the "existential approach" even for simple examples. The "impurity witness" approach, however, terminated on all the examples mentioned above with the correct answer, with the theorem prover taking less than 1 s on each example. Please see [4] for more information about the examples used in our evaluation.

7 Related Work

The previous work that is most closely related to our work is by Barnett et al. [1, 2]. Their approach is based on the same notion of observational purity as our approach. Their approach is structurally similar to ours, in terms of needing an invariant, and using an inductive check for both the validity of the invariant as well as the uniqueness of return values for a given argument. However, their approach is based on a more complex notion of invariant than our approach, which relates pairs of global states, and does not use a function symbol to represent recursive calls within the procedure. Hence, their approach does not extend readily to recursive procedures; they in fact state that "there is a circularity - it would take a delicate argument, and additional conditions, to avoid unsoundness in this case". Our idea of allowing the function symbol in the invariant to represent the recursive call allows recursive procedures to be checked, and also simplifies the specification of the invariant in many cases.

Cok et al. [7] generalize the work of Barnett et al.'s work, and suggest classifying procedures into categories "pure", "secret", and "query". The "query" procedures are observationally pure. Again, recursive procedures are not addressed.

Naumann [3] proposes a notion of observational purity that is also the same as ours. Their paper gives a rigorous but manual methodology for proving the observational purity of a given procedure. Their methodology is not similar to ours; rather, it is based finding a *weakly pure* procedure that simulates the given procedure as far as externally visible state changes and the return value are concerned. They have no notion of an invariant that uses a function symbol that represents the procedure, and they don't explicitly address the checking of recursive procedures.

There exists a significant body of work on identifying differences between two similar procedures. For instance, differential assertion checking [8] is a representative from this body, and is for checking if two procedures can ever start from the same state but end in different states such that exactly one of the ending states fails a given assertion. Their approach is based on logical reasoning, and accommodates recursive procedures. Our impurity witness approach has some similarity with their approach, because it is based on comparing the given procedure with itself. However, our comparison is stricter, because in our setting, starting with a common argument value but from different global states that are both within the invariant should not cause a difference in the return value. Furthermore, technically our approach is different because we use an invariant that refers to a function symbol that represents the procedure being checked, which is not a feature of their invariants. Partush et al. [9] solve a similar problem as differential assertion checking, but using abstract interpretation instead of logical reasoning.

There is a substantial body of work on checking if a procedure is *pure*, in the sense that it does not modify any objects that existed before the procedure was invoked, and does not modify any global variables. Sălcianu et al. [10] describe a static analysis to check purity and Madhavan et al. [11] present an abstract-interpretation based generalization of this analysis. Various tools exist, such as JML [12] and Spec# [13], that use logical techniques based on annotations to prove procedures as pure. Purity is a more restrictive notion than observational purity; procedures such as our 'factCache' example are observationally pure, but not pure because they use as well as update state that persists between calls to the procedure.

References

1. Barnett, M., Naumann, D.A., Schulte, W., Sun, Q.: 99.44% pure: useful abstractions in specifications. In: ECOOP Workshop on Formal Techniques for Java-like Programs (FTfJP) (2004)
2. Barnett, M., Naumann, D.A., Schulte, W., Sun, Q.: Allowing state changes in specifications. In: Müller, G. (ed.) ETRICS 2006. LNCS, vol. 3995, pp. 321–336. Springer, Heidelberg (2006). https://doi.org/10.1007/11766155_23

3. Naumann, D.A.: Observational purity and encapsulation. Theor. Comput. Sci. **376**(3), 205–224 (2007)
4. Arora, H., Komondoor, R., Ramalingam, G.: Checking observational purity of procedures. CoRR https://arxiv.org/abs/1902.05436 (2019)
5. Flanagan, C., Saxe, J.B.: Avoiding exponential explosion: generating compact verification conditions. In: Conference Record of POPL 2001: The 28th ACM SIGPLAN-SIGACT Symposium on Principles of Programming Languages, London, UK, 17–19 January 2001, pp. 193–205 (2001)
6. Leino, K.R.M.: This is Boogie 2. Manuscript KRML 178(131) (2008)
7. Cok, D.R., Leavens, G.T.: Extensions of the theory of observational purity and a practical design for JML. In: Seventh International Workshop on Specification and Verification of Component-Based Systems (SAVCBS 2008). Number CS-TR-08-07 in Technical report, School of EECS, UCF, vol. 4000 (2008)
8. Lahiri, S.K., McMillan, K.L., Sharma, R., Hawblitzel, C.: Differential assertion checking. In: Proceedings of the 2013 9th Joint Meeting on Foundations of Software Engineering, pp. 345–355. ACM (2013)
9. Partush, N., Yahav, E.: Abstract semantic differencing for numerical programs. In: Logozzo, F., Fähndrich, M. (eds.) SAS 2013. LNCS, vol. 7935, pp. 238–258. Springer, Heidelberg (2013). https://doi.org/10.1007/978-3-642-38856-9_14
10. Sălcianu, A., Rinard, M.: Purity and side effect analysis for Java programs. In: Cousot, R. (ed.) VMCAI 2005. LNCS, vol. 3385, pp. 199–215. Springer, Heidelberg (2005). https://doi.org/10.1007/978-3-540-30579-8_14
11. Madhavan, R., Ramalingam, G., Vaswani, K.: Purity analysis: an abstract interpretation formulation. In: Yahav, E. (ed.) SAS 2011. LNCS, vol. 6887, pp. 7–24. Springer, Heidelberg (2011). https://doi.org/10.1007/978-3-642-23702-7_6
12. Leavens, G.T., et al.: JML reference manual (2008)
13. Barnett, M., Leino, K.R.M., Schulte, W.: The Spec# programming system: an overview. In: Barthe, G., Burdy, L., Huisman, M., Lanet, J.L., Muntean, T. (eds.) CASSIS 2004. LNCS, vol. 3362, pp. 49–69. Springer, Heidelberg (2005). https://doi.org/10.1007/978-3-540-30569-9_3

9

Business Process Privacy Analysis in PLEAK

Aivo Toots[1,2], Reedik Tuuling[1], Maksym Yerokhin[2], Marlon Dumas[2],
Luciano García-Bañuelos[2], Peeter Laud[1], Raimundas Matulevičius[2],
Alisa Pankova[1], Martin Pettai[1], Pille Pullonen[1,2(✉)], and Jake Tom[2]

[1] Cybernetica AS, Tallinn, Estonia
`{aivo.toots,reedik.tuuling,peeter.laud,alisa.pankova,martin.pettai,`
`pille.pullonen}@cyber.ee`
[2] University of Tartu, Tartu, Estonia
`{aivo.toots,maksym.yerokhin,marlon.dumas,luciano.garcia-banuelos,`
`raimundas.matulevicius,pille.pullonen,jake.tom}@ut.ee`

Abstract. PLEAK is a tool to capture and analyze privacy-enhanced
business process models to characterize and quantify to what extent the
outputs of a process leak information about its inputs. PLEAK incorporates an extensible set of analysis plugins, which enable users to inspect
potential leakages at multiple levels of detail.

1 Introduction

Data minimization is a core tenet of the European General Data Protection
Regulation (GDPR) [2]. According to GDPR, usage of private data should be
limited to the purpose for which it has been collected. To verify compliance with
this principle, privacy analysts need to determine who has access to the data and
what private information these data may disclose. Business process models are
a rich source of metadata to support this analysis. Indeed, these models capture
which tasks are performed by whom, what data are taken as input and output
by each task, and what data are exchanged with external actors. Process models
are usually captured using the Business Process Model and Notation (BPMN).

This paper introduces PLEAK[1] – the first tool to analyze privacy-enhanced
BPMN models in order to characterize and quantify to what extent the outputs
of a process leak information about its inputs. The top level (Boolean level,
Sect. 2), tell us whether or not a given data in the process may reveal information
about a given input. The middle level, the qualitative level (Sect. 3), goes further
by indicating which attributes of (or functions over) a given input data object are
potentially leaked by each output, and under what conditions this leakage may
occur. The lower level quantifies to what extent a given output leaks information
about an input, either in terms of a sensitivity measure (Sect. 4) or in terms of
the guessing advantage that an attacker gains by having the output (Sect. 5).

---

[1] https://pleak.io (account: *demo@example.com*, password: *pleakdemo*, manual:
https://pleak.io/wiki/, source code: https://github.com/pleak-tools/).

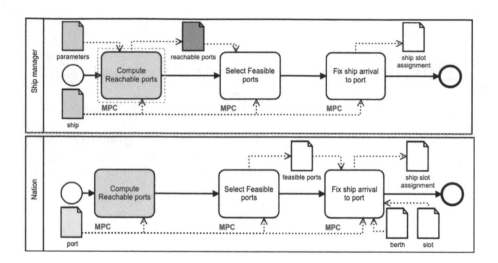

Fig. 1. Aid distribution process

To illustrate the capabilities of PLEAK, we refer to an "aid distribution" process in Fig. 1. This process starts when a nation requests aid from the international community to handle an emergency and a country offers to route a ship to help transport people and/or goods. The goal of the process is to allocate a port and a berth to the ship but not to reveal information about ships that are unable to help or the parameters of the ports. The process uses a type of privacy-enhancing technology (PET) known as secure multiparty computation (MPC). MPC allows participants to perform joint computations such that none of the parties gets to see the data of the other parties, but can learn the output depending on the private inputs. Given a ship, a deadline and the list of ports, task "Compute reachable ports" retrieves the list of ports reachable by the deadline. Tasks with identical names in different pools denote MPC computations carried out jointly by multiple stakeholders. Task "Select feasible ports" retrieves ports with the capacity to host the ship. The third task selects a port, a berth, and a slot for the ship, and discloses them to both participants.

Related Work. We are interested in privacy analysis of business processes and in this space Anica [1] is closest to our work. However, PLEAK's analysis is more fine-grained. Anica allows designers to see that a given object O1 may contain information derived from a sensitive data object O2, but it can neither explain how the data in O2 is derived from O1 (cf. Leaks-When analysis) nor to what extent the data in O2 leaks information from O1 (cf. sensitivity and guessing advantage analysis). In addition, they are interested in security levels and our high level analysis looks at PETs deployed in the process.

2   PE-BPMN Editor and Simple Disclosure Analysis

The model in Fig. 1 is captured Privacy-Enhanced BPMN (PE-BPMN) [7,8]. PE-BPMN uses stereotypes to distinguish used PETs, e.g. MPC or homomorphic encryption, that affect which data is protected in the process. The PE-BPMN editor allows users to attach stereotypes to model elements and to enter the stereotype's parameters where applicable. The editor integrates a checker, which verifies stereotype specific restrictions. For example, that: (1) when a task has an MPC stereotype, there is at least one other "twin" task with the same label in another pool, since an MPC computation involves at least two parties; (2) when one of these tasks is enabled, the other twin tasks is eventually enabled; and (3) the joint computation has at least one input and one output.

Given a valid PE-BPMN model, PLEAK runs a binary privacy analysis, which produces a *simple disclosure report* and data dependency matrix. The disclosure report in Fig. 2 tells us whether or not a stakeholder gets to see a given data object. In the report "V" indicates that a data object (in columns) is visible to a stakeholder (in rows). Marker "H" (hidden) is used for data with cryptographic protection, e.g. encrypted data. Row "shared over" refers to the network service provider, who may also see some of the data (e.g. unencrypted data objects).

#	berth	feasible ports	parameters	port	reachable ports	ship	ship slot assignment	slot
Nation	V	V	-	V	-	-	V	V
Ship manager	-	-	V	-	V	V	V	-
Shared over	-	-	-	-	-	-	-	-

Fig. 2. Simple disclosure report for the aid distribution process in Fig. 1

3 Qualitative Leaks-When Analysis

Leaks-When analysis [3] is a technique that takes as input a SQL workflow and determines, for each (output, input) pair which attributes, if any, of the input object are disclosed by the output object and under which conditions. A SQL workflow is a BPMN process model in which every data object corresponds to a database table, defined by a table schema, and every task is a SQL query that transforms the input tables of the task into its output tables. Figure 3 shows a sample collaborative SQL workflow – a variant of the "aid distribution" example where the disclosure of information about ships to the aid-requesting country is made incrementally. The figure shows the SQL workflow alongside the query corresponding to task "Select reachable ports". All data processing tasks and input data objects are specified analogously.

To perform a Leaks-When analysis, the user selects one or more output data objects and clicks the "SQL LeaksWhen" button. The Leaks-When analysis shows one tab for each output data object and one report for each column in the output table. The report is generated by extracting all runs of the workflow and applying dataflow analysis techniques to each run in order to infer all relevant data dependencies. An example of a leaks-when report (in graphical form) is shown in Fig. 4. The first input to *Filter* is the disclosed value (leaks branch), e.g. the arrival time. The second input (when branch) is the condition of outputting the first input, e.g. that the arrival time is less than the deadline and the ship has the required name. Each Leaks-When report ends with such filter but the rest of the graph aggregates the computations described in SQL.

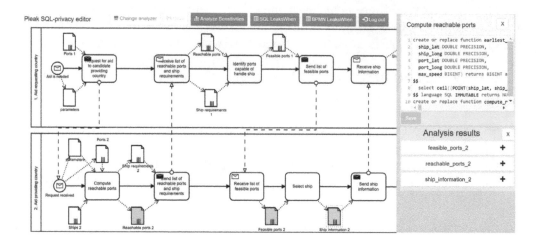

Fig. 3. Aid distribution SQL workflow in PLEAK SQL editor

4   Sensitivity Analysis and Differential Privacy

The *sensitivity of a function* is the expected maximum change in the output, given a change in the input of the function. Sensitivity is the basis for calibrating the amount of noise to be added to prevent leakages on statistical database queries using a differential privacy mechanism [6]. Differential privacy ensures that it is difficult for an attacker, who observes the query output, to distinguish between two input databases that are sufficiently "close" to each other, e.g. differ

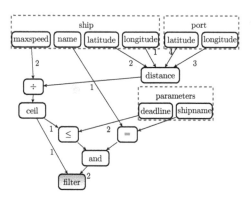

Fig. 4. Sample leaks-when report

in one row. PLEAK tells the user how to sample noise to achieve differential privacy, and how this affects the correctness of the output. PLEAK provides two methods – global and local – to quantify sensitivity of a task in a SQL workflow or of an entire SQL workflow. These methods can be applied to queries that output aggregations (e.g. count, sum, min, max).

Global sensitivity analysis [5] takes as input a database schema and a query, and computes the theoretical bounds for sensitivity, which are suitable for any instance of the database. This shows how the output changes if we add (remove) a row to (from) some input table. The analysis output is a matrix that shows the sensitivity w.r.t. each input table separately. It supports only COUNT queries.

Sometimes, the global sensitivity may be very large or even infinite. *Local sensitivity* analysis is an alternative approach, which requires as input not only a schema and a query, but also a particular instance of the underlying database, and it tells how the output changes with the change *from the given input*. Using the database instance improves the amount of noise needed to ensure differential privacy w.r.t. the number of rows. Moreover, it supports COUNT, SUM, MIN, MAX aggregations, and allows to capture more interesting distances between input tables, such as change in a particular attribute of some row. In PLEAK, we have investigated a particular type of local sensitivity, called *derivative sensitivity* [4], which is in first place adapted to continuous functions, and is closely related to function derivative. PLEAK uses derivative sensitivity to quantify the required amount of noise as described in [4].

An example of derivative sensitivity analysis output is shown in Fig. 5a. It tells that the derivative sensitivity w.r.t. the *Ship* table is 4, and that a differential privacy level of $\varepsilon = 1$ can be achieved using smoothness parameter $\beta = 0.05$. To this end, we would have to add an amount of (Laplacian) noise such that the relative error of the output is 74%. More precisely, if the correct output is y, the noised answer will be between $0.26y$ and $1.74y$ with probability 80%. A tutorial on sensitivity analyzer can be found at https://pleak.io/wiki/sql-derivative-sensitivity-analyser. More examples can be found in the full version of this paper [9].

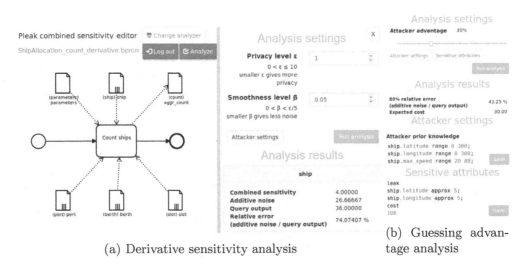

(a) Derivative sensitivity analysis

(b) Guessing advantage analysis

Fig. 5. Examples of quantitative analysis

5   Attacker's Guessing Advantage

While function sensitivity as defined in Sect. 4 can be used directly to compute the noise required to achieve ε-differential privacy, it is in general not clear which ε is good enough, and the "goodness" depends on the data and the query [6]. We want a more standard security measure, such as guessing advantage, defined as the difference between the posterior (after observing the output) and prior (before observing the output) probabilities of attacker guessing the input.

The *guessing advantage* analysis of PLEAK takes as input the desired upper bound on attacker's advantage, which ranges between 0% and 100%. The user specifies particular subset of attributes that the attacker is trying to guess for some data table record, within given precision range. The user may define prior knowledge of the attacker, which is currently expressed as an upper and a lower bound on an attribute. The analyzer internally converts these values to a suitable ε, and computes the noise required to achieve the bound on attacker's advantage.

Figure 5b shows an example parameters and output of this analysis. The attacker already knows that the longitude and latitude of a ship are in the range [0...300] while the speed is in [20...80]. His goal is to learn the location of any ship with a precision of 5 units. If we want to bound the guessing advantage by 30% using differential privacy, the relative error of the output will be 43.25%. For a tutorial see https://pleak.io/wiki/sql-guessing-advantage-analyser.

Acknowledgements. The research was funded by Estonian Research Council under IUT27-1 and IUT20-55 and by the Air Force Research laboratory (AFRL) and Defense Advanced Research Projects Agency (DARPA) under contract FA8750-16-C-0011. The views expressed are those of the authors and do not reflect the official policy or position of the Department of Defense or the U.S. Government.

References

1. Accorsi, R., Lehmann, A.: Automatic information flow analysis of business process models. In: Barros, A., Gal, A., Kindler, E. (eds.) BPM 2012. LNCS, vol. 7481, pp. 172–187. Springer, Heidelberg (2012). https://doi.org/10.1007/978-3-642-32885-5_13
2. Colesky, M., Hoepman, J., Hillen, C.: A critical analysis of privacy design strategies. In: IEEE Security and Privacy Workshops (SP), pp. 33–40. IEEE (2016)
3. Dumas, M., García-Bañuelos, L., Laud, P.: Disclosure analysis of SQL workows. In: 5th International Workshop on Graphical Models for Security. Springer, Heidelberg (2018)
4. Laud, P., Pankova, A., Pettai, M.: Achieving differential privacy using methods from calculus (2018). http://arxiv.org/abs/1811.06343
5. Laud, P., Pettai, M., Randmets, J.: Sensitivity analysis of SQL queries. In: Proceedings of the 13th Workshop on Programming Languages and Analysis for Security, PLAS 2018, pp. 2–12. ACM, New York (2018)
6. Lee, J., Clifton, C.: How much is enough? Choosing ϵ for differential privacy. In: Lai, X., Zhou, J., Li, H. (eds.) ISC 2011. LNCS, vol. 7001, pp. 325–340. Springer, Heidelberg (2011). https://doi.org/10.1007/978-3-642-24861-0_22

7. Pullonen, P., Matulevičius, R., Bogdanov, D.: PE-BPMN: privacy-enhanced business process model and notation. In: Carmona, J., Engels, G., Kumar, A. (eds.) BPM 2017. LNCS, vol. 10445, pp. 40–56. Springer, Cham (2017). https://doi.org/10.1007/978-3-319-65000-5_3
8. Pullonen, P., Tom, J., Matulevičius, R., Toots, A.: Privacy-enhanced BPMN: enabling data privacy analysis in business processes models. Softw. Syst. Model. (2019). https://link.springer.com/article/10.1007/s10270-019-00718-z
9. Toots, A., et al.: Business process privacy analysis in pleak (2019). http://arxiv.org/abs/1902.05052

10

Efficient Model Synchronization by Automatically Constructed Repair Processes

Lars Fritsche[1]([✉]) [iD], Jens Kosiol[2][iD], Andy Schürr[1][iD], and Gabriele Taentzer[2][iD]

[1] TU Darmstadt, Darmstadt, Germany
{lars.fritsche,andy.schuerr}@es.tu-darmstadt.de
[2] Philipps-Universität Marburg, Marburg, Germany
{kosiolje,taentzer}@mathematik.uni-marburg.de

Abstract. Model synchronization, i.e., the task of restoring consistency between two interrelated models after a model change, is a challenging task. Triple Graph Grammars (TGGs) specify model consistency by means of rules. They can be used to automatically derive specifications of edit operations for single models and repair rules that propagate model changes to related models. model (re-)synchronization activities more effectively, a construction mechanism for *short-cut* rules has been recently developed. They describe consistency-preserving complex edit operations across model boundaries. We show that edit and repair rules can be derived from *short-cut* rules. As proof of concept, we implemented the construction and application of *short-cut* edit and repair rules in eMoflon. Our evaluation shows that *short-cut*-rule-based repair processes have considerably decreased data loss and improved runtime compared to former model synchronization processes in eMoflon.

Keywords: Model synchronization · Triple Graph Grammars · Short-cut rule

1 Introduction

Model-driven engineering has become an important technique to cope with the increasing complexity of modern software systems. In the field of Concurrent Engineering [7], for example, products are no longer realized in series but allow parallel tasks. Each of these tasks has its view onto the product and, as a view evolves, it may become inconsistent with the other ones. Keeping views synchronized by checking and preserving their consistency can be a challenging problem which is not only subject to ongoing research but also of practical interest for industrial applications such as stated above.

Triple Graph Grammars (TGGs) [24] are a declarative, rule-based bidirectional transformation approach that aims to synchronize models stemming from different views (usually called *domains* in the TGG literature). Their purpose is to define a consistency relationship between pairs of models in a rule-based manner by defining traces between their elements. Given a finite set of rules that define how both models co-evolve, a TGG can be automatically *operationalized* into *source* and *forward rules*. The source rules of an operationalized TGG can be used to build up models of one domain while forward rules translate them to models of the other domain, thereby establishing traces between their elements. From a synchronization point of view, source rules specify edit operations to change one model while forward rules specify repair operations to synchronize model changes with one another [16,19,24]. Even though both, the translation and the synchronization process, are formally defined and sound, there are in fact several practical issues that arise for model synchronization from (potentially transitive) dependencies between rule applications: To synchronize changed models, popular TGG approaches do not always fix inconsistencies locally but revert all dependent rule applications and start a retranslation process. However, this kind of synchronization often deletes and recreates a lot of model elements to reestablish model consistency, potentially losing information that is local to just one model and wasting processing time. Existing solutions for this problem are rather ad hoc and come without any guarantee to reestablish the consistency of modified models [12,14].

As a new solution to this synchronization problem, we derive *repair rules* from *short-cut* rules [8] that we recently introduced to handle complex consistency-preserving model updates more effectively and efficiently. The construction of *short-cut* rules is a kind of sequential rule composition that allows to replace a rule application with another one while preserving involved model elements (instead of deleting and re-creating them). We used *short-cut* rules to describe model changes exchanging one edit step by another one. Since in this paper we want to use *short-cut* rules for model synchronization as well, they have to be operationalized into *source* and *forward* rules.

Our formal contributions (in Sect. 4) are two-fold: As *short-cut* rules may be non-monotonic, i.e., may be deleting, we formalize the operationalization of non-monotonic TGG rules which decomposes short-cut rules into (semantically equivalent sequences of) source (edit) and forward (repair) rules. Moreover, we obtain sufficient conditions under which an application of a *short-cut* rule preserves the consistency of related pairs of models. This was left to future work in [8]. Together, this constitutes the correctness of our approach using operationalized *short-cut* rules for model synchronization.

Practically, we implement our synchronization approach in eMoflon [21], a state-of-the-art bidirectional graph transformation tool, and evaluate it (Sect. 5). The results show that the construction of *short-cut* repair rules enables us to react to model changes in a less invasive way by preserving information and increasing the performance. We thus contribute to a more comprehensive research trend in the bx-community towards *Least Change* synchronization [5]. Before presenting these results in detail, we illustrate our approach using an example in (Sect. 2) and recall some preliminaries in (Sect. 3). Finally, we discuss related work in (Sect. 6) and conclude with pointers to future work in (Sect. 7). A technical report that includes additional preliminaries, all proofs, and the rule set used for our evaluation (including more complex examples) is available online [9].

2   Introductory Example

We motivate the use of *short-cut* repair processes by synchronizing a Java AST (abstract syntax tree) model and a custom documentation model. For model synchronization, we consider a Java AST model as *source* model and its documentation model as *target* model, i.e., changes in a Java AST model have to be transferred to its documentation model. There are correspondence links in between such that both models become correlated.

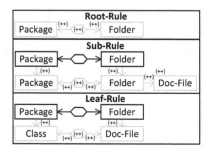

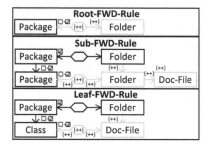

Fig. 1. Example: TGG rules (Color figure online)

Fig. 2. Example: TGG forward rules

TGG rules. Figure 1 shows the rule set of our running example consisting of three TGG rules: *Root-Rule* creates a root *Package* together with a root *Folder* and a correspondence link in between. This rule has an empty precondition and only creates elements which are depicted in green and with the annotation (++). *Sub-Rule* creates a *Package* and *Folder* hierarchy given that an already correlated *Package* and *Folder* pair exists. Finally, *Leaf-Rule* creates a *Class* and a *Doc-File* under the same precondition as *Sub-Rule*.

These rules can be used to generate consistent triple graphs in a synchronized way consisting of source, correspondence, and target graph. A more general scenario of model synchronization is, however, to restore the consistency of a triple graph that has been altered on just one side. For this purpose, each TGG rule has to be operationalized to two kinds of rules: *source* rules enable changes of source models which is followed by translating this model to the target domain with *forward* rules. As *source* rules for single models are just projections of TGG rules to one domain, we do not show them explicitly.

Forward translation rules. Figure 2 depicts the *forward* rules. Using these rules, we can translate the Java AST model depicted on the source side of the triple graph in Fig. 3(a) to a documentation model such that the result is the complete graph in Fig. 3(a). To obtain this result we apply *Root-FWD-Rule* at the root

Package, *Sub-FWD-Rule* at *Packages* p and subP, and finally *Leaf-FWD-Rule* at *Class* c. To guide the translation process, context elements that have already been translated are annotated with ☑ in *forward* rules. A formerly created source element gets the marking □ → ☑ to indicate that applying the rule will mark this element as translated; a formalization of this marking is given in [20]. Note that *Root-FWD-Rule* can always be applied when *Sub-FWD-Rule* is applicable which can lead to untranslated edges. For simplicity, we assume that the correct rule is applied which in praxis can be achieved through negative application conditions [15].

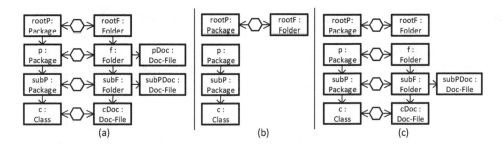

Fig. 3. Exemplary synchronization scenario

Model synchronization. Given the triple graph in Fig. 3(a), a user might want to change a sub *Package* such as p to be a root *Package*, e.g., as could be the case when the project is split up into multiple projects. Since p was created and translated as a sub *Package* rather than a root element, this change introduces an inconsistency. To resolve this issue, one approach is to revert the translation of p into f and re-translate p with an appropriate translation rule such as *Root-FWD-Rule*. Reverting the former translation step may lead to further inconsistencies as we remove elements that were needed as context elements by other rule applications. The result is a reversion of all translation steps except for the first one which translated the original root element. The result is shown in Fig. 3(b). Now, we can re-translate the unmarked elements yielding the result graph in (c). This example shows that this synchronization approach may delete and re-create a lot of similar structures which appears to be inefficient. Second, it may lose information that exists on the target side only, e.g., a use case may be assigned to a document which does not have a representation in the corresponding Java project.

Model synchronization with short-cut repair. In [8] we introduced short-cut rules as a kind of rule composition mechanism that allows to replace a rule application by another one while preserving elements (instead of deleting and re-creating them). In our example, *Root-Rule* and *Sub-Rule* overlap in elements as the first rule can be completely embedded into the latter one. Figure 4 depicts two possible short-cut rules based on *Root-Rule* and *Sub-Rule*. While the upper short-cut

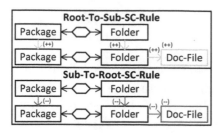

Fig. 4. Short-cut rules (Color figure online)

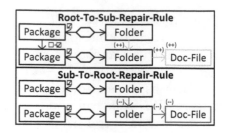

Fig. 5. Repair rules

rule replaces *Root-Rule* with *Sub-Rule*, the lower short-cut rule replaces *Sub-Rule* with *Root-Rule*. Both short-cut rules preserve the model elements on both sides and solely create elements that do not yet exist (++), or delete those depicted in red and annotated with (−−). They are constructed by overlapping both original rules such that each created element that can be mapped to the other rule becomes context and as such, is not touched. When a created element cannot be mapped because it only appears in the replacing rule, it is created. Consequently, an element is deleted if the created element only appears in the replaced rule. Finally, context elements occurring in both rules appear also in the short-cut rule while overlapped context elements appear only once. Using *Sub-To-Root-SC-Rule* enables the user to transform the triple graph in Fig. 3(a) directly to the one in (c).

Yet, these rules can still not cope with the change of a single model since short-cut rules transform both models at once as TGG rules usually do. Hence, in order to be able to handle the deleted edge between rootP and p, we have to forward operationalize short-cut rules, thereby obtaining *short-cut repair* rules. Figure 5 depicts the resulting *short-cut repair* rules derived from *short-cut* rules in Fig. 4. A non-monotonic TGG-rule is forward operationalized by removing deleted elements from the rule's source graphs as they should not be present after a source rule application. *Short-cut repair* rules allow to propagate source graph changes directly to target graphs to restore consistency. In our example, after having transformed Package p into a root element, the rule of choice is *Sub-To-Root-Repair-Rule* which transforms Folder f in Fig. 3(a) into a root element and deletes the superfluous *Doc-File*. The result is again the consistent triple graph depicted in Fig. 3(c). This repair allows to skip the costly reversion process with the intermediate result in Fig. 3(b). Note that applying *Sub-To-Root-Repair-Rule* at arbitrary matches may have undesired consequences: One could, e.g., delete the edge between two *Folders* even if the matched *Packages* are still connected. Our Theorem 8 characterizes matches where such violations of the language of the grammar cannot happen. In our implementation, we exploit an incremental pattern matcher to identify valid matches. Using suitable *negative application conditions* [6] would be an alternative approach.

3　Preliminaries

To understand our formal contributions, we assume familiarity with the basics of double-pushout rewriting in graph transformation and, more generally in adhesive categories [6,18] as well as the definition of TGGs and in particular, their operationalizations [24]. Here, we recall non-basic preliminaries for our work which are the construction of short-cut rules, the notion of sequential independence, and a (simple) categorical definition of partial maps.

In [8], we introduced short-cut rules as a new way of sequential composition for monotonic rules. Given an inverse rule of a monotonic rule (i.e., a rule that only deletes) and a monotonic rule, a short-cut rule combines their respective actions into a single rule. Its construction allows to identify elements that are deleted by the first rule as re-created by the second one. These elements are preserved in the resulting short-cut rule. A *common kernel*, i.e., a common subrule of both, serves to identify how the two rules overlap and which elements are preserved instead of being deleted and re-created. We recall their construction since our construction of repair rules is based on it. Examples are depicted in Fig. 4.

Definition 1 (Short-cut rule). *In an adhesive category C, given two monotonic rules $r_i : L_i \hookrightarrow R_i$, $i = 1, 2$, and a common kernel rule $k : L_\cap \hookrightarrow R_\cap$ for them, the Short-cut rule $r_1^{-1} \ltimes_k r_2 := (L \xleftarrow{l} K \xrightarrow{r} R)$ is computed by executing the following steps depicted in Figs. 6 and 7:*

1. *The union $L_\cup$ of L_1 and L_2 along $L_\cap$ is computed as pushout (2).*
2. *The LHS L of the short-cut rule $r_1^{-1} \ltimes_k r_2$ is computed as pushout (3a).*
3. *The RHS R of the short-cut rule $r_1^{-1} \ltimes_k r_2$ is computed as pushout (3b).*
4. *The interface K of the short-cut rule $r_1^{-1} \ltimes_k r_2$ is computed as pushout (4).*
5. *Morphisms $l : K \to L$ and $r : K \to R$ are obtained by the universal property of K.*

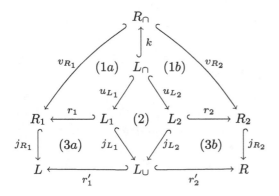

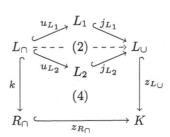

Fig. 6. Construction of LHS and RHS of short-cut rule $r_1^{-1} \ltimes_k r_2$

Fig. 7. Construction of interface K of $r_1^{-1} \ltimes_k r_2$

Sequential independence of two rule applications intuitively means that none of these applications enables the other one. This implies that the order of their application may be switched. The definition of sequential independence can be extended to a sequence of rule applications longer than 2. In Theorem 8, we will use this to identify language-preserving applications of short-cut rules.

Definition 2 (Sequential independence). *Given two rules* $p_i = (L_i \overset{l_i}{\hookleftarrow} K_i \overset{r_i}{\hookrightarrow} R_i)$ *with* $i = 1, 2$, *two direct transformations* $G \Rightarrow_{p_1,m_1} H_1$ *and* $H_1 \Rightarrow_{p_2,m_2} H_2$ *via the rules* r_1 *and* r_2 *are sequentially independent if there exist two morphisms* $d_1 : R_1 \to D_2$ *and* $d_2 : L_2 \to D_1$ *as depicted below such that* $n_1 = f_2 \circ d_1$ *and* $m_2 = f_1 \circ d_2$.

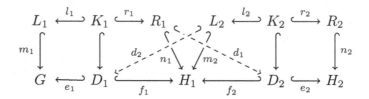

Given rules $p = (L \hookleftarrow K \hookrightarrow R)$ *and* $p_i = (L_i \hookleftarrow K_i \hookrightarrow R_i)$ *with* $1 \leq i \leq t$, *a transformation* $G_t \Rightarrow_{p,m} H$ *is sequentially independent from a sequence of transformations* $G_0 \Rightarrow_{p_1,m_1} G_1 \Rightarrow_{p_2,m_2} \cdots \Rightarrow_{p_t,m_t} G_t, t \geq 2$ *if first,* $G_t \Rightarrow_{p,m} H$ *and* $G_{t-1} \Rightarrow_{p_t,m_t} G_t$ *are sequentially independent and then, the arising transformations* $G_{t-1} \Rightarrow_{p,e_t \circ d_2^t} G_t'$ *and* $G_{t-2} \Rightarrow_{p_{t-1},m_{t-1}} G_{t-1}$ *are sequentially independent and so forth back to the transformations* $G_0 \Rightarrow_{p_1,m_1} G_1$ *and* $G_1 \Rightarrow_{p,e_2 \circ d_2^2} G_2'$ *(where* $e_i : D_i \hookrightarrow G_{i-1}$ *is given by the transformation and* $d_2^i : L \hookrightarrow D_i$ *exists by sequential independence as in the figure above).*

To formalize the application of non-monotonic TGG rules, we need to consider triple graphs with partial morphisms from correspondence to source (or target) graphs. For expressing such triple graphs categorically, we recall a simple definition of partial morphisms [23] to be used in Sect. 4.1. An elaborated theory of triple graphs with partial morphisms is out of scope of this paper.

Definition 3 (Partial morphism. Commuting square with partial morphisms). *A partial morphism* a *from an object* A *to an object* B *is a(n equivalence class of) span(s)* $A \overset{\iota_A}{\hookleftarrow} A' \overset{a}{\to} B$ *where* ι_A *is a monomorphism (denoted by* $\hookrightarrow$*). A partial morphism is denoted as* $a : A \dashrightarrow B$; A' *is called the* domain *of* a. *A diagram with two partial morphisms* a *and* c *as depicted as square (1) in Fig. 8 is said to be* commuting *if there exists a (necessarily unique) morphism* $x : A' \to C'$ *such that both arising squares (2) and (3) in Fig. 9 commute.*

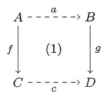

Fig. 8. Square of partial morphisms

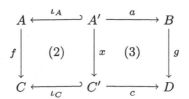

Fig. 9. Commuting square of partial morphisms

4 Constructing Language-Preserving Repair Rules

The general idea of this paper is to use *short-cut repair* rules allowing an optimized model synchronization process based on TGGs. To this end, we operationalize short-cut rules being constructed from the rules of a given TGG. Since those rules are not necessarily monotonic, we generalize the well-known operationalization of TGG rules to the non-monotonic case and show that the basic property is still valid: An application of a source rule followed by an application of the corresponding forward rule is equivalent to applying the original rule instead. This is the content of Sect. 4.1. Constructing *shortspscut* rules in [8], we identified the following problem: Applying a short-cut rule derived from rules of a given grammar might lead to an instance that is not part of the language defined by that grammar. Therefore, in Sect. 4.2, we provide sufficient conditions for applications of short-cut rules leading to instances of the grammar-defined language only. Combining both results ensures the correctness of our approach, i.e., a *shortspscut* repair rule actually propagates a model change from the source to the target model if it is correctly matched.

4.1 Operationalization of Generalized TGG Rules

Since the operationalization of TGG rules has been introduced for monotonic rules only, we extend the theory to general triple rules and, moreover, allow for partial morphisms from correspondence to source and target graph in triple graphs. We split a rule on triple graphs into a *source rule* that only affects the source part and a *forward rule* that affects correspondence and target part.

Definition 4 (TGG rule). *Let the category of triple graphs and graph morphisms be given. A triple rule p is a span of triple graph morphisms*

$$p = ((L_S \xleftarrow{\sigma_L} L_C \xrightarrow{\tau_L} L_T) \xleftarrow{(l_S, l_C, l_T)} (K_S \xleftarrow{\sigma_K} K_C \xrightarrow{\tau_K} K_T) \xrightarrow{(r_S, r_C, r_T)} (R_S \xleftarrow{\sigma_R} R_C \xrightarrow{\tau_R} R_T))$$

which, wherever possible, are abbreviated by

$$p = (L_{SCT} \xleftarrow{(l_S, l_C, l_T)} K_{SCT} \xrightarrow{(r_S, r_C, r_T)} R_{SCT}).$$

Rules p_S and p_F are called source rule *and* forward rule *of p.*

$$p_S = ((L_S \leftarrow \emptyset \rightarrow \emptyset) \xleftarrow{(l_S, id_\emptyset, id_\emptyset)} (K_S \leftarrow \emptyset \rightarrow \emptyset) \xrightarrow{(r_S, id_\emptyset, id_\emptyset)} (R_S \leftarrow \emptyset \rightarrow \emptyset)),$$

$$p_F = (R_S L_{CT} \xleftarrow{(id_{R_S}, l_C, l_T)} R_S K_{CT} \xrightarrow{(id_{R_S}, r_C, r_T)} R_{SCT})$$

with $\emptyset$ being the empty graph. In $R_S L_{CT} = (R_S \xleftarrow{} L_C \xrightarrow{TL} L_T)$, the morphism from L_C to R_S may be partial and is defined by the span $(L_C \xleftarrow{l_C} K_C \xrightarrow{r_S \circ \sigma_K} R_S)$ with $\sigma_K : K_C \hookrightarrow R_C$. Target and backward rules p_T and p_B are defined symmetrically in the other direction.

Given a TGG, a short-cut repair rule *is a forward rule p_F of a short-cut rule $p = r_1^{-1} \bowtie_k r_2$ where r_1, r_2 are (monotonic) rules of the TGG, i.e., a repair rule is an operationalized short-cut rule.*

The above definition is motivated by our application scenario, i.e., the case where a user edits the source (or target) model independently of the other parts. The partial morphism in the forward rule reflects that a model change may introduce a situation where the result is no longer a triple graph. A deleted source element may have a preimage in the correspondence graph that is not deleted as well. In the example *short-cut* rules in Fig. 4, this problem does not occur since edges are deleted only. But in general, this definition of p_S has the disadvantage that often, p_S is not applicable to any triple graph since the result would not be one.

In practical applications, however, the source rule specifies a user edit action that is performed on the source part only, ignoring correspondence and target graphs. The fact that the result is not a triple graph any longer is not a technical problem. A missing source element that should be referenced by a correspondence element gives information about a location that needs some repair. Therefore, we define the application of a source rule such that the resulting triple graph is allowed to be partial. Furthermore, forward rules may be applied to partial triple graphs allowing for dangling correspondence relations.

Definition 5 (Constructing an operationalized rule application). *Let a triple graph rule $p = (L_{SCT} \xleftarrow{(l_S, l_C, l_T)} K_{SCT} \xrightarrow{(r_S, r_C, r_T)} R_{SCT})$ with source rule p_S and forward rule p_F be given. An operationalized rule application $G \Rightarrow_{p_S, m_S} G' \Rightarrow_{p_F, m_F} H$ is constructed as follows:*

1. *The rule $p_S^{\mathrm{pr}} = L_S \xleftarrow{l_S} K_S \xrightarrow{r_S} R_S$ is the projection of p_S to its source part.*
2. *Given a match m_S^{pr} for p_S^{pr}, construct the transformation $t_S^{\mathrm{pr}} : G_S \Rightarrow_{p_S^{\mathrm{pr}}, m_S^{\mathrm{pr}}} H_S$, called* source application *and inducing the span $G_S \xleftarrow{f_S} D_S \xrightarrow{g_S} H_S$.*
3. *The transformation t_S^{pr} can be extended to the transformation $t_S : G = (G_S \xleftarrow{\sigma_G} G_C \xrightarrow{\tau_G} G_T) \Rightarrow_{p_S, m_S} G' = (H_S \xleftarrow{} G_C \xrightarrow{\tau_G} G_T)$ via p_S at match m_S. The partial morphism $G_C \dashrightarrow H_S$ is given as the span $G_C \hookleftarrow G_C' \rightarrow H_S$ that arises as pullback of the co-span $G_C \rightarrow G_S \hookleftarrow D_S$ as depicted in Fig. 10, i.e., as morphism $g_S \circ p_D : G_C \dashrightarrow H_S$ with domain G_C'.*
4. *Given co-match $n_S : R_S \hookrightarrow H_S$ and matches $m_X : L_X \hookrightarrow G_X$ with $X \in \{C, T\}$ such that both arising squares are commuting, i.e., $m_F = (n_S, m_C, m_T)$ is a morphism of partial triple graphs, construct transformation $t_F : G' \Rightarrow_{p_F, m_F} H = (H_S \xleftarrow{\sigma_H} H_C \xrightarrow{\tau_H} H_T)$, called* forward application, *using transformations $G_X \Rightarrow_{p_X, m_X} H_X$ for $X \in \{C, T\}$ if they exist*

and if there are morphisms $\sigma'_D : D_C \to H_S$ and $\tau_D : D_C \to D_T$ such that $H_S D_C D_T \hookrightarrow H_S G_C G_T$ and $R_S K_C K_T \hookrightarrow H_S D_C D_T$ are triple morphisms.

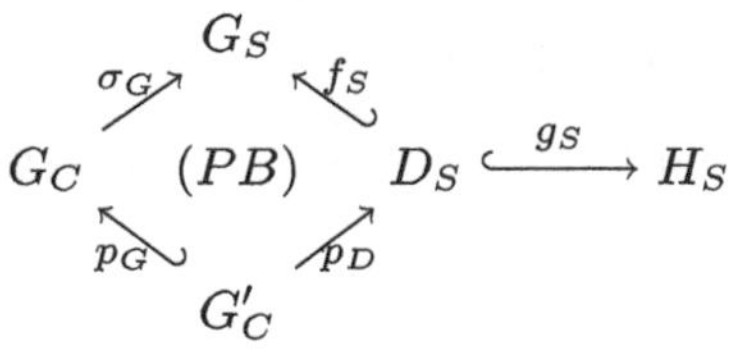

$$G_S$$
$$\sigma_G \nearrow \quad \overset{f_S}{\nwarrow}$$
$$G_C \quad (PB) \quad D_S \overset{g_S}{\longleftrightarrow} H_S$$
$$p_G \nwarrow \quad \nearrow p_D$$
$$G'_C$$

Fig. 10. Retrieval of partial morphism $G_C \dashrightarrow H_S$

In the setting of this paper, it is enough to allow for partial morphisms only in the input graph and not in the output graph of a forward rule application. Intuitively this means that such an application deletes those elements from the correspondence graph that could not be mapped to elements in the source graph any longer and additionally deletes the preimages in the correspondence graph of all deleted elements from the target graph as well (if there are any). The next lemma states that the application of a source rule is well-defined, i.e., that the mentioned partial morphism actually exists.

Lemma 6 (Correctness of application of source rules). *Let a (non-monotonic) triple graph rule*

$$p = (L_{SCT} \overset{(l_S, l_C, l_T)}{\longleftarrow} K_{SCT} \overset{(r_S, r_C, r_T)}{\longrightarrow} R_{SCT})$$

with source rule p_S and projection p_S^{pr} to the source part be given. Given a match m_S for p_S to a triple graph $G = (G_S \overset{\sigma_G}{\longleftarrow} G_C \overset{\tau_G}{\longrightarrow} G_T)$ such that $G_S \Rightarrow_{p_S^{pr}, m_S} H_S$, the partial morphism $D_C \dashrightarrow H_S$ as described in Definition 5 exists.

The next theorem states that a sequential application of a source and a forward rule indeed coincides with an application of the original rule as long as the matches are consistent. This means that the forward rule has to match the RHS R_S of the source rule again and the LHS L_C of the correspondence rule needs to be matched in such a way that all elements not belonging to the domain of the partial morphism from correspondence to source part in the input model are deleted. The forward rule application defined in Definition 5 fulfills this condition by construction.

Theorem 7 (Synthesis of rule applications). *Let a triple graph rule p with source and forward rules p_S and p_F be given. If there are applications $G \Rightarrow_{p_S, m_S} G'$ with co-match n_S and $G' \Rightarrow_{p_F, m_F} H$ with $m_F = (n_S, m_C, m_T)$ as constructed above, then there is an application $G \Rightarrow_{p, m} H$ with $m = (m_S, m_C, m_T)$.*

4.2   Language-Preserving Short-Cut Rules

In this section we identify sufficient conditions for an application of a short-cut rule that guarantee the result to be an element of the language of the original grammar. Since our conditions apply to arbitrary adhesive categories and are not specific for TGGs, we present the result in its general form.

Theorem 8 (Characterization of valid applications). *In an adhesive category $\mathcal{C}$, given a sequence of transformations*

$$G \Rightarrow_{r,m} G_0 \Rightarrow_{p_1,m_1} G_1 \Rightarrow_{p_2,m_2} \cdots \Rightarrow_{p_t,m_t} G_t \Rightarrow_{r^{-1}\ltimes_k r',m_{sc}} H$$

with rules $p_1, \ldots, p_t$ and $r^{-1} \ltimes_k r'$ being the short-cut rule of monotonic rules $r : L \hookrightarrow R$ and $r' : L' \hookrightarrow R'$ along a common kernel k, there is a match m' for r' in G and a transformation sequence

$$G \Rightarrow_{r',m'} G'_1 \Rightarrow_{p_1,m'_1} \cdots G'_{t-1} \Rightarrow_{p_t,m'_t} H,$$

provided that

1. *the application of $r^{-1} \ltimes_k r'$ with match m_{sc} is sequentially independent of the sequence of transformations $G_0 \Rightarrow_{p_1,m_1} G_1 \Rightarrow_{p_2,m_2} \cdots \Rightarrow_{p_t,m_t} G_t$ and*
2. *the thereby implied match m'_{sc} for $r^{-1} \ltimes_k r'$ in G_0, restricted to the RHS R of r, equals the co-match $n : R \hookrightarrow G_0$ of the transformation $G \Rightarrow_{r,m} G_0$ (i.e., $m'_{sc} \circ j_R = n$ where j_R embeds R into the LHS of $r^{-1} \ltimes_k r'$ as in Fig. 6).*

In particular, given a grammar $GG = (\mathcal{R}, S)$ such that $r, r', p_1, \ldots, p_t \in \mathcal{R}$ and $G \in \mathcal{L}(GG)$, then $H \in \mathcal{L}(GG)$.

Independence of the short-cut rule application $t_{sc} : G_t \Rightarrow_{r^{-1}\ltimes_k r',m_{sc}} H$ from the preceding transformation sequence $t : G \Rightarrow G_t$ requires the existence of morphisms in two directions: morphisms d_2^i from the LHS of the short-cut rule to the context objects D_i arising in t and morphisms d_1^i from the right-hand sides R_i of the rules p_i to the context object of t_{sc} (shifted further and further to the beginning of the sequence). In the case of (typed triple) graphs, the existence of morphisms d_2^i ensures that none of the rule applications in t enabled the transformation t_{sc}. The existence of morphisms d_1^i ensures that the transformation t_{sc} does not delete structure needed to perform the transformation sequence t.

Application to model synchronization. The results in Theorems 7 and 8 are the formal basis for an automatic construction of repair rules. Theorem 7 ensures that a suitable edit action followed by application of a repair rule at the right match is equivalent to the application of a short-cut rule. Thus, whenever an edit action on the source model (or symmetrically the target model) corresponds to the source-action (target-action) of a short-cut rule, application of the corresponding forward (backward) rule synchronizes the model again. Since the language of a TGG is defined by its rules, every valid model can be reached from every other valid model by inverse application of some of the rules of the grammar followed by normal application of some rules. Often, edit actions are rather small steps (or at least consist of those). Thus, it is not unreasonable to expect that many typical edit actions can be realized as short-cut rules as these formalize the inverse application of a rule followed by application of a normal one. Theorem 8 characterizes the matches for short-cut rules at which application stays in the language of the TGG. For operational short-cut rules, this can either be used for detecting invalid edit actions or determining valid matches for synchronizing forward rules.

5   Implementation and Evaluation

Implementation. Our implementation[1] of an optimized model synchronizer is based on the existing EMF-based general purpose graph and model transformation tool eMoflon [21]. It offers support for rule-based unidirectional and bidirectional graph transformations where the latter is based on TGGs. To support an effective model synchronizer, we automatically calculate a small but useful subset of all possible short-cut rules. This is done by overlapping as many created elements as possible and only varying in the way that context elements are mapped onto each other. These selected short-cut rules are operationalized to get repair rules that allow us to repair broken links similar to our example in Sect. 2. The model synchronization process is based on an *incremental graph pattern matcher* that tracks all matches that dis-/appear due to model changes. Thus, it offers the ability to react to model changes without the need to recompute matches from scratch. Our implementation uses this technique by processing all those matches marked as broken by the pattern matcher after a model change. A broken match is the starting point to find a repair match as it is defined by the co-match of the performed model change and has to be extended. If the pattern matcher can extend a broken match to a repair match, the corresponding *short-cut* repair rule can be applied. Otherwise, we fall back to the old synchronization strategy of revoking the current step. This completely automatized synchronization process ensures that we are able to restore consistency as long as the edited domain model still resides in the language of our TGG.

Evaluation. Our experimental setup consists of 23 TGG rules (shown in our technical report [9]) that specify consistency between Java AST and custom documentation models and 37 short-cut rules derived from our TGG rule set. A small modified excerpt of this rule set was given in Sect. 2. For this evaluation, however, we define consistency not only between *Package* and *Folder* hierarchies but also between type definitions, e.g., *Classes* and *Interfaces*, and *Methods* with their corresponding documentation entries. We extracted five models from Java projects hosted on Github using the tool MoDisco [4] and translated them into our own documentation structure. Also, we generated five synthetic models consisting of n-level *Package* hierarchies with each non-leaf*Package* containing five sub-*Packages* and each leaf *Package* containing five *Classes*. Given such Java

---

[1] Both the implementation and evaluation workspace can be accessed via https://github.com/Arikae00/FASE19_eMoflon-evaluation.

models, we refactored each model in three different scenarios such as by moving a *Class* from one *Package* to another or completely relocating a *Package*. Then we used eMoflon to synchronize these changes in order to restore consistency to the documentation model, with and without *repair rules*.

These synchronization steps are subject to our evaluation and we pose the following research questions: **(RQ1)** *For different kinds of changes, how many elements can be preserved that would otherwise be deleted and recreated?* **(RQ2)** *How does our new approach affect the runtime performance?* **(RQ3)** *Are there specific scenarios in which our approach performs especially good or bad?*

Repair rules were developed to avoid unnecessary deletions of elements by reverting too many rule applications in order to restore consistency as shown exemplary in Sect. 2. This means that model changes where our approach should perform especially good, have to target rule applications close to the beginning of a rule sequence as this possibly renders many rule applications invalid. This means that altering a root *Package* by creating a new *Package* as root would imply that many rule applications have to be reverted to synchronize the changes correctly (Scenario 1). In contrast, our approach might perform poorly when a model change does not inflict a large cascade of invalid rule applications. Hence, we move *Classes* between *Packages* to measure if the effort of applying *repair rules* does infer a performance loss when both the new and old algorithm do not have to repair many broken rule applications (Scenario 2). Finally, we simulate a scenario between the first two by relocating leaf *Packages* (Scenario 3).

Table 1. Legacy vs. new synchronizer – Time in sec. and number of created elements

Models	Both Trans.		Legacy Synchronization						Synchro. by Repair Rules					
			Scen. 1		Scen. 2		Scen. 3		Scen. 1		Scen. 2		Scen. 3	
	Sec	Elts	Sec	Elts	Sec	Elts	Sec	Elts	Sec	Elts	Sec	Elts	Sec	Elts
lang.List	0.3	25	0.2	20	–	–	0.06	5	0.2	0	–	–	0.03	0
tgg.core	6.4	1.6k	39	1.6k	3.8	99	0.64	17	0.8	0	0.11	0	0.05	0
modisco.java	9.9	3.2k	228	3.3k	18.6	192	3.6	33	2.5	0	0.2	0	0.09	0
eclipse.graphiti	20.7	6.5k	704	6.5k	63.9	490	5.65	25	6.1	0	0.21	0	0.09	0
eclipse.compare	10.74	3.8k	83	3.7k	3.1	76	2.36	47	0.7	0	0.08	0	0.04	0
synthetic $n = 1$	0.3	35	0.32	30	0.2	30	0.03	1	0.1	0	0.05	0	0.03	0
synthetic $n = 2$	0.9	160	1.03	155	0.3	30	0.03	1	0.1	0	0.05	0	0.02	0
synthetic $n = 3$	2.8	785	6	780	0.4	30	0.04	1	0.1	0	0.07	0	0.02	0
synthetic $n = 4$	13.5	3.9k	86.3	3.9k	1.2	30	0.08	1	0.4	0	0.14	0	0.04	0
synthetic $n = 5$	91.5	20k	2731	20k	17.4	30	0.14	1	1.5	0	0.37	0	0.09	0

Table 1 depicts the measured times (Sec) and the number of created elements (Elts) in each scenario. Each created element also represents a deleted element, e.g., through revoking and reapplying a rule or applying a repair rule that creates and deletes elements. In more detail, the table shows measurements for the initial translation of the MoDisco model into the documentation structure and synchronization steps for each scenario using the legacy synchronizer without *repair rules* and the new synchronizer with *repair rules*.

W.r.t. our research questions stated above, we interpret this table as follows: The right columns of the table show clearly that using repair rules preserves all those elements in our scenarios that would otherwise be deleted and recreated by the legacy algorithm[2] **(RQ1)**. The runtime shows a significant performance gain for Scenario 1 including a worst-case model change **(RQ2)**. *Repair rules* do not introduce an overhead compared to the legacy algorithm as can be seen for the synthetic time measurements in Scenario 3 where only one rule application has to be repaired or reapplied. **(RQ2)**. Our new approach excels when the cascade of invalidated rule applications is long. Even if this is not the case, it does not introduce any measurable overhead compared to the legacy algorithm as shown in Scenarios 2 and 3 **(RQ3)**.

Threats to validity. Our evaluation is based on five real world and five synthetic models. Of course, there exists a wide range of projects that differ significantly from each other due to their size, purpose, and developer styles. Thus, the results may probably differ for other projects. Nonetheless, we argue that the four larger projects extracted from Github are representative since they are part of established tools from the Eclipse community. In this evaluation, we selected three edit operations that are representative w.r.t. their dependency on other edit operations. They may not be representative w.r.t. other aspects such as size or kind of change, which seems to be of minor importance in this context. Also we limited our evaluation to one TGG rule set due to space issues. However, in our experience the approach shows similar results for a broader range of TGGs which can be accessed through eMoflon.

6   Related Work

Reuse in existing work on TGGs. Several approaches to model synchronization based on TGGs suffer from the fact that the revocation of a certain rule application triggers the revocation of all dependent rule applications as well [12,16,19]. Especially from a practical point of view such cascades of deletions shall be avoided: In [10], Giese and Hildebrandt propose rules that save nodes instead of deleting and then re-creating them. Their examples can be realized by our construction of *repair rules*. But they do not present a general construction or proof of correctness. This is left as future work in [11] again, where other aspects of [10] are formalized and proven to be correct.

In [3], Blouin et al. added a specially designed repair rule to the rules of their case study to avoid information loss. Greenyer et al. [14] also propose to not directly delete elements but to mark them for deletion and allow for reuse of these marked elements in other rule applications. But this approach comes without any formalization or proof of correctness as well. Again, the given example can be realized as short-cut repair. These uncontrolled and informal approaches are

---

[2] Scenario 1: We expect the new root element to already be translated.

potentially harmful. Re-using elements wrongly may lead to, e.g., containment cycles or unconnected data. Hence, providing precise and sufficient conditions for correct re-use of data is highly desirable as re-use may improve scalability and decrease data-loss. Our short-cut rules formalize when data can be correctly reused. In summary, we do not only offer a unifying principle behind different practically used improvements of TGGs but also give a precise formalization that allows for automatic construction of the rules needed. Thereby, we present conditions under which rule applications lead to valid outputs.

Comparison to other bx approaches. Anjorin et al. [2] compared three state-of-the-art bx tools, namely eMoflon [21] (rule-based), mediniQVT [1] (constraint-based) and BiGUL [17] (bx programming language) w.r.t. model synchronization. They point out that synchronization with eMoflon is faster than with both other tools as the runtime of these tools correlates with the overall model size while the runtime of eMoflon correlates with the size of the changes done by edit operations. Furthermore, eMoflon was the only tool able to solve all but one synchronization scenario. One scenario was not solved because it deleted more model elements than absolutely necessary in that case. Using short-cut repair rules, we can solve the remaining scenario and moreover, can further increase eMoflons model synchronization performance.

Change-preserving model repair. Change-preserving model repair as presented in [22, 25] is closely related to our approach. Assuming a set of consistency-preserving rules and a set of edit rules to be given, each edit rule is accompanied by one or more repair rules completing the edit step, if possible. Such a complement rule is considered as repair rule of an edit rule w.r.t. an overarching consistency-preserving rule. Operationalized TGG rules fit into that approach but provide more structure: As graphs and rules are structured in triples, a source rule is also an edit rule being complemented by a forward rule. In contrast to that approach, source and forward rules can be automatically deduced from a given TGG rule. By our use of short-cut rules we introduce a pre-processing step to first enlarge the sets of consistency-preserving rules and edit rules.

Generalization of correspondence relation. Golas et al. provide a formalization of TGGs in [13] which allows to generalize correspondence relations between source and target graphs as well. They use special typings for the source, target, and correspondence parts of a TGG and for edges between a correspondence part and source and target part instead of using graph morphisms. That approach also allows for partial correspondence relations. But it makes the deletion of elements more complex as it becomes important how many incident edges a node has (at least in the double-pushout approach). We therefore opted for introducing triple graphs with partial morphisms. They allow us to just delete a node without caring if it is needed within an existing correspondence relation.

7 Conclusion

Model synchronization, i.e., the task of restoring consistency between two models after a model change, poses challenges to modern bx approaches and tools: We expect them to synchronize changes without losing data in the process, thus, preserving information and furthermore, we expect them to show a reasonable performance. While Triple Graph Grammars (TGGs) provide the means to perform model synchronization tasks in general, both requirements cannot always be fulfilled since basic TGG rules do not define the adequate means to support intermediate model editing. Therefore, we propose additional edit operations being short-cut rules, a special form of generalized TGG rules that allow to take back one edit action and to perform an alternative one. In our evaluation, we show that operationalized short-cut rules allow for a model synchronization with considerably decreased data loss and improved runtime.

To better cope with practical application scenarios, we like to extend our approach by formally incorporating type inheritance, application conditions and attributes in the model synchronization process. Since all of these have been formalized in the setting of ($\mathcal{M}$-)adhesive categories and our present work uses that framework as well, these extensions are prepared but up to future work. Propagating changes from one domain to another is basically done here by operationalizing short-cut rules. A more challenging task is what we call model integration where related pairs of models are edited concurrently and have to be synchronized. These model edits may be in conflict across model boundaries. It is up to future work to allow short-cut rules in model integration. Our hope is to decrease data loss and to improve runtime of model integration tasks as well.

References

1. Ikv++: Medini QVT. http://projects.ikv.de/qvt
2. Anjorin, A., Diskin, Z., Jouault, F., Ko, H., Leblebici, E., Westfechtel, B.: Benchmarx reloaded: a practical benchmark framework for bidirectional transformations. In: Proceedings of the 6th International Workshop on Bidirectional Transformations co-located with The European Joint Conferences on Theory and Practice of Software, BX@ETAPS 2017, Uppsala, Sweden, 29 April 2017, pp. 15–30 (2017). http://ceur-ws.org/Vol-1827/paper6.pdf
3. Blouin, D., Plantec, A., Dissaux, P., Singhoff, F., Diguet, J.-P.: Synchronization of models of rich languages with triple graph grammars: an experience report. In: Di Ruscio, D., Varró, D. (eds.) ICMT 2014. LNCS, vol. 8568, pp. 106–121. Springer, Cham (2014). https://doi.org/10.1007/978-3-319-08789-4_8
4. Brunelière, H., Cabot, J., Dupé, G., Madiot, F.: MoDisco: a model driven reverse engineering framework. Inf. Softw. Technol. **56**(8), 1012–1032 (2014). https://doi.org/10.1016/j.infsof.2014.04.007
5. Cheney, J., Gibbons, J., McKinna, J., Stevens, P.: On principles of least change and least surprise for bidirectional transformations. J. Object Technol. **16**(1), 3:1–3:31 (2017). https://doi.org/10.5381/jot.2017.16.1.a3
6. Ehrig, H., Ehrig, K., Prange, U., Taentzer, G.: Fundamentals of Algebraic Graph Transformation. Monographs in Theoretical Computer Science. Springer, Heidelberg (2006). https://doi.org/10.1007/3-540-31188-2

7. Eppinger, S.D.: Model-based approaches to managing concurrent engineering. J. Eng. Des. **2**(4), 283–290 (1991). https://doi.org/10.1080/09544829108901686

8. Fritsche, L., Kosiol, J., Schürr, A., Taentzer, G.: Short-cut rules. Sequential composition of rules avoiding unnecessary deletions. In: Mazzara, M., Ober, I., Salaün, G. (eds.) STAF 2018. LNCS, vol. 11176, pp. 415–430. Springer, Cham (2018). https://doi.org/10.1007/978-3-030-04771-9_30

9. Fritsche, L., Kosiol, J., Schürr, A., Taentzer, G.: Optimizing TGG-based model synchronization by automatic short-cut repair processes: extended version. Technical report, Philipps-Universität Marburg (2019). https://www.uni-marburg.de/fb12/arbeitsgruppen/swt/forschung/publikationen/2019/FKST19-TR.pdf

10. Giese, H., Hildebrandt, S.: Efficient model synchronization of large-scale models. Technical report 28, Hasso-Plattner-Institut (2009)

11. Giese, H., Hildebrandt, S., Lambers, L.: Bridging the gap between formal semantics and implementation of triple graph grammars. Softw. Syst. Model. **13**(1), 273–299 (2014). https://doi.org/10.1007/s10270-012-0247-y

12. Giese, H., Wagner, R.: From model transformation to incremental bidirectional model synchronization. Softw. Syst. Model. **8**(1), 21–43 (2009). https://doi.org/10.1007/s10270-008-0089-9

13. Golas, U., Lambers, L., Ehrig, H., Giese, H.: Toward bridging the gap between formal foundations and current practice for triple graph grammars. In: Ehrig, H., Engels, G., Kreowski, H.J., Rozenberg, G. (eds.) ICGT 2012. LNCS, vol. 7562, pp. 141–155. Springer, Heidelberg (2012). https://doi.org/10.1007/978-3-642-33654-6_10

14. Greenyer, J., Pook, S., Rieke, J.: Preventing information loss in incremental model synchronization by reusing elements. In: France, R.B., Kuester, J.M., Bordbar, B., Paige, R.F. (eds.) ECMFA 2011. LNCS, vol. 6698, pp. 144–159. Springer, Heidelberg (2011). https://doi.org/10.1007/978-3-642-21470-7_11

15. Hermann, F., Ehrig, H., Golas, U., Orejas, F.: Efficient analysis and execution of correct and complete model transformations based on triple graph grammars. In: Proceedings of the First International Workshop on Model-Driven Interoperability. pp. 22–31. MDI 2010. ACM, New York (2010). https://doi.org/10.1145/1866272.1866277

16. Hermann, F., et al.: Model synchronization based on triple graph grammars: correctness, completeness and invertibility. Softw. Syst. Model. **14**(1), 241–269 (2015). https://doi.org/10.1007/s10270-012-0309-1

17. Ko, H., Zan, T., Hu, Z.: BiGUL: a formally verified core language for putback-based bidirectional programming. In: Proceedings of the 2016 ACM SIGPLAN Workshop on Partial Evaluation and Program Manipulation, PEPM 2016, St. Petersburg, FL, USA, 20–22 January 2016, pp. 61–72 (2016). https://doi.org/10.1145/2847538.2847544

18. Lack, S., Sobociński, P.: Adhesive and quasiadhesive categories. Theor. Inform. Appl. **39**(3), 511–545 (2005). https://doi.org/10.1051/ita:2005028

19. Lauder, M., Anjorin, A., Varró, G., Schürr, A.: Efficient model synchronization with precedence triple graph grammars. In: Ehrig, H., Engels, G., Kreowski, H.J., Rozenberg, G. (eds.) ICGT 2012. LNCS, vol. 7562, pp. 401–415. Springer, Heidelberg (2012). https://doi.org/10.1007/978-3-642-33654-6_27

20. Leblebici, E., Anjorin, A., Fritsche, L., Varró, G., Schürr, A.: Leveraging incremental pattern matching techniques for model synchronisation. In: de Lara, J., Plump, D. (eds.) ICGT 2017. LNCS, vol. 10373, pp. 179–195. Springer, Cham (2017). https://doi.org/10.1007/978-3-319-61470-0_11

21. Leblebici, E., Anjorin, A., Schürr, A.: Developing eMoflon with eMoflon. In: Di Ruscio, D., Varró, D. (eds.) ICMT 2014. LNCS, vol. 8568, pp. 138–145. Springer, Cham (2014). https://doi.org/10.1007/978-3-319-08789-4_10

22. Ohrndorf, M., Pietsch, C., Kelter, U., Kehrer, T.: Revision: a tool for history-based model repair recommendations. In: Proceedings of the 40th International Conference on Software Engineering: Companion Proceeedings, ICSE 2018, Gothenburg, Sweden, 27 May–03 June 2018, pp. 105–108. ACM (2018). https://doi.org/10.1145/3183440.3183498

23. Robinson, E., Rosolini, G.: Categories of partial maps. Inf. Comput. **79**(2), 95–130 (1988). https://doi.org/10.1016/0890-5401(88)90034-X

24. Schürr, A.: Specification of graph translators with triple graph grammars. In: Mayr, E.W., Schmidt, G., Tinhofer, G. (eds.) WG 1994. LNCS, vol. 903, pp. 151–163. Springer, Heidelberg (1995). https://doi.org/10.1007/3-540-59071-4_45

25. Taentzer, G., Ohrndorf, M., Lamo, Y., Rutle, A.: Change-preserving model repair. In: Huisman, M., Rubin, J. (eds.) FASE 2017. LNCS, vol. 10202, pp. 283–299. Springer, Heidelberg (2017). https://doi.org/10.1007/978-3-662-54494-5_16

11

DeepFault: Fault Localization for Deep Neural Networks

Hasan Ferit Eniser[1]([⊠]) [iD], Simos Gerasimou[2] [iD], and Alper Sen[1] [iD]

[1] Bogazici University, Istanbul, Turkey
{hasan.eniser,alper.sen}@boun.edu.tr
[2] University of York, York, UK
simos.gerasimou@york.ac.uk

Abstract. Deep Neural Networks (DNNs) are increasingly deployed in safety-critical applications including autonomous vehicles and medical diagnostics. To reduce the residual risk for unexpected DNN behaviour and provide evidence for their trustworthy operation, DNNs should be thoroughly tested. The DeepFault whitebox DNN testing approach presented in our paper addresses this challenge by employing suspiciousness measures inspired by fault localization to establish the hit spectrum of neurons and identify suspicious neurons whose weights have not been calibrated correctly and thus are considered responsible for inadequate DNN performance. DeepFault also uses a suspiciousness-guided algorithm to synthesize new inputs, from correctly classified inputs, that increase the activation values of suspicious neurons. Our empirical evaluation on several DNN instances trained on MNIST and CIFAR-10 datasets shows that DeepFault is effective in identifying suspicious neurons. Also, the inputs synthesized by DeepFault closely resemble the original inputs, exercise the identified suspicious neurons and are highly adversarial.

Keywords: Deep Neural Networks · Fault localization · Test input generation

1 Introduction

Deep Neural Networks (DNNs) [33] have demonstrated human-level capabilities in several intractable machine learning tasks including image classification [10], natural language processing [56] and speech recognition [19]. These impressive achievements raised the expectations for deploying DNNs in real-world applications, especially in safety-critical domains. Early-stage applications include air traffic control [25], medical diagnostics [34] and autonomous vehicles [5]. The responsibilities of DNNs in these applications vary from carrying out well-defined tasks (e.g., detecting abnormal network activity [11]) to controlling the entire behaviour system (e.g., end-to-end learning in autonomous vehicles [5]).

Despite the anticipated benefits from a widespread adoption of DNNs, their deployment in safety-critical systems must be characterized by a high degree of dependability. Deviations from the expected behaviour or correct operation, as expected in safety-critical domains, can endanger human lives or cause significant financial loss. Arguably, DNN-based systems should be granted permission for use in the public domain only after exhibiting high levels of trustworthiness [6].

Software testing is the de facto instrument for analysing and evaluating the quality of a software system [24]. Testing enables at one hand to reduce the risk by proactively finding and eliminating problems (*bugs*), and on the other hand to evidence, through using the testing results, that the system actually achieves the required levels of safety. Research contributions and advice on best practices for testing conventional software systems are plentiful; [63], for instance, provides a comprehensive review of the state-of-the-art testing approaches.

Nevertheless, there are significant challenges in applying traditional software testing techniques for assessing the quality of DNN-based software [54]. Most importantly, the little correlation between the behaviour of a DNN and the software used for its implementation means that the behaviour of the DNN cannot be explicitly encoded in the control flow structures of the software [51]. Furthermore, DNNs have very complex architectures, typically comprising thousand or millions of parameters, making it difficult, if not impossible, to determine a parameter's contribution to achieving a task. Likewise, since the behaviour of a DNN is heavily influenced by the data used during training, collecting enough data that enables exercising all potential DNN behaviour under all possible scenarios becomes a very challenging task. Hence, there is a need for systematic and effective testing frameworks for evaluating the quality of DNN-based software [6].

Recent research in the DNN testing area introduces novel white-box and black-box techniques for testing DNNs [20,28,36,37,48,54,55]. Some techniques transform valid training data into adversarial through mutation-based heuristics [65], apply symbolic execution [15], combinatorial [37] or concolic testing [55], while others propose new DNN-specific coverage criteria, e.g., neuron coverage [48] and its variants [35] or MC/DC-inspired criteria [52]. We review related work in Section 6. These recent advances provide evidence that, while traditional software testing techniques are not directly applicable to testing DNNs, the sophisticated concepts and principles behind these techniques, if adapted appropriately, could be useful to the machine learning domain. Nevertheless, none of the proposed techniques uses *fault localization* [4,47,63], which can identify parts of a system that are most responsible for incorrect behaviour.

In this paper, we introduce *DeepFault*, the first fault localization-based white-box testing approach for DNNs. The objectives of DeepFault are twofold: (i) *identification* of *suspicious* neurons, i.e., neurons likely to be more responsible for incorrect DNN behaviour; and (ii) *synthesis* of new inputs, using correctly classified inputs, that exercise the identified suspicious neurons. Similar to conventional fault localization, which receives as input a faulty software and outputs a ranked list of suspicious code locations where the software may be defective [63], DeepFault *analyzes* the behaviour of neurons of a DNN after training to establish their hit spectrum and *identifies* suspicious neurons by employing suspiciousness measures. DeepFault employs a suspiciousness-guided algorithm to *synthesize* new inputs, that achieve high activation values for suspicious neurons, by modifying correctly classified inputs. Our empirical evaluation on the popular publicly available datasets MNIST [32] and CIFAR-10 [1] provides evidence that DeepFault can identify neurons which can be held responsible for insufficient network performance. DeepFault can also synthesize new inputs, which closely resemble the original inputs, are highly adversarial and increase the activation values of the identified suspicious neurons. To the best of our knowledge, DeepFault is the first research attempt that introduces *fault localization* for DNNs to identify suspicious neurons and synthesize new, likely adversarial, inputs.

Overall, the main contributions of this paper are:

- The DeepFault approach for whitebox testing of DNNs driven by fault localization;
- An algorithm for identifying suspicious neurons that adapts suspiciousness measures from the domain of spectrum-based fault localization;
- A suspiciousness-guided algorithm to synthesize inputs that achieve high activation values of potentially suspicious neurons;
- A comprehensive evaluation of DeepFault on two public datasets (MNIST and CIFAR-10) demonstrating its feasibility and effectiveness;

The reminder of the paper is structured as follows. Section 2 presents briefly DNNs and fault localization in traditional software testing. Section 3 introduces *DeepFault* and Section 4 presents its open-source implementation. Section 5 describes the experimental setup, research questions and evaluation carried out. Sections 6 and 7 discuss related work and conclude the paper, respectively.

2 Background

2.1 Deep Neural Networks

We consider Deep Learning software systems in which one or more system modules is controlled by DNNs [13]. A typical feed-forward DNN comprises multiple interconnected neurons organised into several layers: the *input* layer, the *output* layer and at least one *hidden* layer (Fig. 1). Each DNN layer comprises a sequence of neurons. A *neuron* denotes a computing unit that applies a *nonlinear activation function* to its inputs and transmits the result to neurons in the successive layer. Commonly used

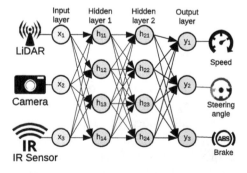

Fig. 1. A four layer fully-connected DNN that receives inputs from vehicle sensors (camera, LiDAR, infrared) and outputs a decision for speed, steering angle and brake.

activation functions are sigmoid, hyperbolic tangent, ReLU (Rectified Linear Unit) and leaky ReLU [13]. Except from the input layer, every neuron is connected to neurons in the successive layer with *weights*, i.e., edges, whose values signify the strength of a connection between neuron pairs. Once the DNN architecture is defined, i.e., the number of layers, neurons per layer and activation functions, the DNN undergoes a *training process* using a large amount of labelled training data to find weight values that minimise a *cost function*.

In general, a DNN could be considered as a parametric multidimensional function that consumes input data (e.g, raw image pixels) in its input layer, extracts *features*, i.e., semantic concepts, by performing a series of nonlinear transformations in its *hidden layers*, and, finally, produces a decision that matches the effect of these computations in its *output layer*.

2.2 Software Fault Localization

Fault localization (FL) is a white box testing technique that focuses on identifying source code elements (e.g., statements, declarations) that are more likely to contain faults. The general FL process [63] for traditional software uses as inputs a program P, corresponding to the system under test, and a test suite T, and employs an FL technique to test P against T and establish subsets that represent the passed and failed tests. Using these sets and information regarding program elements $p \in P$, the FL technique extracts fault localization data which is then employed by an FL measure to establish the "suspiciousness" of each program element p. Spectrum-based FL, the most studied class of FL techniques, uses program traces (called program spectra) of successful and failed test executions to establish for program element p the tuple (e_s, e_f, n_s, n_f). Members e_s and e_f (n_s and n_f) represent the number of times the corresponding program element has been (has not been) executed by tests, with success and fail, respectively. A spectrum-based FL measure consumes this list of tuples and ranks the program elements in decreasing order of suspiciousness enabling software engineers to inspect program elements and find faults effectively. For a comprehensive survey of state-of-the-art FL techniques, see [63].

3 DeepFault

In this section, we introduce our DeepFault whitebox approach that enables to systematically test DNNs by identifying and localizing highly erroneous neurons across a DNN. Given a pre-trained DNN, DeepFault, whose workflow is shown in Fig. 2, performs a series of *analysis*, *identification* and *synthesis* steps to identify highly erroneous DNN neurons and synthesize new inputs that exercise erroneous neurons. We describe the DeepFault steps in Sections 3.1, 3.2 and 3.3.

We use the following notations to describe DeepFault. Let $\mathcal{N}$ be a DNN with l layers. Each layer $L_i, 1 \leq i \leq l$, consists of s_i neurons and the total number of neurons in $\mathcal{N}$ is given by $s = \sum_{i=1}^{l} s_i$. Let also $n_{i,j}$ be the j-th neuron in the i-th layer. When the context is clear, we use $n \in \mathcal{N}$ to denote any neuron which is part of the DNN $\mathcal{N}$ irrespective of its layer. Likewise, we use N_H to denote the neurons which belong to the hidden layers of N, i.e., $N_H = \{n_{ij} | 1 < i < l, 1 \leq j \leq s_j\}$. We use $\mathcal{T}$ to denote the set of test inputs from the input domain of $\mathcal{N}$, $t \in \mathcal{T}$ to denote a concrete input, and $u \in t$ for an element of t. Finally, we use the function $\phi(t, n)$ to signify the output of the activation function of neuron $n \in \mathcal{N}$.

3.1 Neuron Spectrum Analysis

The first step of DeepFault involves the analysis of neurons within a DNN to establish suitable neuron-based attributes that will drive the detection and localization of faulty neurons. As highlighted in recent research [18, 48], the adoption of whitebox testing techniques provides additional useful insights regarding internal neuron activity and network behaviour. These insights cannot be easily extracted through black-box DNN testing, i.e., assessing the performance of a DNN considering only the decisions made given a set of test inputs $\mathcal{T}$.

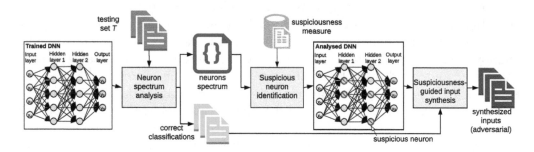

Fig. 2. DeepFault workflow.

DeepFault initiates the identification of suspicious neurons by establishing attributes that capture a neuron's execution pattern. These attributes are defined as follows. Attributes $attr_n^{as}$ and $attr_n^{af}$ signify the number of times neuron n was active (i.e., the result of the activation function $\phi(t, n)$ was above the predefined threshold) and the network made a successful or failed decision, respectively. Similarly, attributes $attr_n^{ns}$ and $attr_n^{nf}$ cover the case in which neuron n is not active. DeepFault analyses the behaviour of neurons in the DNN hidden layers, under a specific test set $\mathcal{T}$, to assemble a *Hit Spectrum (HS)* for each neuron, i.e., a tuple describing its dynamic behaviour. We define formally the HS as follows.

Definition 1. Given a DNN $\mathcal{N}$ and a test set $\mathcal{T}$, we say that for any neuron $n \in \mathcal{N}_H$ its hit spectrum is given by the tuple $HS_n = (attr_n^{as}, attr_n^{af}, attr_n^{ns}, attr_n^{nf})$.

Note that the sum of each neuron's HS should be equal to the size of $\mathcal{T}$.

Clearly, the interpretation of a hit spectrum (cf. Definition 1) is meaningful only for neurons in the hidden layers of a DNN. Since neurons within the input layer L_1 correspond to elements from the input domain (e.g., pixels from an image captured by a camera in Fig. 1), we consider them to be "correct-by-construction". Hence, these neurons cannot be credited or held responsible for a successful or failed decision made by the network. Furthermore, input neurons are always active and thus propagate one way or another their values to neurons in the following layer. Likewise, neurons within the output layer L_l simply aggregate values from neurons in the penultimate layer L_{l-1}, multiplied by the corresponding weights, and thus have limited influence in the overall network behaviour and, accordingly, to decision making.

3.2 Suspicious Neurons Identification

During this step, DeepFault consumes the set of hit spectrums, derived from DNN analysis, and identifies *suspicious* neurons which are likely to have made significant contributions in achieving inadequate DNN performance (low accuracy/high loss). To achieve this identification, DeepFault employs a spectrum-based suspiciousness measure which computes a suspiciousness score per neuron using spectrum-related information. Neurons with the highest suspiciousness score are more likely to have been trained unsatisfactorily and, hence, contributing more to incorrect DNN decisions. This indicates that the weights of these neurons need further calibration [13]. We define neuron suspiciousness as follows.

Table 1. Suspiciousness measures used in DeepFault

Suspiciousness Measure	Algebraic Formula
Tarantula [23]:	$\dfrac{attr_n^{\mathrm{af}}/(attr_n^{\mathrm{af}}+attr_n^{\mathrm{nf}})}{attr_n^{\mathrm{af}}/(attr_n^{\mathrm{af}}+attr_n^{\mathrm{nf}})+attr_n^{\mathrm{as}}/(attr_n^{\mathrm{as}}+attr_n^{\mathrm{ns}})}$
Ochiai [42]:	$\dfrac{attr_n^{\mathrm{af}}}{\sqrt{(attr_n^{\mathrm{af}}+attr_n^{\mathrm{nf}})\cdot(attr_n^{\mathrm{af}}+attr_n^{\mathrm{as}})}}$
D* [62]:	$\dfrac{attr_n^{\mathrm{af}*}}{attr_n^{\mathrm{as}}+attr_n^{\mathrm{nf}}}$

$*>0$ is a variable. We used $*=3$, among the most widely explore values [47,63].

Algorithm 1. Identification of suspicious neurons

1:	**function** SUSPICIOUSNEURONSIDENTIFICATION($\mathcal{N}, \mathcal{T}, k$)
2:	$S \leftarrow \emptyset$ ▷ suspiciousness vector
3:	**for all** $n \in N$ **do**
4:	$HS_n \leftarrow \emptyset$ ▷ n-th neuron hit spectrum vector
5:	**for all** $p \in \{as, af, ns, nf\}$ **do**
6:	$a_n^p =$ATTR($\mathcal{T}, p$) ▷ establish attribute for property p
7:	$HS_n = HS_n \cup \{a_n^p\}$ ▷ construct hit spectrum (cf. Def. 1)
8:	$S = S \cup \{$SUSP(HS_n)$\}$ ▷ determine neuron suspiciousness (cf. Def. 2)
9:	SN $= \{n|$SUSP(HS_n) $\in$ SELECT(S, k)$\}$ ▷ select the k most suspicious neurons
10:	**return** SN

Definition 2. Given a neuron $n \in \mathcal{N}_H$ with HS_n being its hit spectrum, a neuron's spectrum-based suspiciousness is given by the function $\text{SUSP}_n :$ $HS_n \rightarrow \mathbb{R}$.

Intuitively, a suspiciousness measure facilitates the derivation of correlations between a neuron's behaviour given a test set $\mathcal{T}$ and the failure pattern of $\mathcal{T}$ as determined by the overall network behaviour. Neurons whose behaviour pattern is *close* to the failure pattern of $\mathcal{T}$ are more likely to operate unreliably, and consequently, they should be assigned higher suspiciousness. Likewise, neurons whose behaviour pattern is *dissimilar* to the failure pattern of $\mathcal{T}$ are considered more trustworthy and their suspiciousness values should be low.

In this paper, we instantiate DeepFault with three different suspiciousness measures, i.e., Tarantula [23], Ochiai [42] and D* [62] whose algebraic formulae are shown in Table 1. The general principle underlying these suspiciousness measures is that the more often a neuron is activated by test inputs for which the DNN made an incorrect decision, and the less often the neuron is activated by test inputs for which the DNN made a correct decision, the more suspicious the neuron is. These suspiciousness measures have been adapted from the domain of fault localization in software engineering [63] in which they have achieved competitive results in automated software debugging by isolating the root causes of software failures while reducing human input. To the best of our knowledge, DeepFault is the first approach that proposes to incorporate these suspiciousness measures into the DNN domain for the identification of defective neurons.

The use of suspiciousness measures in DNNs targets the identification of a set of defective neurons rather than diagnosing an isolated defective neuron. Since the output of a DNN decision task is typically based on the aggregated effects of its neurons (computation units), with each neuron making its own contribution

---

Algorithm 2. New input synthesis guided by the identified suspicious neurons

Input: $SN \leftarrow$ suspicious neurons (Algorithm 1), $step \leftarrow$ step size in gradient ascent $T_s \leftarrow$ test inputs correctly classified by $\mathcal{N}$, $d \leftarrow$ new inputs maximum allowed distance

1: **function** SUSPICIOUSNESSGUIDEDINPUTSYNTHESIS($SN, T_s, d, step$)
2: $\quad NT \leftarrow \emptyset$ $\qquad\qquad\qquad\qquad\qquad\qquad\qquad\qquad\qquad$ ▷ set of synthesized inputs
3: $\quad$ **for all** $t \in T_s$ **do**
4: $\qquad G_t \leftarrow \emptyset$ $\qquad\qquad\qquad\qquad\qquad$ ▷ gradient collection of suspicious neurons
5: $\qquad$ **for all** $n \in SN$ **do**
6: $\qquad\qquad n^v = \phi(t, n)$ $\qquad\qquad\qquad\qquad\qquad$ ▷ determine output of neuron
7: $\qquad\qquad G = \partial n^v / \partial t$ $\qquad\qquad\qquad\qquad$ ▷ establish gradient of neuron for t
8: $\qquad\qquad G_t = G_t \cup \{G\}$ $\qquad\qquad$ ▷ collect gradients of suspicious neurons for t
9: $\qquad t' \leftarrow \emptyset$ $\qquad\qquad\qquad\qquad\qquad$ ▷ initialisation of input to be synthesised
10: $\qquad$ **for all** $u \in t$ **do**
11: $\qquad\qquad u_{gradient} = \sum_{G \in G_t} G/|G_t|$ $\qquad\qquad$ ▷ determine average gradient of u
12: $\qquad\qquad u_{gradient} = \text{GRADIENTCONSTRAINT}(u_{gradient}, d, step)$
13: $\qquad\qquad t' = t' \frown \{\text{DOMAINCONSTRAINTS}(u + u_{gradient})\}$
14: $\quad NT = NT \cup \{t'\}$
15: $\quad$ **return** NT

to the whole computation procedure [13], identifying a single point of failure (i.e., a single defective neuron) has limited value. Thus, after establishing the suspiciousness of neurons in the hidden layers of a DNN, the neurons are ordered in decreasing order of suspiciousness and the $k, 1 \leq l \leq s$, most probably defective (i.e., "undertrained") neurons are selected. Algorithm 1 presents the high-level steps for identifying and selecting the k most suspicious neurons. When multiple neurons achieve the same suspiciousness score, DeepFault resolves ties by prioritising neurons that belong to deeper hidden layers (i.e., they are closer to the output layer). The rationale for this decision lies in fact that neurons in deeper layers are able to learn more meaningful representations of the input space [69].

3.3   Suspiciousness-Guided Input Synthesis

DeepFault uses the selected k most suspicious neurons (cf. Section 3.2) to synthesize inputs that exercise these neurons and could be adversarial (see Section 5). The premise underlying the synthesis is that increasing the activation values of suspicious neurons will cause the propagation of degenerate information, computed by these neurons, across the network, thus, shifting the decision boundaries in the output layer. To achieve this, DeepFault applies targeted modification of test inputs from the test set T for which the DNN made correct decisions (e.g., for a classification task, the DNN determined correctly their ground truth classes) aiming to steer the DNN decision to a different region (see Fig. 2).

Algorithm 2 shows the high-level process for synthesising new inputs based on the identified suspicious neurons. The synthesis task is underpinned by a gradient ascent algorithm that aims at determining the extent to which a correctly classified input should be modified to increase the activation values of suspicious neurons. For any test input $t \in T_s$ correctly classified by the DNN, we extract the value of each suspicious neuron and its gradient in lines 6 and 7, respectively. Then, by iterating over each input dimension $u \in t$, we determine the gradient value $u_{gradient}$ by which u will be perturbed (lines 11–12). The value of $u_{gradient}$ is based on the mean gradient of u across the suspicious neurons controlled by the function GRADIENTCONSTRAINTS. This function uses a test set specific *step* parameter and a distance d parameter to facilitate the synthesis of realistic test inputs that are sufficiently *close*, according to L_∞-norm, to the original inputs. We demonstrate later in the evaluation of DeepFault (cf. Table 4) that these parameters enable the synthesis of inputs similar to the original. The function DOMAINCONSTRAINTS applies domain-specific constraints thus ensuring that u changes due to gradient ascent result in realistic and physically reproducible test inputs as in [48]. For instance, a domain-specific constraint for an image classification dataset involves bounding the pixel values of synthesized images to be within a certain range (e.g., 0–1 for the MNIST dataset [32]). Finally, we append the updated u to construct a new test input t' (line 13).

As we experimentally show in Section 5, the suspiciousness measures used by DeepFault can synthesize adversarial inputs that cause the DNN to misclassify previously correctly classified inputs. Thus, the identified suspicious neurons can be attributed a degree of responsibility for the inadequate network performance meaning that their weights have not been optimised. This reduces the DNN's ability for high generalisability and correct operation in untrained data.

4 Implementation

To ease the evaluation and adoption of the DeepFault approach (cf. Fig. 2), we have implemented a prototype tool on top of the open-source machine learning framework Keras (v2.2.2) [9] with Tensorflow (v1.10.1) backend [2]. The full experimental results summarised in the following section are available on DeepFault project page at https://DeepFault.github.io.

5 Evaluation

5.1 Experimental Setup

We evaluate DeepFault on two popular publicly available datasets. MNIST [32] is a handwritten digit dataset with 60,000 training samples and 10,000 testing samples; each input is a 28×28 pixel image with a class label from 0 to 9. CIFAR-10 [1] is an image dataset with 50,000 training samples and 10,000 testing samples; each input is a 32×32 image in ten different classes (e.g., dog, bird, car).

For each dataset, we study three DNNs that have been used in previous research [1,60] (Table 2). All DNNs have different architecture and number of trainable parameters. For MNIST, we use fully connected neural networks (dense) and for CIFAR-10 we use convolutional neural networks with max-pooling and dropout layers that have been trained to achieve at least 95% and 70% accuracy on the provided test sets, respectively. The column 'Architecture' shows the number of fully connected hidden layers and the number of neurons per layer. Each DNN uses a leaky ReLU [38] as its activation function ($\alpha = 0.01$), which has been shown to achieve competitive accuracy results [67].

We instantiate DeepFault using the suspiciousness measures Tarantula [23], Ochiai [42] and D* [62] (Table 1). We analyse the effectiveness of DeepFault instances using different number of suspicious neurons, i.e., $k \in \{1, 2, 3, 5, 10\}$ and $k \in \{10, 20, 30, 40, 50\}$ for MNIST and CIFAR models, respectively. We also ran preliminary experiments for each model from Table 2 to tune the hyperparameters of Algorithm 2 and facilitate replication of our findings. Since gradient values are model and input specific, the perturbation magnitude should reflect these values and reinforce their impact. We determined empirically that $step = 1$ and $step = 10$ are good values, for MNIST and CIFAR models, respectively, that enable our algorithm to perturb inputs. We also set the maximum allowed distance d to be at most 10% (L_∞) with regards to the range of each input dimension (maximum pixel value). As shown in Table 4, the synthesized inputs are very similar to the original inputs and are rarely constrained by d. Studying other $step$ and d values is part of our future work. All experiments were run on an Ubuntu server with 16 GB memory and Intel Xeon E5-2698 2.20 GHz.

Table 2. Details of MNIST and CIFAR-10 DNNs used in the evaluation.

Dataset	Model Name	# Trainable Params	Architecture	Accuracy
MNIST	MNIST_1	27,420	$<5 \times 30>$	96.6%
	MNIST_2	22,975	$<6 \times 25>$	95.8%
	MNIST_3	18,680	$<8 \times 20>$	95%
CIFAR-10	CIFAR_1	411,434	$<4 \times 128>$	70.1%
	CIFAR_2	724,010	$<2 \times 256>$	72.6%
	CIFAR_3	1,250,858	$<1 \times 512>$	76.1%

5.2 Research Questions

Our experimental evaluation aims to answer the following research questions.

RQ1 (Validation): Can DeepFault find suspicious neurons effectively?
If suspicious neurons do exist, suspiciousness measures used by DeepFault should comfortably outperform a random suspiciousness selection strategy.

RQ2 (Comparison): How do DeepFault instances using different suspiciousness measures compare against each other? Since DeepFault can work with multiple suspiciousness measures, we examined the results produced by DeepFault instances using Tarantula [23], Ochiai [42] and D* [62].

RQ3 (Suspiciousness Distribution): How are suspicious neurons found by DeepFault distributed across a DNN? With this research question, we analyse the distribution of suspicious neurons in hidden DNN layers using different suspiciousness measures.

RQ4 (Similarity): How realistic are inputs synthesized by DeepFault?
We analysed the distance between synthesized and original inputs to examine the extent to which DeepFault synthesizes realistic inputs.

RQ5 (Increased Activations): Do synthesized inputs increase activation values of suspicious neurons? We assess whether the suspiciousness-guided input synthesis algorithm produces inputs that reinforce the influence of suspicious neurons across a DNN.

RQ6 (Performance): How efficiently can DeepFault synthesize new inputs? We analysed the time consumed by DeepFault to synthesize new inputs and the effect of suspiciousness measures used in DeepFault instances.

5.3 Results and Discussion

RQ1 (Validation). We apply the DeepFault workflow to the DNNs from Table 2. To this end, we instantiate DeepFault with a suspiciousness measure, *analyse* a pre-trained DNN given the dataset's test set $\mathcal{T}$, *identify* k neurons with the highest suspiciousness scores and *synthesize* new inputs, from *correctly classified* inputs, that exercise these suspicious neurons. Then, we measure the prediction performance of the DNN on the synthesized inputs using the standard performance metrics: cross-entropy *loss*, i.e., the divergence between output and target distribution, and *accuracy*, i.e., the percentage of correctly classified inputs over all given inputs. Note that DNN analysis is done per class, since the activation pattern of inputs from the same class is similar to each other [69].

Table 3 shows the average loss and accuracy for inputs synthesized by Deep-Fault instances using Tarantula (T), Ochiai (O), D* (D) and a random selection strategy (R) for different number of suspicious neurons k on the MNIST (top) and CIFAR-10 (bottom) models from Table 2. Each cell value in Table 3, except from random R, is averaged over 100 synthesized inputs (10 per class). For R, we collected 500 synthesized inputs (50 per class) over five independent runs, thus, reducing the risk that our findings may have been obtained by chance.

As expected (see Table 3), DeepFault using any suspiciousness measure (T, O, D) obtained considerably lower prediction performance than R on MNIST models. The suspiciousness measures T and O are also effective on CIFAR-10 model, whereas the performance between D and R is similar. These results show that the identified k neurons are actually *suspicious* and, hence, their weights are insufficiently trained. Also, we have sufficient evidence that increasing the activation value of suspicious neurons by slightly perturbing inputs that have been classified correctly by the DNN could transform them into adversarial.

We applied the non-parametric statistical test Mann-Whitney with 95% confidence level [61] to check for statistically significant performance difference between the various DeepFault instances and random. We confirmed the significant difference among T-R and O-R (p-value < 0.05) for all MNIST and CIFAR-10 models and for all k values. We also confirmed the interesting observation that significant difference between D-R exists only for MNIST models (all k values). We plan to investigate this observation further in our future work.

Another interesting observation from Table 3 is the small performance difference of DeepFault instances for different k values. We investigated this further by analyzing the activation values of the next k' most suspicious neurons according to the suspiciousness order given by Algorithm 1. For instance, if $k = 2$ we analysed the activation values of the next $k' \in \{3, , 5, 10\}$ most suspicious neurons. We observed that the synthesized inputs frequently increase the activation values of the k' neurons whose suspiciousness scores are also high, in addition to increasing the values of the top k suspicious neurons.

Considering these results, we have empirical evidence about the existence of *suspicious* neurons which can be responsible for inadequate DNN performance. Also, we confirmed that DeepFault instances using sophisticated suspiciousness measures significantly outperform a random strategy for most of the studied DNN models (except from the D-R case on CIFAR models; see RQ3).

RQ2 (Comparison). We compare DeepFault instances using different suspiciousness measures and carried out pairwise comparisons using the Mann-Whitney test to check for significant difference between T, O, and D*. We show the results of these comparisons on the project's webpage. Ochiai achieves better results on MNIST_1 and MNIST_3 models for various k values. This result suggests that the suspicious neurons reported by Ochiai are more responsible

Table 3. Accuracy and loss of inputs synthesized by DeepFault on MNIST (top) and CIFAR-10 (bottom) datasets. The best results per suspiciousness measure are shown in bold. (k:#suspicious neurons, T:Tarantula, O:Ochiai, D:D*, R:Random)

k	Measure	MNIST_1				MNIST_2				MNIST_3			
		T	O	D	R	T	O	D	R	T	O	D	R
1	Loss	3.55	**6.19**	4.03	2.42	3.48	3.53	**3.97**	2.78	7.35	**8.23**	6.36	3.66
	Accuracy	0.26	**0.16**	0.2	0.59	0.3	**0.2**	0.5	0.49	0.16	**0.1**	0.13	0.39
2	Loss	3.73	**6.08**	3.18	2.67	3.12	3.76	**4.08**	0.9	4.27	**6.81**	6.5	3.06
	Accuracy	**0.16**	0.23	0.4	0.58	0.23	0.23	**0.13**	0.77	0.29	**0.13**	0.26	0.56
3	Loss	4.1	6.19	**6.25**	1.14	2.39	**3.94**	3.04	1.61	3.33	**7.59**	6.98	2.91
	Accuracy	**0.23**	**0.23**	0.33	0.77	0.46	0.26	**0.23**	0.67	0.26	**0.06**	0.16	0.61
5	Loss	4.63	6.68	**6.97**	1.1	2.49	**3.64**	3.48	0.94	4.15	**7.22**	6.47	1.22
	Accuracy	0.23	0.23	**0.13**	0.79	0.26	0.26	**0.2**	0.73	0.16	**0.1**	0.26	0.77
10	Loss	4.97	6.95	**7.4**	1.3	2.08	3.06	**3.82**	0.49	4.45	**7.16**	5.9	0.57
	Accuracy	0.23	**0.2**	0.23	0.75	0.4	**0.23**	0.26	0.86	**0.13**	**0.13**	**0.13**	0.87

k	Measure	CIFAR_1				CIFAR_2				CIFAR_3			
		T	O	D	R	T	O	D	R	T	O	D	R
10	Loss	12.75	**13.49**	1.33	3.25	**8.42**	8.41	0	2.49	**6.12**	1.77	1.12	1.21
	Accuracy	0.2	**0.16**	0.9	0.79	**0.47**	**0.47**	1.0	0.84	**0.62**	0.88	0.92	0.91
20	Loss	**12.79**	12.43	0.45	1.8	**8.81**	6.92	0.32	1.67	**6.12**	1.12	0.96	0.64
	Accuracy	**0.2**	0.22	0.96	0.88	**0.44**	0.55	0.97	0.89	**0.62**	0.92	0.93	0.95
30	Loss	**13.19**	13.13	0.38	1.43	**8.35**	6.32	0.55	0.86	**5.64**	0.76	0.42	0.41
	Accuracy	**0.18**	**0.18**	0.95	0.9	**0.48**	0.6	0.95	0.94	**0.64**	0.93	0.96	0.97
40	Loss	**13.69**	11.92	0.8	1.29	**9.4**	5.01	0.32	0.61	**4.51**	1.12	0.22	0.54
	Accuracy	**0.14**	0.26	0.92	0.91	**0.41**	0.68	0.97	0.95	**0.72**	0.92	0.97	0.96
50	Loss	12.1	**13.37**	0.36	0.9	**9.59**	3.38	0	0.56	**4.67**	0.04	0.64	0.48
	Accuracy	0.24	**0.17**	0.96	0.94	**0.4**	0.78	1.0	0.96	**0.71**	0.98	0.96	0.96

for insufficient DNN performance. D* performs competitively on MNIST_1 and MNIST_3 for $k \in \{3, 5, 10\}$, but its performance on CIFAR-10 models is significantly inferior to Tarantula and Ochiai. The best performing suspiciousness measure in CIFAR models for most k values is, by a great amount, Tarantula.

These findings show that multiple suspiciousness measures could be used for instantiating DeepFault with competitive performance. We also have evidence that DeepFault using D* is ineffective for some complex networks (e.g., CIFAR-10), but there is insufficient evidence for the best performing DeepFault instance. Our findings conform to the latest research on software fault localization which claims that there is no single best spectrum-based suspiciousness measure [47].

RQ3 (Suspiciousness Distribution). We analysed the distribution of suspicious neurons identified by DeepFault instances across the hidden DNN layers.

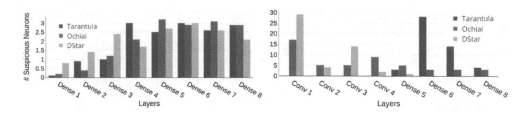

Fig. 3. Suspicious neurons distribution on MNIST_3 (left) and CIFAR_3 (right) models.

Figure 3 shows the distribution of suspicious neurons on MNIST_3 and CIFAR_3 models with $k = 10$ and $k = 50$, respectively. Considering MNIST_3, the majority of suspicious neurons are located at the deeper hidden layers (Dense 4-Dense 8) irrespective of the suspiciousness measure used by DeepFault. This observation holds for the other MNIST models and k values. On CIFAR_3, however, we can clearly see variation in the distributions across the suspiciousness measures. In fact, D* suggests that most of the suspicious neurons belong to initial hidden layers which is in contrast with Tarantula's recommendations. As reported in RQ2, the inputs synthesized by DeepFault using Tarantula achieved the best results on CIFAR models, thus showing that the identified neurons are actually suspicious. This difference in the distribution of suspicious neurons explains the inferior inputs synthesized by D* on CIFAR models (Table 3).

Another interesting finding concerns the relation between the suspicious neurons distribution and the "adversarialness" of synthesized inputs. When suspicious neurons belong to deeper hidden layers, the likelihood of the synthesized input being adversarial increases (cf. Table 3 and Fig. 3). This finding is explained by the fact that initial hidden layers transform input features (e.g., pixel values) into abstract features, while deeper hidden layers extract more semantically meaningful features and, thus, have higher influence in the final decision [13].

RQ4 (Similarity). We examined the distance between original, correctly classified, inputs and those synthesized by DeepFault, to establish DeepFault's ability to synthesize realistic inputs. Table 4 (left) shows the distance between original and synthesized inputs for various distance metrics (L_1 Manhattan, L_2 Euclidean, $L\infty$ Chebyshev) for different k values (# suspicious neurons). The distance values, averaged over inputs synthesized using the DeepFault suspiciousness measures (T, O and D*), demonstrate that the degree of perturbation is similar irrespective of k for MNIST models, whereas for CIFAR models the distance decreases as k increases. Given that a MNIST input consists of 784 pixels, with each pixel taking values in $[0, 1]$, the average perturbation per input is less than 5.28% of the total possible perturbation (L_1 distance). Similarly, for a CIFAR input that comprises 3072 pixels, with each pixel taking values in $\{0, 1, ..., 255\}$, the average perturbation per input is less that 0.03% of the total possible perturbation (L_1 distance). Thus, for both datasets, the difference of synthesized inputs to their original versions is very small. We qualitatively

Table 4. Distance between synthesized and original inputs. The values shown represent minimal perturbation to the original inputs ($< 5\%$ for MNIST and $< 1\%$ for CIFAR-10).

k	MNIST			CIFAR			Susp.	MNIST			CIFAR		
MNIST(CIFAR)	L_1	L_2	L_∞	L_1	L_2	L_∞	measure	L_1	L_2	L_∞	L_1	L_2	L_∞
1(10)	41.4	2.0	0.1	179.07	7216.6	15.46	Tarantula	40.3	1.97	0.1	180.23	6575.6	19.41
2(20)	41.2	1.99	0.1	144.95	5897.4	12.45	Ochiai	41.0	1.98	0.1	110.45	4825.3	7.84
3(30)	40.9	1.98	0.1	124.61	5073.9	10.67	D*	41.5	1.99	0.1	109.4	4823.2	7.39
5(40)	40.7	1.97	0.1	113.45	4579.2	9.89	Random	39.2	1.92	0.1	121.73	4988.1	11.63
10(50)	40.3	1.96	0.1	104.72	4273	9.24							

Fig. 4. Synthesized images (top) and their originals (bottom). For each dataset, suspicious neurons are found using (from left to right) Tarantula, Ochiai, D* and Random.

support our findings by showing in Fig. 4 the synthesized images and their originals for an example set of inputs from the MNIST and CIFAR-10 datasets.

We also compare the distances between original and synthesized inputs based on the suspiciousness measures (Table 4 right). The inputs synthesized by DeepFault instances using T, O or D* are very close to the inputs of the random selection strategy (L_1 distance). Considering these results, we can conclude that DeepFault is effective in synthesizing highly adversarial inputs (cf. Table 3) that closely resemble their original counterparts.

RQ5 (Increasing Activations). We studied the activation values of suspicious neurons identified by DeepFault to examine whether the synthesized inputs increase the values of these neurons. The gradients of suspicious neurons used in our suspiciousness-guided

Table 5. Effectiveness of *suspiciousness-guided input synthesis* algorithm to increase activations values of suspicious neurons.

Datasets	k: MNIST(CIFAR)				
	1(10)	2(20)	3(30)	5(40)	10(50)
MNIST	98%	99%	97%	97%	91%
CIFAR	91%	92%	90%	89%	88%

input synthesis algorithm might be conflicting and a global increase in all suspicious neurons' values might not be feasible. This can occur if some neurons' gradients are negative, indicating a decrease in an input feature's value, whereas other gradients are positive and require to increase the value of the same feature. Table 5 shows the percentage of suspicious neurons k, averaged over all suspiciousness measures for all considered MNIST and CIFAR-10 models from Table 2, whose values were increased by the inputs synthesized by DeepFault. For MNIST models, DeepFault synthesized inputs that increase the suspicious neurons' values with success at least 97% for $k \in \{1, 2, 3, 5\}$, while the average effectiveness for CIFAR models is 90%. These results show the effectiveness of our suspiciousness-guided input synthesis algorithm in generating inputs that increase the activation values of suspicious neurons (see https://DeepFault.github.io).

RQ6 (Performance). We measured the performance of Algorithm 2 to synthesize new inputs (https://DeepFault.github.io). The average time required to synthesize a single input for MNIST and CIFAR models is 1 s and 24.3 s, respectively. The performance of the algorithm depends on the number of suspicious neurons (k), the distribution of those neurons over the DNN and its architecture. For CIFAR models, for instance, the execution time per input ranges between 3 s ($k = 10$) and 48 s ($k = 50$). We also confirmed empirically that more time is taken to synthesize an input if the suspicious neurons are in deeper hidden layers.

5.4 Threats to Validity

Construct validity threats might be due to the adopted experimental methodology including the selected datasets and DNN models. To mitigate this threat, we used widely studied public datasets (MNIST [32] and CIFAR-10 [1]), and applied DeepFault to multiple DNN models of different architectures with competitive prediction accuracies (cf. Table 2). Also, we mitigate threats related to the identification of suspicious neurons (Algorithm 1) by adapting suspiciousness measures from the fault localization domain in software engineering [63].

Internal validity threats might occur when establishing the ability of Deep-Fault to synthesize new inputs that exercise the identified suspicious neurons. To mitigate this threat, we used various distance metrics to confirm that the synthesized inputs are close to the original inputs and similar to the inputs synthesized by a random strategy. Another threat could be that the suspiciousness measures employed by DeepFault accidentally outperform the random strategy. To mitigate this threat, we reported the results of the random strategy over five independent runs per experiment. Also, we ensured that the distribution of the randomly selected suspicious neurons resembles the distribution of neurons identified by DeepFault suspiciousness measures. We also used the non-parametric statistical test Mann-Whitney to check for significant difference in the performance of DeepFault instances and random with a 95% confidence level.

External validity threats might exist if DeepFault cannot access the internal DNN structure to assemble the hit spectrums of neurons and establish their suspiciousness. We limit this threat by developing DeepFault using the open-source frameworks Keras and Tensorflow which enable whitebox DNN analysis. We also examined various spectrum-based suspiciousness measures, but other measures can be investigated [63]. We further reduce the risk that DeepFault might be difficult to use in practice by validating it against several DNN instances trained on two widely-used datasets. However, more experiments are needed to assess the applicability of DeepFault in domains and networks with characteristics different from those used in our evaluation (e.g., LSTM and Capsule networks [50]).

6 Related Work

DNN Testing and Verification. The inability of blackbox DNN testing to provide insights about the internal neuron activity and enable identification of corner-case inputs that expose unexpected network behaviour [14], urged researchers to leverage whitebox testing techniques from software engineering [28,35,43,48,54]. DeepXplore [48] uses a differential algorithm to generate inputs that increase neuron coverage. DeepGauge [35] introduces multi-granularity coverage criteria for effective test synthesis. Other research proposes testing criteria and techniques inspired by metamorphic testing [58], combinatorial testing [37], mutation testing [36], MC/DC [54], symbolic execution [15] and concolic testing [55].

Formal DNN verification aims at providing guarantees for trustworthy DNN operation [20]. Abstraction refinement is used in [49] to verify safety properties of small neural networks with sigmoid activation functions, while AI^2 [12] employs abstract interpretation to verify similar properties. Reluplex [26] is an SMT-based approach that verifies safety and robustness of DNNs with ReLUs, and DeepSafe [16] uses Reluplex to identify safe regions in the input space. DLV [60] can verify local DNN robustness given a set of user-defined manipulations.

DeepFault adopts spectrum-based fault localization techniques to systematically identify suspicious neurons and uses these neurons to synthesize new inputs, which is mostly orthogonal to existing research on DNN testing and verification.

Adversarial Deep Learning. Recent studies have shown that DNNs are vulnerable to adversarial examples [57] and proposed search algorithms [8,40,41,44], based on gradient descent or optimisation techniques, for generating adversarial inputs that have a minimal difference to their original versions and force the DNN to exhibit erroneous behaviour. These types of adversarial examples have been shown to exist in the physical world too [29]. The identification of and protection against these adversarial attacks, is another active area of research [45,59]. DeepFault is similar to these approaches since it uses the identified suspicious neurons to synthesize perturbed inputs which as we have demonstrated in Section 5 are adversarial. Extending DeepFault to support the synthesis of adversarial inputs using these adversarial search algorithms is part of our future work.

Fault Localization in Traditional Software. Fault localization is widely studied in many software engineering areas including including software debugging [46], program repair [17] and failure reproduction [21,22]. The research focus in fault localization is the development of identification methods and suspiciousness measures that isolate the root causes of software failures with reduced engineering effort [47]. The most notable fault localization methods are spectrum-based [3,23,30,31,62], slice-based [64] and model-based [39]. Threats to the value of empirical evaluations of spectrum-based fault localization are studied in [53], while the theoretical analyses in [66,68] set a formal foundation about desirable formal properties that suspiciousness measures should have. We refer interested readers to a recent comprehensive survey on fault localization [63].

7 Conclusion

The potential deployment of DNNs in safety-critical applications introduces unacceptable risks. To reduce these risks to acceptable levels, DNNs should be tested thoroughly. We contribute in this effort, by introducing DeepFault, the first fault localization-based whitebox testing approach for DNNs. DeepFault *analyzes* pre-trained DNNs, given a specific test set, to establish the hit spectrum of each neuron, *identifies suspicious neurons* by employing suspiciousness measures and *synthesizes* new inputs that increase the activation values of the suspicious neurons. Our empirical evaluation on the widely-used MNIST and CIFAR-10 datasets shows that DeepFault can identify neurons which can be held responsible for inadequate performance. DeepFault can also synthesize new inputs, which closely resemble the original inputs, are highly adversarial and exercise the identified suspicious neurons. In future work, we plan to evaluate DeepFault on other DNNs and datasets, to improve the suspiciousness-guided synthesis algorithm and to extend the synthesis of adversarial inputs [44]. We will also explore techniques to repair the identified suspicious neurons, thus enabling to reason about the safety of DNNs and support safety case generation [7,27].

References

1. Cifar10 model in keras. https://github.com/keras-team/keras/blob/master/examples/cifar10_cnn.py. Accessed 08 Oct 2018
2. Abadi, M., Barham, P., Chen, J., et al.: TensorFlow: a system for large-scale machine learning. In: 12th USENIX Symposium on Operating Systems Design and Implementation, pp. 265–283 (2016)
3. Abreu, R., Zoeteweij, P., Golsteijn, R., Van Gemund, A.J.: A practical evaluation of spectrum-based fault localization. J. Syst. Softw. **82**(11), 1780–1792 (2009)
4. Artzi, S., Dolby, J., Tip, F., Pistoia, M.: Directed test generation for effective fault localization. In: International Symposium on Software Testing and Analysis (ISSTA), pp. 49–60 (2010)
5. Bojarski, M., Del Testa, D., Dworakowski, D., Firner, B., et al.: End to end learning for self-driving cars (2016)
6. Burton, S., Gauerhof, L., Heinzemann, C.: Making the case for safety of machine learning in highly automated driving. In: Tonetta, S., Schoitsch, E., Bitsch, F. (eds.) SAFECOMP 2017. LNCS, vol. 10489, pp. 5–16. Springer, Cham (2017). https://doi.org/10.1007/978-3-319-66284-8_1
7. Calinescu, R., Weyns, D., Gerasimou, S., Iftikhar, M.U., Habli, I., Kelly, T.: Engineering trustworthy self-adaptive software with dynamic assurance cases. IEEE Trans. Softw. Eng. **44**(11), 1039–1069 (2018)
8. Carlini, N., Wagner, D.: Towards evaluating the robustness of neural networks. In: IEEE Symposium on Security and Privacy (S&P), pp. 39–57 (2017)

9. Chollet, F., et al.: Keras (2015). https://keras.io
10. Cireşan, D., Meier, U., Schmidhuber, J.: Multi-column deep neural networks for image classification. In: Conference on Computer Vision and Pattern Recognition (CVPR), pp. 3642–3649 (2012)
11. Cui, Z., Xue, F., Cai, X., Cao, Y., et al.: Detection of malicious code variants based on deep learning. IEEE Trans. Ind. Inform. **14**(7), 3187–3196 (2018)
12. Gehr, T., Mirman, M., Drachsler-Cohen, D., Tsankov, P., et al.: AI2: safety and robustness certification of neural networks with abstract interpretation. In: IEEE Symposium on Security and Privacy (S&P), pp. 1–16 (2018)
13. Goodfellow, I., Bengio, Y., Courville, A.: Deep Learning. MIT Press (2016). http://www.deeplearningbook.org
14. Goodfellow, I., Papernot, N.: The challenge of verification and testing of machine learning (2017)
15. Gopinath, D., Wang, K., Zhang, M., Pasareanu, C.S., Khurshid, S.: Symbolic execution for deep neural networks. In: arXiv preprint arXiv:1807.10439 (2018)
16. Gopinath, D., Katz, G., Pasareanu, C.S., Barrett, C.: DeepSafe: a data-driven approach for checking adversarial robustness in neural networks. arXiv preprint arXiv:1710.00486 (2017)
17. Goues, C.L., Nguyen, T., Forrest, S., Weimer, W.: GenProg: a generic method for automatic software repair. IEEE Trans. Softw. Eng. **38**(1), 54–72 (2012)
18. Guo, J., Jiang, Y., Zhao, Y., Chen, Q., Sun, J.: DLFuzz: differential fuzzing testing of deep learning systems. In: ACM Joint European Software Engineering Conference and Symposium on the Foundations of Software Engineering (ESEC/FSE), pp. 739–743 (2018)
19. Hinton, G., Deng, L., Yu, D., Dahl, G.E., et al.: Deep neural networks for acoustic modeling in speech recognition: the shared views of four research groups. IEEE Signal Process. Mag. **29**(6), 82–97 (2012)
20. Huang, X., Kwiatkowska, M., Wang, S., Wu, M.: Safety verification of deep neural networks. In: Majumdar, R., Kunčak, V. (eds.) CAV 2017. LNCS, vol. 10426, pp. 3–29. Springer, Cham (2017). https://doi.org/10.1007/978-3-319-63387-9_1
21. Jin, W., Orso, A.: BugRedux: reproducing field failures for in-house debugging. In: International Conference on Software Engineering (ICSE), pp. 474–484 (2012)
22. Jin, W., Orso, A.: F3: fault localization for field failures. In: ACM International Symposium on Software Testing and Analysis (ISSTA), pp. 213–223 (2013)
23. Jones, J.A., Harrold, M.J.: Empirical evaluation of the tarantula automatic fault-localization technique. In: IEEE/ACM International Conference on Automated Software Engineering (ASE), pp. 273–282 (2005)
24. Jorgensen, P.C.: Software Testing: A Craftsman's Approach. Auerbach Publications (2013)
25. Julian, K.D., Lopez, J., Brush, J.S., Owen, M.P., Kochenderfer, M.J.: Policy compression for aircraft collision avoidance systems. In: IEEE Digital Avionics Systems Conference (DASC), pp. 1–10 (2016)
26. Katz, G., Barrett, C., Dill, D.L., Julian, K., Kochenderfer, M.J.: Reluplex: an efficient SMT solver for verifying deep neural networks. In: Majumdar, R., Kunčak, V. (eds.) CAV 2017. LNCS, vol. 10426, pp. 97–117. Springer, Cham (2017). https://doi.org/10.1007/978-3-319-63387-9_5
27. Kelly, T.P.: Arguing safety: a systematic approach to managing safety cases. Ph.D. thesis, University of York, York (1999)
28. Kim, J., Feldt, R., Yoo, S.: Guiding deep learning system testing using surprise adequacy. In: arXiv preprint arXiv:1808.08444 (2018)

29. Kurakin, A., Goodfellow, I., Bengio, S.: Adversarial examples in the physical world. arXiv preprint arXiv:1607.02533 (2016)
30. Landsberg, D., Chockler, H., Kroening, D., Lewis, M.: Evaluation of measures for statistical fault localisation and an optimising scheme. In: Egyed, A., Schaefer, I. (eds.) FASE 2015. LNCS, vol. 9033, pp. 115–129. Springer, Heidelberg (2015). https://doi.org/10.1007/978-3-662-46675-9_8
31. Landsberg, D., Sun, Y., Kroening, D.: Optimising spectrum based fault localisation for single fault programs using specifications. In: International Conference on Fundamental Approaches to Software Engineering (FASE), pp. 246–263 (2018)
32. LeCun, Y.: The MNIST database of handwritten digits (1998). http://yann.lecun.com/exdb/mnist
33. Lecun, Y., Bengio, Y., Hinton, G.: Deep learning. Nature **521**(7553), 436–444 (2015)
34. Litjens, G., Kooi, T., Bejnordi, B.E., et al.: A survey on deep learning in medical image analysis. Med. Image Anal. **42**, 60–88 (2017)
35. Ma, L., Juefei-Xu, F., Zhang, F., Sun, J., et al.: DeepGauge: multi-granularity testing criteria for deep learning systems. In: IEEE/ACM International Conference on Automated Software Engineering (ASE) (2018)
36. Ma, L., Zhang, F., Sun, J., Xue, M., et al.: DeepMutation: mutation testing of deep learning systems. In: IEEE International Symposium on Software Reliability Engineering (ISSRE) (2018)
37. Ma, L., Zhang, F., Xue, M., Li, B., et al.: Combinatorial testing for deep learning systems. In: arXiv preprint arXiv:1806.07723 (2018)
38. Maas, A.L., Hannun, A.Y., Ng, A.Y.: Rectifier nonlinearities improve neural network acoustic models. In: International Conference on Machine Learning (ICML), vol. 30, p. 3 (2013)
39. Mayer, W., Stumptner, M.: Evaluating models for model-based debugging. In: IEEE/ACM International Conference on Automated Software Engineering (ASE), pp. 128–137 (2008)
40. Moosavi-Dezfooli, S.M., Fawzi, A., Frossard, P.: DeepFool: a simple and accurate method to fool deep neural networks. In: IEEE Conference on Computer Vision and Pattern Recognition (CVPR), pp. 2574–2582 (2016)
41. Nguyen, A., Yosinski, J., Clune, J.: Deep neural networks are easily fooled: high confidence predictions for unrecognizable images. In: Conference on Computer Vision and Pattern Recognition (CVPR), pp. 427–436 (2015)
42. Ochiai, A.: Zoogeographic studies on the soleoid fishes found in Japan and its neighbouring regions. Bull. Jpn. Soc. Sci. Fish. **22**, 526–530 (1957)
43. Odena, A., Goodfellow, I.: TensorFuzz: debugging neural networks with coverage-guided fuzzing. arXiv preprint arXiv:1807.10875 (2018)
44. Papernot, N., McDaniel, P., Jha, S., Fredrikson, M., et al.: The limitations of deep learning in adversarial settings. In: International Symposium on Security and Privacy (S&P), pp. 372–387 (2016)
45. Papernot, N., McDaniel, P., Wu, X., Jha, S., Swami, A.: Distillation as a defense to adversarial perturbations against deep neural networks. In: International Symposium on Security and Privacy (S&P), pp. 582–597 (2016)
46. Parnin, C., Orso, A.: Are automated debugging techniques actually helping programmers? In: International Symposium on Software Testing and Analysis (ISSTA), pp. 199–209 (2011)
47. Pearson, S., Campos, J., Just, R., Fraser, G., et al.: Evaluating and improving fault localization. In: International Conference on Software Engineering (ICSE), pp. 609–620 (2017)

48. Pei, K., Cao, Y., Yang, J., Jana, S.: DeepXplore: automated whitebox testing of deep learning systems. In: Symposium on Operating Systems Principles (SOSP), pp. 1–18 (2017)

49. Pulina, L., Tacchella, A.: An abstraction-refinement approach to verification of artificial neural networks. In: Touili, T., Cook, B., Jackson, P. (eds.) CAV 2010. LNCS, vol. 6174, pp. 243–257. Springer, Heidelberg (2010). https://doi.org/10.1007/978-3-642-14295-6_24

50. Sabour, S., Frosst, N., Hinton, G.E.: Dynamic routing between capsules. In: Advances in Neural Information Processing Systems, pp. 3856–3866 (2017)

51. Salay, R., Queiroz, R., Czarnecki, K.: An analysis of ISO26262: using machine learning safely in automotive software. arXiv preprint arXiv:1709.02435 (2017)

52. Seshia, S.A., et al.: Formal specification for deep neural networks. Technical report, University of California at Berkeley (2018)

53. Steimann, F., Frenkel, M., Abreu, R.: Threats to the validity and value of empirical assessments of the accuracy of coverage-based fault locators. In: International Symposium on Software Testing and Analysis (ISSTA), pp. 314–324 (2013)

54. Sun, Y., Huang, X., Kroening, D.: Testing deep neural networks. arXiv preprint arXiv:1803.04792 (2018)

55. Sun, Y., Wu, M., Ruan, W., Huang, X., et al.: Concolic testing for deep neural networks. In: Proceedings of the 33rd ACM/IEEE International Conference on Automated Software Engineering (ASE), pp. 109–119 (2018)

56. Sutskever, I., Vinyals, O., Le, Q.V.: Sequence to sequence learning with neural networks. In: International Conference on Neural Information Processing Systems, pp. 3104–3112 (2014)

57. Szegedy, C., Zaremba, W., Sutskever, I., Bruna, J., et al.: Intriguing properties of neural networks. arXiv preprint arXiv:1312.6199 (2013)

58. Tian, Y., Pei, K., Jana, S., Ray, B.: DeepTest: automated testing of deep-neural-network-driven autonomous cars. In: International Conference on Software Engineering (ICSE), pp. 303–314 (2018)

59. Tramèr, F., Kurakin, A., Papernot, N., Goodfellow, I., et al.: Ensemble adversarial training: attacks and defenses. arXiv preprint arXiv:1705.07204 (2017)

60. Wicker, M., Huang, X., Kwiatkowska, M.: Feature-guided black-box safety testing of deep neural networks. In: International Conference on Tools and Algorithms for the Construction and Analysis of Systems (TACAS), pp. 408–426 (2018)

61. Wohlin, C., Runeson, P., Höst, M., Ohlsson, M.C., et al.: Experimentation in Software Engineering. Springer, Heidelberg (2012). https://doi.org/10.1007/978-3-642-29044-2

62. Wong, W.E., Debroy, V., Gao, R., Li, Y.: The DStar method for effective software fault localization. IEEE Trans. Reliab. **63**(1), 290–308 (2014)

63. Wong, W.E., Gao, R., Li, Y., Abreu, R., Wotawa, F.: A survey on software fault localization. IEEE Trans. Softw. Eng. **42**(8), 707–740 (2016)

64. Wong, W.E., Qi, Y.: Effective program debugging based on execution slices and inter-block data dependency. J. Syst. Softw. **79**(7), 891–903 (2006)

65. Wu, M., Wicker, M., Ruan, W., Huang, X., Kwiatkowska, M.: A game-based approximate verification of deep neural networks with provable guarantees. arXiv preprint arXiv:1807.03571 (2018)

66. Xie, X., Chen, T.Y., Kuo, F.C., Xu, B.: A theoretical analysis of the risk evaluation formulas for spectrum-based fault localization. ACM Trans. Softw. Eng. Methodol. **22**(4), 31–40 (2013)

67. Xu, B., Wang, N., Chen, T., Li, M.: Empirical evaluation of rectified activations in convolutional network. arXiv preprint arXiv:1505.00853 (2015)

68. Yoo, S., Xie, X., Kuo, F.C., Chen, T.Y., Harman, M.: Human competitiveness of genetic programming in spectrum-based fault localisation: theoretical and empirical analysis. ACM Trans. Softw. Eng. Methodol. **26**(1), 4–30 (2017)
69. Zeiler, M.D., Fergus, R.: Visualizing and understanding convolutional networks. In: Fleet, D., Pajdla, T., Schiele, B., Tuytelaars, T. (eds.) ECCV 2014. LNCS, vol. 8689, pp. 818–833. Springer, Cham (2014). https://doi.org/10.1007/978-3-319-10590-1_53

12

Automatic Modeling of Opaque Code for JavaScript Static Analysis

Joonyoung Park[1,2]([✉])(iD), Alexander Jordan[1]([✉])(iD), and Sukyoung Ryu[2]([✉])(iD)

[1] Oracle Labs Australia, Brisbane, Australia
{joonyoung.p.park,alexander.jordan}@oracle.com
[2] KAIST, Daejeon, Republic of Korea
{sryu.cs,gmb55}@kaist.ac.kr

Abstract. Static program analysis often encounters problems in analyzing library code. Most real-world programs use library functions intensively, and library functions are usually written in different languages. For example, static analysis of JavaScript programs requires analysis of the standard built-in library implemented in host environments. A common approach to analyze such *opaque code* is for analysis developers to build models that provide the semantics of the code. Models can be built either manually, which is time consuming and error prone, or automatically, which may limit application to different languages or analyzers. In this paper, we present a novel mechanism to support automatic modeling of opaque code, which is applicable to various languages and analyzers. For a given static analysis, our approach automatically computes analysis results of opaque code via dynamic testing during static analysis. By using testing techniques, the mechanism does not guarantee *sound* over-approximation of program behaviors in general. However, it is fully automatic, is scalable in terms of the size of opaque code, and provides more precise results than conventional over-approximation approaches. Our evaluation shows that although not all functionalities in opaque code can (or should) be modeled automatically using our technique, a large number of JavaScript built-in functions are approximated soundly yet more precisely than existing manual models.

Keywords: Automatic modeling · Static analysis · Opaque code · JavaScript

1 Introduction

Static analysis is widely used to optimize programs and to find bugs in them, but it often faces difficulties in analyzing library code. Since most real-world programs use various libraries usually written in different programming languages, analysis developers should provide analysis results for libraries as well. For example, static analysis of JavaScript apps involves analysis of the builtin functions implemented in host environments like the V8 runtime system written in C++.

A conventional approach to analyze such *opaque code* is for analysis developers to create models that provide the analysis results of the opaque code. Models approximate the behaviors of opaque code, they are often tightly integrated with specific static analyzers to support precise abstract semantics that are compatible with the analyzers' internals.

Developers can create models either manually or automatically. Manual modeling is complex, time consuming, and error prone because developers need to consider all the possible behaviors of the code they model. In the case of JavaScript, the number of APIs to be modeled is large and ever-growing as the language evolves. Thus, various approaches have been proposed to model opaque code automatically. They create models either from specifications of the code's behaviors [2,26] or using dynamic information during execution of the code [8,9,22]. The former approach heavily depends on the quality and format of available specifications, and the latter approach is limited to the capability of instrumentation or specific analyzers.

In this paper, we propose a novel mechanism to model the behaviors of opaque code to be used by static analysis. While existing approaches aim to create general models for the opaque code's behaviors, which can produce analysis results for all possible inputs, our approach computes specific results of opaque code during static analysis. This on-demand modeling is specific to the abstract states of a program being analyzed, and it consists of three steps: sampling, run, and abstraction. When static analysis encounters opaque code with some abstract state, our approach generates samples that are a subset of all possible inputs of the opaque code by concretizing the abstract state. After evaluating the code using the concretized values, it abstracts the results and uses it during analysis. Since the sampling generally covers only a small subset of infinitely many possible inputs to opaque code, our approach does not guarantee the soundness of the modeling results just like other automatic modeling techniques.

The sampling strategy should select well-distributed samples to explore the opaque code's behaviors as much as possible and to avoid redundant ones. Generating too few samples may miss too much behaviors, while redundant samples can cause the performance overhead. As a simple yet effective way to control the number of samples, we propose to use *combinatorial testing* [11].

We implemented the proposed automatic modeling as an extension of SAFE, a JavaScript static analyzer [13,17]. For opaque code encountered during analysis, the extension generates concrete inputs from abstract states, and executes the code dynamically using the concrete inputs via a JavaScript engine (Node.js in our implementation). Then, it abstracts the execution results using the operations provided by SAFE such as lattice-*join* and our over-approximation, and resumes the analysis.

Our paper makes the following contributions:

- We present a novel way to handle opaque code during static analysis by computing a precise on-demand model of the code using (1) input samples that represent analysis states, (2) dynamic execution, and (3) abstraction.

- We propose a combinatorial sampling strategy to efficiently generate well-distributed input samples.
- We evaluate our tool against hand-written models for large parts of JavaScript's builtin functions in terms of precision, soundness, and performance.
- Our tool revealed implementation errors in existing hand-written models, demonstrating that it can be used for automatic testing of static analyzers.

In the remainder of this paper, we present our Sample-Run-Abstract approach to model opaque code for static analysis (Sect. 2) and describe the sampling strategy (Sect. 3) we use. We then discuss our implementation and experiences of applying it to JavaScript analysis (Sect. 4), evaluate the implementation using ECMAScript 5.1 builtin functions as benchmarks (Sect. 5), discuss related work (Sect. 6), and conclude (Sect. 7).

2 Modeling via Sample-Run-Abstract

Our approach models opaque code by designing a universal model, which is able to handle arbitrary opaque code. Rather than generating a specific model for each opaque code statically, it produces a single general model, which produces results for given states using concrete semantics via dynamic execution. We call this universal model the *SRA model*.

In order to create the SRA model for a given static analyzer $\mathcal{A}$ and a dynamic executor $\mathcal{E}$, we assume the following:

- The static analyzer $\mathcal{A}$ is based on abstract interpretation [6]. It provides the abstraction function $\alpha : \wp(S) \to \widehat{S}$ and the concretization function $\gamma : \widehat{S} \to \wp(S)$ for a set of concrete states S and a set of abstract states $\widehat{S}$.
- An abstract domain forms a complete lattice, which has a partial order among its values from $\bot$(bottom) to $\top$(top).
- For a given program point $c \in C$, either $\mathcal{A}$ or $\mathcal{E}$ can identify the code corresponding to the point.

Then, the SRA model consists of the following three steps:

- *Sample* : $\widehat{S} \to \wp(S)$
  For a given abstract state $\widehat{s} \in \widehat{S}$, *Sample* chooses a finite set of elements from $\gamma(\widehat{s})$, a possible set of values for $\widehat{s}$. Because it is, in the general case, impossible to execute opaque code dynamically with all possible inputs, *Sample* should select representative elements efficiently as we discuss in the next section.
- *Run* : $C \times S \to S$
  For a given program point and a concrete state at this point, *Run* generates executable code corresponding to the point and state, executes the code, and returns the result state of the execution.
- *Abstract* : $\wp(S) \to \widehat{S}$
  For a given set of concrete states, *Abstract* produces an abstract state that encompasses the concrete states. One can apply α to each concrete state, join

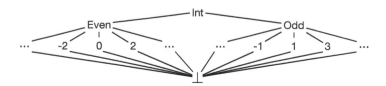

Fig. 1. An abstract domain for even and odd integers

all the resulting abstract states, and optionally apply an over-approximation heuristic, comparable to widening $Broaden : \widehat{S} \rightarrow \widehat{S}$ to mitigate missing behaviors of the opaque code due to the under-approximate sampling.

We write the SRA model as $\Downarrow_{SRA}: C \times \widehat{S} \rightarrow \widehat{S}$ and define it as follows:

$$
\begin{aligned}
\Downarrow_{SRA} (c, \widehat{s}) = \quad & Abstract(\{Run(c, s) \quad | \quad s \in Sample(\widehat{s})\}) \\
= & Broaden(\bigsqcup\{\alpha(\{Run(c, s)\}) \quad | \quad s \in Sample(\widehat{s})\})
\end{aligned}
$$

We now describe how $\Downarrow_{SRA}$ works using an example abstract domain for even and odd integers as shown in Fig. 1. Let us consider the code snippet x := abs(x) at a program point c where the library function abs is opaque. We use maps from variables to their concrete values for concrete states, maps from variables to their abstract values for abstract states, and the identity function for $Broaden$ in this example.

Case $\widehat{s}_1 \equiv [\mathtt{x} : n]$ where n is a constant integer:

$$
\begin{aligned}
\Downarrow_{SRA} (c, \widehat{s}_1) &= \bigsqcup\{\alpha(\{Run(c, s)\}) \quad | \quad s \in Sample(\widehat{s}_1)\} \\
&= \bigsqcup\{\alpha(\{Run(c, s)\}) \quad | \quad s \in \{[\mathtt{x} : n]\}\} \\
&= \bigsqcup\{\alpha(\{Run(c, [\mathtt{x} : n])\})\} \\
&= \bigsqcup\{\alpha(\{[\mathtt{x} : |n|]\})\} \\
&= [\mathtt{x} : |n|]
\end{aligned}
$$

Because the given abstract state $\widehat{s}_1$ contains a single abstract value corresponding to a single concrete value, $Sample$ produces the set of all possible states, which makes $\Downarrow_{SRA}$ provide a sound and also the most precise result.

Case $\widehat{s}_2 \equiv [\mathtt{x} : \mathtt{Even}]$:

$$
\begin{aligned}
\Downarrow_{SRA} (c, \widehat{s}_2) &= \bigsqcup\{\alpha(\{Run(c, s)\}) \quad | \quad s \in Sample(\widehat{s}_2)\} \\
&= \bigsqcup\{\alpha(\{Run(c, s)\}) \quad | \quad s \in \{[\mathtt{x} : -2], [\mathtt{x} : 0], [\mathtt{x} : 2]\}\} \\
&= \bigsqcup\{\alpha(\{[\mathtt{x} : 0], [\mathtt{x} : 2]\})\} \\
&= [\mathtt{x} : \mathtt{Even}]
\end{aligned}
$$

When $Sample$ selects three elements from the set of all possible states represented by $\widehat{s}_2$, executing abs results in $\{[\mathtt{x} : 0], [\mathtt{x} : 2]\}$. Since joining these two abstract states produces **Even**, $\Downarrow_{SRA}$ models the correct behavior of abs by taking advantage of the abstract domain.

Case $\widehat{s}_3 \equiv [\texttt{x} : \texttt{Int}]$:

$\Downarrow_{SRA} (c, \widehat{s}_3)$
$= \bigsqcup\{\alpha(\{Run(c, s)\}) \mid s \in Sample(\widehat{s}_3)\}$
$= \bigsqcup\{\alpha(\{Run(c, s)\}) \mid s \in Sample(\widehat{s}_2) \cup Sample([\texttt{x} : \texttt{Odd}])\}$
$= \bigsqcup\{\alpha(\{Run(c, s)\}) \mid s \in \{[\texttt{x} : -2], [\texttt{x} : -1], [\texttt{x} : 0], [\texttt{x} : 1], [\texttt{x} : 2], [\texttt{x} : 3]\}\}$
$= \bigsqcup\{\alpha(\{[\texttt{x} : 0], [\texttt{x} : 1], [\texttt{x} : 2], [\texttt{x} : 3]\})\}$
$= [\texttt{x} : \texttt{Int}]$

When an abstract value has a finite number of elements that are immediately below it in the abstract domain lattice, our sampling strategy selects samples from them recursively. Thus, in this example, $Sample([\texttt{x} : \texttt{Int}])$ becomes the union of $Sample([\texttt{x} : \texttt{Even}])$ and $Sample([\texttt{x} : \texttt{Odd}])$. We explain this recursive sampling strategy in Sect. 3.

Case $\widehat{s}_4 \equiv [\texttt{x} : \texttt{Odd}]$:

$\Downarrow_{SRA} (c, \widehat{s}_4) = \bigsqcup\{\alpha(\{Run(c, s)\}) \mid s \in Sample(\widehat{s}_4)\}$
$= \bigsqcup\{\alpha(\{Run(c, s)\}) \mid s \in \{[\texttt{x} : -1], [\texttt{x} : 1]\}\}$
$= \bigsqcup\{\alpha(\{[\texttt{x} : 1]\})\}$
$= [\texttt{x} : 1]$

While $\Downarrow_{SRA}$ produces sound and precise results for the above three cases, it does not guarantee soundness; it may miss some behaviors of opaque code due to the limitations of the sampling strategy. Let us assume that $Sample([\texttt{x} : \texttt{Odd}])$ selects $\{[\texttt{x} : -1], [\texttt{x} : 1]\}$ this time. Then, the model produces an unsound result $[\texttt{x} : 1]$, which does not cover odd integers, because the selected values explore only partial behaviors of **abs**. When the number of possible states at a call site of opaque code is infinite, the sampling strategy can lead to unsound results. A well-designed sampling strategy is crucial for our modeling approach; it affects the analysis performance and soundness significantly. The approach is precise thanks to under-approximated results from sampling, but entails a tradeoff between the analysis performance and soundness depending on the number of samples. In the next section, we propose a strategy to generate samples for various abstract domains and to control sample sizes effectively.

3   Combinatorial Sampling Strategy

We propose to use a combinatorial sampling strategy (inspired by combinatorial testing) by the types of values that an abstract domain represents. The domains represent either *primitive* values like number and string, or *object* values like tuple, set, and map. Based on combinatorial testing, our strategy is recursively defined on the hierarchy of abstract domains used to represent program states. Assume that $\widehat{a}, \widehat{b} \in \widehat{A}$ are abstract values that we want to concretize using *Sample*.

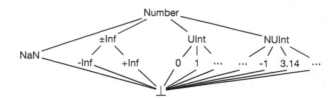

Fig. 2. The SAFE number domain for JavaScript

3.1   Abstract Domains for Primitive Values

To explain our sampling strategy for primitive abstract domains, we use the `DefaultNumber` domain from SAFE as an example. `DefaultNumber` represents JavaScript numbers with subcategories as shown in Fig. 2. The subcategories are NaN (not a number), ±Inf (positive/negative infinity), UInt (unsigned integer), and NUInt (not an unsigned integer, which is a negative integer or a floating point number).

Case $|\gamma(\widehat{a})| = constant$:

$$Sample(\widehat{a}) = \gamma(\widehat{a})$$

When $\widehat{a}$ represents a finite number of concrete values, *Sample* simply takes all the values. For example, ±Inf has two possible values, +Inf and -Inf. Therefore, $Sample(\pm\text{Inf}) = \{\text{+Inf}, \text{-Inf}\}$.

Case $|\gamma(\widehat{a})| = \infty$ and $|\{\widehat{b} \in \widehat{A} \mid \forall \widehat{x} \sqsubset \widehat{a}.\ \widehat{b} \not\sqsubset \widehat{x}\}| = constant$:

$$Sample(\widehat{a}) = \bigcup_{\widehat{b}} Sample(\widehat{b})$$

When $\widehat{a}$ represents an infinite number of concrete values, but it *covers* (that is, is immediately preceded by) a finite number of abstract values in the lattice, *Sample* applies to each predecessor recursively and merges the concrete results by set union. Note that, "*y* covers *x*" holds whenever $x \sqsubset y$ and there is no z such that $x \sqsubset z \sqsubset y$. The number of samples increases linearly in this step. Number falls into this case. It represents infinitely many numbers, but it covers four abstract values in the lattice: NaN, ±Inf, UInt, and NUInt.

Case $|\gamma(\widehat{a})| = \infty$ and $|\{\widehat{b} \in A \mid \forall \widehat{x} \sqsubset \widehat{a}.\ \widehat{b} \not\sqsubset \widehat{x}\}| = \infty$:

$$Sample(\widehat{a}) = H(\gamma(\widehat{a}))$$

When $\widehat{a}$ represents infinitely many concrete values and also covers infinitely many abstract values, we make the number of samples finite by applying a heuristic injection H of seed samples. For seed samples, we propose the following guidelines to manually select them:

- Use a small number of commonly used values. Our conjecture is that common values will trigger the same behavior in opaque code repeatedly.
- Choose values that have special properties for known operators. For example, for each operator, select the minimum, maximum, identity, and inverse elements, if any.

In the `DefaultNumber` domain example, `UInt` and `NUInt` fall into this case. For the evaluation of our modeling approach in Sect. 5, we selected seed samples based on the guidelines as follows:

$$Sample(\text{UInt}) = \{0, 1, 3, 10, 9999\}$$
$$Sample(\text{NUInt}) = \{-10, -3, -1, -0.5, -0, 0.5, 3.14\}$$

We experimentally show that this simple heuristic works well for automatic modeling of JavaScript builtin functions.

3.2 Abstract Domains for Object Values

Our sampling strategy for object abstract domains consists of four steps. To sample from a given abstract object $\widehat{a} \in \widehat{A}$, we assume the following:

- A concrete object $a \in \gamma(\widehat{a})$ is a map from fields to their values: $Map[F, V]$.
- Abstract domains for fields and values are $\widehat{F}$ and $\widehat{V}$, respectively.
- The abstract domain $\widehat{A}$ provides two helper functions: $mustF : \widehat{A} \to \wp(F)$ and $mayF : \widehat{A} \to \widehat{F}$. The $mustF(\widehat{a})$ function returns a set of fields that $\forall a \in \gamma(\widehat{a})$ must have, and $mayF(\widehat{a})$ returns an abstract value $\widehat{f} \in \widehat{F}$ representing a set of fields that $\exists a \in \gamma(\widehat{a})$ may have.

Then, the sampling strategy follows the next four steps:

1. Sampling fields
   In order to construct sampled objects, it first samples a finite number of fields. JavaScript provides open objects, where fields can be added and removed dynamically, and fields can be referenced not only by string literals but also by arbitrary expressions of string values. Thus, this step collects fields from a finite set of fields that all possible objects should contain (F_{must}) and samples from a possibly infinite set of fields that some possible objects may (but not must) contain (F_{may}):

$$F_{must} = mustF(\widehat{a})$$
$$F_{may} = Sample(mayF(\widehat{a})) \setminus F_{must}$$

2. Abstracting values for the sampled fields
   For the fields in F_{must} and F_{may} sampled from the given abstract object $\widehat{a}$, it constructs two maps from fields to their abstract values, M_{must} and M_{may}, respectively, of type $Map[F, \widehat{V}]$:

$$M_{must} = \lambda f \in F_{must}.\ \alpha(\{a(f) \mid a \in \gamma(\widehat{a})\})$$
$$M_{may} = \lambda f \in F_{may}\ .\ \alpha(\{a(f) \mid a \in \gamma(\widehat{a})\})$$

3. Sampling values
   From M_{must} and M_{may}, it constructs another map $M_s : F \to \wp(V_\sharp)$, where $V_\sharp = V \cup \{\sharp\}$ denotes a set of values and the absence of a field $\sharp$, by applying $Sample$ to the value of each field in F_{must} and F_{may}. The value of each field in F_{may} contains $\sharp$ to denote that the field may not exist in M_s:

$$M_s = \lambda f \in F_{must} \cup F_{may} \cdot \begin{cases} Sample(M_{must}(f)) & \text{if } f \in F_{must} \\ Sample(M_{may}(f)) \cup \{\sharp\} & \text{if } f \in F_{may} \end{cases}$$

4. Choosing samples by combinatorial testing
   Finally, since a number of all combinations from M_s, $\prod_{f \in Domain(M_s)} |M_s(f)|$, grows exponentially, the last step limits the number selections. We solve this selection problem by reducing it to a traditional testing problem with combinatorial testing [3]. Combinatorial testing is a well-studied problem and efficient algorithms for generating test cases exist. It addresses a similar problem to ours, increasing dynamic coverage of code under test, but in the context of finding bugs:

   > "The most common bugs in a program are generally triggered by either a single input parameter or an interaction between pairs of parameters."

   Thus, we apply each-used or pair-wise testing (1 or 2-wise) as the last step.

   Now, we demonstrate each step using an abstract array object $\widehat{a}$, whose length is greater than or equal to 2 and the elements of which are true or false. We write $\top_b$ to denote an abstract value such that $\gamma(\top_b) = \{\text{true}, \text{false}\}$.

- Assumptions
    - A concrete array object a is a map from indices to boolean values: $Map[\text{UInt}, \text{Boolean}]$.
    - For given abstract object $\widehat{a}$, $mustF(\widehat{a}) = \{0, 1\}$ and $mayF(\widehat{a}) = \text{UInt}$.
    - From Sect. 3.1, we sample $\{0, 1, 3, 10, 9999\}$ for UInt.
    - $k\text{-}wise(M)$ generates a set of minimum number of test cases satisfying all the requirements of $k\text{-}wise$ testing for a map M. It constructs a test case by choosing one element from a set on each field.
- Step 1: Sampling fields

$$F_{must} = \{0, 1\}$$
$$F_{may} = Sample(\text{UInt}) \setminus \{0, 1\} = \{3, 10, 9999\}$$

- Step 2: Abstracting values for the sampled fields

$$M_{must} = [0 \mapsto \top_b, 1 \mapsto \top_b]$$
$$M_{may} = [3 \mapsto \top_b, 10 \mapsto \top_b, 9999 \mapsto \top_b]$$

- Step 3: Sampling values

$$M_s = [\quad 0 \mapsto \{\text{true}, \text{false}\}, \quad 1 \mapsto \{\text{true}, \text{false}\},$$
$$3 \mapsto \{\text{true}, \text{false}, \sharp\}, 10 \mapsto \{\text{true}, \text{false}, \sharp\},$$
$$9999 \mapsto \{\text{true}, \text{false}, \sharp\} \qquad]$$

- Step 4: Choosing samples by combinatorial testing
   The number of all combinations $\prod_{f \in Domain(M_s)} |M_s(f)|$ is 108 even after sampling fields and values in an under-approximate manner. We can avoid such

explosion of samples and manage well-distributed samples by using combinatorial testing. With each-used testing, three combinations can cover every element in a set on each field at least once:

$$1\text{-}wise(M_s) =$$
$$\{ [0 \mapsto \texttt{true}, \quad 1 \mapsto \texttt{false}, 3 \mapsto \texttt{true}, \quad 10 \mapsto \nexists, \qquad 9999 \mapsto \nexists],$$
$$[0 \mapsto \texttt{false}, 1 \mapsto \texttt{true}, \quad 3 \mapsto \texttt{false}, 10 \mapsto \texttt{false}, 9999 \mapsto \texttt{true}],$$
$$[0 \mapsto \texttt{false}, 1 \mapsto \texttt{true}, \quad 3 \mapsto \nexists, \qquad 10 \mapsto \texttt{true}, \quad 9999 \mapsto \texttt{false}] \}$$

With pair-wise testing, 12 samples can cover every pair of elements from different sets at least once.

4 Implementation

We implemented our automatic modeling approach for JavaScript because of its large number of builtin APIs and complex libraries, which are all opaque code for static analysis. They include the functions in the ECMAScript language standard [1] and web standards such as DOM and browser APIs. We implemented the modeling as an extension of SAFE [13,17], a JavaScript static analyzer. When the analyzer encounters calls of opaque code during analysis, it uses the SRA model of the code.

Sample. We applied the combinatorial sampling strategy for the SAFE abstract domains. Of the abstract domains for primitive JavaScript values, UInt, NUInt, and OtherStr represent an infinite number of concrete values (c.f. third case in Sect. 3.1) and thus require the use of heuristics. We describe the details of our heuristics and sample sets in Sect. 5.1.

We implemented the *Sample* step to use "each-used sample generation" for object abstract domains by default. In order to generate more samples, we added three options to apply pair-wise generation:

- ThisPair generates pairs between the values of this and heap,
- HeapPair among objects in the heap, and
- ArgPair among property values in an arguments object.

As an exception, we use the all-combination strategy for the DefaultDataProp domain representing a JavaScript property, consisting of a value and three booleans: writable, enumerable, and configurable. Note that *field* is used for language-independent objects and *property* is for JavaScript objects. The number of their combinations is limited to 2^3. We consider a linear increase of samples as acceptable. The *Sample* step returns a finite set of concrete states, and each element in the set, which in turn contains concrete values only, is passed to the *Run* step.

Run. For each concrete input state, the *Run* step obtains a result state by executing the corresponding opaque code in four steps:

1. Generation of executable code
   First, *Run* populates object values from the concrete state. We currently omit the JavaScript scope-chain information, because the library functions that we analyze as opaque code are independent from the scope of user code. It derives executable code to invoke the opaque code and adds argument values from the static analysis context.
2. Execution of the code using a JavaScript engine
   Run executes the generated code using the JavaScript `eval` function on Node.js. Populating objects and their properties from sample values before invoking the opaque function may throws an exception. In such cases, *Run* executes the code once again with a different sample value. If the second sample value also throws an exception during population of the objects and their properties, it dismisses the code.
3. Serialization of the result state
   After execution, the result state contains the objects from the input state, the return value of the opaque code, and all the values that it might refer to. Also, any mutation of objects of the input state as well as newly created objects are captured in this way. We use a snapshot module of SAFE to serialize the result state into a JSON-like format.
4. Transfer of the state to the analyzer
   The serialized snapshot is then passed to SAFE, where it is parsed, loaded, and combined with other results as a set of concrete result states.

Abstract. To abstract result states, we mostly used existing operations in SAFE, like lattice-*join*, and also implemented an over-approximation heuristic function, *Broaden*, comparable to widening. We use *Broaden* for property name sets in JavaScript objects, because *mayF* of a JavaScript abstract object can produce an abstract value that denotes an infinite set of concrete strings, and because $\Downarrow_{SRA}$ cannot produce such an abstract value from simple sampling and *join*. Thus, we regard all possibly absent properties as sampled properties. Then, we implemented the *Broaden* function merging all possibly absent properties into one abstract property representing any property, when the number of absent properties is greater than a certain threshold proportional to a number of sampled properties.

5   Evaluation

We evaluated the $\Downarrow_{SRA}$ model in two regards, (1) the feasibility of replacing existing manual models (RQ1 and RQ2) and (2) the effects of our heuristic H on the analysis soundness (RQ3). The research questions are as follow:

- **RQ1: Analysis performance of $\Downarrow_{SRA}$**
  Can $\Downarrow_{SRA}$ replace existing manual models for program analysis with decent performance in terms of soundness, precision, and runtime overhead?

– **RQ2: Applicability of $\Downarrow_{SRA}$**
  Is $\Downarrow_{SRA}$ broadly applicable to various builtin functions of JavaScript?
– **RQ3: Dependence on heuristic H**
  How much is the performance of $\Downarrow_{SRA}$ affected by the heuristics?

After describing the experimental setup for evaluation, we present our answers to the research questions with quantitative results, and discuss the limitations of our evaluation.

5.1 Experimental Setup

In order to evaluate the $\Downarrow_{SRA}$ model, we compared the analysis performance and applicability of $\Downarrow_{SRA}$ with those of the existing manual models in SAFE. We used two kinds of subjects: browser benchmark programs and builtin functions. From 34 browser benchmarks included in the test suite of SAFE, a subset of V8 Octane[1], we collected 13 of them that invoke opaque code. Since browser benchmark programs use a small number of opaque functions, we also generated test cases for 134 functions in the ECMAScript 5.1 specification.

Each test case contains abstract values that represent two or more possible values. Because SAFE uses a finite number of abstract domains for primitive values, we used all of them in the test cases. We also generated 10 abstract objects. Five of them are manually created to represent arbitrary objects:

OBJ1 has an arbitrary property whose value is an arbitrary primitive.
OBJ2 is a property descriptor whose `"value"` is an arbitrary primitive, and the others are arbitrary booleans.
OBJ3 has an arbitrary property whose value is OBJ2.
OBJ4 is an empty array whose `"length"` is arbitrary.
OBJ5 is an arbitrary-length array with an arbitrary property

The other five objects were collected from SunSpider benchmark programs by using Jalangi2 [20] to represent frequently used abstract objects. We counted the number of function calls with object arguments and joined the most used object arguments in each program. Out of 10 programs that have function calls with object arguments, we discarded four programs that use the same objects for every function call, and one program that uses an argument with 2500 properties, which makes manual inspection impossible. We joined the first 10 concrete objects for each argument of the following benchmark to obtain abstract objects: 3d-cube.js, 3d-raytrace.js, access-binary-trees.js, regexp-dna.js, and string-fasta.js. For 134 test functions, when a test function consumes two or more arguments, we restricted each argument to have only an expected type to manage the number of test cases. Also, we used one or minimum number of arguments for functions with variable number of arguments.

In summary, we used 13 programs for RQ1, and 134 functions with 1565 test cases for RQ2 and RQ3. All experiments were on a 2.9 GHz quad-core Intel Core i7 with 16 GB memory machine.

---

[1] https://github.com/chromium/octane.

5.2   Answers to Research Questions

Answer to RQ1. We compared the precision, soundness, and analysis time of the SAFE manual models and the $\Downarrow_{SRA}$ model. Table 1 shows the precision and soundness for each opaque function call, and Table 2 presents the analysis time and number of samples for each program.

As for the precision, Table 1 shows that $\Downarrow_{SRA}$ produced more precise results than manual models for 9 (19.6%) cases. We manually checked whether each result of a model is sound or not by using the partial order function ($\sqsubseteq$) implemented in SAFE. We found that all the results of the SAFE manual models for the benchmarks were sound. The $\Downarrow_{SRA}$ model produced an unsound result for only one function: `Math.random`. While it returns a floating-point value in the range $[0, 1)$, $\Downarrow_{SRA}$ modeled it as `NUInt`, instead of the expected `Number`, because it missed 0.

As shown in Table 2, on average $\Downarrow_{SRA}$ took 1.35 times more analysis time than the SAFE models. The table also shows the number of context-sensitive opaque function calls during analysis (#Call), the maximum number of samples (#Max), and the total number of samples (#Total). To understand the runtime overhead better, we measured the proportion of elapsed time for each step. On average, *Sample* took 59%, *Run* 7%, *Abstract* 17%, and the rest 17%. The experimental results show that $\Downarrow_{SRA}$ provides high precision while slightly sacrificing soundness with modest runtime overhead.

Answer to RQ2. Because the benchmark programs use only 15 opaque functions as shown in Table 1, we generated abstracted arguments for 134 functions out of 169 functions in the ECMAScript 5.1 builtin library, for which SAFE has manual models. We semi-automatically checked the soundness and precision of the $\Downarrow_{SRA}$ model by comparing the analysis results with their expected results. Table 3 shows the results in terms of test cases (left half) and functions (right half). The **Equal** column shows the number of test cases or functions, for which both models provide equal results that are sound. The **SRA Pre.** column shows the number of such cases where the $\Downarrow_{SRA}$ model provides sound and more precise results than the manual model. The **Man. Uns.** column presents the number of such cases where $\Downarrow_{SRA}$ provides sound results but the manual one provides unsound results, and **SRA Uns.** shows the opposite case of **Man. Uns.** Finally, **Not Comp.** shows the number of cases where the results of $\Downarrow_{SRA}$ and the manual model are incomparable.

The $\Downarrow_{SRA}$ model produced sound results for 99.4% of test cases and 94.0% of functions. Moreover, $\Downarrow_{SRA}$ produced more precise results than the manual models for 33.7% of test cases and 50.0% of functions. Although $\Downarrow_{SRA}$ produced unsound results for 0.6% of test cases and 6.0% of functions, we found soundness bugs in the manual models using 1.3% of test cases and 7.5% of functions. Our experiments showed that the automatic $\Downarrow_{SRA}$ model produced less unsound results than the manual models. We reported the manual models producing unsound results to SAFE developers with the concrete examples that were generated in the *Run* step, which revealed the bugs.

Table 1. Precision and soundness by functions in the benchmarks

Function	Precision and Soundness		
	Equal Precise	More Precise	Unsound
`Array, Array.prototype.join, Array.prototype.push`	15	5	0
`Date, Date.prototype.getTime`	0	4	0
`Error`	5	0	0
`Math.cos, Math.max, Math.pow, Math.sin, Math.sqrt`	11	0	0
`Math.random`	0	0	1
`Number.prototype.toString`	1	0	0
`String, String.prototype.substring`	4	0	0
Total	36	9	1
Proportion	78.3%	19.6%	2.2%

Table 2. Analysis time overhead by programs in the benchmarks

Program	Manual		$\Downarrow_{SRA}$				Increased
	Time(ms)	#Call	Time(ms)	#Call	#Max	#Total	Time Ratio
3d-morph.js	1,423	50	2,641	50	16	408	1.86
access-binary-trees.js	1,926,132	10	1,784,866	10	16	95	0.93
access-fannkuch.js	1,615	31	2,627	31	15	413	1.63
access-nbody.js	10,125	132	25,564	324	16	4,274	2.52
access-nsieve.js	1,019	6	1,126	6	16	54	1.10
bitops-nsieve-bits.js	282	1	343	1	2	2	1.22
math-cordic.js	574	2	662	2	2	4	1.15
math-partial-sums.js	1,613	99	4,703	99	16	916	2.92
math-spectral-norm.js	10,702	6	10,986	6	16	96	1.03
string-fasta.js	22,170	78	6,147	30	226	2,555	0.28
navier-stokes.js	4,662	20	5,104	20	2	40	1.09
richards.js	86,013	85	88,902	85	54	4,018	1.03
splay.js	259,073	423	217,863	422	56	11,492	0.84
Total	2,325,404	943	2,151,533	1,086	453	24,367	1.35

Answer to RQ3. The sampling strategy plays an important role in the performance of $\Downarrow_{SRA}$ especially for soundness. Our sampling strategy depends on two factors: (1) manually sampled sets via the heuristic H and (2) each-used or pair-wise selection for object samples. We used manually sampled sets for three abstract values: UInt, NUInt, and OtherStr. To sample concrete values from them, we used three methods: Base simply follows the guidelines described in Sect. 3.1, Random generates samples randomly, and Final denotes the heuristics determined by our trials and errors to reach the highest ratio of sound results. For object samples, we used three pair-wise options: HeapPair, ThisPair, and Arg-Pair. For various sampling configurations, Table 4 summarizes the ratio of sound

Table 3. Precision and soundness for the builtin functions

Object	#Test Case							#Function						
	Equal	SRA Pre.	Man. Uns.	Man. Pre.	SRA Uns.	Not Comp.	Total	Equal	SRA Pre.	Man. Uns.	Man. Pre.	SRA Uns.	Not Comp.	Total
Array	59	144	1	0	0	0	174	8	7	1	0	0	0	16
Boolean	37	2	3	0	0	0	42	1	0	3	0	0	0	4
Date	74	241	0	2	1	1	319	8	35	0	2	1	1	47
Global	7	1	0	0	0	0	8	1	1	0	0	0	0	2
Math	106	5	0	0	6	0	117	11	2	0	0	5	1	18
Number	41	71	0	3	0	1	116	1	6	0	0	0	0	8
Object	370	24	7	1	3	5	410	12	2	5	0	2	0	21
String	300	70	9	0	0	0	379	3	14	1	0	0	0	18
Total	994	528	20	6	10	7	1565	45	67	10	2	8	2	134
Proportion	63.5%	33.7%	1.3%	0.4%	0.6%	0.4%	100%	33.6%	50.0%	7.5%	1.5%	6.0%	1.5%	100%

Table 4. Soundness and sampling cost for the builtin functions

Sampling Configuration						Builtin Function		
Set Heuristic			Pair Option			Sound Result Ratio	#Ave.	#Max
UInt	NUInt	Other	HeapPair	ThisPair	ArgPair			
Base	Base	Base	F	F	F	85.0%	17.4	41
Random	Random	Random	F	F	F	84.9%	17.4	41
Final	Final	Final	F	F	F	92.1%	32.6	98
			F	F	T	93.5%	38.1	226
			F	T	F	95.0%	181.9	4312
			F	T	T	95.5%	276.8	11752
			T	F	F	96.2%	323.0	7220
			T	F	T	97.4%	397.5	16498
			T	T	F	99.2%	513.7	11988
			T	T	T	99.4%	677.6	16498

results, the average and maximum numbers of samples for the test cases used in RQ2.

The table shows that **Base** and **Random** produced sound results for 85.0% and 84.9% (the worst case among 10 repetitions) of the test cases, respectively. Even without any sophisticated heuristics or pair-wise options, $\Downarrow_{SRA}$ achieved a decent amount of sound results. Using more samples collected by trials and errors with **Final** and all three pair-wise options, $\Downarrow_{SRA}$ generated sound results for 99.4% of the test cases by observing more behaviors of opaque code.

5.3   Limitations

A fundamental limitation of our approach is that the $\Downarrow_{SRA}$ model may produce unsound results when the behavior of opaque code depends on values that $\Downarrow_{SRA}$ does not support via sampling. For example, if a sampling strategy calls the `Date` function without enough time intervals, it may not be able to sample different results. Similarly, if a sampling strategy does not use 4-wise combinations for property descriptor objects that have four components, it cannot produce all the possible combinations. However, at the same time, simply applying more complex strategies like 4-wise combinations may lead to an explosion of samples, which is not scalable.

Our experimental evaluation is inherently limited to a specific use case, which poses a threat to validity. While our approach itself is not dependent on a particular programming language or static analysis, the implementation of our approach depends on the abstract domains of SAFE. Although the experiments used well-known benchmark programs as analysis subjects, they may not be representative of all common uses of opaque functions in JavaScript applications.

6 Related Work

When a textual specification or documentation is available for opaque code, one can generate semantic models by mining them. Zhai *et al.* [26] showed that natural language processing can successfully generate models for Java library functions and used them in the context of taint analysis for Android applications. Researchers also created models automatically from types written in WebIDL or TypeScript declarations to detect Web API misuses [2, 16].

Given an executable (e.g. binary) version of opaque code, researchers also synthesized code by sampling the inputs and outputs of the code [7, 10, 12, 19]. Heule *et al.* [8] collected partial execution traces, which capture the effects of opaque code on user objects, followed by code synthesis to generate models from these traces. This approach works in the absence of any specification and has been demonstrated on array-manipulating builtins.

While all of these techniques are a-priori attempts to generate general-purpose models of opaque code, to be usable for other analyses, researchers also proposed to construct models during analysis. Madsen *et al.*'s approach [14] infers models of opaque functions by combining pointer analysis and use analysis, which collects expected properties and their types from given application code. Hirzel *et al.* [9] proposed an online pointer analysis for Java, which handles native code and reflection via dynamic execution that ours also utilizes. While both approaches use only a finite set of pointers as their abstract values, ignoring primitive values, our technique generalizes such online approaches to be usable for all kinds of values in a given language.

Opaque code does matter in other program analyses as well such as model checking and symbolic execution. Shafiei and Breugel [22] proposed *jpf-nhandler*, an extension of Java PathFinder (JPF), which transfers execution between JPF and the host JVM by on-the-fly code generation. It does not need concretization and abstraction since a JPF object represents a concrete value. In the context of symbolic execution, concolic testing [21] and other hybrid techniques that combine path solving with random testing [18] have been used to overcome the problems posed by opaque code, albeit sacrificing completeness [4].

Even when source code of external libraries is available, substituting external code with models rather than analyzing themselves is useful to reduce time and memory that an analysis takes. Palepu *et al.* [15] generated summaries by abstracting concrete data dependencies of library functions observed on a training execution to avoid heavy execution of instrumented code. In model checking, Tkachuk *et al.* [24,25] generated over-approximated summaries of environments by points-to and side-effect analyses and presented a static analysis tool OCSEGen [23]. Another tool Modgen [5] applies a program slicing technique to reduce complexities of library classes.

7   Conclusion

Creating semantic models for static analysis by hand is complex, time-consuming and error-prone. We present a Sample-Run-Abstract approach ($\Downarrow_{SRA}$) as a promising way to perform static analysis in the presence of opaque code using automated on-demand modeling. We show how $\Downarrow_{SRA}$ can be applied to the abstract domains of an existing JavaScript static analyzer, SAFE. For benchmark programs and 134 builtin functions with 1565 abstracted inputs, a tuned $\Downarrow_{SRA}$ produced more sound results than the manual models and concrete examples revealing bugs in the manual models. Although not all opaque code may be suitable for modeling with $\Downarrow_{SRA}$, it reduces the amount of hand-written models a static analyzer should provide. Future work on $\Downarrow_{SRA}$ could focus on orthogonal testing techniques that can be used for sampling complex objects, and practical optimizations, such as caching of computed model results.

Acknowledgment. This work has received funding from National Research Foundation of Korea (NRF) (Grants NRF-2017R1A2B3012020 and 2017M3C4A7068177).

References

1. ECMAScript Language Specification. Edition 5.1. http://www.ecma-international. org/publications/standards/Ecma-262.htm
2. Bae, S., Cho, H., Lim, I., Ryu, S.: SAFEWAPI: web API misuse detector for web applications. In: Proceedings of the 22nd ACM SIGSOFT International Symposium on Foundations of Software Engineering, pp. 507–517. ACM (2014)
3. Black, R.: Pragmatic Software Testing: Becoming an Effective and Efficient Test Professional. Wiley, Hoboken (2007)
4. Cadar, C., Sen, K.: Symbolic execution for software testing: three decades later. Commun. ACM **56**(2), 82–90 (2013)
5. Ceccarello, M., Tkachuk, O.: Automated generation of model classes for Java PathFinder. ACM SIGSOFT Softw. Eng. Notes **39**(1), 1–5 (2014)
6. Cousot, P., Cousot, R.: Abstract interpretation: a unified lattice model for static analysis of programs by construction or approximation of fixpoints. In: Proceedings of the 4th ACM SIGACT-SIGPLAN Symposium on Principles of Programming Languages, pp. 238–252. ACM (1977)
7. Gulwani, S., Harris, W.R., Singh, R.: Spreadsheet data manipulation using examples. Commun. ACM **55**(8), 97–105 (2012)

8. Heule, S., Sridharan, M., Chandra, S.: Mimic: computing models for opaque code. In: Proceedings of the 2015 10th Joint Meeting on Foundations of Software Engineering, pp. 710–720. ACM (2015)
9. Hirzel, M., Dincklage, D.V., Diwan, A., Hind, M.: Fast online pointer analysis. ACM Trans. Program. Lang. Syst. (TOPLAS) **29**(2), 11 (2007)
10. Jha, S., Gulwani, S., Seshia, S.A., Tiwari, A.: Oracle-guided component-based program synthesis. In: Proceedings of the 32nd ACM/IEEE International Conference on Software Engineering, vol. 1, pp. 215–224. ACM (2010)
11. Kuhn, D.R., Wallace, D.R., Gallo, A.M.: Software fault interactions and implications for software testing. IEEE Trans. Softw. Eng. **30**(6), 418–421 (2004)
12. Lau, T., Domingos, P., Weld, D.S.: Learning programs from traces using version space algebra. In: Proceedings of the 2nd International Conference on Knowledge Capture, pp. 36–43. ACM (2003)
13. Lee, H., Won, S., Jin, J., Cho, J., Ryu, S.: SAFE: formal specification and implementation of a scalable analysis framework for ECMAScript. In: FOOL 2012: 19th International Workshop on Foundations of Object-Oriented Languages, p. 96. Citeseer (2012)
14. Madsen, M., Livshits, B., Fanning, M.: Practical static analysis of JavaScript applications in the presence of frameworks and libraries. In: Proceedings of the 2013 9th Joint Meeting on Foundations of Software Engineering, pp. 499–509. ACM (2013)
15. Palepu, V.K., Xu, G., Jones, J.A.: Improving efficiency of dynamic analysis with dynamic dependence summaries. In: Proceedings of the 28th IEEE/ACM International Conference on Automated Software Engineering, pp. 59–69. IEEE Press (2013)
16. Park, J.: JavaScript API misuse detection by using TypeScript. In: Proceedings of the Companion Publication of the 13th International Conference on Modularity, pp. 11–12. ACM (2014)
17. Park, J., Ryou, Y., Park, J., Ryu, S.: Analysis of JavaScript web applications using SAFE 2.0. In: 2017 IEEE/ACM 39th International Conference on Software Engineering Companion (ICSE-C), pp. 59–62. IEEE (2017)
18. Păsăreanu, C.S., Rungta, N., Visser, W.: Symbolic execution with mixed concrete-symbolic solving. In: Proceedings of the 2011 International Symposium on Software Testing and Analysis, pp. 34–44. ACM (2011)
19. Qi, D., Sumner, W.N., Qin, F., Zheng, M., Zhang, X., Roychoudhury, A.: Modeling software execution environment. In: 2012 19th Working Conference on Reverse Engineering (WCRE), pp. 415–424. IEEE (2012)
20. Sen, K., Kalasapur, S., Brutch, T., Gibbs, S.: Jalangi: a selective record-replay and dynamic analysis framework for JavaScript. In: Proceedings of the 2013 9th Joint Meeting on Foundations of Software Engineering, pp. 488–498. ACM (2013)
21. Sen, K., Marinov, D., Agha, G.: CUTE: a concolic unit testing engine for C. In: ACM SIGSOFT Software Engineering Notes, vol. 30, pp. 263–272. ACM (2005)
22. Shafiei, N., Breugel, F.V.: Automatic handling of native methods in Java PathFinder. In: Proceedings of the 2014 International SPIN Symposium on Model Checking of Software, pp. 97–100. ACM (2014)
23. Tkachuk, O.: OCSEGen: open components and systems environment generator. In: Proceedings of the 2nd ACM SIGPLAN International Workshop on State Of the Art in Java Program Analysis, pp. 9–12. ACM (2013)
24. Tkachuk, O., Dwyer, M.B.: Adapting side effects analysis for modular program model checking, vol. 28. ACM (2003)

25. Tkachuk, O., Dwyer, M.B., Pasareanu, C.S.: Automated environment generation for software model checking. In: Proceedings of the 18th IEEE International Conference on Automated Software Engineering, pp. 116–127. IEEE (2003)
26. Zhai, J., Huang, J., Ma, S., Zhang, X., Tan, L., Zhao, J., Qin, F.: Automatic model generation from documentation for Java API functions. In: 2016 IEEE/ACM 38th International Conference on Software Engineering (ICSE), pp. 380–391. IEEE (2016)

13

Formal Verification of Safety & Security Related Timing Constraints for a Cooperative Automotive System

Li Huang[1] and Eun-Young Kang[2(✉)]

[1] School of Data and Computer Science, Sun Yat-Sen University, Guangzhou, China
huang1223@mail2.sysu.edu.cn
[2] The Maersk Mc-Kinney Moller Institute, University of Southern Denmark,
Odense, Denmark
eyk@mmmi.sdu.dk

Abstract. Modeling and analysis of timing constraints is crucial in real-time automotive systems. Modern vehicles are interconnected through wireless networks which creates vulnerabilities to external malicious attacks. Violations of cyber-security can cause safety related accidents and serious damages. To identify the potential impacts of security related threats on safety properties of interconnected automotive systems, this paper presents analysis techniques that support verification and validation (V&V) of safety & security (S/S) related timing constraints on those systems: Probabilistic extension of S/S timing constraints are specified in PrCcsl (probabilistic extension of clock constraint specification language) and the semantics of the extended constraints are translated into verifiable Uppaal models with stochastic semantics for formal verification. A set of mapping rules are proposed to facilitate the translation. An automatic translation tool, namely ProTL, is implemented based on the mapping rules. Formal verification are performed on the S/S timing constraints using Uppaal-SMC under different attack scenarios. Our approach is demonstrated on a cooperative automotive system case study.

Keywords: Automotive system · Safety and security · PrCcsl · Uppaal-SMC

1 Introduction

Model based development (MBD) is rigorously applied in automotive systems in which the software controllers interact with physical environments. The continuous time behaviors of those systems often rely on complex dynamics as well as on stochastic behaviors. Formal verification and validation (V&V) technologies are indispensable and highly recommended for development of safe and reliable automotive systems [11, 12]. Conventional V&V, i.e., testing and model checking have limitations in terms of assessing the reliability of hybrid systems due to both stochastic and non-linear dynamical features. To ensure the reliability of safety critical hybrid dynamic systems, *statistical model checking (SMC)* techniques have been proposed [7,8,19]. These techniques for fully stochastic models validate probabilistic performance properties of given deterministic (or stochastic) controllers in given stochastic environments.

Modern vehicles are being equipped with communication devices and interconnected with each other through wireless networks. Vehicular Ad Hoc Networks (VANET) [28] are the technologies of wireless networks that establish communication among vehicles and roadside units (RSU). Nevertheless vehicular communication contributes to the safety and efficiency of traffic, it introduces vulnerabilities to vehicles. Transmitted information can be corrupted or modified by attackers, resulting in serious safety consequences (e.g., rear-end collision). Analysis of the potential impacts of cyber-security violations on safety properties is crucial in automotive systems. However, traditional automotive system design often addresses the correctness of safety properties without consideration of security breaches. There is still a lack of techniques that enable an integrated analysis of safety & security (S/S) properties. Moreover, message transmission in VANET that pertains to S/S requires restrictions by time deadlines [10]. In this paper, we focus on S/S related timing constraints and propose analysis techniques that support formal verification on interconnected automotive systems.

EAST-ADL [9,22] is an architectural description language for modeling of automotive systems. The latest release of EAST-ADL has adopted the time model proposed in Timing Augmented Description Language (TADL2) [5], which expresses and composes basic timing constraints, i.e., repetition rates, end-to-end delays. TADL2 specializes the time model of MARTE, the UML profile for Modeling and Analysis of Real-Time and Embedded systems [30]. MARTE provides CCSL, a Clock Constraint Specification Language, that supports specification of both logical and dense timing constraints, as well as functional causality constraints [16,23]. A probabilistic extension of CCSL, called PrCCSL [14], has been proposed to formally specify timing constraints associated with stochastic properties in weakly-hard real-time systems [4], i.e., a bounded number of constraints violations would not lead to system failures when the results of the violations are negligible.

In this paper, we present a formal analysis of S/S related timing constraints for interconnected automotive systems at the design level: 1. To identify vulnerabilities of automotive systems under malicious attacks, we adopt and modify the behavioral model of a cooperative automotive system (CAS) [13] in UPPAAL-SMC by adding it with the models of an RSU-aided (RAISE) communication protocol in VANET and malicious attacks. The modification results in a refined behavioral model of the system, i.e., more details in terms of vehicular communication and security breaches are depicted; 2. Probabilistic extension of S/S timing constraints are specified in PrCCSL and the semantics of the extended constraints are translated into verifiable models with stochastic semantics for formal verification; 3. A set of mapping rules are proposed to facilitate the translation, based on which an automatic translation tool ProTL is implemented;

4. Formal verification is performed on the S/S timing constraints using UPPAAL-SMC under different attack scenarios.

The paper is organized as follows: Sect. 2 presents an overview of PrCCSL and UPPAAL-SMC. CAS is introduced as a running example in Sect. 3. Section 4.1 presents the UPPAAL-SMC model of CAS complemented with model of RAISE protocol and three types of attacks. S/S related timing constraints are specified in PrCCSL and translated into verifiable UPPAAL-SMC models in Sect. 5. The applicability of our approach is demonstrated by performing verification on CAS case study in Sect. 6. Sections 7 and 8 present related works and conclusion.

2 Preliminary

In our framework, S/S related timing constraints are specified in PrCCSL. UPPAAL-SMC is employed to perform formal verification on the timing constraints.

2.1 Probabilistic Extension of Clock Constraint Specification Language (PrCCSL)

PrCCSL [14] is a probabilistic extension of CCSL [3,23] for formal specification of timing constraints associated with stochastic behaviors. In PrCCSL, a clock represents a sequence of (possibly infinite) instants. An event is a clock and the occurrences of an event correspond to a set of ticks of the clock. PrCCSL provides two types of clock constraints, i.e., *expressions* and *relations*, to specify the progression/occurrences of clocks. An *expression* derives new clocks from the already defined clocks [3]. Let $c1, c2 \in C$, ITE (if-then-else) *expression*, denoted as $\beta ? c1 : c2$, defines a new clock that behaves either as $c1$ or as $c2$ according to the value of the boolean variable/formula β. DelayFor (denoted $ref\ (d) \rightsquigarrow base$) results in a new clock by delaying the reference clock ref for d ticks (or d time units) of a *base* clock. FilterBy ($c \triangleq base\ \blacktriangledown\ u(v)$) builds a new clock c by filtering the instants of a *base* clock according to a binary word $w=u(v)$, where u is the *prefix* and v is the *period*. "(v)" denotes the infinite repetition of v. This expression results in a clock c that $\forall\ k\ \in N^+$, if the kth bit in w is 1, then at the kth tick of *base*, c ticks.

A *relation* limits the occurrences among different events, which are defined based on run and history. A run corresponds to an execution of the system model where the clocks tick/progress. The history of a clock c represents the number of times the clock c has ticked prior to the current step.

Definition 1 (Run). *A* run *R consists of a finite set of consecutive steps where a set of clocks tick at each step i. The set of clocks ticking at step i is denoted as $R(i)$, i.e., for all i, $0 \leqslant i \leqslant n$, $R(i) \in R$, where n is the number of steps of R.*

Definition 2 (History). *The* history *of clock c in a run R is a function: H_R^c: $\mathbb{N} \rightarrow \mathbb{N}$. $H_R^c(i)$ indicates the number of times the clock c has ticked prior to step i in run R, which is initialized as 0 at step 0. It is defined as: (1) $H_R^c(0) = 0$;*

(2) $\forall\, i \in \mathbb{N}^+$, $c \notin R(i) \implies H_R^c(i+1) = H_R^c(i)$; (3) $\forall\, i \in \mathbb{N}^+$, $c \in R(i) \implies H_R^c(i+1) = H_R^c(i) + 1$.

A probabilistic *relation* in PrCCSL is satisfied if and only if the probability of the *relation* constraint being satisfied is greater than or equal to the probability threshold $p \in [0,\ 1]$. Given k runs $= \{R_1, \ldots, R_k\}$, the probabilistic `subclock`, `coincidence`, `exclusion` and `precedence` in PrCCSL are defined as follows:

Probabilistic Subclock: $c1 \subseteq_p c2 \iff Pr[c1 \subseteq c2] \geqslant p$, where $Pr[c1 \subseteq c2] = \frac{1}{k} \sum_{j=1}^{k} \{R_j \models c1 \subseteq c2\}$, representing the ratio of `runs` that satisfies the relation out of k `runs`. A `run` R_j satisfies the `subclock` relation between $c1$ and $c2$ "if $c1$ ticks, $c2$ must tick" holds at every step i in R_j, s.t., $(R_j \models c1 \subseteq c2) \iff (\forall i\ 0 \leqslant i \leqslant n,\ c1 \in R(i) \implies c2 \in R(i))$. "$R_j \models c1 \subseteq c2$" returns 1 if R_j satisfies $c1 \subseteq c2$, otherwise it returns 0.

Probabilistic Coincidence: $c1 \equiv_p c2 \iff Pr[c1 \equiv c2] \geqslant p$, where $Pr[c1 \equiv c2] = \frac{1}{k} \sum_{j=1}^{k} \{R_j \models c1 \equiv c2\}$, which represents the ratio of `runs` that satisfies the `coincidence` relation out of k `runs`. A `run`, R_j satisfies the `coincidence` relation on $c1$ and $c2$ if the assertion holds: $\forall i, 0 \leqslant i \leqslant n, (c1 \in R(i) \implies c2 \in R(i)) \wedge (c2 \in R(i) \implies c1 \in R(i))$. In other words, the satisfaction of `coincidence` relation is established when the two conditions "if $c1$ ticks, $c2$ must tick" and "if $c2$ ticks, $c1$ must tick" hold at every step.

Probabilistic Exclusion: $c1 \#_p c2 \iff Pr[c1 \# c2] \geqslant p$, where $Pr[c1 \# c2] = \frac{1}{k} \sum_{j=1}^{k} \{R_j \models c1 \# c2\}$, indicating the ratio of `runs` that satisfies the `exclusion` relation out of k `runs`. A `run`, R_j, satisfies the `exclusion` relation on $c1$ and $c2$ if $\forall i, 0 \leqslant i \leqslant n, (c1 \in R(i) \implies c2 \notin R(i)) \wedge (c2 \in R(i) \implies c1 \notin R(i))$, i.e., for every step, if $c1$ ticks, $c2$ must not tick and vice versa.

Probabilistic Precedence: $c1 \prec_p c2 \iff Pr[c1 \prec c2] \geqslant p$, where $Pr[c1 \prec c2] = \frac{1}{k} \sum_{j=1}^{k} \{R_j \models c1 \prec c2\}$, which denotes the ratio of `runs` that satisfies the `precedence` relation out of k `runs`. A `run` R_j satisfies the `precedence` relation if the condition $\forall i, 0 \leqslant i \leqslant n, (H_R^{c1}(i) \geqslant H_R^{c2}(i))$ and $(H_R^{c2}(i) = H_R^{c1}(i)) \implies (c2 \notin R(i))$ hold, i.e., the history of $c1$ is greater than or equal to the history of $c2$, and $c2$ must not tick when the history of the two clocks are equal.

2.2 UPPAAL-SMC

UPPAAL-SMC [31] performs the probabilistic analysis of properties by monitoring simulations of the complex hybrid system in a given stochastic environment and using results from the statistics to determine whether the system satisfies the property with some degree of confidence. UPPAAL-SMC provides a number of queries related to the stochastic interpretation of Timed Automata (STA)

[8] and they are as follows, where N and *bound* indicate the number of simulations to be performed and the time bound on the simulations respectively:
1. *Probability Estimation* estimates the probability of a requirement property ϕ being satisfied for a given STA model within the time bound: $Pr[bound]\ \phi$;
2. *Hypothesis Testing* checks if the probability of ϕ is satisfied within a certain probability P_0: $Pr[bound]\ \phi \geq P_0$; 3. *Simulations*: UPPAAL-SMC runs multiple simulations on the STA model and the k (state-based) properties/expressions $\phi_1, ..., \phi_k$ are monitored and visualized along the simulations: *simulate* N [$\leq$ *bound*]$\{\phi_1, ..., \phi_k\}$.

3 Running Example

A cooperative automotive system (CAS) [13] is adopted to illustrate our approaches. CAS includes distributed and coordinated sensing, control, and actuation over three vehicles (denoted as v_i, where $i \in \{0, 1, 2\}$) which are running in the same lane. As shown in Fig. 1, a lead vehicle (v_0) runs automatically by recognizing traffic signs on the road. The following vehicle must set its desired velocity identical to that of its immediate preceding vehicle. Vehicles should maintain sufficient braking distance to avoid rear-end collision while remaining close enough to guarantee communication quality. Vehicle movement relies on availability of environmental information, e.g., traffic signs, obstacles, etc. The position of v_i is represented by Cartesian coordinate (x_i, y_i), where x_i and y_i are distances measured from the vehicle to the two fixed perpendicular lines, i.e., x-axis and y-axis, respectively.

Fig. 1. Overview of Cooperative Automotive System

The cooperative driving of CAS requires prompt and secure information transmission among vehicles. We adopt a roadside unit aided (RAISE) [33] communication protocol in VANET to achieve the data transmission. Each vehicle periodically broadcasts its own position and velocity to its immediate following vehicle through wireless connection. The authentication of the identities of each vehicle and verification of messages sent by the vehicles is performed by RSU. For further details of RAISE, refer to Sect. 4.1. The following S/S properties on CAS are considered:
R1. The follower vehicle should not overtake its leading vehicle when the vehicles run at a positive direction of x-axis.
R2. When the lead vehicle detects a stop sign, all the three vehicles must stop within a given time, e.g., 2000 ms.

R3. If the distance between a vehicle and its preceding vehicle is less than minimum safety distance, the vehicle should decelerate within a certain time (200 ms).

R4. If the distance between a vehicle and its preceding vehicle is greater than the maximum safety distance (e.g., 100 m), the vehicle should accelerate within a certain time, e.g., 300 ms.

R5. When the lead vehicle starts to turn left (or turn right), the two follower vehicles should finish turning and run in the same lane within a given time.

R6. Authenticity: If a vehicle receives a message, its preceding vehicle must have sent a corresponding message before, i.e., the protocol should be resistant to message spoofing attack.

R7. Secrecy: Symmetric keys of vehicles should be kept confidential to attackers. R8. Integrity: The content of messages must not be modified during transmission, i.e., the protocol should be resistant to message falsification attack.

R9. Freshness: The vehicles should not accept an "obsolete" message, namely, the difference between the current time and the *timestamp* of the accepted message should be less than the predefined time threshold.

R10. The symmetric key agreement (i.e., mutual authentication) process between RSU and three vehicles should be completed within a certain time, e.g., 600 ms.

R11. A vehicle should send messages to its subsequent vehicle periodically with a period 200 ms and a jitter 100 ms.

Among the above S/S requirements, R1–R5 are safety [20] properties, which specify that the system should not cause undesirable results on its environment and aim at protecting human lives, health and assets from being damaged. R6–R11 are security properties, which refer to the inability of the environment to affect the system in an undesirable way and aim to guarantee the confidentiality and integrity of transmitted information. The interdependencies among those S/S properties are conditional dependencies [17], i.e., violations of security properties can lead to the violations on safety properties. The events associated with those S/S properties can be interpreted as logical clocks in PrCCSL, which provides a way to express S/S properties in the logical time manner [16]. Therefore, S/S properties can be interpreted as logical timing constraints, i.e., the temporal and causality clock *relations* in PrCCSL.

The methodology for analysis of S/S related timing constraints in this paper can be generalized in Fig. 2. First, on the basis of the existing behavioral model of CAS described in [13], we enhance the CAS model by augmenting (parallelly composing) it with models of RAISE protocol and malicious attacks, resulting in a refined CAS model regarding vehicular communication characteristics and security-related adversary interference. Second, we specify S/S timing constraints (R1–R11) in PrCCSL and translate the PrCCSL specifications into corresponding STA and probabilistic queries. Finally, we combine the model of CAS and the STA of PrCCSL specifications, and perform formal verification based on the combined model using UPPAAL-SMC.

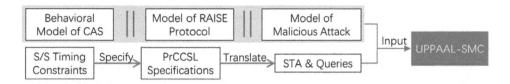

Fig. 2. Methodology for analysis of S/S timing constraints

4   Modeling and Refinement of CAS in UPPAAL-SMC

The behaviors of CAS are modeled as a network of stochastic timed automata (NSTA) in UPPAAL-SMC described in [13]. In this section, we refine the CAS model by adding it with the models of RAISE protocol and security attacks.

4.1   Modeling of RAISE Protocol in UPPAAL-SMC

We present a simplified version of RAISE protocol [33] and its UPPAAL-SMC model. The original RAISE protocol is modified to facilitate the communication mechanism of CAS, i.e., each follower vehicle receives messages from its immediate preceding vehicle and RSU. Furthermore, timing constraints are also appended to restrict the time duration of each step (e.g., encryption and decryption) during communication process. There are two phases in RAISE protocol, i.e., *symmetric key agreement* and *information transmission*.

1. **Symmetric key agreement (SKA)** is performed to obtain symmetric key k_i for guaranteeing security of communication and generates pseudo identities ID_i of vehicles for covering their real identities. The shared symmetric key between RSU and v_i is $k_i = g^{ab}$, where g, a, b are three positive random numbers. As shown in Fig. 3, $Encry(msg, k)$ ($Decry(msg, k)$) denotes the encryption (decryption) of message msg with key k, where k can be either a public key or symmetric key. $Sign(msg, k)$ generates signature of msg with a private key k. We use PK_i to denote the public key of v_i and SK_i to represent the corresponding private key. "$||$" is the concatenation operation on messages.

Initially, v_i randomly picks g and a (step 1), encrypts "$g||a$" and sends the encrypted result (m_i) to RSU (step 2). Upon receiving m_i, RSU decrypts the message (step 3). It then generates b and ID_i, signs and sends the signed message (rm_i) to v_i (step 4 and 5). v_i verifies the rm_i's signature (step 6) and sends back the signature of $g||a||b||ID_i$ (step 7). Finally, RSU verifies the signature s_i (step 8). If all the steps are completed correctly, the key agreement process succeeds.

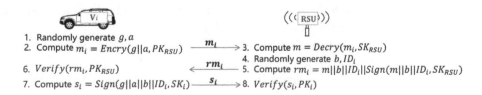

Fig. 3. Symmetric key agreement in RAISE

2. **Information transmission (IT)** initiates after the SKA is completed. The traffic information (i.e, brake, direction, position and speed) of v_i is integrated into a message $msg_i = brake_i||direction_i||x_i||y_i||speed_i$. As presented in Fig. 4, initially, v_i generates the message authentication code (MAC) of msg_i with the symmetric key k_i (generated in SKA). Then, v_i concatenates the MAC code with

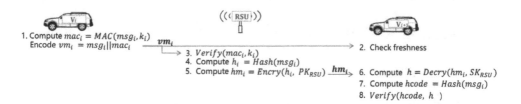

Fig. 4. Information transmission in RAISE

msg_i and sends it to RSU and v_{i+1} (step 1). Upon receiving vm_i, v_{i+1} checks the freshness of the message (step 2), i.e., if the time interval between the current time and the time when vm_i is sent is greater than the predefined threshold, v_{i+1} drops vm_i. At the same time, RSU checks the authenticity of vm_i (step 3). If mac_i is correct, RSU computes the hash code h_i of message msg_i (step 4). Afterwards, it encrypts h_i and sends the encrypted result hm_i to v_{i+1} (step 5). v_{i+1} decrypts hm_i and get the hash code h (step 6). Furthermore, to ensure the consistency of the message, v_{i+1} itself also computes the hash code of msg_i (step 7). It then verifies whether the hash code calculated by itself is the same as the decrypted hash code and decides to accept or reject msg_i (step 8).

To model RAISE in UPPAAL-SMC, interactions among vehicles and RSU (i.e., sending/receiving messages) are modeled by *synchronization channels* [31] and global variables. The cryptographic operations in RAISE refer to public and private key encryption and decryption, i.e., a message encrypted by public key can be decrypted using the corresponding private key, and vice versa. The automaton of `cryptographic device` [6] is adopted to model the encryption and decryption. Figure 5 presents the STA capturing behaviors of vehicle v_i and RSU in SKA. *startEn* (resp. *startDe*) and *finDe* (resp. *finEn*) are channels for indicating the starting and finishing of encryption (resp. decryption). The encryption/decryption result is denoted *en_res/de_res*. In the STA, names of locations indicate the corresponding steps pictured in Fig. 3.

IT phase from v_0 to v_1 is established with the help of RSU, modeled as the STA shown in Fig. 6 (the transmission from v_1 to v_2 can be modeled similarly). The behaviors of v_0 (sender), v_1 (receiver) and RSU in the IT phase are modeled in `IT_v0`, `IT_v1` and `IT_RSU` STA, respectively.

The SKA (or IT) succeeds if each step of the SKA (IT) is completed correctly within a given time interval, modeled by invariant "t ≤ d" (the value of d varies in different steps). If timeout occurs (i.e., "t ≥ d"), *fail* location will be activated and the procedure is restarted from the initial step.

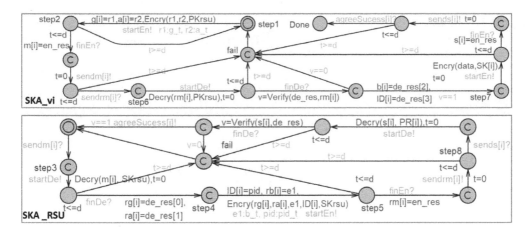

Fig. 5. UPPAAL-SMC model of SKA

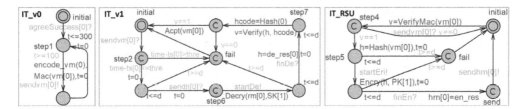

Fig. 6. UPPAAL-SMC model of IT

4.2 Modeling of Attacks in UPPAAL-SMC

We present the modeling of three types of attacks commonly used in the security analysis, i.e., message falsification, message replaying and message spoofing attacks [2]. The models of attacks are illustrated in Fig. 7, where the ls parameter ($ls \in [0, 100]$) serves as an indicator of level of adversarial strength while qc ($qc \in [0, 100]$) is an indicator of the adversarial channel quality.

Message Falsification Attack (MFA) aims to falsify messages transmitted from v_i to v_{i+1}, which is modeled as MFA STA in Fig. 7. As described earlier, in RAISE, RSU verifies the authenticity of messages by checking the correctness of the MAC code of messages. To deceive the RSU on the validity of the modified message and avoid exposing itself to RSU, MFA attempts to obtain the symmetric key and utilizes the key to compute the MAC code of the falsified message. At s1 state, MFA eavesdrops on rm_i (generated at step 5 in Fig. 3), which contains the information for symmetric key generation (i.e., g, a, b). It tries to decrypt rm_i when receiving it via $sendrm[i]$?. The probability that the decryption can succeed is $ls\%$, modeled by probabilistic choices [31] (dashed edges) with probability weight as $\frac{ls}{100}$ and $\frac{100-ls}{100}$. If the decryption succeeds, MFA obtains the symmetric key of v_i based on the decrypted result ($getKey(de\_res)$). Finally, it modifies the content of message using the key, and tries to send the modified message to v_{i+1} ($sendvm[i]$!). The probability that the message can be sent successfully is

(100-qc)%. In our setting, MFA modifies the $speed_i$ field in the message into a random value in [100, 120], and changes the direction as $direction_i = 4$, which indicates that the v_i is running at the positive direction on y-axis.

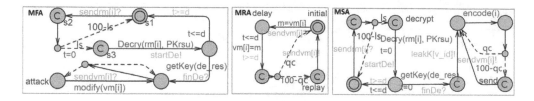

Fig. 7. STA of attacks

Message Replaying Attack (MRA) targets to replay obsolete messages that contain old information. The MRA STA represents an MRA that replays messages sent by v_i. Upon capturing a message (via $sendvm[i]$?), MRA stores the message ($m = vm[i]$) and tries to replay it at a later time (i.e., after *10* s). The probability that the attacker can replay the message successfully is (100-qc)%.

Message Spoofing Attack (MSA) impersonates a vehicle (v_i) in order to inject fraudulent information into its subsequent vehicle (v_{i+1}). Similar to MFA, MSA STA first obtains the symmetric key of v_i by detecting and decrypting rm_i. It then fabricates a new message whose content is "$brake_i = 0$, $speed_i = 0$, $direction_i = 4$, $x_i = 0$, $y_i = 10$" (denoted "$encode(i)$") and tries to send the message to v_{i+1} ($sendvm[i]$!), with the probability of the message being sent successfully as (100-qc)%.

5 Representation of S/S Related Timing Constraints in UPPAAL-SMC

To enable the formal verification of S/S related timing constraints (given in Sect. 3), we first investigate how to specify those constraints in PrCcSL. Then, translation from PrCcSL specifications of the constraints into verifiable STA is demonstrated. Furthermore, a tool ProTL that supports the automatic transformation based on the proposed translation rules is introduced.

5.1 Specifications of S/S Related Timing Constraints in PrCCSL

The specifications of R1–R11 are presented in Table 1, where ac is a clock that always ticks while nc represents a clock that never ticks. R1 is specified as an **exclusion** *relation* between $xdir$ (the event that the vehicles are running at the positive direction of x-axis) and $ovtake$ (the event that the position of follower v_1 on x-axis is greater than that of leader v_0). Similarly, R7 and R9 can be specified as **exclusion** *relations*.

In the specification of R2, $stopD$ is a clock generated by delaying $stopSign$ (the event that the leader vehicle detects a stop sign) for 2000 ms. $vstop$ refers

Table 1. PrCCSL specifications of R1–R11

Req	PrCCSL Specification
R1	$xdir \triangleq dir = 1?\ ac : nc,\ ovtake \triangleq x_1 \geq x_0\ ?\ ac : nc,\ xdir\ \#_{0.95}\ ovtake$
R2	$stopSign \triangleq sign = 5\ ?\ signRec : nc,\ stopD \triangleq stopSign\ (2000) \rightsquigarrow ms,$ $vstop \preceq_{0.95} stopD$
R3	$vUnsafeDe \triangleq vUnsafe\ (200) \rightsquigarrow ms,\ vDec \prec_{0.95} vUnsafeDe$
R4	$vFarDisDe \triangleq vFarDis\ (300) \rightsquigarrow ms,\ startAcc \prec_{0.95} vFarDisDe$
R5	$v0TurnDe \triangleq v0Turn\ (3000) \rightsquigarrow ms,\ finTurn \preceq_{0.95} v0TurnDe$
R6	$msgRec \subseteq_{0.95} msgSent$
R7	$leakK\ \#_{0.95}\ ac$
R8	$validMsg \triangleq rMsg = sMsg\ ?\ msgRec : nc,\ msgRec \equiv_{0.95} validMsg$
R9	$oldMsg \triangleq time - ts > thre\ ?\ msgAcpt : nc,\ msgAcpt\ \#_{0.95}\ oldMsg$
R10	$startSKADe \triangleq startSKA\ (600) \rightsquigarrow ms,\ finSKA \prec_{0.95} startSKADe$
R11	$fclk \triangleq msgSent\ \blacktriangledown 01(1),\ sentDe1 \triangleq msgSent\ (100) \rightsquigarrow ms,$ $sentDe2 \triangleq msgSent\ (300) \rightsquigarrow ms,\ sentDe1 \preceq_{0.95} fclk,$ $fclk \preceq_{0.95} sentDe2$

to the event that three vehicles are completely stopped, which should occur no later than *stopD*. Hence, R2 is expressed as a `causality` *relation* between *vstop* and *stopD*. R3–R5 can be specified in a similar manner.

R6 (authenticity) is expressed as a `subclock` *relation* between *msgRec* and *msgSent*, where *msgRec* (*msgSent*) represents the event that a message is received (sent) by the follower (leader) vehicle. R8 is specified as a `coincidence` *relation* between *msgRec* and *validMsg*, where *validMsg* is a clock that ticks with *msgRec* when the received message *rMsg* is identical with the sent message *sMsg* (i.e., $rMsg == sMsg$). For R10, *startSKA* (*finSKA*) represents the starting (completion) of SKA. *startSKADe* is a clock constructed by delaying *startSKA* for 600 ms. R10 delimits that *finSKA* must occur before *startSKADe*. R11 states that two consecutive occurrences of *msgSent* must has a interval of [*period* − *jitter, period* + *jitter*]ms (i.e., [100, 300] ms). In the specification of R11, *fclk* is a clock generated by filtering out the 1st tick of *msgSent*. *sentDe1* and *sentDe2* are two clocks generated by delaying *msgSent* for 100 ms and 300 ms. R11 can be interpreted as: $\forall i \in \mathbb{N}^+$, the ith tick of *fclk* should occur later than the ith tick of *sentDe1* but prior to the ith tick of *sentDe2*.

5.2 Translation of PrCCSL into STA

We present how the S/S related timing constraints specified in PrCCSL can be transformed into STA and probabilistic queries in UPPAAL-SMC. We first describe how clock tick and history (introduced in Sect. 2) can be represented in UPPAAL-SMC. Using the mapping, we then demonstrate that *expressions* and *relations* in PrCCSL can be translated into STA and queries.

In the earlier work [14], the semantics of PrCCSL operators are translated into STA based on discrete time, i.e., the continuous physical time is discretized into a set of equalized steps. As a result, two clock instants are still considered coincident even if they are one time step apart. To alleviate this restriction and enable the representation of PrCCSL that pertains to continuous real-time semantics, the mapping patterns are refined: two clock instants are coinstantaneous only if the time difference between them is insignificant, i.e., the time difference between them is less than a positive infinitesimal value e, e.g., $e = 0.000001$.

In PrCCSL, a logical clock represents an event and the instants of the clock correspond to the occurrences of the event. A logical clock c is represented as a *synchronization channel* $c!$ in UPPAAL-SMC. The history of c is modeled as the STA shown in Fig. 8: whenever c occurs ($c?$), the value of its history is increased by 1 (i.e., $h++$).

Fig. 8. History

Based on the mapping patterns of tick and history, the PrCCSL *expressions* (including ITE, DelayFor and filterBy), as well as *relations* (including subclock, coincidence, exclusion and precedence), can be represented as STA and queries shown in Fig. 9.

The STA of *expressions* trigger the ticks of the new clock (denoted *res!*) based on the occurrences of existed clocks. To represent *relations*, observer STA that capture the semantics of standard subclock, coincidence, exclusion and precedence *relations* are constructed. Each observer STA contains a *"fail"* location (see Fig. 9), which indicates the violation of the corresponding *relation*. Recall the definition of PrCCSL in Sect. 2, the probability of a *relation* being satisfied is interpreted as a ratio of runs that satisfies the *relation* among all runs. It is specified as *Hypothesis Testing* queries in UPPAAL-SMC, H_0: $\frac{m}{k} \geqslant p$ against H_1: $\frac{m}{k} < p$, where m is the number of runs satisfying the given *relation* out of all k runs. As a result, the probabilistic *relations* are interpreted as the query (see Fig. 9): $Pr[bound]([\ ] \neg STA.fail) \geq p$, which means that the probability of the *"fail"* location of the observer STA never being reached should be greater than or equal to p. The STA of *expressions* and *relations* are composed to the system NSTA in parallel. Then, the probabilistic analysis is performed over the composite NSTA that enables us to verify the S/S related timing constraints over the entire system using UPPAAL-SMC.

Tool support: Manual translation of PrCCSL specifications into UPPAAL models for verification can be time-consuming and error-prone. To improve the accuracy and efficiency of translation, we implement a tool ProTL (Probabilistic-CCSL TransLator) [26] that provides a push-button transformation from PrCCSL specifications into corresponding STA & queries. Furthermore, verification and simulation support is provided in ProTL by employing the UPPAAL-SMC as the backend analysis engine. ProTL encompasses the following features: (1) An editor for editing PrCCSL specification of requirements (stored as *".txt"* files); (2) Automated transformation of PrCCSL specifications into UPPAAL-SMC STA; (3) Integration of the STA and the system behavioral model (imported by users); (4) A configuration palette for setting parameters (e.g., time bound of simula-

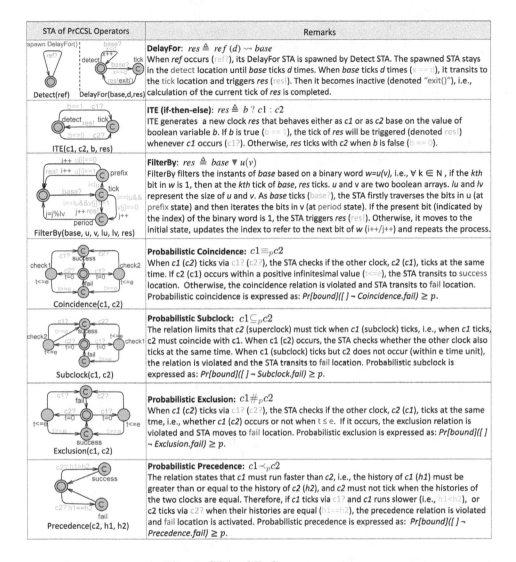

STA of PrCCSL Operators	Remarks
Detect(ref) DelayFor(base,d,res)	**DelayFor:** $res \triangleq ref\,(d) \rightsquigarrow base$ When *ref* occurs (ref?), its DelayFor STA is spawned by Detect STA. The spawned STA stays in the detect location until *base* ticks *d* times. When *base* ticks *d* times (x == d), it transits to the tick location and triggers *res* (res!). Then it becomes inactive (denoted "exit()"), i.e., calculation of the current tick of *res* is completed.
ITE(c1, c2, b, res)	**ITE (if-then-else):** $res \triangleq b\,?\,c1:c2$ ITE generates a new clock *res* that behaves either as *c1* or as *c2* base on the value of boolean variable *b*. If *b* is true (b == 1), the tick of *res* will be triggered (denoted res!) whenever *c1* occurs (c1?). Otherwise, *res* ticks with *c2* when *b* is false (b == 0).
FilterBy(base, u, v, lu, lv, res)	**FilterBy:** $res \triangleq base \blacktriangledown u(v)$ FilterBy filters the instants of *base* based on a binary word $w=u(v)$, i.e., $\forall\,k \in N$, if the *kth* bit in *w* is 1, then at the *kth* tick of *base*, *res* ticks. *u* and *v* are two boolean arrays. *lu* and *lv* represent the size of *u* and *v*. As *base* ticks (base?), the STA firstly traverses the bits in *u* (at prefix state) and then iterates the bits in *v* (at period state). If the present bit (indicated by the index) of the binary word is 1, the STA triggers *res* (res!). Otherwise, it moves to the initial state, updates the index to refer to the next bit of *w* (i++/j++) and repeats the process.
Coincidence(c1, c2)	**Probabilistic Coincidence:** $c1 \equiv_p c2$ When *c1* (*c2*) ticks via c1? (c2?), the STA checks if the other clock, *c2* (*c1*), ticks at the same time. If c2 (c1) occurs within a positive infinitesimal value (t<=e), the STA transits to success location. Otherwise, the coincidence relation is violated and STA transits to fail location. Probabilistic coincidence is expressed as: *Pr[bound]([ ] ¬ Coincidence.fail) ≥ p*.
Subclock(c1, c2)	**Probabilistic Subclock:** $c1 \subseteq_p c2$ The relation limits that *c2* (superclock) must tick when *c1* (subclock) ticks, i.e., when *c1* ticks, *c2* must coincide with *c1*. When c1 (c2) occurs, the STA checks whether the other clock also ticks at the same time. When c1 (subclock) ticks but c2 does not occur (within e time unit), the relation is violated and the STA transits to fail location. Probabilistic subclock is expressed as: *Pr[bound]([ ] ¬ Subclock.fail) ≥ p*.
Exclusion(c1, c2)	**Probabilistic Exclusion:** $c1 \#_p c2$ When *c1* (*c2*) ticks via c1? (c2?), the STA checks if the other clock, *c2* (*c1*), ticks at the same tme, i.e., whether *c1* (*c2*) occurs or not when t ≤ e. If it occurs, the exclusion relation is violated and STA moves to fail location. Probabilistic exclusion is expressed as: *Pr[bound]([ ] ¬ Exclusion.fail) ≥ p*.
Precedence(c2, h1, h2)	**Probabilistic Precedence:** $c1 \prec_p c2$ The relation states that *c1* must run faster than *c2*, i.e., the history of *c1* (*h1*) must be greater than or equal to the history of *c2* (*h2*), and *c2* must not tick when the histories of the two clocks are equal. Therefore, if *c1* ticks via c1? and *c1* runs slower (i.e., h1<h2), or *c2* ticks via c2? when their histories are equal (h1==h2), the precedence relation is violated and fail location is activated. Probabilistic precedence is expressed as: *Pr[bound]([ ] ¬ Precedence.fail) ≥ p*.

Fig. 9. STA of PrCCSL operators

tion, number of simulations) used for verification and simulation; (5) Automatic generation of probabilistic queries (introduced in Sect. 2) based on user-specified parameters; (6) Capability of performing verification and simulation on PrCCSL specifications against the integrated model and generated queries.

The GUI of ProTL is implemented by applying the Python package TKIN-TER [27]. The implementation of *Translator* is achieved by the ANother Tool for Language Recognition (ANTLR) [24], a parser generator that can constructs lexical parsers for a language by analyzing user-defined syntax of the language. We specified the syntax of PrCCSL in Backus-Naur Form (BNF) and apply ANTLR to generate a *parser* that can analyze and recognize encodings in the format of PrCCSL. The *parser* reads the PrCCSL specifications and generates abstract syntax trees (AST), i.e., an intermediate form that has tree structures.

By traversing AST, the information (i.e., operators and parameters) of PrCcsL can be extracted and utilized for generation of corresponding STA.

6 Experiment

To identify vulnerabilities of system to external malicious attackers, we combine the refined CAS system model (including the models of RAISE protocol) with models of three different attackers. Formal verification on S/S related timing constraints (R1–R11) for the combined model is performed by UPPAAL-SMC. The combined CAS model contains the stochastic behaviors in terms of the unpredictable environments (e.g., the traffic signs are randomly recognized by the leader vehicle of CAS and the probability of each sign type occurring is equally set as 16.7%), as well as the indeterministic behaviors modeled by weighted probability choices in the STA of attacks (see Fig. 7). In our setting, ls and qc are configured as 10 and 90, respectively. To estimate the probability of an attack being launched on CAS successfully, *Probability Estimation* query is applied to check the probability that the "*attack*" location in each attack STA is reachable from the system NSTA. The time bound of the verification is set as 10000. The probability of message falsification, message replaying and message spoofing attack being successfully completed by the corresponding attacker is within the range of [0.109, 0.209], [0.563, 0.663] and [0.143, 0.243], respectively.

In our experiments, S/S related timing constraints are specified in PrCcsL and transformed into STA using ProTL. Each constraint is specified as a PrCcsL *relation* (as described in Sect. 5.1) whose probability threshold is 95%. The verification results are demonstrated in Table 2, in which "√" denotes the corresponding requirement is satisfied while "×" indicates the violation of the requirement: Under the message replaying attack, all the S/S timing constraints are established as valid with 95% level of confidence. In the message falsification attack, the secrecy and integrity properties (R7 and R8), as well as three safety properties (R3–R5), are violated. The MSA damages the authenticity (R6) and secrecy (R7) of communication, and leads to the violations of four safety properties, i.e., R1 and R3–R5.

Table 2. Verification results of timing constraints under different attacks

Attacks	R1	R2	R3	R4	R5	R6	R7	R8	R9	R10	R11	Average Time	Mem (Mb)
Message Falsification	√	√	×	×	×	√	×	×	√	√	√	40.20	57.94
Message Replaying	√	√	√	√	√	√	√	√	√	√	√	68.33	61.49
Message Spoofing	×	√	×	×	×	×	×	√	√	√	√	58.11	40.23

The experiment results indicate the severity of impacts on safety and security caused by the demonstrated attacks on CAS: No requirement is violated under MRA scenario while the MSA causes the violations of most safety properties.

When CAS is attached with the STA of MSA or MFA, the secrecy of symmetric key is violated. With the obtained symmetric key, MSA can masquerade message as legitimate vehicles and MFA is able to tamper the content of messages without being detected, leading to the violations of authenticity (R6) and integrity (R7) respectively. To explore how the malicious attackers can influence the safety of system, we conduct simulation by using *Simulations* queries. The simulation results in Fig. 10 illustrate how an MSA drives the system to undesirable states.

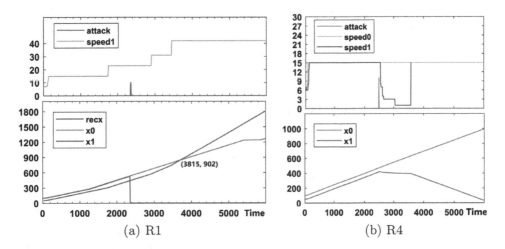

(a) R1   (b) R4

Fig. 10. Simulation results of R1 and R4: (a) At *Time* = 2345, the attack occurs (indicated by the rising edge of the red line). MSA sends the fabricated position information of V_0 to V_1 (the value of *recx* becomes 0), which tricks V_1 to think that the distance between V_0 and V_1 exceeds the maximum limit. V_1 keeps increasing its speed (*speed*1) and thus leading to the collision (indicated by $x_0 == x_1$) at *Time* = 3815, which violates R1. (b) When an attack takes place at *Time* = 2496 (indicated by the rising edge of the blue line), V_1 receives the message from the attacker and is deluded into believing that the speed of V_0 is 0. Therefore, V_1 keeps decreasing its speed even if the distance between V_0 and V_1 becomes greater than 100 m, which violates R4. (Color figure online)

7   Related Work

Formal verification of (non)-functional properties of automotive systems containing stochastic behaviors were investigated in several works [13–15]. In these works, systems are by default resilient to security threats and the safety properties are analyzed under no malicious attack scenarios, which is inadequate for design of automotive systems interconnected via wireless communications. Combined analysis of safety and security (S/S) properties for interconnected cyber physical systems have been addressed in earlier works [1,21,29], which are however, limited to theoretical frameworks and high-level descriptions of S/S properties without the support for formal verification. Pedroza et al. [25] proposed a SysML based environment called AVATAR for the formal verification of S/S properties, which enables assessment of the impacts of cyber-security threats on functional safety. Wardell et al. [32] proposed an approach for identifying security vulnerabilities of industrial control systems by modeling malicious attacks as PROMELA models amenable to formal verification. However, those approaches lack precise probabilistic annotations specifying stochastic properties regarding to S/S aspects. Kumar et al. [18] introduced the attack-fault trees formalism for descriptions of attack scenarios and conducted formal analysis by using UPPAAL-SMC to obtain quantitative estimation on impacts of system failures or security threats. On the other hand, our work is based on the probabilistic extension of S/S related timing constraints with the focus on probabilistic verification of the extended constraints.

8   Conclusion

This paper presents a model-based approach for probabilistic formal analysis of safety and security (S/S) related timing constraints for interconnected automotive system in EAST-ADL at the early design phase. The behavioral model of automotive system in UPPAAL-SMC is refined by adding the models of vehicular communication protocol and malicious attacks, which facilitates to exploit the impacts of adversary environment on S/S of the system. Timing constraints are specified in PrCCSL and translated into stochastic timed automata (STA) amenable to formal verification using UPPAAL-SMC. A set of translation rules from PrCCSL to STA, as well as the corresponding tool support for automating the translation are provided. We demonstrate our approach by performing formal verification on a cooperative automotive system (CAS) case study. Although, we have shown the one-to-one mapping patterns from a subset of PrCCSL operators to STA for conducting formal verification on timing constraints using UPPAAL-SMC, as ongoing work, systematic and formal translation techniques covering a full set of PrCCSL constraints are further studied. Furthermore, new features of ProTL with respect to analysis of UPPAAL-SMC models involving wider range of variable/query types (e.g., *urgent channels*, *bounded integers*) are further developed.

Acknowledgment. This work is supported by the EASY project funded by NSFC, a collaborative research between Sun Yat-Sen University and University of Southern Denmark.

References

1. Abdo, H., Kaouk, M., Flaus, J.M., Masse, F.: A safety/security risk analysis approach of industrial control systems: a cyber bowtie-combining new version of attack tree with bowtie analysis. Comput. Secur. **72**, 175–195 (2018)
2. Amoozadeh, M., et al.: Security vulnerabilities of connected vehicle streams and their impact on cooperative driving. IEEE Commun. Mag. **53**(6), 126–132 (2015)
3. André, C.: Syntax and semantics of the clock constraint specification language (CCSL). Ph.D. thesis, Inria (2009)

4. Bernat, G., Burns, A., Llamosi, A.: Weakly hard real-time systems. Trans. Comput. **50**(4), 308–321 (2001)
5. Blom, H., et al.: TIMMO-2-USE timing model, tools, algorithms, languages, methodology, use cases. Technical report, TIMMO-2-USE (2012)
6. Corin, R., Etalle, S., Hartel, P.H., Mader, A.: Timed model checking of security protocols. In: ACM Workshop on Formal Methods in Security Engineering (FMSE), pp. 23–32. ACM (2004)
7. David, A., et al.: Statistical model checking for stochastic hybrid systems. In: Hybrid Systems and Biology (HSB), pp. 122–136. EPTCS (2012)
8. David, A., Larsen, K.G., Legay, A., Mikučionis, M., Poulsen, D.B.: UPPAAL-SMC tutorial. Int. J. Softw. Tools Technol. Transf. **17**(4), 397–415 (2015)
9. EAST-ADL: EAST-ADL specification v2.1.9. Technical report, MAENAD (2011). https://www.maenad.eu/public/EAST-ADL-Specification_M2.1.9.1.pdf
10. Engoulou, R.G., Bellaïche, M., Pierre, S., Quintero, A.: VANET security surveys. Comput. Commun. **44**, 1–13 (2014)
11. IEC 61508: Functional safety of electrical electronic programmable electronic safety related systems (2010)
12. ISO 26262-6: Road vehicles functional safety part 6. Product development at the software level (2011)
13. Kang, E.Y., Huang, L., Mu, D.: Formal verification of energy and timed requirements for a cooperative automotive system. In: ACM/SIGAPP Symposium On Applied Computing (SAC), pp. 1492–1499. ACM (2018)
14. Kang, E.-Y., Mu, D., Huang, L.: Probabilistic verification of timing constraints in automotive systems using UPPAAL-SMC. In: Furia, C.A., Winter, K. (eds.) IFM 2018. LNCS, vol. 11023, pp. 236–254. Springer, Cham (2018). https://doi.org/10.1007/978-3-319-98938-9_14
15. Kang, E.Y., Mu, D., Huang, L., Lan, Q.: Verification and validation of a cyber-physical system in the automotive domain. In: IEEE International Conference on Software Quality, Reliability and Security Companion (QRS), pp. 326–333. IEEE (2017)
16. Khan, A.M., Mallet, F., Rashid, M.: Combining SysML and MARTE/CCSL to model complex electronic systems. In: Information Systems Engineering (ICISE), pp. 12–17. IEEE (2016)
17. Kriaa, S., Pietre-Cambacedes, L., Bouissou, M., Halgand, Y.: A survey of approaches combining safety and security for industrial control systems. Reliab. Eng. Syst. Saf. **139**, 156–178 (2015)
18. Kumar, R., Stoelinga, M.: Quantitative security and safety analysis with attack-fault trees. In: High Assurance Systems Engineering (HASE), pp. 25–32. IEEE (2017)
19. Legay, A., Viswanathan, M.: Statistical model checking: challenges and perspectives. Int. J. Softw. Tools Technol. Transf. **17**(4), 369–376 (2015)
20. Line, M.B., Nordland, O., Røstad, L., Tøndel, I.A.: Safety vs. Security. In: International Conference on Probabilistic Safety Assessment and Management (PSAM) (2006)
21. Macher, G., Höller, A., Sporer, H., Armengaud, E., Kreiner, C.: A combined safety-hazards and security-threat analysis method for automotive systems. In: Koornneef, F., van Gulijk, C. (eds.) SAFECOMP 2015. LNCS, vol. 9338, pp. 237–250. Springer, Cham (2015). https://doi.org/10.1007/978-3-319-24249-1_21
22. MAENAD (2011). http://www.maenad.eu/
23. Mallet, F., De Simone, R.: Correctness issues on MARTE/CCSL constraints. Sci. Comput. Program. **106**, 78–92 (2015)

24. Parr, T.: The definitive ANTLR 4 reference. Pragmatic Bookshelf (2013)
25. Pedroza, G., Apvrille, L., Knorreck, D.: Avatar: a SysML environment for the formal verification of safety and security properties. In: New Technologies of Distributed Systems (NOTERE), pp. 1–10. IEEE (2011)
26. ProTL. https://sites.google.com/view/protl
27. Tkinter: Python interface to Tcl/Tk. https://docs.python.org/3/library/tkinter.html
28. Raya, M., Hubaux, J.P.: Securing vehicular Ad Hoc networks. J. Comput. Secur. **15**(1), 39–68 (2007)
29. Sabaliauskaite, G., Mathur, A.P.: Aligning cyber-physical system safety and security. In: Cardin, M.A., Krob, D., Lui, P., Tan, Y., Wood, K. (eds.) Complex Systems Design & Management Asia, pp. 41–53. Springer, Cham (2015). https://doi.org/10.1007/978-3-319-12544-2_4
30. Specification, O.: UML profile for MARTE: modeling and analysis of real-time embedded systems. Technical report, Object Management Group (2011)
31. UPPAAL-SMC. http://people.cs.aau.dk/~adavid/smc/
32. Wardell, D.C., Mills, R.F., Peterson, G.L., Oxley, M.E.: A method for revealing and addressing security vulnerabilities in cyber-physical systems by modeling malicious agent interactions with formal verification. Proc. Comput. Sci. **95**, 24–31 (2016)
33. Zhang, C., Lin, X., Lu, R., Ho, P.H., Shen, X.: An efficient message authentication scheme for vehicular communications. IEEE Trans. Veh. Technol. **57**(6), 3357–3368 (2008)

14

Offline Delta-Driven Model Transformation with Dependency Injection

Artur Boronat[(✉)][iD]

Department of Informatics,
University of Leicester, Leicester, UK
aboronat@le.ac.uk

Abstract. When model transformations are used to implement consistency relations between very large models (VLMs), incrementality plays a cornerstone role in the realization of practical consistency maintainers. State-of-the-art model transformation engines with support for incrementality normally rely on a publish-subscribe model for linking model updates − deltas − to the application of model transformation rules, in so called dependencies, at run time. These deltas can then be propagated along an already executed model transformation. A small number of such engines use domain-specific languages (DSLs) for representing model deltas offline in order to enable their use in asynchronous, event-based execution environments.

The principal contribution of this work is the design of a forward delta propagation mechanism for incremental execution of model transformations, which decouples dependency tracking from delta propagation using two innovations. First, the publish-subscribe model is replaced with dependency injection, physically decoupling domain models from consistency maintainers. Second, a standardized representation of model deltas is reused, facilitating interoperability with EMF-compliant tools, both for defining deltas and for processing them asynchronously. This procedure has been implemented in a model transformation engine, whose performance has been evaluated empirically using the VIATRA CPS benchmark. In the experiments performed, the new transformation engine shows gains in the form of several orders of magnitude in the initial phase of the incremental execution of the benchmark model transformation and delta propagation is performed in real time, independently of the size of the models involved, whereas the up-to-now best-performant approach is dependent.

Keywords: Mappings between languages · Traceability · Incremental model transformation · Performance benchmark

1 Introduction

Significant issues in the application of Model-Driven Engineering (MDE) in large-scale industrial problems stem from interoperability and scalability of current MDE tools [1,16,17]. Model transformation, widely accepted as the *heart and soul* of MDE [23], deals with model manipulation either by translating models or by synchronizing them. Current tool support for model transformation is a key root cause for many of the bottlenecks hampering scalability in MDE [2,8]. This is particularly crucial when transformations are used to implement consistency maintainers between very large models (VLMs), consisting of milions of elements. In this context, incrementality ensures that only those parts of the model that are inconsistent or that have been modified – a model delta – are transformed or, more precisely, propagated along an already executed transformation [11,12].

Current state-of-the-art approaches that support incremental execution of model transformations share common features: the delta propagation mechanism is usually decoupled from the delta detection mechanism in order to facilitate maintainability of the consistency maintainer; and deltas are represented either in memory for synchronous notification or offline, with dedicated domain-specific languages, for asynchronous notification. The most mature tools rely on a publish/subscribe mechanism, where model deltas are notified at run time whenever a model is updated. This notification mechanism is synchronous and loosely couples model updates with the delta propagation mechanism, facilitating maintainability of the underlying transformation engine after fixing the type of notification. However, it usually requires an observer for each object that can be modified, with a consequent impact on performance, and the model transformation must be live, in memory, in order to listen for changes. These problems can be avoided by using offline deltas. The publish/subscribe mechanism can be extended to enable asynchronous delta notification but this is normally achieved by using dedicated domain-specific languages to represent deltas offline, which do not involve standardized formats, hindering the interoperability of those transformation engines in existing modeling tool ecosystems.

In this paper, the design of a forward delta propagation procedure is presented for executing model transformations in incremental mode that can handle documented change scenarios [4], i.e. documents representing a change to a given source model. Such documents are defined with the EMF change model [24], both conceptually and implementation-wise, guaranteeing interoperability with EMF-compliant tools. This design decision replaces a publish/subscribe notification with dependency injection: each notification is directly performed by the implementation of the domain model at run time by injecting the dependency corresponding to the model update that has been performed. Aspect-oriented programming is used to weave code into an already existing implementation of a domain model totally decoupling domain models from the consistency maintainer at design time. The proposed forward delta propagation procedure has been implemented in YAMTL [6], a model transformation engine for VLMs, enabling the execution of model transformations both in batch mode and in incremental mode without additional user specification overhead. This new extension dramatically improves the performance of the batch execution mode when dealing with sparse model deltas, which can be propagated in real time (i.e. in μs.).

This work is structured as follows: Sect. 2 provides a self-contained description of the class of model transformations supported using a class diagram to relational schema model transformation; Sect. 3 presents the forward propagation procedure implemented in the model transformation engine together with the main innovations; Sect. 4 discusses the performance of the transformation engine with an adaptation of the VIATRA CPS benchmark; Sect. 5 discusses related work from reactive and bidirectional model transformation.

2   Model Transformation: A Running Example

The type of model transformations that are considered in this work are classified as unidirectional and out-place. For example, when considering the well-known example that maps class diagrams to relational schemas, a class diagram is used by queries to extract information and a relational schema is built from scratch. If we consider a graph transformation perspective, both models are considered to form part of the same graph in order to enable transformation by rewriting. In that case, we are only considering transformations where the two models are two clearly disjoint subgraphs and where rewriting is performed deterministically.

In this work, model transformations are represented using an implementation-agnostic graphical syntax, quite close to that used in the graph transformation literature. In this representation, metamodels are given as class diagrams, the abstract syntax of models is given as object diagrams and model transformations are represented as a collection of rules, where each rule is defined as a pair of model patterns, called left-hand side (LHS) and right-hand side (RHS). The notion of metamodel, model and model pattern correspond to those of type graph, attributed graph with containments and node inheritance, and graph pattern in the graph transformation literature [5, 10]. For example, the rules A->C and R->FK of Fig. 1 map attributes to columns. The $ before a variable denotes string interpolation.

Graph patterns in rules can be augmented with universally quantified variables (represented by an overlaid box). Moreover, rules are augmented with a when clause to express conditions that must be satisfied by the variables in LHS, and with a where clause to indicate how variables from LHS and from RHS are related via the application of other rules, expressed as two graph patterns. Formulas in a when clause may be expressed in conjunctive form, as all filter conditions must be satisfied in order for the rule to be applied, whereas formulas in a where clause may be expressed in disjunctive form (assuming mutually exclusive conditions), as all the side effects expressed in a where clause must be evaluated. The variables of RHS of the main rule must appear either in the LHS of the main rule or in the RHS of a where transformation step. The rule C->T of Fig. 1 illustrates how to map a class to a table with a primary key column PK_COL and for each attribute A whose type is a DataType, the corresponding column is obtained by applying a rule, with the rule A->C, and for each attribute OTHER whose type is the class C, matched in LHS of the main rule, a new foreign key column is added to the table T, with the rule R->FK.

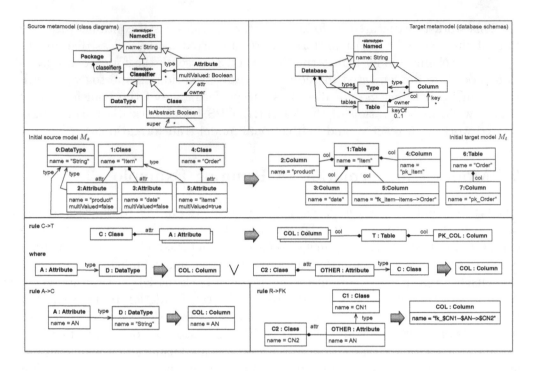

Fig. 1. Metamodels, example and transformation rules.

From an operational point of view, transformation rules are applied unidirectionally from LHS to RHS performing an out-place transformation following two steps. First, during the *matching phase*, matches for the rules in the model transformation are found as long as they are not shared by different rules and these are included in a set *matchPool*. A match is formally defined as a graph morphism from LHS to the source graph, which satisfies the **when** conditions, but it is represented as a map from variables to object identifiers for the sake of presentation in this paper.

Second, during the *execution phase*, each match is processed by triggering the application of a transformation rule, which is represented as a transformation step, denoted by $r : \overrightarrow{in \mapsto \varsigma} \rightarrow \overrightarrow{out \mapsto \varsigma}$, which consists of a labelled pair of two matches, the match for the input pattern of the rule, which enables its application, and the match for the output pattern of the rule, with the objects that result from applying the rule. When a rule is applied, the source model is only used for query purposes but the target model is constructed by adding the pattern of the RHS instantiated with values from the variables both in the LHS and in the RHS of **where** transformation steps. In addition, **where** transformation steps may further expand the structure of the target model. This execution model resembles the application of forward rules used in triple graph grammars (TGGs) [22], where the source graph is annotated as rules are applied and only the target graph is constructed together with a link in a correspondence graph, where each link denotes a transformation step.

3   Delta-Driven Model Transformations

This section presents the mechanism to propagate documented deltas δ_t from a source model M_s to a target model M_t in an incremental way, when the (unidirectional) synchronization correspondence between these two models is represented with a model transformation t as described in the previous section. This has been implemented in the YAMTL transformation engine [6], which has been extended with two modes of execution: *initialization*, the transformation is executed in batch mode but, additionally, tracks those parts of the source model involved in transformation steps as *dependencies*; *propagation*, the transformation is executed incrementally for a given source delta.

In order for a model transformation to be executed in propagation mode, it first needs to be executed in initialization mode in order both to create transformation steps and to inject the dependencies that facilitate the analysis of the impact of changes in the already executed model transformation. Therefore, the transformation t is applied to M_s using the original batch semantics [6] while injecting dependencies in the transformation engine. Once the initialization is done, any number of source forward deltas δ_s can be propagated.

Given a source documented delta δ_s between a source model M_s, already synchronized with a target model M_t via a model transformation $t : M_s \xrightarrow{*} M_t$ (where $\xrightarrow{*}$ denotes a sequence of transformation steps), and an updated source model M_s', the transformation engine propagates the model update δ_s along t. The effect of this forward propagation is the application of an update δ_t on the target model M_t.

In the following subsections, we explain the different phases of the new execution modes, initialization and propagation, in more detail. As the initialization mode faithfully corresponds to the batch execution of a model transformation, the discussion of this mode focuses on the type of dependencies that are injected in the transformation engine in Sect. 3.1. The discussion on the propagation mode focuses on how deltas are represented in Sect. 3.2. Then, the two main phases of the propagation execution mode, namely impact analysis and delta propagation, are explained in Sects. 3.3 and 3.4, respectively.

3.1   Dependency Injection

When running a model transformation in initialization mode, the engine monitors the source model and whenever an object ς is matched or a feature call, represented as a pair (ς, f) of an EMF object ς and a feature name f, is performed, a dependency is injected into the dependency registry. A dependency thereby links either an object ς or a feature call (ς, f) to transformation steps $r : \overrightarrow{in \mapsto \varsigma} \rightarrow \overrightarrow{out \mapsto \varsigma}$ in which it is used. Such dependencies are detected both during the matching phase and during the execution phase.

In the matching phase, while finding a match for a rule, the engine keeps track of all of the feature calls used in both element and rule `when` conditions. When a match is found to be valid, the collection of dependencies is injected into the dependency registry for the transformation step that uses that match. Otherwise,

Table 1. Analysis of dependencies for the initial MT $t : M_s \xrightarrow{*} M_t$ of Fig. 2.

Rule	Source Match	Target Match	Dependencies from M_s
C->T	$c \mapsto 1$	$t \mapsto 1,$	$(1,\texttt{name}), (1,\texttt{att}),$
		$\texttt{pk\_col} \mapsto 4$	$(5, \texttt{type}), (5, \texttt{multiValued})$
C->T	$c \mapsto 4$	$t \mapsto 6, \texttt{pk\_col} \mapsto 7$	$(4, \texttt{name}), (4, \texttt{attr})$
A->C	$\texttt{att} \mapsto 2$	$\texttt{col} \mapsto 2$	$(2, \texttt{name})$
A->C	$\texttt{att} \mapsto 3$	$\texttt{col} \mapsto 3$	$(3, \texttt{name})$
R->FK	$\texttt{ref} \mapsto 5$	$\texttt{fk\_col} \mapsto 5$	$(5,\texttt{name}), (5,\texttt{type}),$
		$\texttt{fk\_col} \mapsto 5$	$(1, \texttt{name}), (4,\texttt{name})$

when the match is not valid, the collected dependencies are discarded. Additionally, when inserting a match in the *matchPool*, the transformation engine also records reverse matches as injected dependencies between matched objects ς and the transformation step in which they are matched.

Dependencies may also be found when executing a transformation step, e.g., while executing initialization expressions associated with attributes in model patterns in RHS and in **where** clauses. In such cases, the transformation engine injects a dependency for the transformation step every time a feature call in the source model is detected. As a result, note that several transformation steps may depend on the same object ς, when rules have more than one single input element, or on the same feature call (ς, f).

Table 1 shows the dependencies that are found when executing the transformation of Fig. 1 in initialization mode from model M_s. Each row in the table represents a transformation step, where: the source match indicates where the rule has been applied, the target match indicates what objects were created, and dependencies refers to the set of feature calls associated with a transformation step. Reverse matches are extracted from source matches, by reading them in the opposite direction.

Dependency injection is configured with an aspect whose pointcut matches feature calls under a user-defined namespace. Hence, the model transformation engine is entirely decoupled from the domain model at design time. They become tightly coupled at compilation time and, hence, at run time.

3.2 Representable Deltas

The EMF change model [24] is used to represent deltas to an instance of any other EMF model. It is built-in in EMF and, therefore, available for any EMF-compliant tool. In this section, we describe how a documented delta is represented with the EMF change model and how it can be automatically defined given any potentially *live* atomic update.

A delta consists of a `ChangeDescription` which contains a map of `objectChanges`, which refer to those objects that are updated and, for each such object, it contains a list of `FeatureChanges`. A `FeatureChange` (FC) refers to the structural feature that needs to be updated and provides the new value. For single-valued attributes, a `FeatureChange` contains the new `dataValue` if the feature is an attribute. For references and multi-valued attributes, a `FeatureChange` includes a containment reference `listChanges` pointing to `ListChange`. `ListChange`s are used to represent addition to, removal from, or movement *within* the given feature values. In particular, movement only captures when an object changes to a different index within the collection. However, it does not capture structural changes, e.g. change of container, which are represented as a removal from and an addition to the corresponding containment references. When a `FeatureChange` refers to a containment reference, objects to be added are pointed by `objectsToAttach` and objects to be removed are pointed by `objectsToDetach`.

`FeatureChange`s capture when a feature value is updated for an object but EMF also permits adding and removing root objects to a resource, representing the model in memory, which need not be contained by any other object. Such changes are considered to be performed on the resource itself and are represented with `ResourceChange`s, one for each changed resource. A `ResourceChange` (`RC`) contains the `ListChange`s for the root objects of the corresponding resource, similarly to multi-valued features. For a more detailed explanation of the EMF change model, we refer the reader to [24].

Table 2 shows a classification of atomic model updates that are representable with the EMF change model as explained above. Note that moving and object structurally, case 12 − *move (inter.)*, − is represented in a composite delta by two opposite actions, removing the object either from the root contents of the resource − if it is a root object (case 2) − or from a containment reference − if it is a contained object (case 10) − and adding it either to the root contents of the resource − if it is to become a root object (case 1) − or to another containment reference in another container object (case 9). This case is not captured by the EMF change model explicitly but the transformation engine is able to infer it, as explained in the following section.

Table 2. Summary of model update types, with their representation in EMF.

Cases	Granularity	Level	Feature	Delta action	Delta representation	DO	DFC
1,2	atomic	root		add/remove	`RC::listChanges`	✓	
3	atomic	root		move (intra.)	`RC::listChanges`		
4,5	atomic	any	single-valued att	add/remove	FC		✓
6,7	atomic	any	multi-valued att	add/remove	`FC::listChanges`	✓	✓
8	atomic	any	multi-valued att	move (intra.)	`FC::listChanges`		✓
9,10	atomic	any	ref	add/remove	`FC::listChanges`		✓
11	atomic	any	ref	move (intra.)	`FC::listChanges`		✓
12	composite	any	containment ref	move (inter.)	opposite remove and add actions in cases $\{2, 10\}/\{1, 9\}$		✓

A delta, which may represent atomic and composite changes, is defined as an instance of the EMF change model and can be serialized. EMF also provides facilities for applying them and reversing them. Furthermore, EMF provides a change recorder, which enables recording *live updates* as a `ChangeDescription` for either a root object, a collection of root objects, a resource or a resource set. The resulting `ChangeDescription` is the representation of a *history scenario* [4], from the updated model to the original one, which is optimized. That is, atomic changes for the same feature of the same object may be discarded or merged, as long as the optimization process preserves reversibility. Hence, reversing the recorded delta may yield less changes than were originally made. Reversed deltas represent *documented scenarios* and can be propagated along a model transformation, as discussed in subsequent sections.

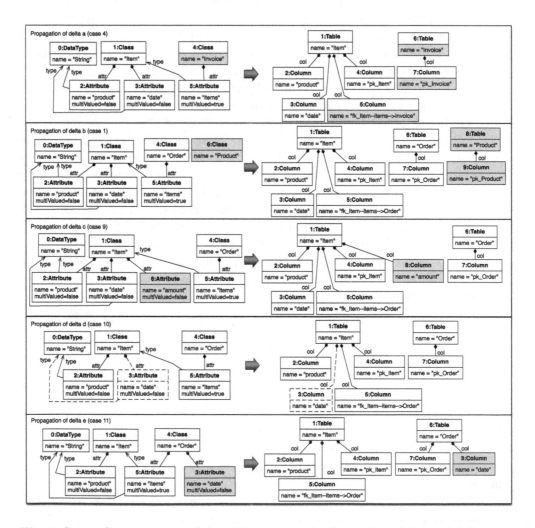

Fig. 2. Source/target metamodels, initial synchronized models and forward delta propagation (a–e).

The EMF change recorder enables the possibility of deferring the observation of updates to the point in which they occur, saving memory resources, and interoperability. Furthermore, recorded (history) deltas can be regarded as a rollback mechanism for implementing transactional model updates, which may be performed live.

Figure 2 shows examples of documented deltas, defined over the source model M_s of the running example. Such deltas are representable as EMF model changes, i.e. operationally, but are graphically depicted using the abstract syntax of M_s, using their state-based representation for the sake of presentation. Additions and updates, including moves, are highlighted in grey colour. Objects that are added, and thus created, have a new identifier. Objects that are updated and/or moved preserve their identifier. Removals are highlighted by using dashed lines for the contour lines of the corresponding shapes. The given deltas are instantiations of case 4 (delta a), changing the name of the class Order to Invoice; case 1 (delta b), adding a root class Product; case 9 (delta c), adding a single-valued attribute amount to class Item; case 10 (delta d), removing the attribute date from class Item; and case 11 (delta e), structurally moving the attribute date from class Item to class Order.

In the following subsections, the different phases of the procedure for forward propagation of source deltas is discussed and the aforementioned examples will be used for illustrating them.

3.3   Impact Analysis

In this subsection, we discuss how source documented deltas are analyzed in order to determine which transformation steps are affected by source changes. This analysis is comprised of three main steps: identification of atomic model updates from a documented delta, initialization of locations for newly enabled rules, and marking of transformation steps impacted by changes.

Identification of atomic model updates. In the first step, the transformation engine infers which objects and which feature calls have been impacted by changes. For objects, it also infers whether an object has been added or removed, ignoring if the object is moved, either within the same collection or structurally.

For affected objects, such information is recorded in the set DO of *dirty objects* of the form $(\varsigma, ctype)$, where ς is the affected object and *ctype* is the type of change from the set { ADD, DEL}. To obtain a dirty object from the delta, FeatureChanges and ResourceChanges are traversed considering two cases: when an object ς is added either to a containment feature (for a FeatureChange) or to the root contents of the resource (for a ResourceChange) and such object is not removed elsewhere in the delta, either from a containment reference or from the root contents of the resource; and, similarly, when an object is deleted and it is not added elsewhere in the delta. DO is augmented with $(\varsigma,$ ADD) in the first case and with $(\varsigma,$ DEL) in the second case.

For affected feature calls, such information is recorded in the set DFC of *dirty feature calls* of the form (ς, f), where ς is an object and f is a feature

Table 3. Impact analysis of source deltas a–e.

	Case	DO	DFC	Rule	Source Match	Target Match	$matchPool_\Delta$	dirty?
a	4	–	(4, name)	C->T	$c \mapsto 4$	$t \mapsto 6, pk\_col \mapsto 7$	✓	✓
b	1	(6, ADD)	–	C->T	$c \mapsto 6$		✓	
c	9		(1, attr)	C->T	$c \mapsto 1$	$t \mapsto 1, pk\_col \mapsto 4$	✓	✓
		(6, ADD)		A->C	$att \mapsto 6$		✓	
d	10		(1, attr)	C->T	$c \mapsto 1$	$t \mapsto 1, pk\_col \mapsto 4$	✓	✓
		(3, DEL)		A->C	$att \mapsto 3$	$col \mapsto 3$		✓
e	11	–	(1, attr),	C->T	$c \mapsto 1$	$t \mapsto 1, pk\_col \mapsto 4$	✓	✓
			(4, attr)	C->T	$c \mapsto 4$	$t \mapsto 6, pk\_col \mapsto 7$	✓	✓

name. For each `FeatureChange` of an `ObjectChange`, the dirty feature call (ς, f) with the object ς referred by the `ObjectChange` and the feature name f referred to by the `FeatureChange` is added to DFC.

Table 2 shows how atomic model update types are represented using the EMF change model (column *delta representation*), internally, using the sets DO and DFC. Table 3 shows the sets DO of dirty objects and DFC of dirty feature calls for the source deltas of Fig. 2. Note that the sets DO and DFC decouple the transformation engine from the EMF change model and provide another entry point for defining deltas programmatically, which can be used for capturing atomic *live changes* received via EMF adapters.

Initialization of delta locations. For each dirty object (ς, ADD), the object ς is added to the extent associated with $type(o)$ in the location map used for delta propagation. This potentially enables new matches when rules are matched during the delta propagation phase.

Marking of impacted transformation steps. In this step, transformation steps that are affected by the atomic changes in the source delta are marked as dirty. For each dirty object $(\varsigma, \text{ADD}) \in DO$, the extent of type `type(`ς`)` is augmented with ς. This will potentially enable new matches for some rule during the change propagation phase. For each dirty object $(\varsigma, \text{DEL}) \in DO$, we obtain the list of transformation steps that are affected from the map of reverse matches. Such transformation steps will then remain transient and the objects in their target match will not be linked to other objects in the target models. In particular, note that when processing root objects or a containment reference, an object that is removed in the delta is not present in the updated source model and, therefore, it does not trigger the transformation step that had been executed in the initial transformation.

For each dirty feature call $(\varsigma, f) \in DFC$ we obtain the list of transformation steps that are affected from the registry of dependencies. For each such transformation step, the satisfaction of its source match is checked. If such source match is still valid, then it is inserted into $matchPool_\Delta$, the pool of matches that are used to schedule rule applications during the change propagation phase.

For each atomic change in Fig. 2, Table 3 shows the marking of transformation steps that are (re-)scheduled according to the dependencies of Table 1. In particular, if a transformation step is re-scheduled, its current source and target matches are included, it is marked as dirty and included in $matchPool_\Delta$. If a transformation step is not to be re-executed, it is simply marked as dirty. New transformation steps, with fresh matches due to new objects, are scheduled in $matchPool_\Delta$. This last step is actually achieved by augmenting the corresponding type extent with the new objects and the matches are scheduled during the change propagation phase, explained in the next subsection.

3.4   Change Propagation

After the impact analysis phase, delta propagation proceeds by executing a model transformation using the matching and execution phases, as outlined in Sect. 2. Figure 2 illustrates the propagation of source deltas according to the model transformation of Fig. 1. We highlight how incrementality has been considered in these two phases below.

Matching Phase. During the matching phase (in batch/initialization execution mode), matches for a given rule are found by traversing objects from the extent of the types associated with the elements of the source pattern of the rule, with the constraints specified in the form of graphical patterns and **when** conditions. In propagation mode, the transformation engine employs the same pattern matching algorithm but it fetches objects from the location map used for delta propagation, initialized during the change impact analysis phase. Therefore, new matches may be found for objects that have been created by the source delta. Those matches are inserted both into $matchPool$ and $matchPool_\Delta$, scheduling new transformation steps. Table 3 shows that two new transformation steps are scheduled, one for rule C->T in delta b, and one for rule A->C in delta c.

Execution Phase. During the execution phase, transformation steps determined by the matches in $matchPool_\Delta$ are executed. Such matches originate from the impact analysis phase, corresponding to transformation steps that are *dirty* and need to be re-executed, and from the matching phase above, corresponding to new transformation steps.

The re-execution of a transformation step is performed as in the batch/initialization mode but for the creation of transformation steps. Whereas a newly scheduled transformation step needs to get its output objects initialized (instantiated for output elements), a dirty transformation step *reuses* the objects of the target match and unsets their features. This avoids loss of contextual information, which is not affected by changes, when re-executing a transformation step. In particular, those references to output objects that emerge from the external context are preserved. On the other hand, references from those output objects are re-calculated by re-executing the transformation step. It is worth noting that the transformation engine uses **where** clauses to define references to objects that are created by other rules, which in turn uses a cache mechanism to avoid re-executing the transformation step that produced it. Therefore, when a dirty transformation rule is re-executed, the initialization of output element bindings are performed again. However, those bindings that are initialized in a **where** clause are also initialized incrementally. That is, only those objects that belong to a match of a new scheduled transformation step will be transformed from scratch. References to already initialized objects will be simply fetched. Hence, the granularity of the target delta is as fine grained (at binding level) as the source delta for the underlying graph structure of the model.

4 Performance Analysis

For the empirical analysis of the incremental execution of model transformations in YAMTL using the propagation procedure presented above, we have used the VIATRA CPS benchmark [27]. The transformation *YAMTL-incr* implemented for our model transformation engine passes the sanity checks of the benchmark. The software artifacts used in this section and the results obtained are publicly available in a GitHub repository [7] and YAMTL is available at https://yamtl. github.io/.

This evaluation is an extension of the one performed for the batch component of the VIATRA CPS benchmark in [6]. From the original VIATRA CPS benchmark, two incremental variants of the transformation implemented with *EMF-IncQuery* have been selected: *ExplicitTraceability* (EXPL) [25] and *QueryResultTraceability* (QRT) [26], out of which the first one is the best performing solution up to now. These transformations have been extracted as independent Java projects. Classes implementing them have been kept intact in the new projects, including their namespaces, so that errors are not introduced due to lack of expertise. Although these two transformations produce results that are different from the other transformations, the main differences are due to reordering of multi-valued references and we have considered them valid for this evaluation. On the other hand, a benchmark measurement harness considering the best practices recommended by the VIATRA team [13] was developed in order both to fine-tune measurements and to crosscheck results. This harness removes dependencies to other components of the VIATRA CPS benchmark so that experiments can be run locally.

In the present work, we aimed at answering the following research questions: *(RQ1)* Does *YAMTL-incr* show any performance penalty w.r.t. its execution in batch mode (*YAMTL-batch*)? *(RQ2)* Does *YAMTL-incr* show any improvement in performance w.r.t *EXPL* or *QRT* during initialization phase? *(RQ3)* And during propagation phase?

From the scenarios provided in the original benchmark, the scenarios *client-server* and *statistic based* [29] were considered. The CPS model generator [28] was used to obtain the input models to be used for the analysis so that their size depends on a logarithmic factor. The biggest models considered, in the client server scenario, consist of millions of nodes (10.16M) and edges (27.53M) and are, hence, VLMs.

For each tool and scenario, the experiments are run in isolation, i.e. in a separate Java process. For each of the input models, an initial experiment is performed to warm up the JVM and, then, twelve more experiments to measure performance. Each experiment consists of four phases: model load and engine initialization, initial transformation, delta propagation and model storage. In between each execution phase, the harness sends hints to the JVM to run garbage collection and waits for one second before proceeding on to the next phase. The first phase includes the instantiation of a fresh engine instance, avoiding interference between experiments as caches are not reused. The delta propagation phase includes the application of the delta to the source model and its propagation. Only initial transformation and delta propagation times have been considered in the quantitative analysis. For the results the median obtained for each of these two phases out of ten experiments is used, after removing the minimum and the maximum results.

In both solutions *EXPL* [25] and *QRT* [26], the delta is applied to the source model by directly modifying the resource containing the model. In the solution with YAMTL such delta was recorded and persisted using the EMF change model as described in Sect. 3.2. To analyze whether this feature could become a threat to validity, a separate experiment was run by excluding the query part of the model update (searching for the objects to be updated) in the solution *EXPL* but this change did not affect performance results perceptibly and the original solutions provided by the authors of the VIATRA CPS benchmark were considered. Therefore, the actions performed during the propagation phase are equivalent in all of the evaluated solutions.

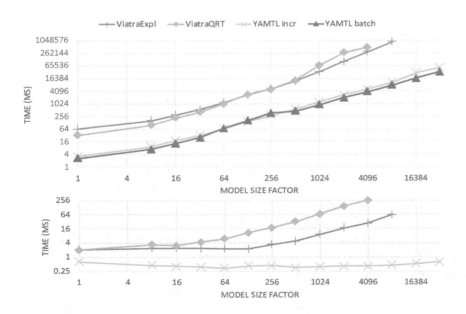

Fig. 3. Performance of initialization (top) and delta propagation (bottom).

Figure 3 shows the performance results obtained both for the initial model transformation and for forward delta propagation for the models generated for the client-server scenario. Scales both for time (ms.) along Y axis and for model size factors along X axis are logarithmic allowing us to compare the scalability of the different approaches. In the initialization phase, we have included the execution of YAMTL in batch mode (*YAMTL-batch*) over the source model, and it can be seen that tracking dependencies incurs a small penalty. However, the other two solutions (*EXPL* and *QRT*) operate several orders of magnitude slower. In the propagation phase, it can be observed that while *YAMTL-incr* exhibits a constant propagation time (in μs.) for the source delta, the cost of the other solutions depends on the size of the input model. Furthermore, for the other incremental approaches, when both initial and propagation time are combined their performance worsens due to their costly initialization phase.

5   Related Work

In this section, we discuss techniques used in related work for achieving incrementality in both reactive and bidirectional model transformation.

Reactive model transformation [3, 21] enable the propagation of model updates from source models to target models on demand. State-of-the-art tool support relies on notification mechanisms, enabling live detection of source model updates either for immediate processing, as in VIATRA [3], or for deferred processing, as in ReactiveATL [21]. In these approaches, source model update notifications are usually fine-grained and kept in memory. Such notifications can only be detected when the transformation engine is in memory (live) as well. The use of a notification mechanism means that models are *loosely coupled* to the transformation engine. Working with offline model updates, as in the proposed delta propagation procedure, completely decouples detection of deltas from the transformation engine, freeing model update developers from the overhead of having the transformation infrastructure in memory. The latter is only needed for propagating changes but not for defining them. In reactive approaches, when an observer receives an update notification, information about the intent of the overall model delta, i.e. the contextual information relating different atomic updates, is lost. This problem is avoided using documented deltas, which may be serialized, enabling their processing − e.g. aggregating composite changes like the *move operation* − and optimization − reduction of atomic operations that are cancelled when composed. We refer the reader to [9] for an additional discussion of delta-based model updates against state-based model updates.

Among bidirectional model transformation approaches, Triple Graph Grammars (TGG), introduced in [22], are a declarative approach for specifying bidirectional consistency relations between models. Although our approach is not bidirectional, it is worth comparing how incrementality is supported in operational TGG rules. Incrementality was first introduced in TGG synchronization in [11,12]. Efficient approaches for TGG synchronization [18–20] avoid analyzing the whole model by relying on dependencies which hint at the impact of a model update directly. Precedence-based approaches [18, 20] keep a binary precedence relation over the set of model elements in order to determine when creation or deletion of a model element affects another one. While [18] overestimates the actual dependencies by defining them at the type level, others underestimate them relying on user feedback [20] or on special correspondences [12]. [19] decouples impact analysis of model updates from consistency restoration by delegating the former to VIATRA's incremental pattern matcher, which has a built-in dependency tracker, and by defining operational rules using a reactive model transformation approach. However, these two phases are still tightly coupled using a synchronous communication mechanism between the incremental pattern matcher and the synchronization procedure since the pattern matcher may trigger revocations/applications of forward marking rules after revoking/applying one of them. That is, the model synchronization procedure uses the pattern matcher to know when synchronization terminates. In the delta propagation mechanism proposed in the present work, either the revocation of applied transformation steps or the creation of new transformation steps cannot trigger further applications because rule matches are computed against the source model and they are unique, that is the same match cannot enable two different rules. A new transformation step may be found when new elements are inserted in the source model. On the other hand, when a transformation step is revoked, no other rule can be applied or a conflict would have been detected when the rule was applied the first time.

Some transformation engines with support for bidirectional transformations, like NMF [14, 15], support the offline representation of model deltas. However, to the best of our knowledge, none of the aforementioned approaches uses a standardized notation for them, such as the EMF model change, which can be regarded as the de-facto standard for representing model deltas in the EMF modeling tool ecosystem.

6   Concluding Remarks

The main contribution of this work is the design of a delta propagation procedure for executing delta-driven model transformations, which has been implemented in YAMTL. The novelty of the approach consists in the use of a standardized representation of model deltas, which facilitates interoperability with EMF-compliant tools, and in the use of dependency injection mechanism, which allows the transformation engine to be aware of model updates without having to rely on a publish-subscribe infrastructure. The VIATRA CPS benchmark has been used to justify that *(1)* the initialization transformation in YAMTL is several orders of magnitude faster than the up-to-now fastest incremental solutions and that *(2)* propagation of sparse deltas can be performed in real time for VLMs, independently of their size, whereas other solutions show a clear dependence on their size. Hence, YAMTL shows satisfactory scalability in incremental execution of model transformations on VLMs. Additional studies with larger classes of models will be considered in future work.

References

1. Baker, P., Loh, S., Weil, F.: Model-driven engineering in a large industrial context — Motorola case study. In: Briand, L., Williams, C. (eds.) MODELS 2005. LNCS, vol. 3713, pp. 476–491. Springer, Heidelberg (2005). https://doi.org/10. 1007/11557432_36

2. Benelallam, A., Gómez, A., Tisi, M., Cabot, J.: Distributing relational model transformation on mapreduce. J. Syst. Softw. **142**, 1–20 (2018)

3. Bergmann, G., et al.: VIATRA 3: a reactive model transformation platform. In: Kolovos, D., Wimmer, M. (eds.) ICMT 2015. LNCS, vol. 9152, pp. 101–110. Springer, Cham (2015). https://doi.org/10.1007/978-3-319-21155-8_8

4. Bergmann, G., Ráth, I., Varró, G., Varró, D.: Change-driven model transformations - change (in) the rule to rule the change. Softw. Syst. Model. **11**(3), 431–461 (2012)

5. Biermann, E., Ermel, C., Taentzer, G.: Formal foundation of consistent EMF model transformations by algebraic graph transformation. Softw. Syst. Model. **11**(2), 227–250 (2012)

6. Boronat, A.: Expressive and efficient model transformation with an internal DSL of Xtend. In: MODELS 2018, pp. 78–88. ACM (2018)

7. Boronat, A.: YAMTL evaluation repository with the incremental component of the VIATRA CPS benchmark (2018). https://github.com/yamtl/viatra-cps-incr-benchmark

8. Daniel, G., Jouault, F., Sunyé, G., Cabot, J.: Gremlin-ATL: a scalable model transformation framework. In: ASE, pp. 462–472. IEEE Computer Society (2017)

9. Diskin, Z., Xiong, Y., Czarnecki, K., Ehrig, H., Hermann, F., Orejas, F.: From state- to delta-based bidirectional model transformations: the symmetric case. In: Whittle, J., Clark, T., Kühne, T. (eds.) MODELS 2011. LNCS, vol. 6981, pp. 304–318. Springer, Heidelberg (2011). https://doi.org/10.1007/978-3-642-24485-8_22

10. Ehrig, H., Ehrig, K., Prange, U., Taentzer, G.: Fundamentals of Algebraic Graph Transformation. Springer, Heidelberg (2006). https://doi.org/10.1007/3-540-31188-2

11. Giese, H., Wagner, R.: Incremental model synchronization with triple graph grammars. In: Nierstrasz, O., Whittle, J., Harel, D., Reggio, G. (eds.) MODELS 2006. LNCS, vol. 4199, pp. 543–557. Springer, Heidelberg (2006). https://doi.org/10. 1007/11880240_38

12. Giese, H., Wagner, R.: From model transformation to incremental bidirectional model synchronization. Softw. Syst. Model. **8**(1), 21–43 (2009)

13. Harmath, D., Ráth, I.: VIATRA/query/FAQ: performance optimization guidelines (2016). https://wiki.eclipse.org/VIATRA/Query/FAQ#Performance_optimization _guidelines

14. Hinkel, G.: Change propagation in an internal model transformation language. In: Kolovos, D., Wimmer, M. (eds.) ICMT 2015. LNCS, vol. 9152, pp. 3–17. Springer, Cham (2015). https://doi.org/10.1007/978-3-319-21155-8_1

15. Hinkel, G., Burger, E.: Change propagation and bidirectionality in internal transformation DSLs. Softw. Syst. Model. **18**(1), 249–278 (2017)

16. Hutchinson, J., Whittle, J., Rouncefield, M., Kristoffersen, S.: Empirical assessment of MDE in industry. In: ICSE, pp. 471–480. ACM (2011)

17. Kolovos, D.S., Paige, R.F., Polack, F.A.C.: The grand challenge of scalability for model driven engineering. In: Chaudron, M.R.V. (ed.) MODELS 2008. LNCS, vol. 5421, pp. 48–53. Springer, Heidelberg (2009). https://doi.org/10.1007/978-3-642-01648-6_5

18. Lauder, M., Anjorin, A., Varró, G., Schürr, A.: Efficient model synchronization with precedence triple graph grammars. In: Ehrig, H., Engels, G., Kreowski, H.-J., Rozenberg, G. (eds.) ICGT 2012. LNCS, vol. 7562, pp. 401–415. Springer, Heidelberg (2012). https://doi.org/10.1007/978-3-642-33654-6_27

19. Leblebici, E., Anjorin, A., Fritsche, L., Varró, G., Schürr, A.: Leveraging incremental pattern matching techniques for model synchronisation. In: de Lara, J., Plump, D. (eds.) ICGT 2017. LNCS, vol. 10373, pp. 179–195. Springer, Cham (2017). https://doi.org/10.1007/978-3-319-61470-0_11

20. Orejas, F., Pino, E.: Correctness of incremental model synchronization with triple graph grammars. In: Di Ruscio, D., Varró, D. (eds.) ICMT 2014. LNCS, vol. 8568, pp. 74–90. Springer, Cham (2014). https://doi.org/10.1007/978-3-319-08789-4_6

21. Perez, S.M., Tisi, M., Douence, R.: Reactive model transformation with ATL. Sci. Comput. Program. **136**, 1–16 (2017)

22. Schürr, A.: Specification of graph translators with triple graph grammars. In: Mayr, E.W., Schmidt, G., Tinhofer, G. (eds.) WG 1994. LNCS, vol. 903, pp. 151–163. Springer, Heidelberg (1995). https://doi.org/10.1007/3-540-59071-4_45

23. Sendall, S., Kozaczynski, W.: Model transformation: the heart and soul of model-driven software development. IEEE Softw. **20**(5), 42–45 (2003)

24. Steinberg, D., Budinsky, F., Paternostro, M., Merks, E.: EMF: Eclipse Modeling Framework 2.0., 2nd edn. Addison-Wesley Professional (2009)

25. VIATRA Team: Explicit traceability M2M transformation (2016). https://github.com/viatra/viatra-docs/blob/master/cps/Explicit-traceability-M2M-transformation.adoc

26. VIATRA Team: Query result traceability M2M transformation (2016). https://github.com/viatra/viatra-docs/blob/master/cps/Query-result-traceability-M2M-transformation.adoc

27. VIATRA Team: VIATRA CPS benchmark (cps to deployment transformation) (2016). https://github.com/viatra/viatra-docs/blob/master/cps/CPS-to-Deployment-Transformation.adoc

28. VIATRA Team: VIATRA CPS benchmark (model generator) (2016). https://github.com/viatra/viatra-docs/blob/master/cps/Model-Generator.adoc

29. VIATRA Team: VIATRA CPS benchmark (scenario specification) (2016). https://github.com/viatra/viatra-cps-benchmark/wiki/Benchmark-specification#cases

15

KUPC: A Formal Tool for Modeling and Verifying Dynamic Updating of C Programs

Jiaqi Qian[1], Min Zhang[1(✉)], Yi Wang[2], and Kazuhiro Ogata[3]

[1] Shanghai Key Lab of Trustworthy Computing,
ECNU, Shanghai, China
`zhangmin@sei.ecnu.edu.cn`
[2] GCCIS, Rochester Institute of Technology,
Rochester, NY, USA
[3] Japan Advanced Institute of Science and Technology, Nomi, Japan

Abstract. Dynamic Software Updating (DSU) is a useful technique for updating running software without incurring any downtime. Its correctness must be guaranteed because updating a running software is a complicated and safety-critical process. In this paper, we present a formal tool called KUPC for modeling and verifying dynamic updating of C programs. The tool is built on $\mathbb{K}$–a formal semantic framework for programming languages. We formalize a patch-based dynamic updating mechanism in $\mathbb{K}$ based on the formal executable operational semantics of C. The formalization automatically yields an interpreter and several verification tools, which can be used to formally analyze the correctness of dynamic updating for C programs. To our knowledge, KUPC is the first formal tool for code-level verification of dynamic software updating.

1 Introduction

Software systems require frequent updating to fixate defects, improve performance, and add new features. For those systems providing 24×7 service commitment, Dynamic Software Updating (DSU) is a useful technique as it does not incur system downtime while updating [5]. Such systems are becoming prevalent with the diffusion of Internet of Things (IoT) and Cyber-Physical Systems (CPS), where additions, modifications, and removal of behaviors could be done in a quick and localized fashion. There is a comprehensive survey on DSU [10].

The difficulty of guaranteeing the correctness of dynamic updating is a fundamental barrier when we adopt this technique widely as expected. Correctness is crucial to those systems that need dynamic updating because they are usually safety-critical and highly-dependable. Meanwhile, dynamically updating a running software system is a complicated process, and it is difficult to predict all possible updating results. In order to update a program successfully while it is running in practice one has to know everything about that program [6]. However, it still lacks effective methodologies and tools to help understand all possible behaviors of running programs caused by updating.

Formal methods are rigorous approaches to program verification. Some attempts have been made on applying formal methods to DSU [3,4]. The existing approaches suffer one or more difficulties as follows. In some approaches formalizing a dynamic update may require abstraction of target programs. Such abstraction is usually done manually. It requires both formal methods expertise and human intellection to interpret target programs. Some approaches [1,11] lack tool support while developing such tools needs substantial efforts.

To mitigate the above difficulties, we present a formal tool called KUPC for modeling and verifying dynamic updating of C programs in this paper. KUPC is built upon the formalization of a DSU tool called `Ginseng` [8] for C programs. We formalize the updating strategy of `Ginseng` atop the operational semantics of C in the formal semantic framework called $\mathbb{K}$ [9]. From the formalization, $\mathbb{K}$ automatically generates several tools that can be used for formal analysis of dynamic updating of C programs. According to our knowledge, KUPC is the first tool for the code-level formal verification of dynamic software updating.

KUPC has the following three features. (1) KUPC is focused on the code-level verification of dynamic updating. It does not require any abstraction or transformation of target C programs that are subject to dynamic updating. (2) The verification functionalities of KUPC are automatically generated from the formalization of dynamic updating mechanisms. No extra effort is needed on the implementation. (3) The formalization is built upon the operational semantics of the C language. One can easily develop similar tools for the formal analysis of dynamic updating of other languages such as Java and Python, whose operational semantics have already been formally defined in $\mathbb{K}$.

2 KUPC Design

Patch-based DSU. Many DSU tools achieve dynamic updating by injecting patches into running programs [10]. A patch contains all updating contents, e.g., new functions and data. Figure 1 (left) is an overview of the patch-based updating process. An old-version program is first made updatable by attaching additional version information, wrapping user-defined types, and inserting possible updating points. They are achieved by the two operations called *Dependants Updating* and *Restriction Generating*. Next, a patch file *p1.c* is generated and complied by comparing the differences between old and new programs. After an update request is invoked, a DSU tool checks whether it is safe to inject the compiled patch whenever the running program reaches a pre-specified updating point. Safety means that the behavior of the updated program is consistent with the expectation. It is guaranteed by the adopted updating policies in DSU tools.

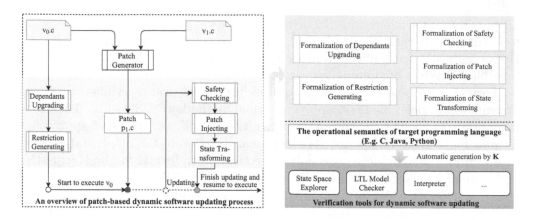

Fig. 1. Patch-based dynamic updating and its formalization using $\mathbb{K}$

If it is safe, the patch is injected and the running program state is transformed into the new version by a transformation function that is predefined in the patch. The patched program continues to execute from the new state. If updating at this point is not safe, the program continues to execute the old version.

It is worth mentioning that the entire updating process is atomically performed, that is, the execution keeps being suspended until the completion of the updating. Updating in an atomic manner is the most consistent approach that simplifies the updating process and reduces unexpected errors.

The $\mathbb{K}$ Framework. $\mathbb{K}$ [9] is a state-of-art semantic framework for programming languages. Many mainstream languages such as C and Java have been completely defined in $\mathbb{K}$. One only needs to focus on the formalization of an updating mechanism using the pre-defined operational semantics of the targeted language. After formalizing the updating mechanism, $\mathbb{K}$ automatically generates several analysis tools such as program interpreter, state space explorer, and model checker.

Formalization of dynamic updating strategy in $\mathbb{K}$. The basic idea of formalizing a dynamic updating mechanism using $\mathbb{K}$ is to formalize the functionalities of the mechanism on the basis of the operational semantics of the target programming language that the mechanism supports. The right part of Fig. 1 shows the formalization of the patch-based dynamic updating mechanism, consisting of the formalization of the five functionalities, respectively.

The functionalities of an updating mechanism are formalized by a set of rewrite rules. For instance, below is a rewrite rule that formalizes the function of checking the safety of updating a set of functions at an updating point *Loc*.

$$\left\langle TypeSafety(Loc, (\frac{F}{\cdot})\_) \cdots \right\rangle_k \quad \begin{array}{l} \langle \cdots Loc \mapsto (\_, \_, Re) \cdots \rangle_{restriction} \\ \langle \cdots F \mapsto T \quad F_{New} \mapsto T' \cdots \rangle_{types} \end{array}$$
$$when \; ((F \in Re) \wedge (T == T')) \vee (F \notin Re) \quad (\textsc{SafetyChecking})$$

```
 1 struct Road{                    20 void Calculate(int x){      1 struct Road{ // modified structure
 2   int dist;                     21   LoadG();                   2   int dist;
 3 };                              22   Shortest(x);               3   int cost;  // new element
 4 struct City{                    23 }                            4 };
 5   ... // node structure         24 void Query(int x,int y){     5 void Cheapest(int x){ // newly added
 6 };                              25   /* point1 */               6   ... // new function
 7 struct Graph{                   26   Calculate(x);              7 }
 8   ... // Road+City..            27   /* point2 */               8 void PrintR(int x){ // modified
 9 };                              28   PrintR(x,y);               9   ... // print results and
10 struct Graph G;                 29   /* point3 */              10   ... // the cheapest path
11 void Shortest(int x){           30 }                           11 }
12   ... // shortest path..        31 int main(){                 12 void LoadG(){ // modified
13 }                               32   ...                       13   ... // load new data
14 void PrintR(int x){             33   Query(0,6);               14 }
15   ... // print results..        34   ...                       15 void Calculate(int x){  // modified
16 }                               35   Query(0,6);               16   LoadG();
17 void LoadG(){                   36   ...                       17   Shortest(x);
18   ... // load graph data..      37 }                           18   Cheapest(x);
19 }                                                              19 }
```

Fig. 2. The snippets of old-version and new-version programs of a GPS application

In the rule, a pair of brackets is a labeled *cell*, representing a piece of program execution information. $\frac{F}{\cdot}$ means F is deleted from the set if the conduction that follows the keyword *when* is true. The condition says that either F is updatable (represented by $F \notin Re$) or it is un-updatable at the point Loc but its types T and T' (before and after updating, respectively) are the same. Here, Re is the set of un-updatable contents at Loc. If the second argument of *TypeSafety* becomes an empty set, it means all the functions in the set are safe to update.

We totally defined 371 rewrite rules to formalize the updating mechanism of `Ginseng`. We tested the correctness of the rules using the example dynamic updating programs provided in `Ginseng`. These rules are seamlessly compiled by $\mathbb{K}$ together with the rules defined for the operational semantics of C [2]. The compilation yields the formal tool KUPC which supports formal analysis of dynamic updating of C programs in various ways such as simulation, state exploration, and LTL model checking.

3 KUPC Usage

KUPC is equipped with an interpreter to *execute* updatable C programs, a state space explorer to search for all possible updating results, and an LTL model checker to verify temporal properties of dynamic updating. We demonstrate the usage of KUPC using a dynamic updating to a GPS application. The tool, examples and a demo video are available https://github.com/dexter-qjq/KupC.

The program in Fig. 2 (left) is the old version of a GPS system. It calculates the shortest path. In the new version in Fig. 2 (right), the new program not only shows the shortest path, but also finds the most economic path. Three update points are inserted in function `Query` from Line 24 to Line 30.

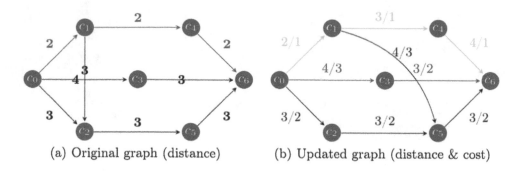

(a) Original graph (distance)   (b) Updated graph (distance & cost)

Fig. 3. The shortest path before and after updating (Color figure online)

Simulating a dynamic updating scenario. Given an original C program annotated with update points, KUPC can compile it with a patch file and generate binary code that is executable on $\mathbb{K}$. During execution, updating is applied once reaching a safe updating point. It simulates the behavior of a dynamic updating to a program that is running on a real-world operating system.

Figure 3 shows the results of the simulation. Figures 3(a) and (b) show the original graph and the updated graph, respectively. When the update takes place at `point1`, the output of first call is the red path in Fig. 3(a). While the second call produces two paths as shown in Fig. 3(b). The red one is the shortest path and the green one is the most economic path.

```
==========================================================================================
Case 1                        |  Case 2                        |  Case 3
Update at: point1             |  Update at: point1             |  Update at: point3
Output: "7km $3; 7km $3"      |  Output: "6km; 7km $3"         |  Output: "6km; 7km $3"
------------------------------------------------------------------------------------------
Case 4                        |  Case 5
Update at: point3             |  Update at:
Output: "6km; 6km"            |  Output: "6km; 6km"
==========================================================================================
```

Fig. 4. All possible updating results searched by the state space explorer of KUPC

Exploring all dynamic updating results. In addition to simulating one possible updating scenario, KUPC can search for all possible updating results by exploring each possible updating point using the state space explorer.

We compile and execute the program `map` with the option `UPSEARCH=1` to invoke the state exploration function. Figure 4 shows all five different updating results. The outputs are divided into two parts by semicolon, representing the results of the two function calls of `Query`, respectively. Case 1 and Case 2 show the results when updating occurs at `point1`. Case 3 and Case 4 are for `point3`. Case 4 shows the result when updating is not performed.

While the dynamic updating occurs during the first call of the function `Query` at `point3` in Case 3, the output of the first call is not affected by updating. The reason is that the updated content will not take effect until the next access after updating. Therefore, the outputs in Case 4 are exactly the same as the ones in Case 5. Updating at `point2` violates the safety policies. Therefore, there is no case corresponding to `point2`. All the updating results searched are valid.

Model checking temporal properties. Dynamic updating is a temporal behavior in that the properties before and after updating may be different. Such differences can be formalized as temporal properties. Another attractive function of KUPC is to verify these temporal properties using LTL model checking.

As an example, we verify whether or not updating in the GPS example can be finally deployed. First, we introduce an atomic proposition called `__update`, which is false before updating and becomes true after the program is updated. Given the command `UPLTLMC = "TrueLtl ULtl __update" ./map`, KUPC returns true, indicating that updating can be eventually performed.

Another property of interest is that the shortest path must become 7 after the system is updated. It can be defined as an LTL formula `__update->(<>(x==7))`, where variable x stores the value of the shortest path. Given the command `UPLTLMC="'('~Ltl__update'\'/Ltl'('TrueLtlULtl'('x==7')''')'''')'"./map`, KUPC returns true, indicating that updating result is correct as expected.

4   Concluding Remarks and Ongoing Work

We have presented the design and implementation of an operational semantics-based verification tool called KUPC for dynamic software updating. Three case studies showed the effectiveness of KUPC for the formal analysis of the dynamic software updating of C programs by simulation, state exploration, and LTL model checking. Semantics-based formalization is promising in providing effective and practical solutions for guaranteeing the correctness of dynamic software updating. For instance, Lounas *et al.* achieved formal verification of dynamic updating of Java programs based on Java's semantics [7]. Compared with their approach, our approach is more general and extendable as 𝕂 provides an elegant semantic framework for the definition of programming languages and an easy-to-use automated verification tool generation service.

KUPC is at a good position for practical code-level verification of DSU. It is directly applicable to the code and shows the feasibility of formalizing a dynamic updating mechanism on the basis of the operational semantics of target programming languages. To verify the dynamic updating of more complex and practical programs, a complete semantics of C including those of standard libraries is needed. The efficiency of KUPC also needs to examine although the efficiency of 𝕂 has been validated [9]. There is ongoing work on these directions.

KUPC has some limitations because of theoretical and practical challenges in the formal verification of DSU. Theoretically, Gutpa *et al.* have shown the undecidability of the reachability of updating points [3]. Another issue is that there is no uniform definition of *correctness* of dynamic updating. The logical correctness of dynamic updating depends on target programs and its formalization relies on programmers' interpretation. Although KUPC does not require any abstraction of target programs, we suspect that certain abstraction is necessary for optimizing efficiency and scalability of the verification. For instance, a function that is not modified in a new version can be considered atomic for verification purpose. It is still an ongoing quest for an appropriate abstraction of target programs for the scalability while maintaining the validity of verification.

References

1. Duggan, D.: Type-based hot swapping of running modules. In: ICFP 2001, vol. 36, pp. 62–73. ACM (2001)
2. Ellison, C., Rosu, G.: An executable formal semantics of C with applications. In: POPL 2012. pp. 533–544. ACM (2012)
3. Gupta, D., Jalote, P., Barua, G.: A formal framework for on-line software version change. IEEE Trans. Soft. Eng. **22**(2), 120–131 (1996)
4. Hayden, C.M., Magill, S., Hicks, M., Foster, N., Foster, J.S.: Specifying and verifying the correctness of dynamic software updates. In: Joshi, R., Müller, P., Podelski, A. (eds.) VSTTE 2012. LNCS, vol. 7152, pp. 278–293. Springer, Heidelberg (2012). https://doi.org/10.1007/978-3-642-27705-4_22
5. Hicks, M., Nettles, S.: Dynamic software updating. ACM Trans. Prog. Lang. Syst. **27**(6), 1049–1096 (2005)
6. Hoare, C.A.R.: Record of a workshop on programming languages for distributed computing. In: Whitby-Strevens, C. (ed.) University of Warwick, p. 54 (1979)
7. Lounas, R., Mezghiche, M., Lanet, J.L.: A formal verification of dynamic updating in a Java-based embedded system. IJCCBS **7**(4), 303–340 (2017)
8. Neamtiu, I., Hicks, M., et al.: Practical dynamic software updating for C. In: PLDI 2006, pp. 72–83. ACM (2006)
9. Rosu, G.: 𝕂: a semantic framework for programming languages and formal analysis tools. In: Dependable Software Systems Engineering, pp. 186–206. IOS Press (2017)
10. Seifzadeh, H., Abolhassani, H., Moshkenani, M.S.: A survey of dynamic software updating. J. Softw. Evol. Process **25**(5), 535–568 (2013)
11. Zhang, M., Ogata, K., Futatsugi, K.: An algebraic approach to formal analysis of dynamic software updating mechanisms. In: APSEC 2012, pp. 664–673. IEEE (2012)

Permissions

All chapters in this book were first published by Springer; hereby published with permission under the Creative Commons Attribution License or equivalent. Every chapter published in this book has been scrutinized by our experts. Their significance has been extensively debated. The topics covered herein carry significant findings which will fuel the growth of the discipline. They may even be implemented as practical applications or may be referred to as a beginning point for another development.

The contributors of this book come from diverse backgrounds, making this book a truly international effort. This book will bring forth new frontiers with its revolutionizing research information and detailed analysis of the nascent developments around the world.

We would like to thank all the contributing authors for lending their expertise to make the book truly unique. They have played a crucial role in the development of this book. Without their invaluable contributions this book wouldn't have been possible. They have made vital efforts to compile up to date information on the varied aspects of this subject to make this book a valuable addition to the collection of many professionals and students.

This book was conceptualized with the vision of imparting up-to-date information and advanced data in this field. To ensure the same, a matchless editorial board was set up. Every individual on the board went through rigorous rounds of assessment to prove their worth. After which they invested a large part of their time researching and compiling the most relevant data for our readers.

The editorial board has been involved in producing this book since its inception. They have spent rigorous hours researching and exploring the diverse topics which have resulted in the successful publishing of this book. They have passed on their knowledge of decades through this book. To expedite this challenging task, the publisher supported the team at every step. A small team of assistant editors was also appointed to further simplify the editing procedure and attain best results for the readers.

Apart from the editorial board, the designing team has also invested a significant amount of their time in understanding the subject and creating the most relevant covers. They scrutinized every image to scout for the most suitable representation of the subject and create an appropriate cover for the book.

The publishing team has been an ardent support to the editorial, designing and production team. Their endless efforts to recruit the best for this project, has resulted in the accomplishment of this book. They are a veteran in the field of academics and their pool of knowledge is as vast as their experience in printing. Their expertise and guidance has proved useful at every step. Their uncompromising quality standards have made this book an exceptional effort. Their encouragement from time to time has been an inspiration for everyone.

The publisher and the editorial board hope that this book will prove to be a valuable piece of knowledge for researchers, students, practitioners and scholars across the globe.

List of Contributors

Min Zhang and Xiaohong Chen
Shanghai Key Laboratory of Trustworthy Computing, ECNU, Shanghai, China

Fu Song
ShanghaiTech University, Shanghai, China

Frédéric Mallet
Université Cote d'Azur, CNRS, Inria, I3S, Nice, France

Marsha Chechik, Rick Salay, Torin Viger, Sahar Kokaly and Mona Rahimi
University of Toronto, Toronto, Canada

Rolf Hennicker
Ludwig-Maximilians-Universität München, Munich, Germany

Alexandre Madeira
CIDMA, University of Aveiro, Aveiro, Portugal
QuantaLab, University of Minho, Braga, Portugal

Alexander Knapp
Universität Augsburg, Augsburg, Germany

Tobias Runge, Ina Schaefer and Thomas Thüm
Software Engineering, TU Braunschweig, Braunschweig, Germany

Loek Cleophas
Software Engineering Technology, TU Eindhoven, Eindhoven, The Netherlands
Information Science, Stellenbosch University, Stellenbosch, South Africa

Derrick Kourie and Bruce W. Watson
Information Science, Stellenbosch University, Stellenbosch, South Africa
Centre for Artificial Intelligence Research, CSIR, Pretoria, South Africa

Joonyoung Park
Oracle Labs Australia, Brisbane, Australia

KAIST, Daejeon, Republic of Korea

Alexander Jordan
Oracle Labs Australia, Brisbane, Australia

Sukyoung Ryu
KAIST, Daejeon, Republic of Korea

Sven Schneider and Leen Lambers
Hasso Plattner Institut, University of Potsdam, Potsdam, Germany

Fernando Orejas
Universitat Politècnica de Catalunya, Barcelona, Spain

Artur Boronat
Department of Informatics, University of Leicester, Leicester, UK

Philip Zweihoff, Stefan Naujokat and Bernhard Steffen
Chair for Programming Systems, TU Dortmund University, Dortmund, Germany

Lars Fritsche and Andy Schürr
TU Darmstadt, Darmstadt, Germany

Jens Kosiol and Gabriele Taentzer
Philipps-Universität Marburg, Marburg, Germany

Aleksandar S. Dimovski
Mother Teresa University, 12 Udarna Brigada 2a, 1000 Skopje, Macedonia

Axel Legay
UCLouvain, Belgium and IRISA/Inria Rennes, Rennes, France

Andrzej Wasowski
IT University of Copenhagen, Rued Langgaards Vej 7, 2300 Copenhagen, Denmark

Li Huang
School of Data and Computer Science, Sun Yat-Sen University, Guangzhou, China

Eun-Young Kang
The Maersk Mc-Kinney Moller Institute, University of Southern Denmark, Odense, Denmark

Himanshu Arora and Raghavan Komondoor
Indian Institute of Science, Bangalore, India

G. Ramalingam
Microsoft Research, Bellevue, WA, USA

Hasan Ferit Eniser and Alper Sen
Bogazici University, Istanbul, Turkey

Simos Gerasimou
University of York, York, UK

Aivo Toots and Pille Pullonen
Cybernetica AS, Tallinn, Estonia
University of Tartu, Tartu, Estonia

Reedik Tuuling, Peeter Laud, Alisa Pankova and Martin Pettai
Cybernetica AS, Tallinn, Estonia

Maksym Yerokhin, Marlon Dumas, Luciano García-Bañuelos, Raimundas Matulevičius and Jake Tom
University of Tartu, Tartu, Estonia

Jiaqi Qian and Min Zhang
Shanghai Key Lab of Trustworthy Computing, ECNU, Shanghai, China

Yi Wang
GCCIS, Rochester Institute of Technology, Rochester, NY, USA

Kazuhiro Ogata
Japan Advanced Institute of Science and Technology, Nomi, Japan

Index